HYDRA CONQUERED THE UNITED STATES, FOLLOWING A LEADER WITH STEVE ROGERS' FACE.

CAPTAIN AMERICA RETURNED, AND HYDRA FELL, BUT A NEW THREAT KNOWN AS THE POWER ELITE
HAS EMERGED AND FRAMED STEVE FOR THE MURDER OF THUNDERBOLT ROSS.

STEVE TURNED HIMSELF IN VOLUNTARILY AND WAS SENT TO THE MYRMIDON, A PRIVATIZED PRISON RUN
BY POWER ELITE MEMBER WOLFGANG VON STRUCKER. BUT SHARON CARTER, FEARING FOR STEVE'S LIFE,
RECRUITED THE MYSTERIOUS DAUGHTERS OF LIBERTY AND THEIR LEADER, THE DRYAD, TO BREAK HIM OUT.

NOW STEVE IS FREE, BUT AFTER THE POWER ELITE'S PROPAGANDA MACHINE DECLARED HIM AND THE
HYDRA SUPREME TO BE ONE AND THE SAME, NICK FURY WILL LEAVE NO STONE UNTURNED UNTIL HE FINDS HIM...

CAPTAIN AMERICA

THE LEGEND OF STEVE

Ta-Nehisi Coates
WRITER

Jason Masters [#13, #15, #17-19],
Sean Izaakse [#13], Niko Walter [#14],
Bob Quinn [#16, #19] & Lucas Werneck [#19]
ARTISTS

Matt Milla
COLOR ARTIST

VC's Joe Caramagna
LETTERER

Alex Ross
COVER ART

Shannon Andrews Ballesteros
ASSISTANT EDITOR

Alanna Smith
ASSOCIATE EDITOR

Tom Brevoort
EDITOR

CAPTAIN AMERICA CREATED BY JOE SIMON & JACK KIRBY

COLLECTION EDITOR JENNIFER GRÜNWALD
ASSISTANT MANAGING EDITOR MAIA LOY
ASSISTANT MANAGING EDITOR LISA MONTALBANO
EDITOR, SPECIAL PROJECTS MARK D. BEAZLEY

VP PRODUCTION & SPECIAL PROJECTS JEFF YOUNGQUIST
BOOK DESIGNER ADAM DEL RE
SVP PRINT, SALES & MARKETING DAVID GABRIEL
EDITOR IN CHIEF C.B. CEBULSKI

CAPTAIN AMERICA BY TA-NEHISI COATES VOL. 3: THE L... printing 2020. ISBN 978-1-302-91441-7. Published by MARVEL
WORLDWIDE, INC., a subsidiary of MARVEL ENTERTAINMEN... ...een any of the names, characters, persons, and/or institutions in
this magazine with those of any living or dead person or inst... ...Creative Officer; DAN BUCKLEY, President, Marvel Entertainment;
JOHN NEE, Publisher; JOE QUESADA, EVP & Creative Director... ...DAVID GABRIEL, VP of Print & Digital Publishing; JEFF YOUNGQUIST,
VP of Production & Special Projects; DAN CARR, Executive D... ...SAN CRESPI, Production Manager; STAN LEE, Chairman Emeritus.
For information regarding advertising in Marvel Comics or o... ...m. For Marvel subscription inquiries, please call 888-511-5480.
Manufactured between 1/31/2020 and 3/3/2020 by LSC...

10 9 8 7 6 5 4 3 2 1

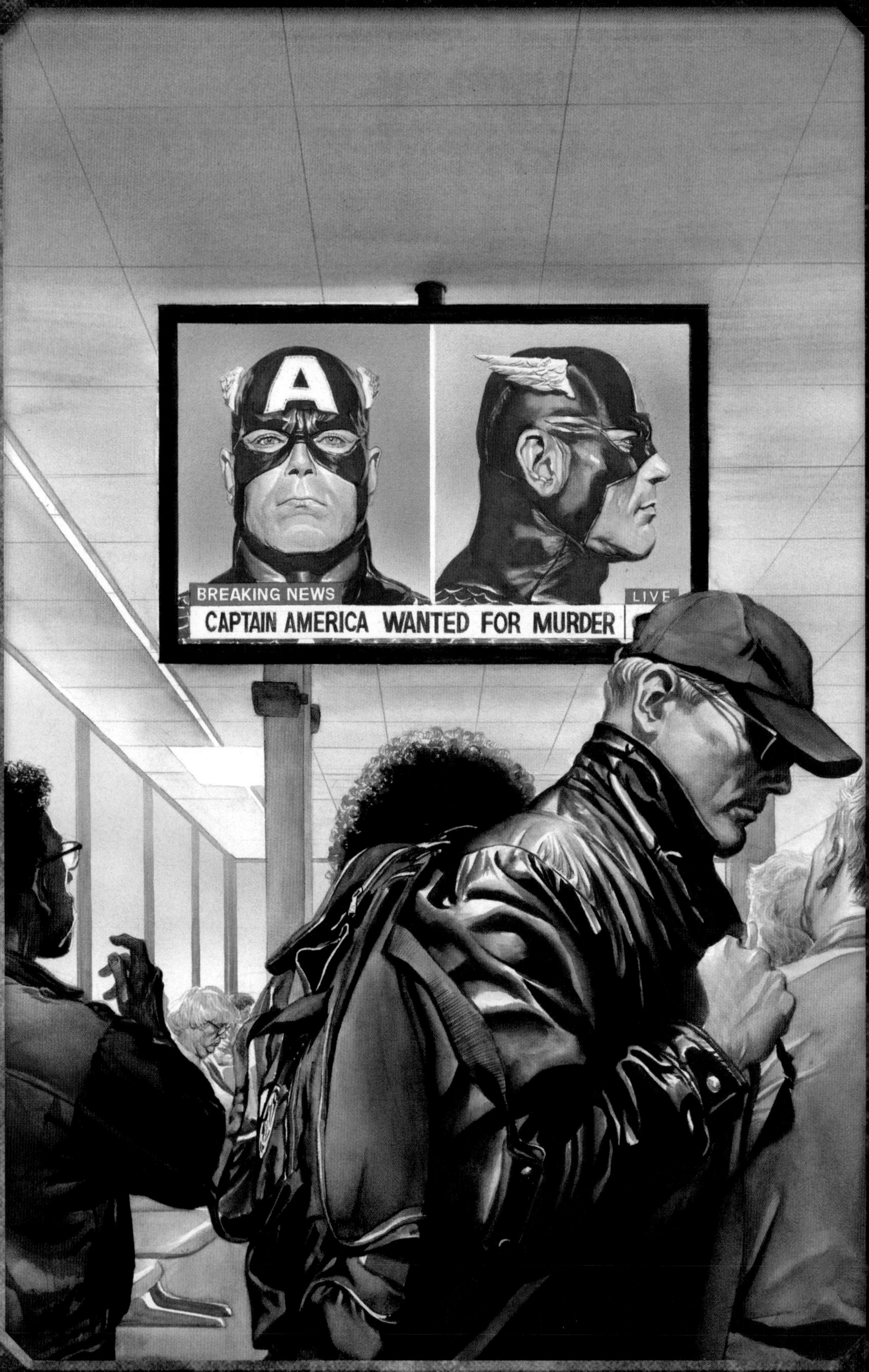
BREAKING NEWS
LIVE
CAPTAIN AMERICA WANTED FOR MURDER

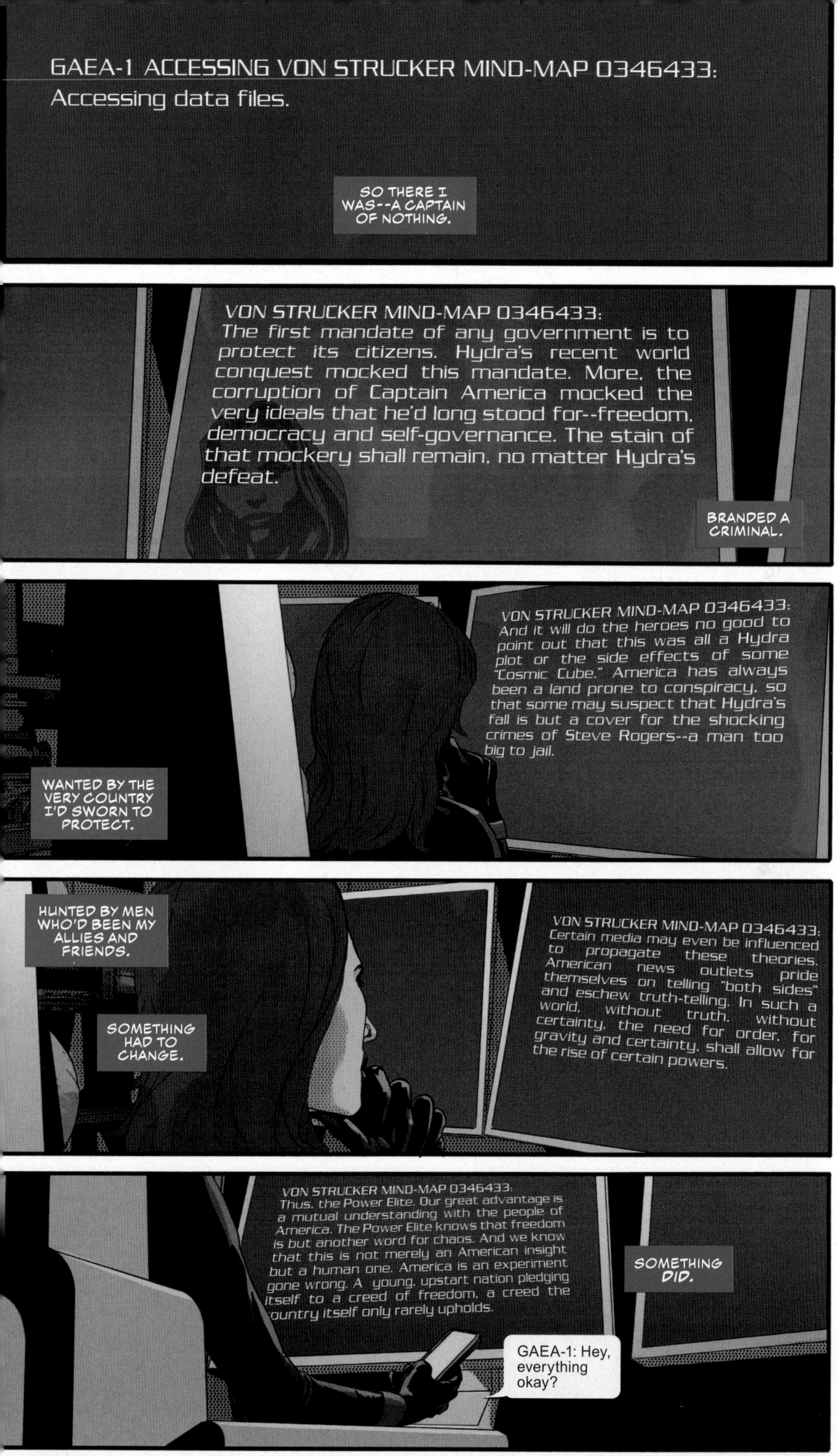
GAEA-1 ACCESSING VON STRUCKER MIND-MAP 0346433:
Accessing data files.
SO THERE I WAS--A CAPTAIN OF NOTHING.
VON STRUCKER MIND-MAP 0346433:
The first mandate of any government is to protect its citizens. Hydra's recent world conquest mocked this mandate. More, the corruption of Captain America mocked the very ideals that he'd long stood for--freedom, democracy and self-governance. The stain of that mockery shall remain, no matter Hydra's defeat.
BRANDED A CRIMINAL.
VON STRUCKER MIND-MAP 0346433:
And it will do the heroes no good to point out that this was all a Hydra plot or the side effects of some "Cosmic Cube." America has always been a land prone to conspiracy, so that some may suspect that Hydra's fall is but a cover for the shocking crimes of Steve Rogers--a man too big to jail.
WANTED BY THE VERY COUNTRY I'D SWORN TO PROTECT.
HUNTED BY MEN WHO'D BEEN MY ALLIES AND FRIENDS.
SOMETHING HAD TO CHANGE.
VON STRUCKER MIND-MAP 0346433:
Certain media may even be influenced to propagate these theories. American news outlets pride themselves on telling "both sides" and eschew truth-telling. In such a world, without truth, without certainty, the need for order, for gravity and certainty, shall allow for the rise of certain powers.
VON STRUCKER MIND-MAP 0346433:
Thus, the Power Elite. Our great advantage is a mutual understanding with the people of America. The Power Elite knows that freedom is but another word for chaos. And we know that this is not merely an American insight but a human one. America is an experiment gone wrong. A young, upstart nation pledging itself to a creed of freedom, a creed the country itself only rarely upholds.
SOMETHING DID.
GAEA-1: Hey, everything okay?

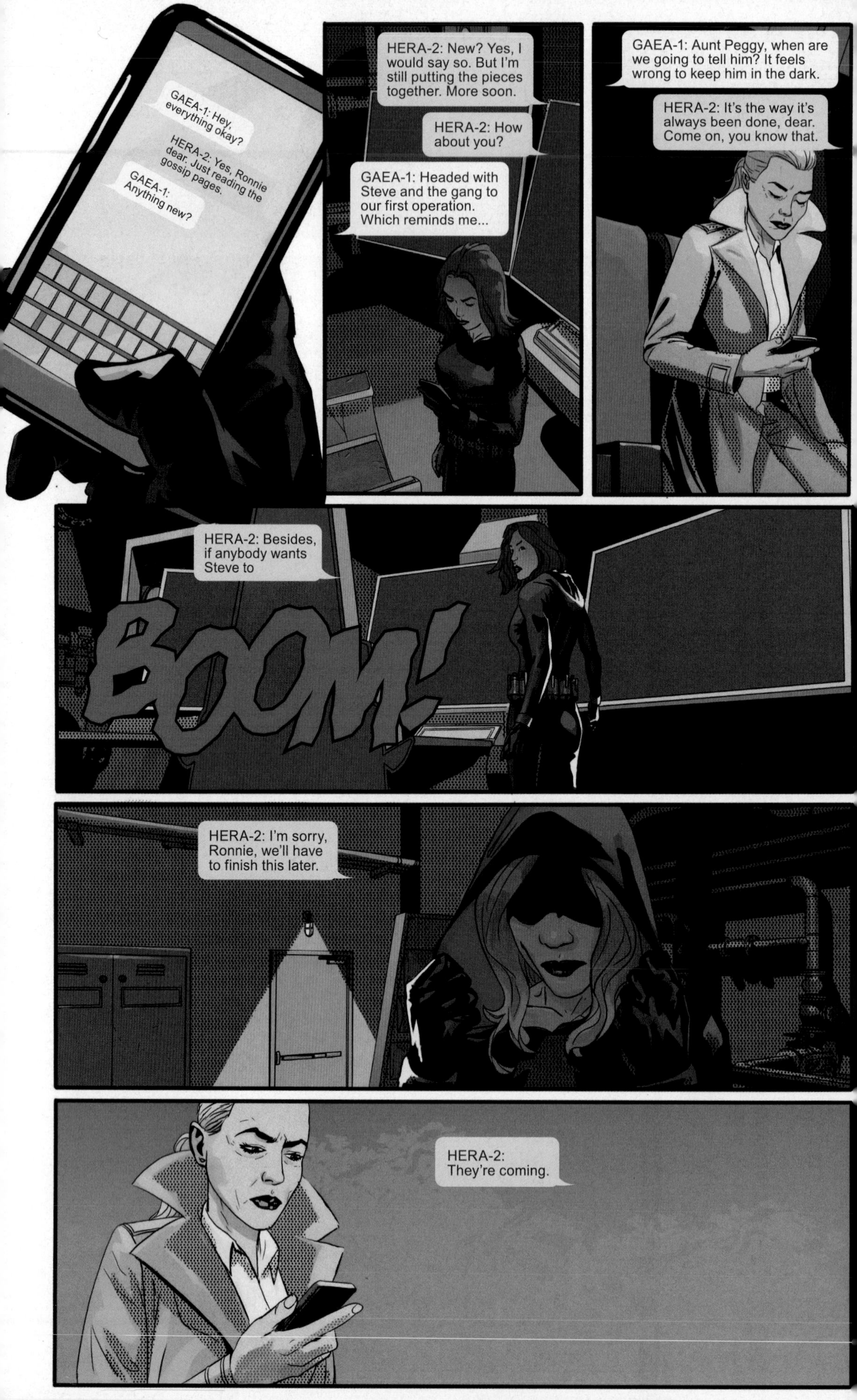
GAEA-1: Hey, everything okay?
HERA-2: Yes, Ronnie dear. Just reading the gossip pages.
GAEA-1: Anything new?
HERA-2: New? Yes, I would say so. But I'm still putting the pieces together. More soon.
HERA-2: How about you?
GAEA-1: Headed with Steve and the gang to our first operation. Which reminds me...
GAEA-1: Aunt Peggy, when are we going to tell him? It feels wrong to keep him in the dark.
HERA-2: It's the way it's always been done, dear. Come on, you know that.
HERA-2: Besides, if anybody wants Steve to
BOOM!
HERA-2: I'm sorry, Ronnie, we'll have to finish this later.
HERA-2: They're coming.

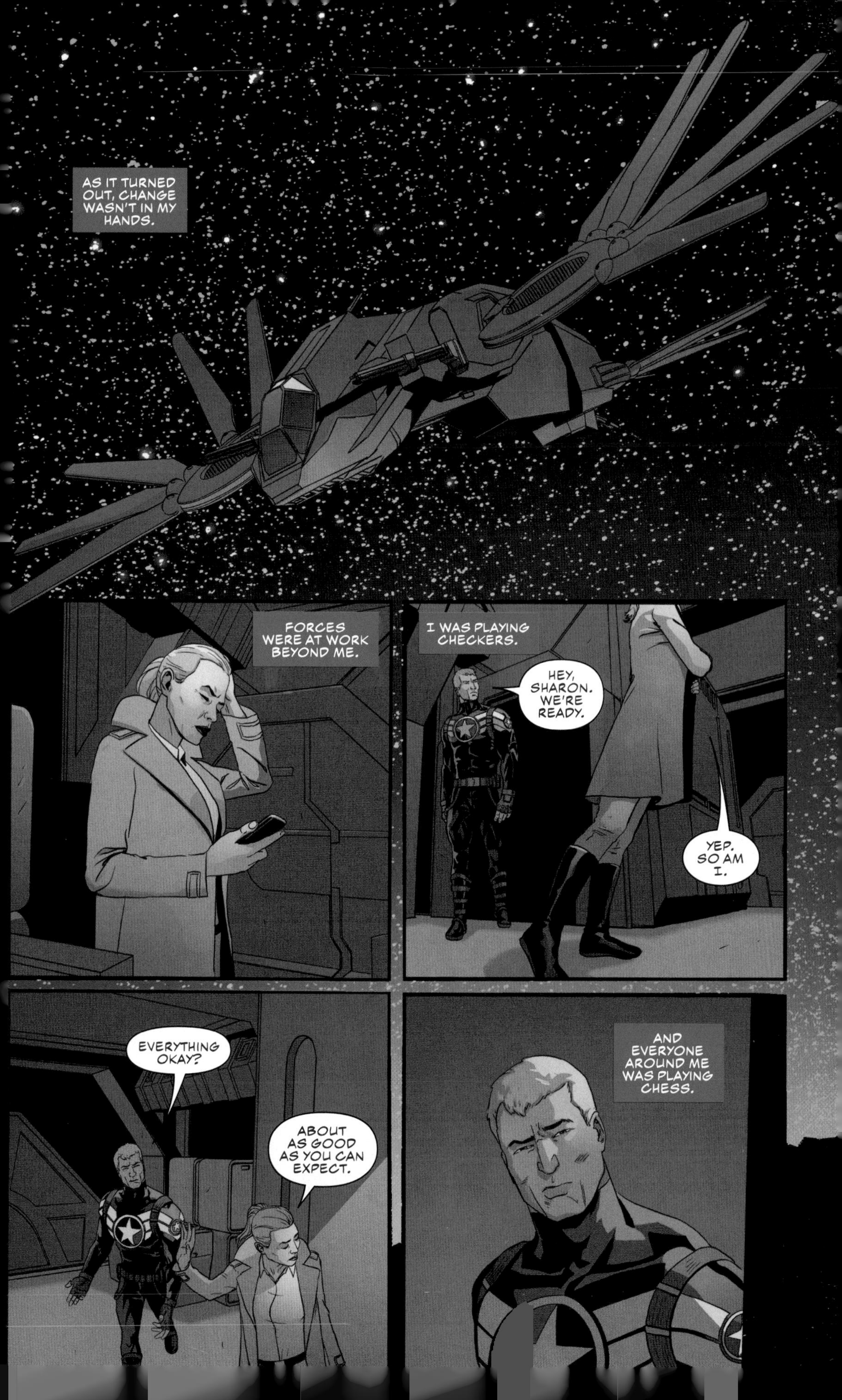
AS IT TURNED OUT, CHANGE WASN'T IN MY HANDS.
FORCES WERE AT WORK BEYOND ME.
I WAS PLAYING CHECKERS.
HEY, SHARON. WE'RE READY.
YEP. SO AM I.
EVERYTHING OKAY?
ABOUT AS GOOD AS YOU CAN EXPECT.
AND EVERYONE AROUND ME WAS PLAYING CHESS.

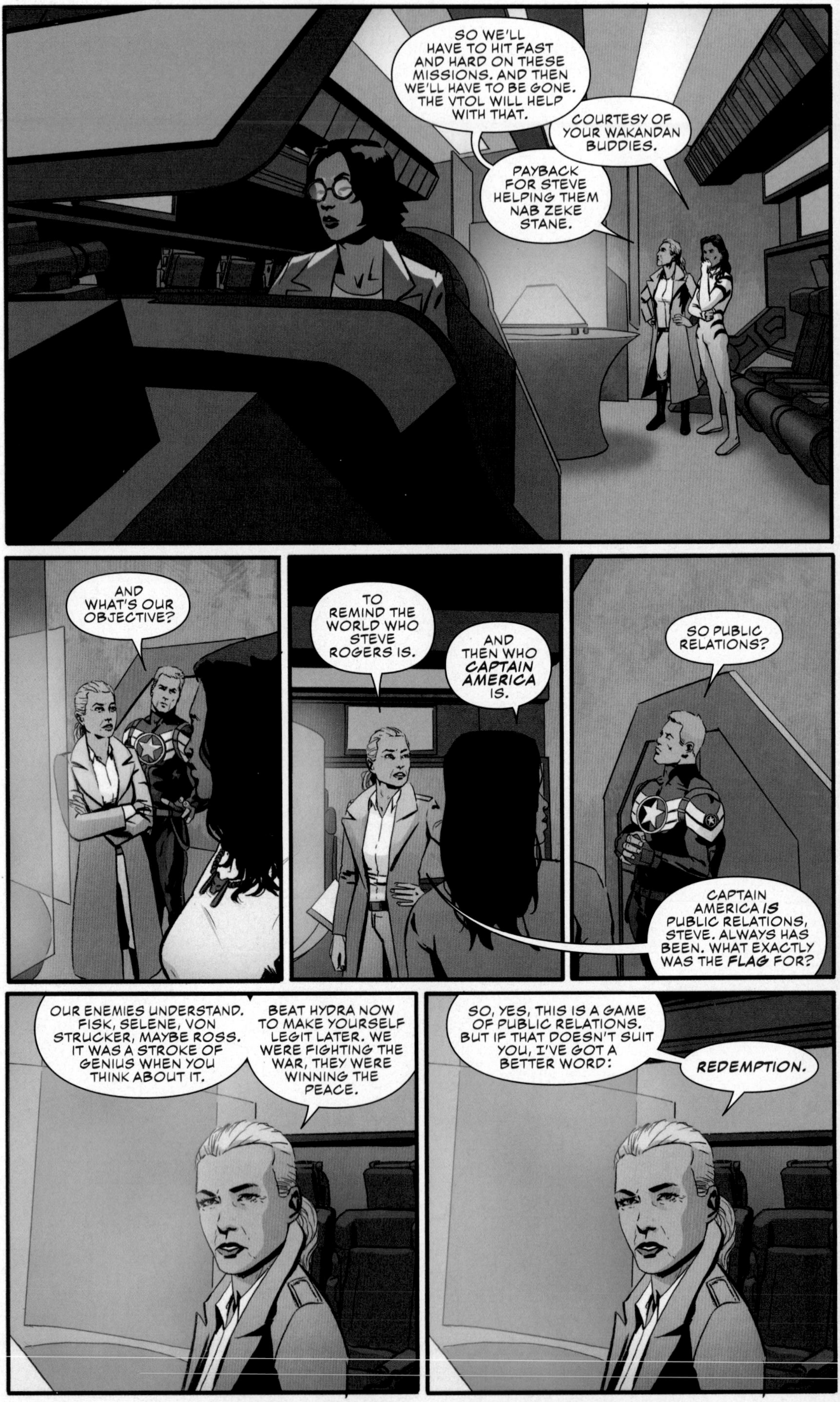
SO WE'LL HAVE TO HIT FAST AND HARD ON THESE MISSIONS. AND THEN WE'LL HAVE TO BE GONE. THE VTOL WILL HELP WITH THAT.
COURTESY OF YOUR WAKANDAN BUDDIES.
PAYBACK FOR STEVE HELPING THEM NAB ZEKE STANE.
AND WHAT'S OUR OBJECTIVE?
TO REMIND THE WORLD WHO STEVE ROGERS IS.
AND THEN WHO CAPTAIN AMERICA IS.
SO PUBLIC RELATIONS?
CAPTAIN AMERICA IS PUBLIC RELATIONS, STEVE. ALWAYS HAS BEEN. WHAT EXACTLY WAS THE FLAG FOR?
OUR ENEMIES UNDERSTAND. FISK, SELENE, VON STRUCKER, MAYBE ROSS. IT WAS A STROKE OF GENIUS WHEN YOU THINK ABOUT IT.
BEAT HYDRA NOW TO MAKE YOURSELF LEGIT LATER. WE WERE FIGHTING THE WAR, THEY WERE WINNING THE PEACE.
SO, YES, THIS IS A GAME OF PUBLIC RELATIONS. BUT IF THAT DOESN'T SUIT YOU, I'VE GOT A BETTER WORD:
REDEMPTION.

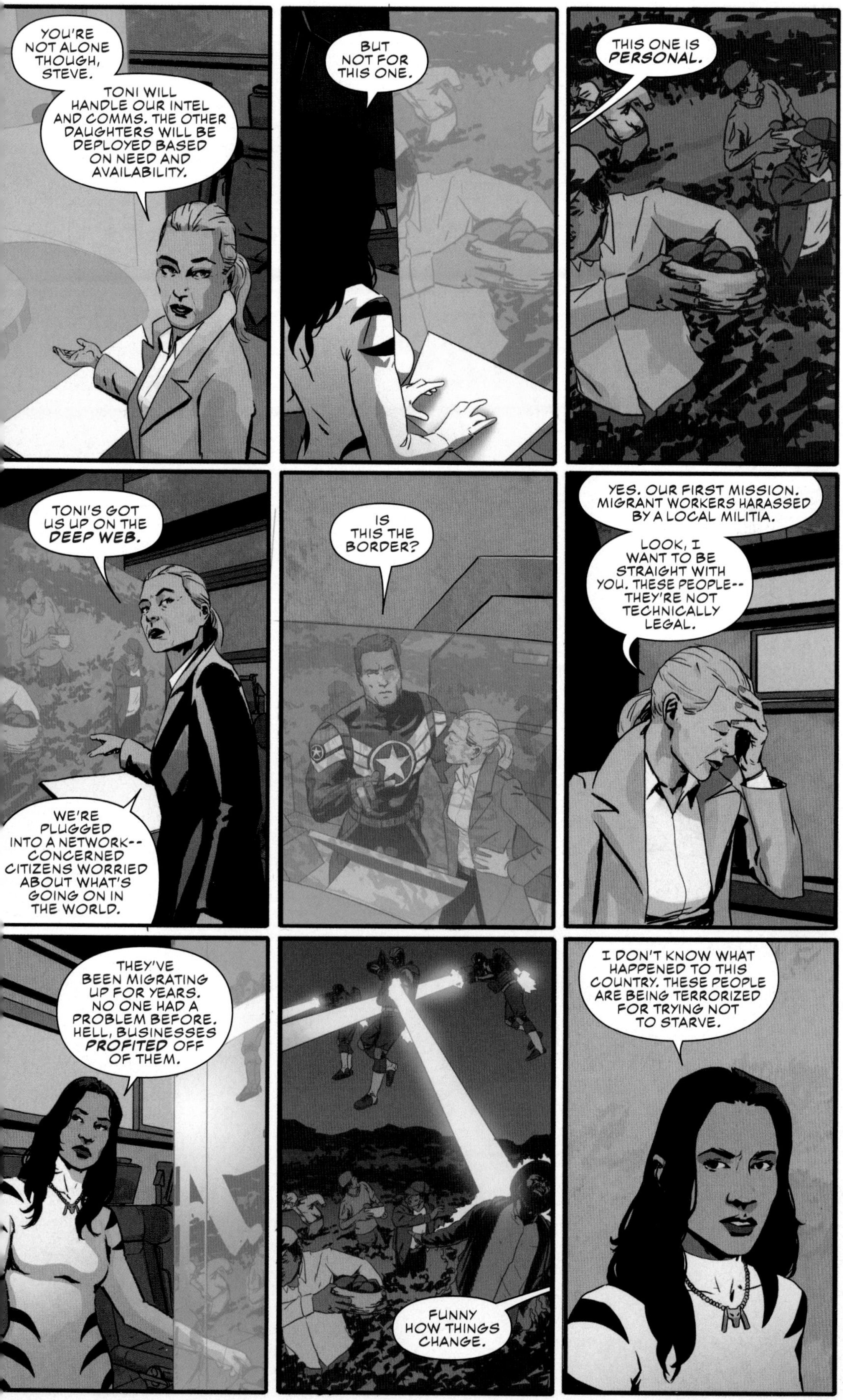
YOU'RE NOT ALONE THOUGH, STEVE.
TONI WILL HANDLE OUR INTEL AND COMMS. THE OTHER DAUGHTERS WILL BE DEPLOYED BASED ON NEED AND AVAILABILITY.
BUT NOT FOR THIS ONE.
THIS ONE IS PERSONAL.
TONI'S GOT US UP ON THE DEEP WEB.
WE'RE PLUGGED INTO A NETWORK-- CONCERNED CITIZENS WORRIED ABOUT WHAT'S GOING ON IN THE WORLD.
IS THIS THE BORDER?
YES. OUR FIRST MISSION. MIGRANT WORKERS HARASSED BY A LOCAL MILITIA.
LOOK, I WANT TO BE STRAIGHT WITH YOU. THESE PEOPLE-- THEY'RE NOT TECHNICALLY LEGAL.
THEY'VE BEEN MIGRATING UP FOR YEARS. NO ONE HAD A PROBLEM BEFORE. HELL, BUSINESSES PROFITED OFF OF THEM.
FUNNY HOW THINGS CHANGE.
I DON'T KNOW WHAT HAPPENED TO THIS COUNTRY. THESE PEOPLE ARE BEING TERRORIZED FOR TRYING NOT TO STARVE.

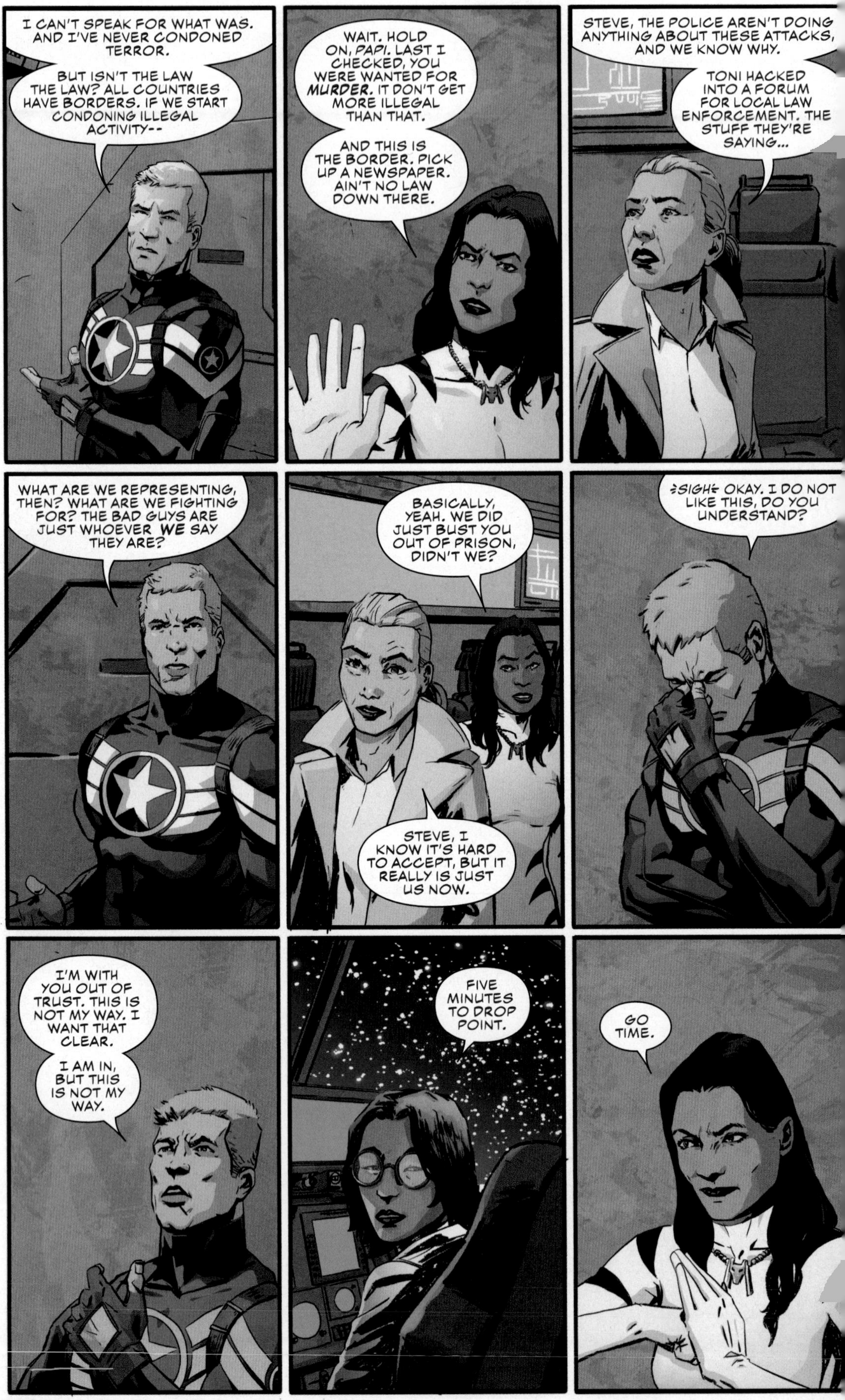
I CAN'T SPEAK FOR WHAT WAS. AND I'VE NEVER CONDONED TERROR.
BUT ISN'T THE LAW THE LAW? ALL COUNTRIES HAVE BORDERS. IF WE START CONDONING ILLEGAL ACTIVITY--
WAIT. HOLD ON, PAPI. LAST I CHECKED, YOU WERE WANTED FOR MURDER. IT DON'T GET MORE ILLEGAL THAN THAT.
AND THIS IS THE BORDER. PICK UP A NEWSPAPER. AIN'T NO LAW DOWN THERE.
STEVE, THE POLICE AREN'T DOING ANYTHING ABOUT THESE ATTACKS, AND WE KNOW WHY.
TONI HACKED INTO A FORUM FOR LOCAL LAW ENFORCEMENT. THE STUFF THEY'RE SAYING...
WHAT ARE WE REPRESENTING, THEN? WHAT ARE WE FIGHTING FOR? THE BAD GUYS ARE JUST WHOEVER WE SAY THEY ARE?
BASICALLY, YEAH. WE DID JUST BUST YOU OUT OF PRISON, DIDN'T WE?
STEVE, I KNOW IT'S HARD TO ACCEPT, BUT IT REALLY IS JUST US NOW.
SIGH OKAY. I DO NOT LIKE THIS, DO YOU UNDERSTAND?
I'M WITH YOU OUT OF TRUST. THIS IS NOT MY WAY. I WANT THAT CLEAR.
I AM IN, BUT THIS IS NOT MY WAY.
FIVE MINUTES TO DROP POINT.
GO TIME.

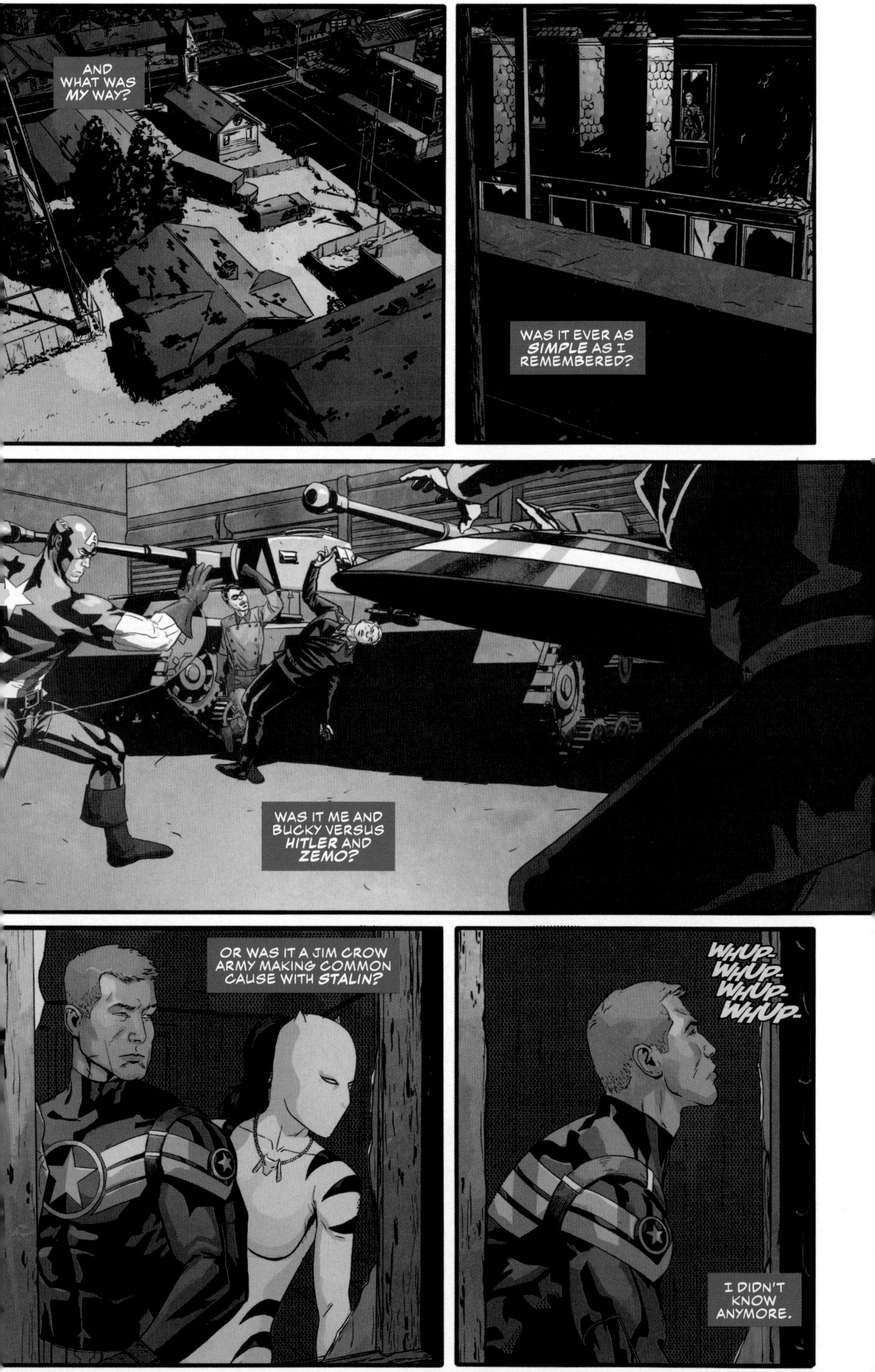
AND WHAT WAS MY WAY?
WAS IT EVER AS SIMPLE AS I REMEMBERED?
WAS IT ME AND BUCKY VERSUS HITLER AND ZEMO?
OR WAS IT A JIM CROW ARMY MAKING COMMON CAUSE WITH STALIN?
WHUP- WHUP- WHUP- WHUP-
I DIDN'T KNOW ANYMORE.

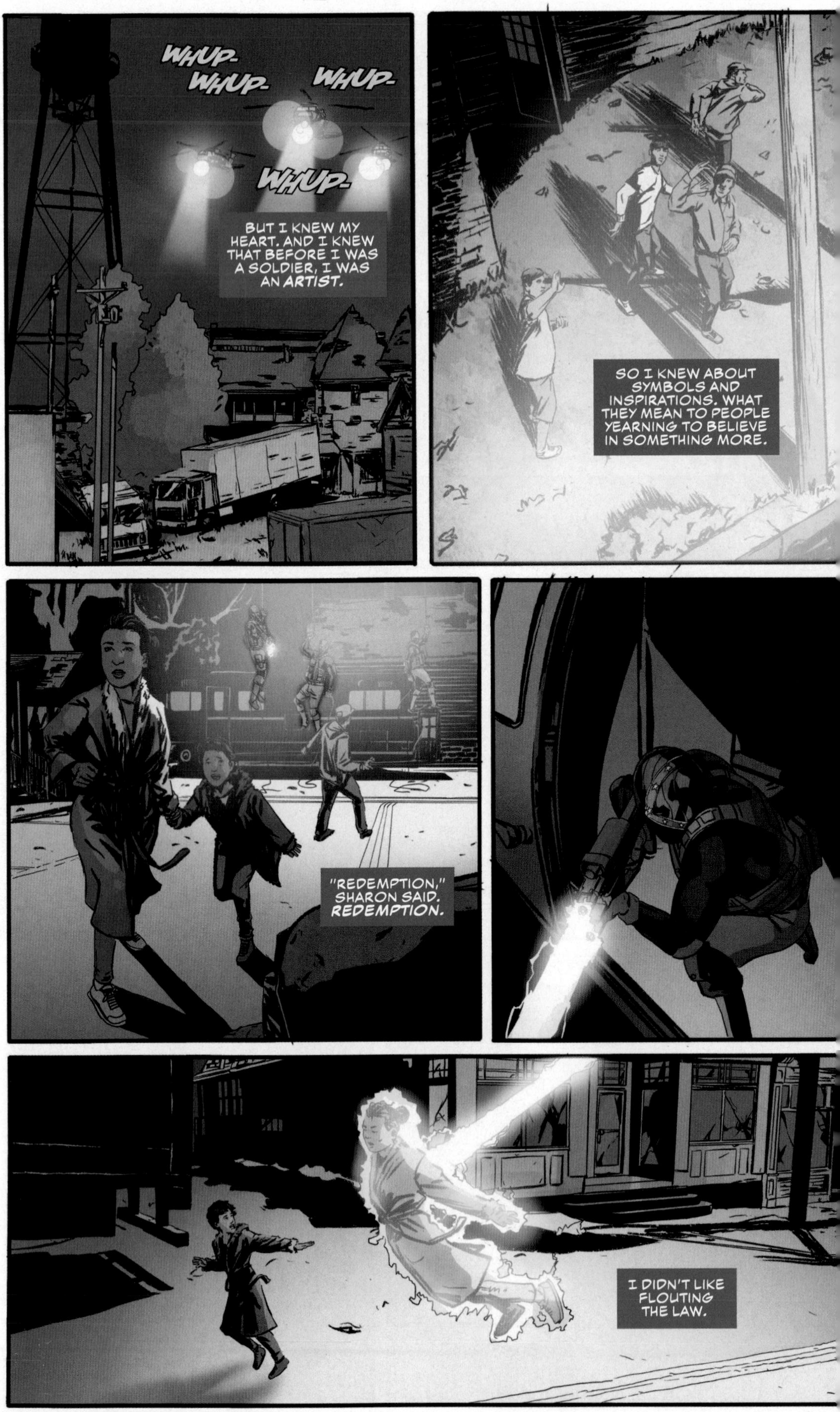
WHUP-
WHUP-
WHUP-
WHUP-
BUT I KNEW MY HEART. AND I KNEW THAT BEFORE I WAS A SOLDIER, I WAS AN ARTIST.
SO I KNEW ABOUT SYMBOLS AND INSPIRATIONS. WHAT THEY MEAN TO PEOPLE YEARNING TO BELIEVE IN SOMETHING MORE.
"REDEMPTION," SHARON SAID. REDEMPTION.
I DIDN'T LIKE FLOUTING THE LAW.

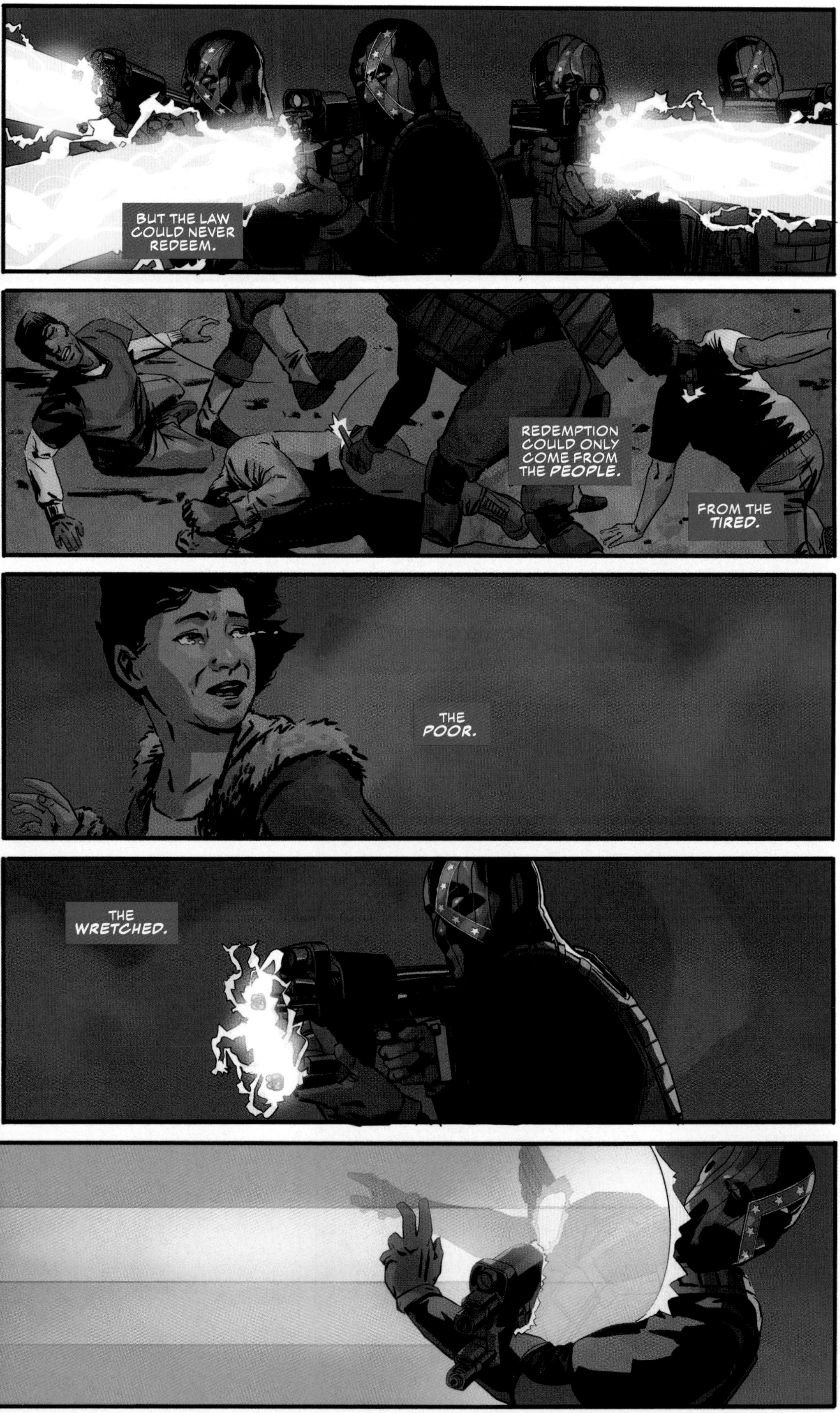

BUT THE LAW COULD NEVER REDEEM.
REDEMPTION COULD ONLY COME FROM THE PEOPLE.
FROM THE TIRED.
THE POOR.
THE WRETCHED.

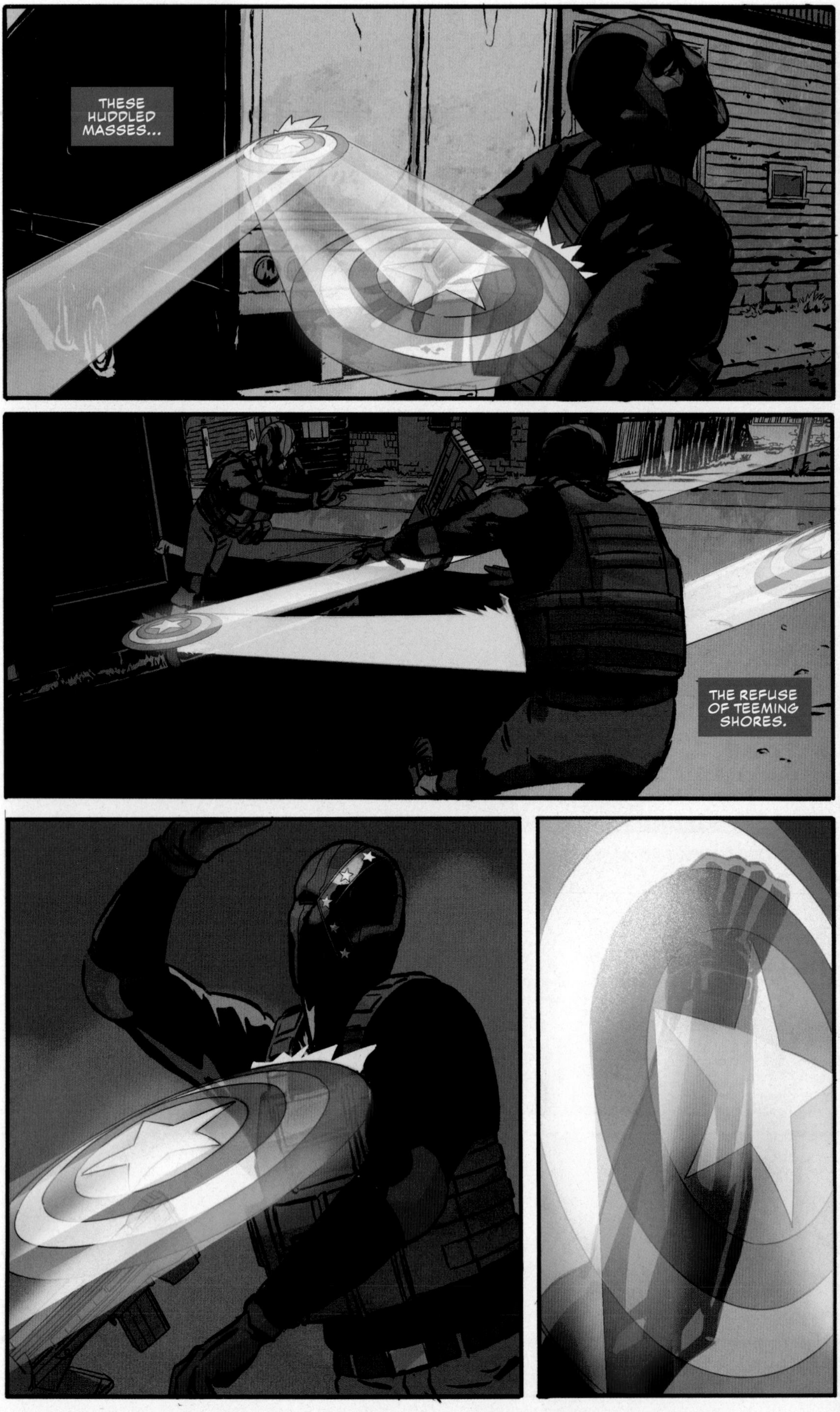

THESE HUDDLED MASSES...
THE REFUSE OF TEEMING SHORES.

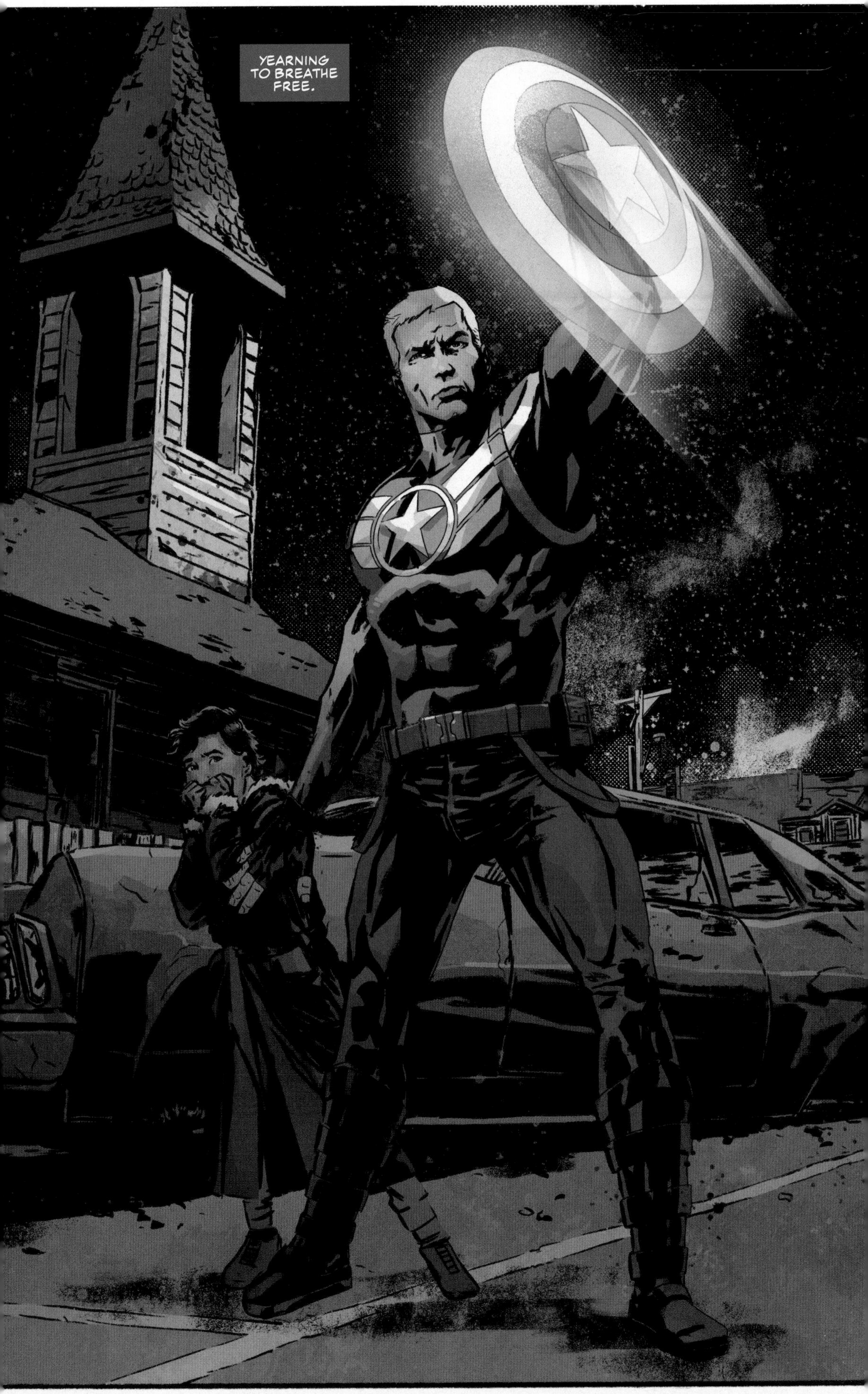
YEARNING TO BREATHE FREE.

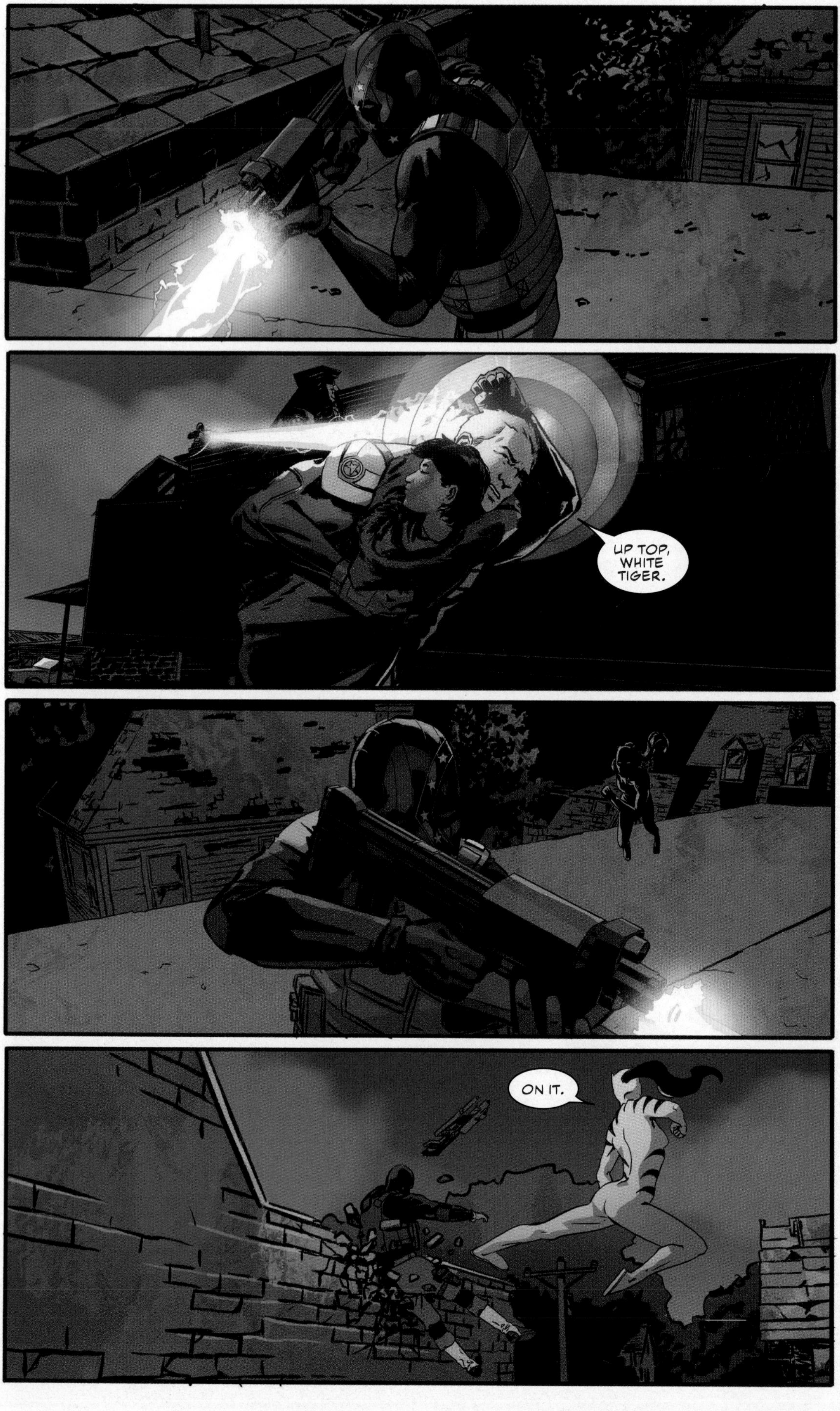
UP TOP, WHITE TIGER.
ON IT.

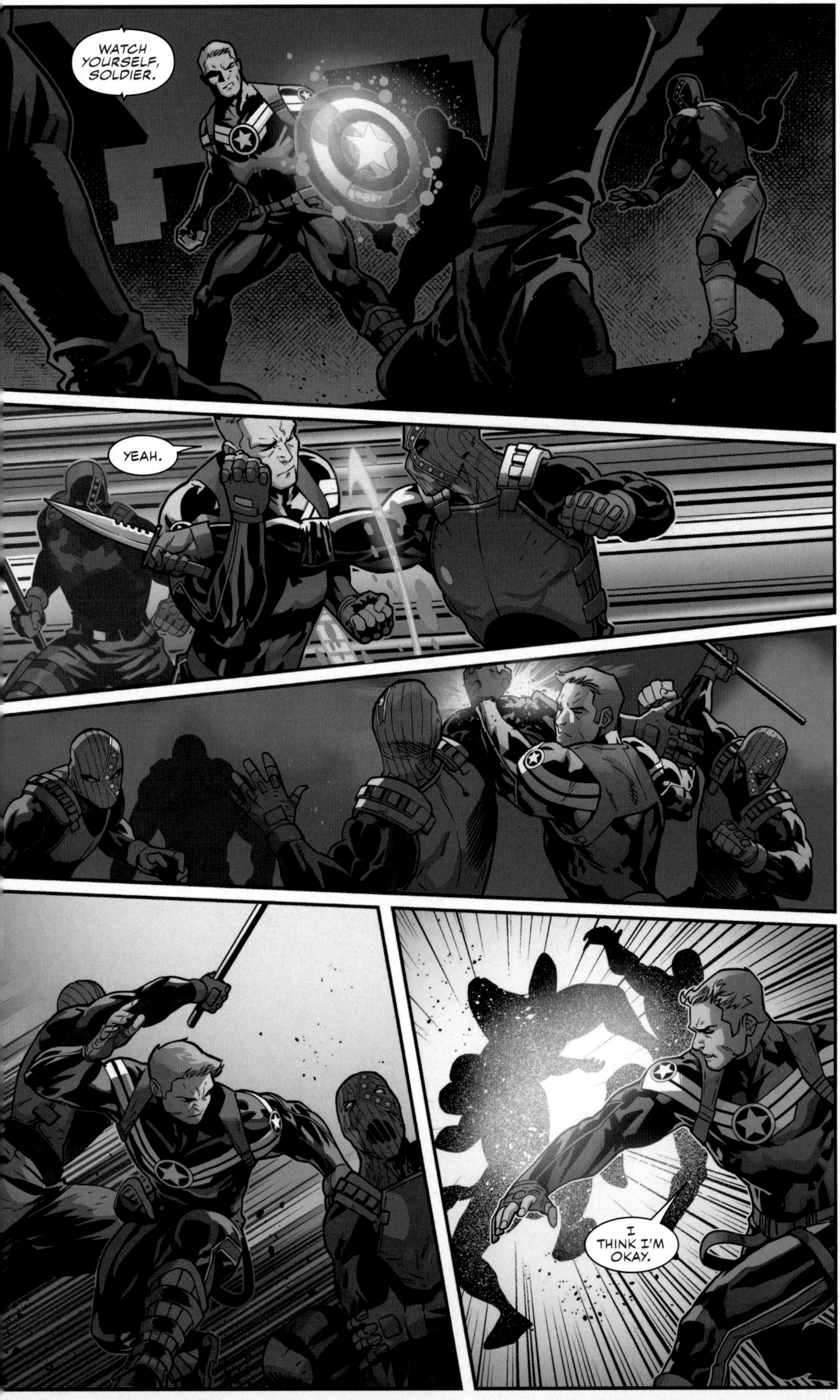
WATCH YOURSELF, SOLDIER.
YEAH.
I THINK I'M OKAY.

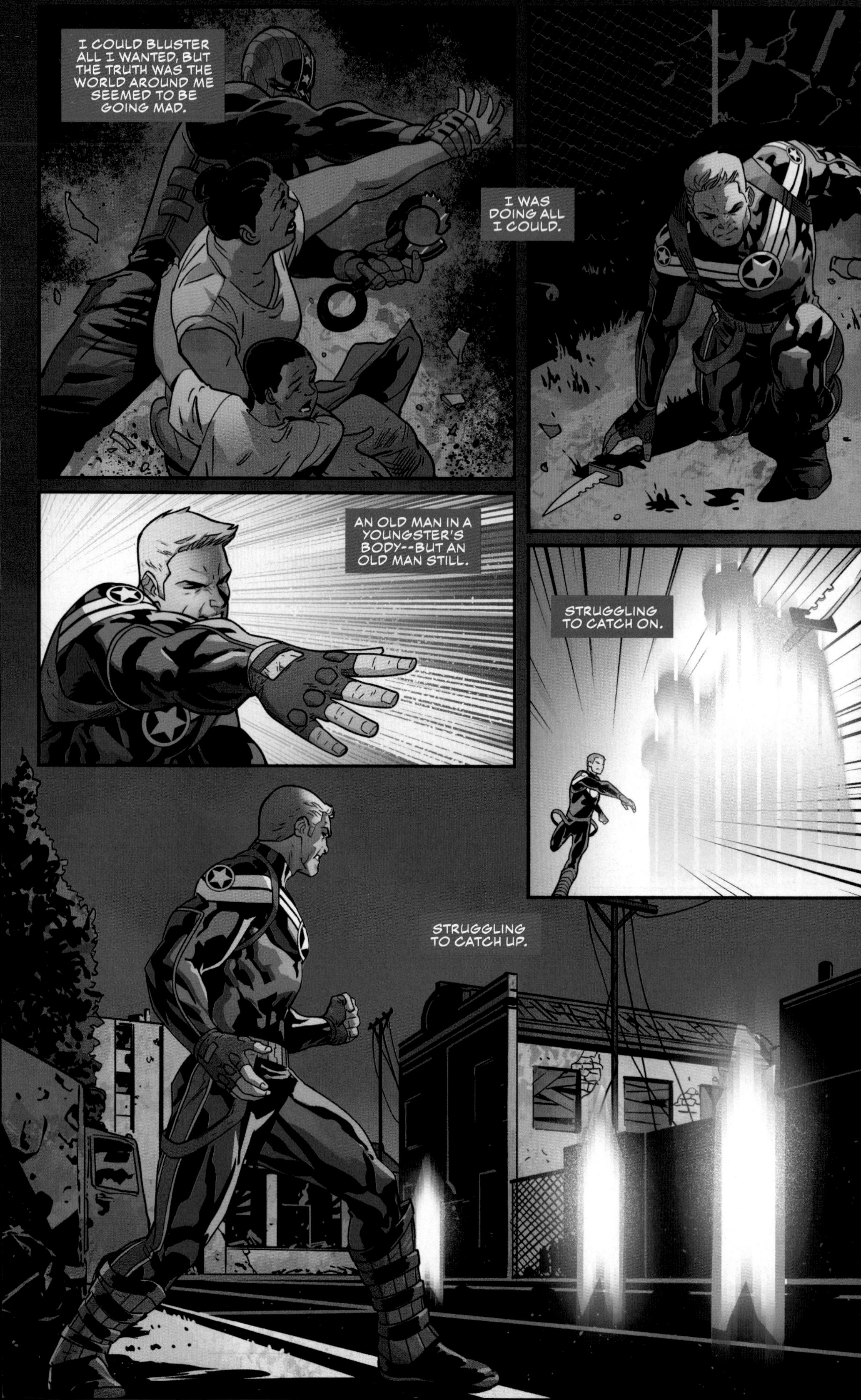
I COULD BLUSTER ALL I WANTED, BUT THE TRUTH WAS THE WORLD AROUND ME SEEMED TO BE GOING MAD.
I WAS DOING ALL I COULD.
AN OLD MAN IN A YOUNGSTER'S BODY--BUT AN OLD MAN STILL.
STRUGGLING TO CATCH ON.
STRUGGLING TO CATCH UP.

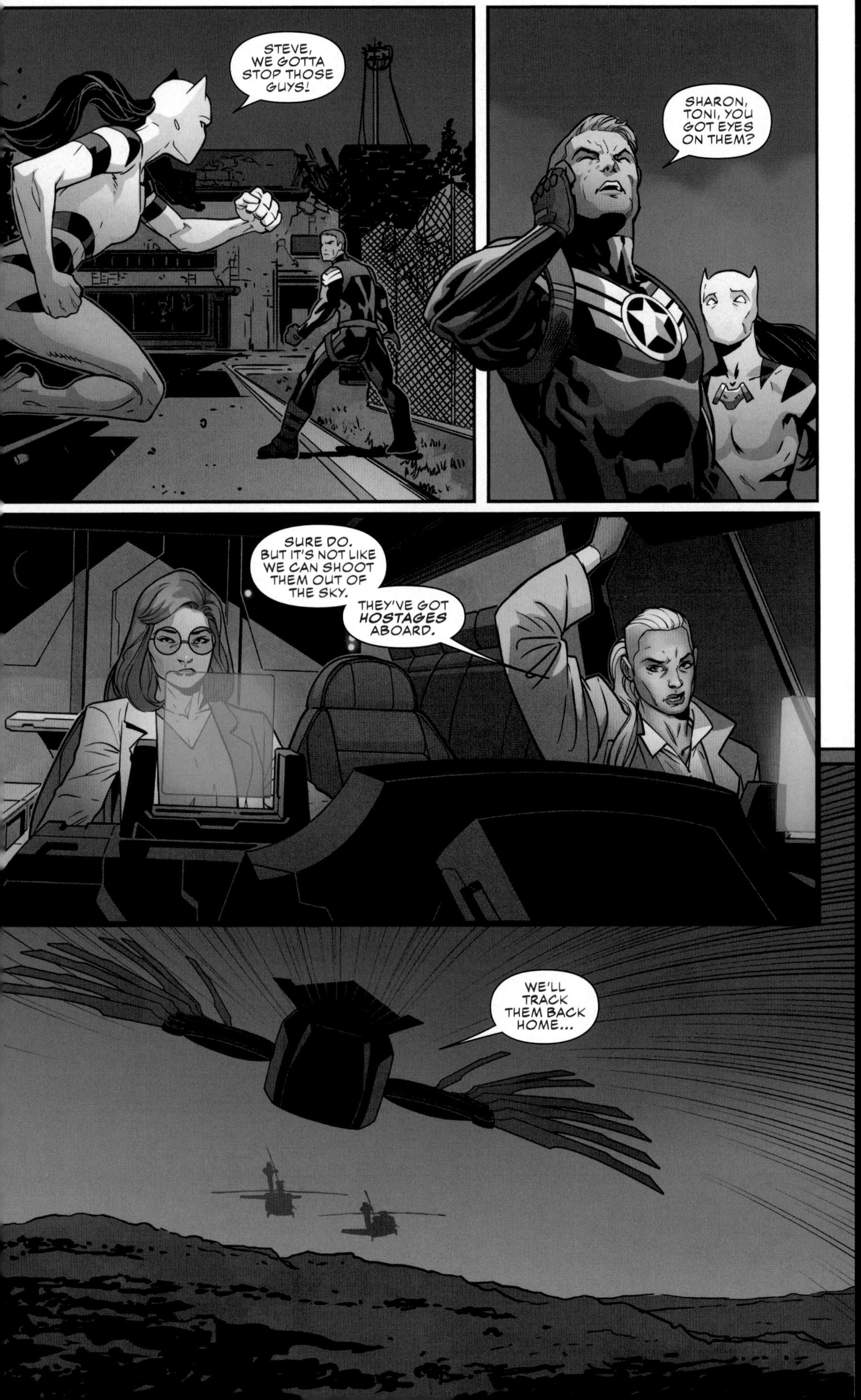
STEVE, WE GOTTA STOP THOSE GUYS!
SHARON, TONI, YOU GOT EYES ON THEM?
SURE DO. BUT IT'S NOT LIKE WE CAN SHOOT THEM OUT OF THE SKY.
THEY'VE GOT HOSTAGES ABOARD.
WE'LL TRACK THEM BACK HOME...

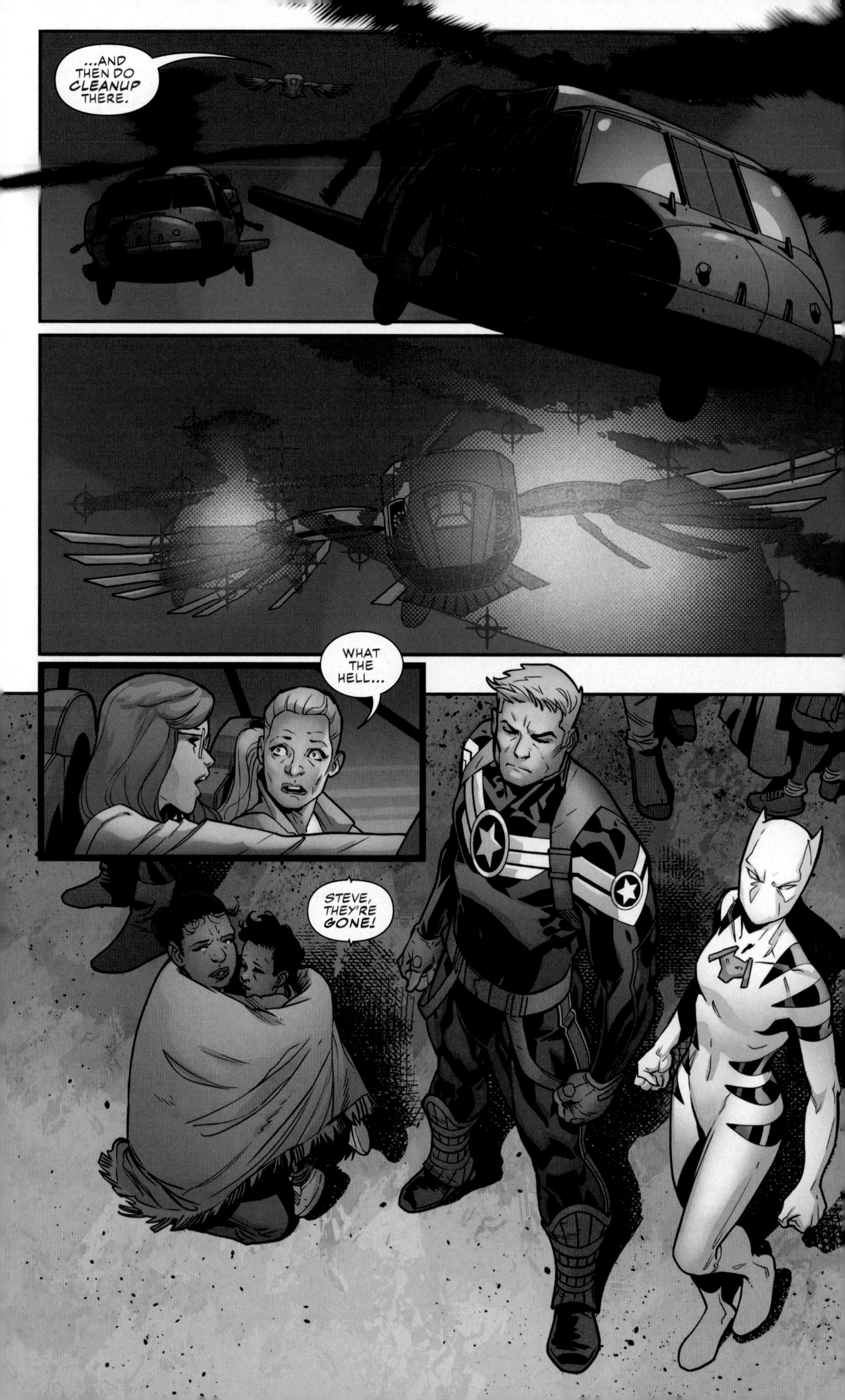
...AND THEN DO CLEANUP THERE.
WHAT THE HELL...
STEVE, THEY'RE GONE!

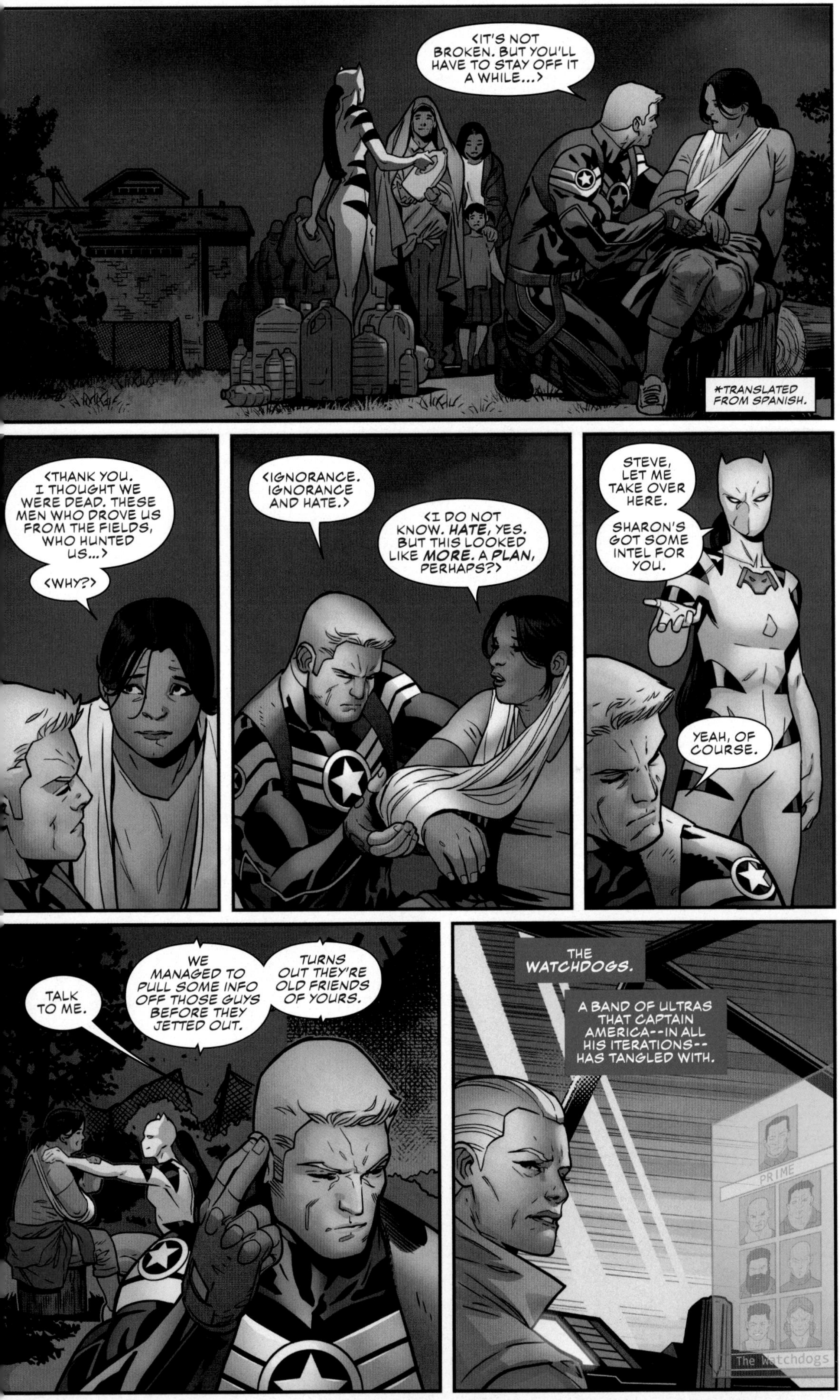

<IT'S NOT BROKEN. BUT YOU'LL HAVE TO STAY OFF IT A WHILE...>
*TRANSLATED FROM SPANISH.
<THANK YOU. I THOUGHT WE WERE DEAD. THESE MEN WHO DROVE US FROM THE FIELDS, WHO HUNTED US...>
<WHY?>
<IGNORANCE. IGNORANCE AND HATE.>
<I DO NOT KNOW. **HATE**, YES. BUT THIS LOOKED LIKE **MORE**. A **PLAN**, PERHAPS?>
STEVE, LET ME TAKE OVER HERE.
SHARON'S GOT SOME INTEL FOR YOU.
YEAH, OF COURSE.
TALK TO ME.
WE MANAGED TO PULL SOME INFO OFF THOSE GUYS BEFORE THEY JETTED OUT.
TURNS OUT THEY'RE OLD FRIENDS OF YOURS.
THE **WATCHDOGS.**
A BAND OF ULTRAS THAT CAPTAIN AMERICA--IN ALL HIS ITERATIONS--HAS TANGLED WITH.
PRIME
The Watchdogs

ALL MY OLD BUDDIES WERE COMING OUT TO HAUNT.

SOME WEREN'T MUCH OF A SURPRISE.

BUT THERE WERE OTHERS I NEVER SAW COMING.

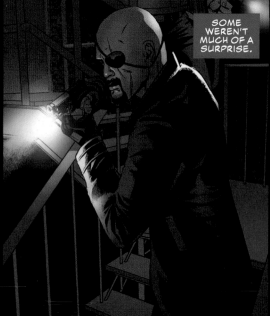

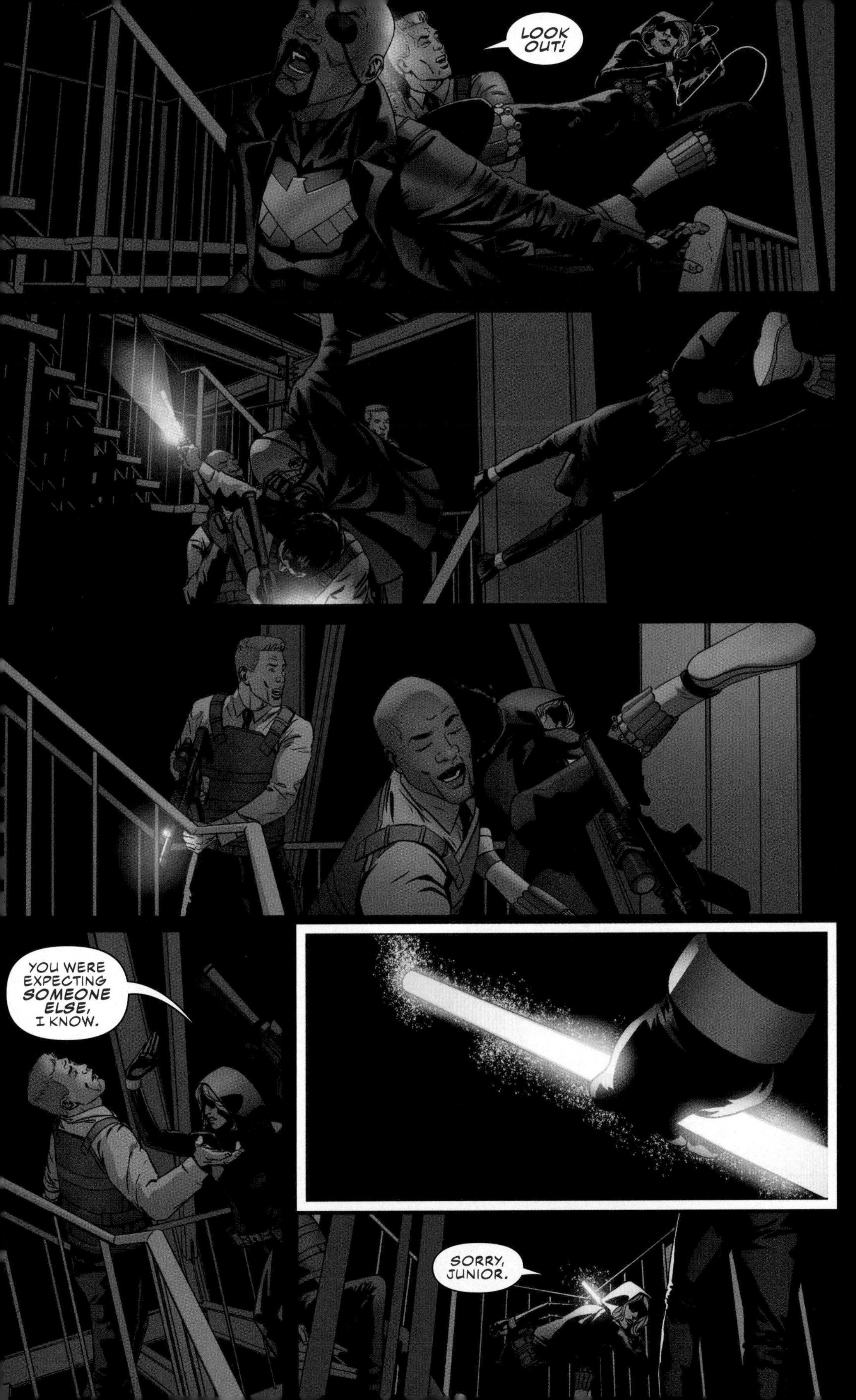
LOOK OUT!
YOU WERE EXPECTING SOMEONE ELSE, I KNOW.
SORRY, JUNIOR.

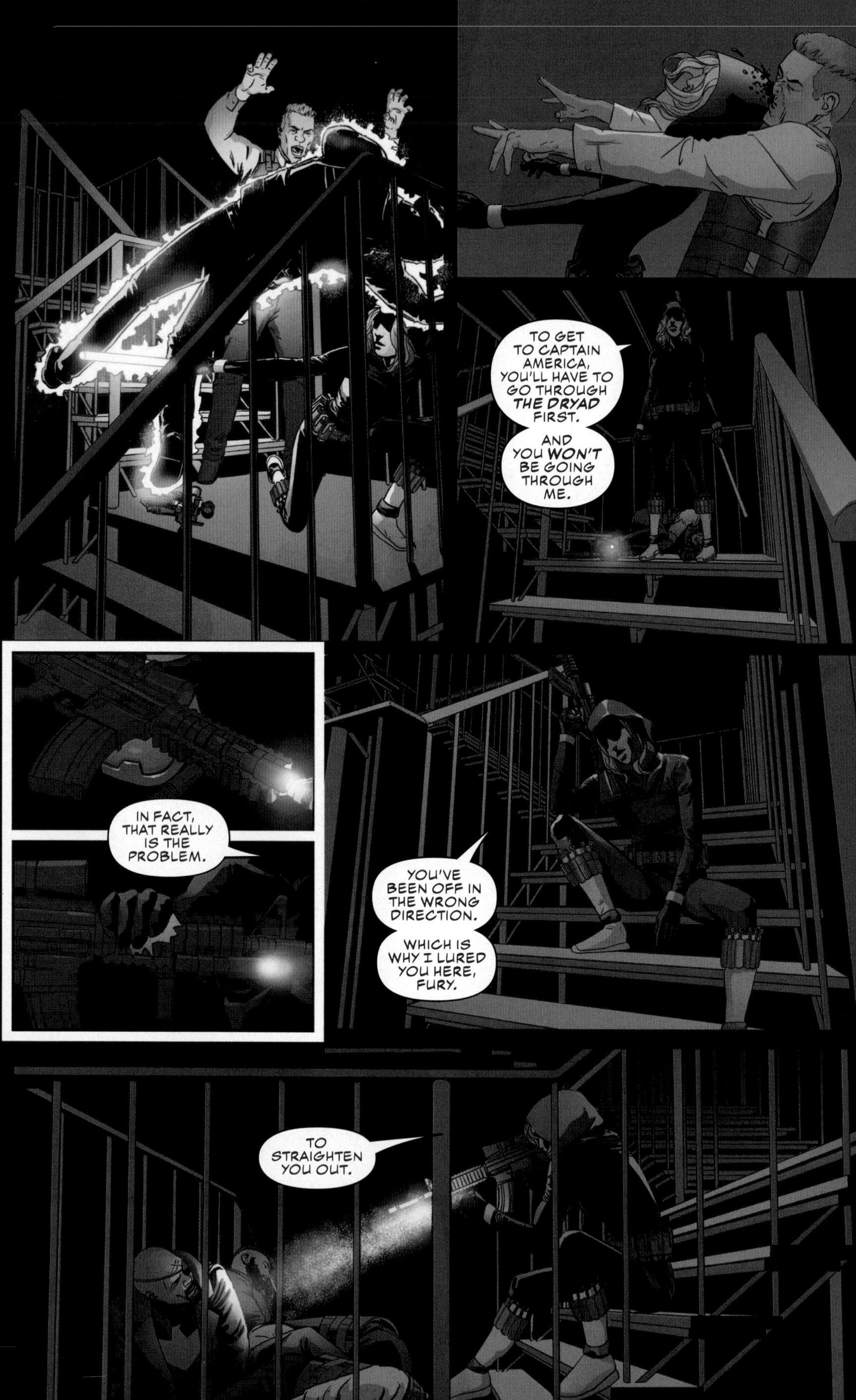
TO GET TO CAPTAIN AMERICA, YOU'LL HAVE TO GO THROUGH THE DRYAD FIRST.
AND YOU WON'T BE GOING THROUGH ME.
IN FACT, THAT REALLY IS THE PROBLEM.
YOU'VE BEEN OFF IN THE WRONG DIRECTION.
WHICH IS WHY I LURED YOU HERE, FURY.
TO STRAIGHTEN YOU OUT.

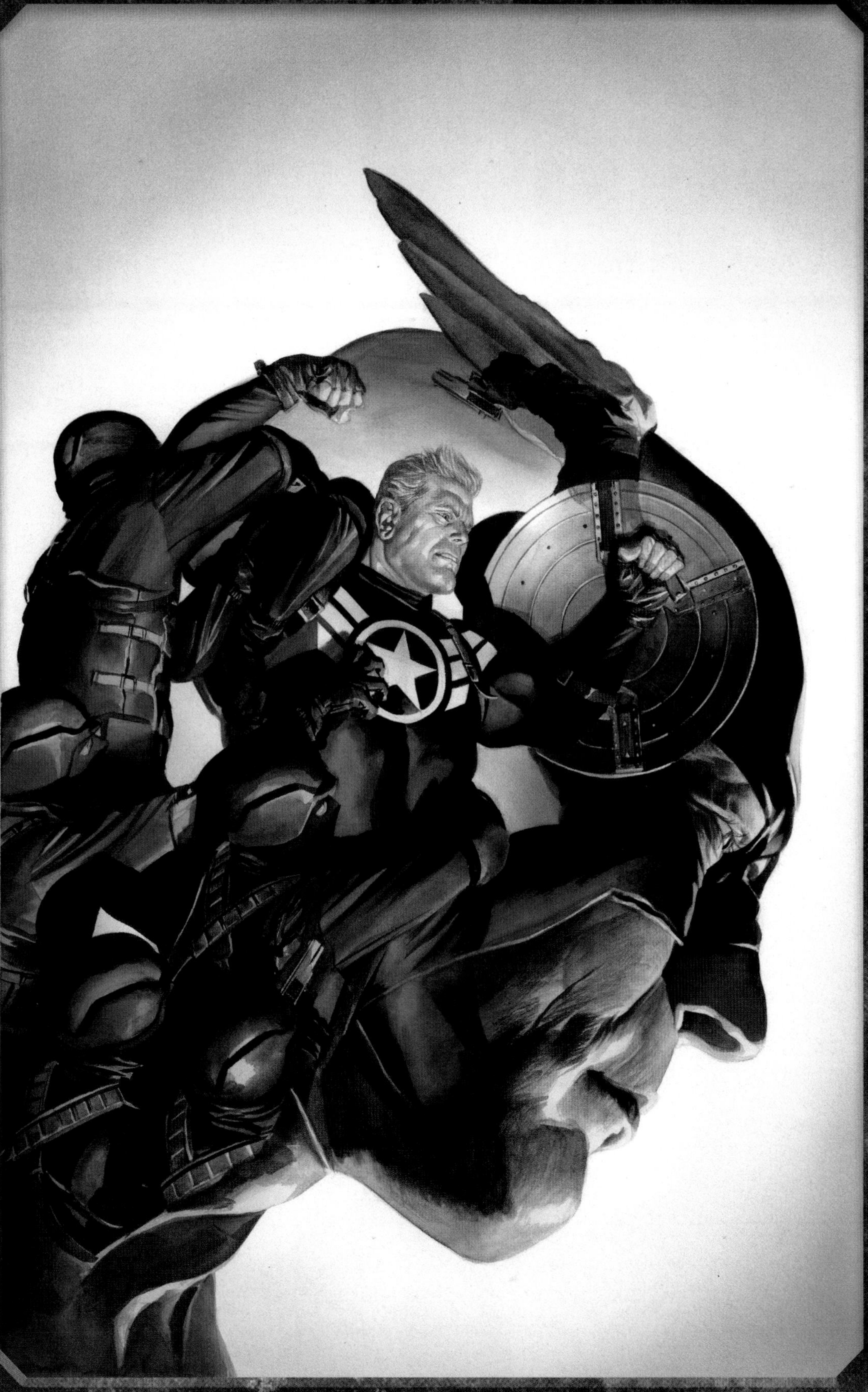

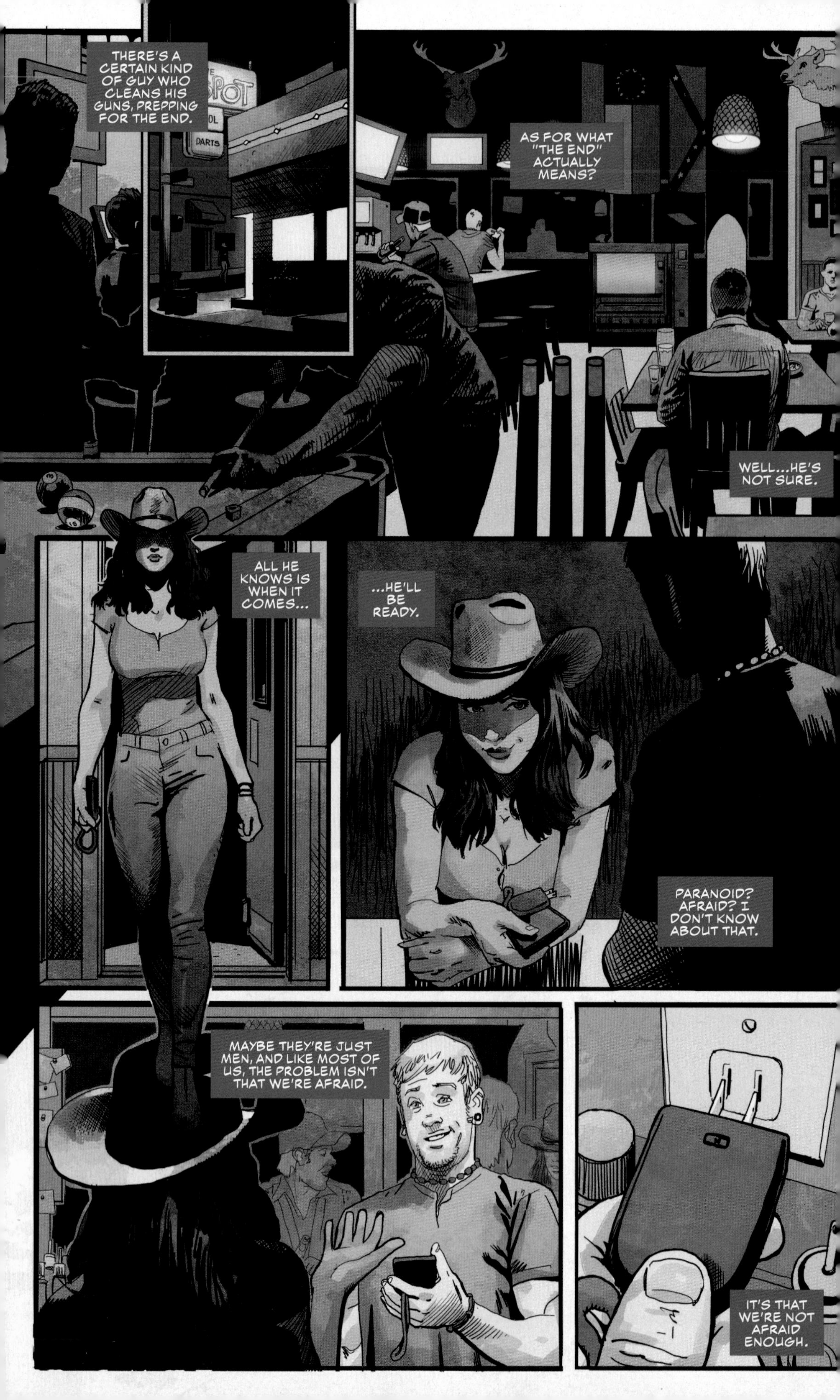

THERE'S A CERTAIN KIND OF GUY WHO CLEANS HIS GUNS, PREPPING FOR THE END.
SPOT
DARTS
AS FOR WHAT "THE END" ACTUALLY MEANS?
WELL...HE'S NOT SURE.
ALL HE KNOWS IS WHEN IT COMES...
...HE'LL BE READY.
PARANOID? AFRAID? I DON'T KNOW ABOUT THAT.
MAYBE THEY'RE JUST MEN, AND LIKE MOST OF US, THE PROBLEM ISN'T THAT WE'RE AFRAID.
IT'S THAT WE'RE NOT AFRAID ENOUGH.

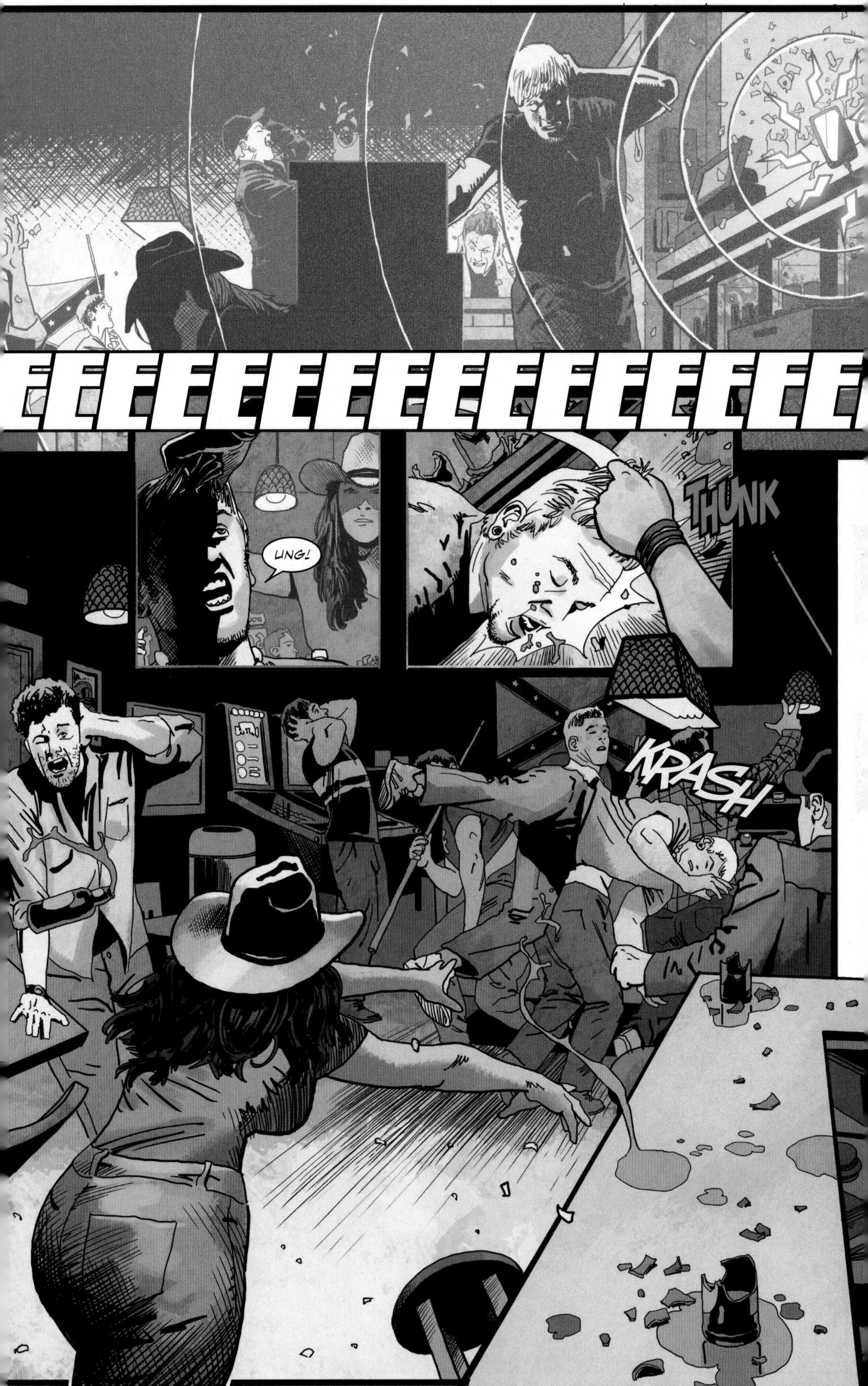
EEEEEEEEEEEEEEE
UNG!
THUNK
KRASH

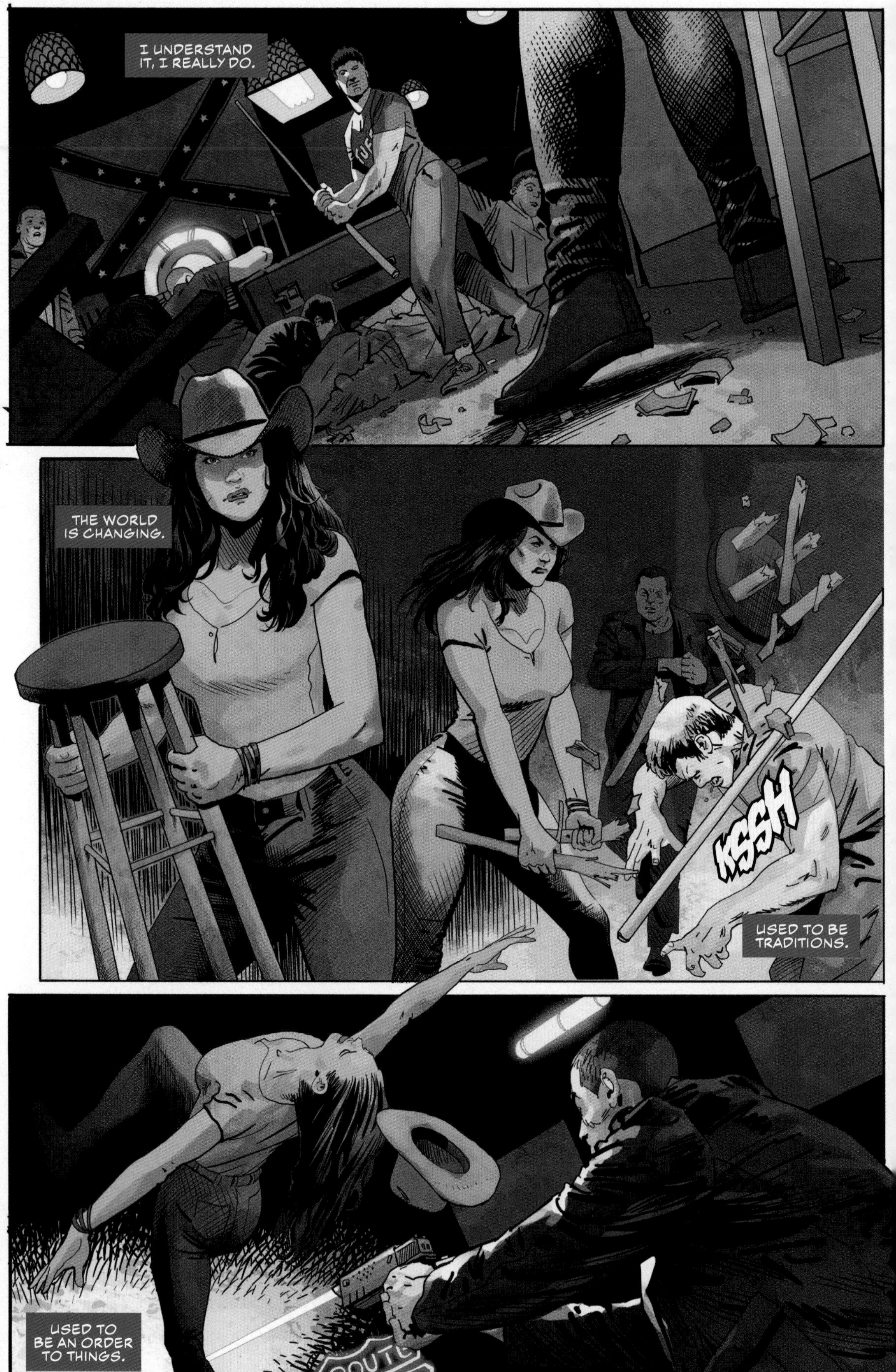
I UNDERSTAND IT, I REALLY DO.
THE WORLD IS CHANGING.
KSSH
USED TO BE TRADITIONS.
USED TO BE AN ORDER TO THINGS.
ROUTE 66

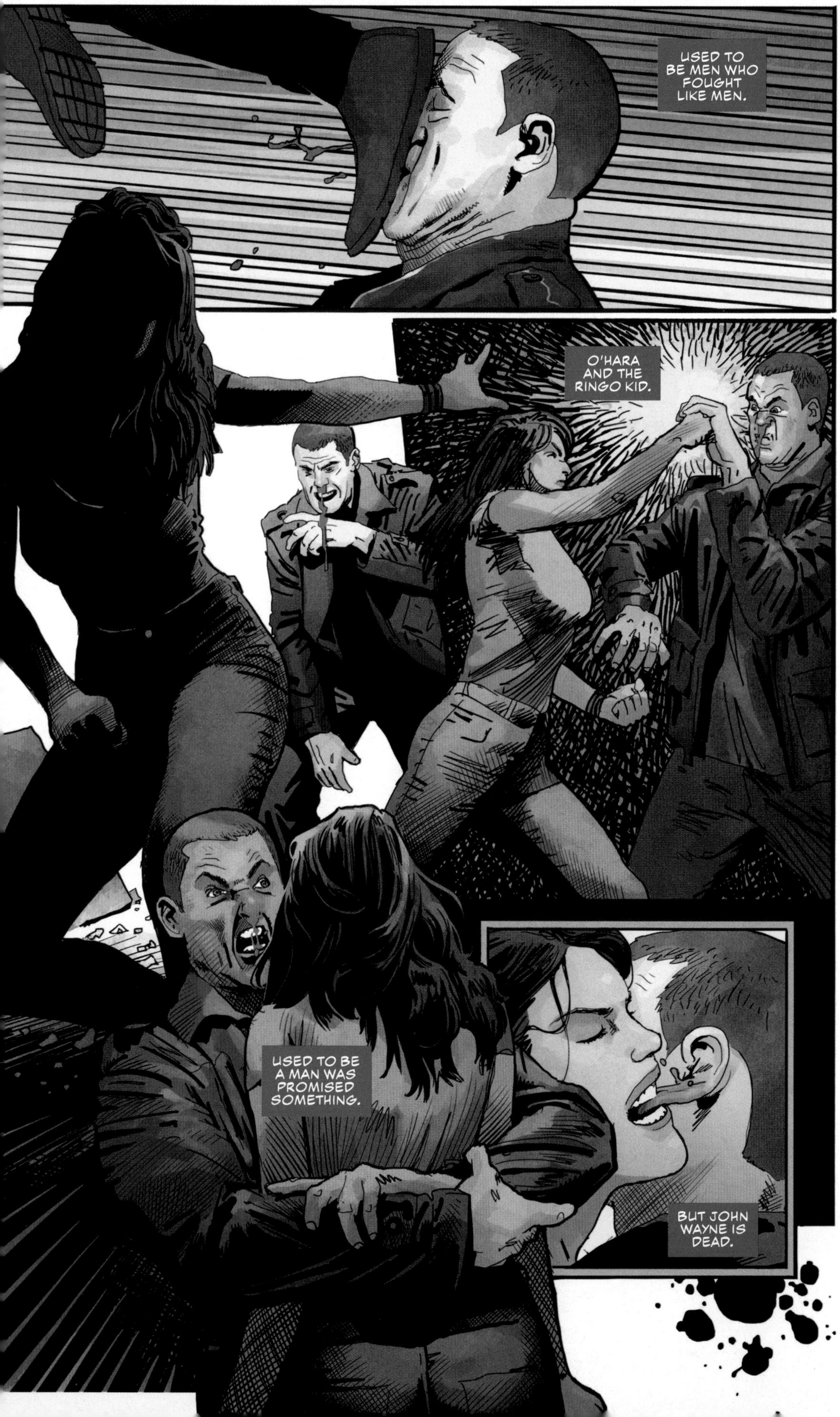
USED TO BE MEN WHO FOUGHT LIKE MEN.
O'HARA AND THE RINGO KID.
USED TO BE A MAN WAS PROMISED SOMETHING.
BUT JOHN WAYNE IS DEAD.

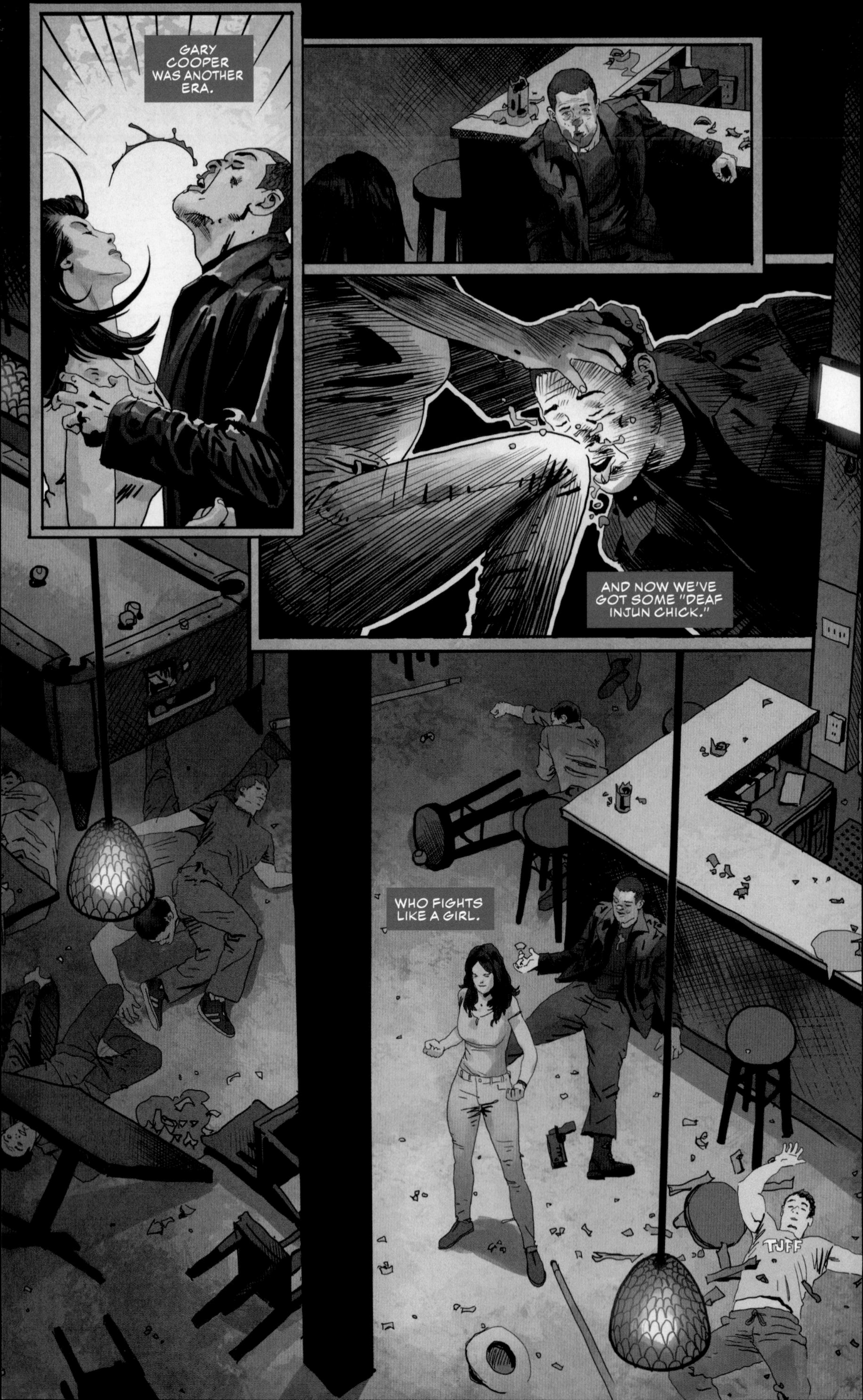
GARY COOPER WAS ANOTHER ERA.
AND NOW WE'VE GOT SOME "DEAF INJUN CHICK."
WHO FIGHTS LIKE A GIRL.
TUFF

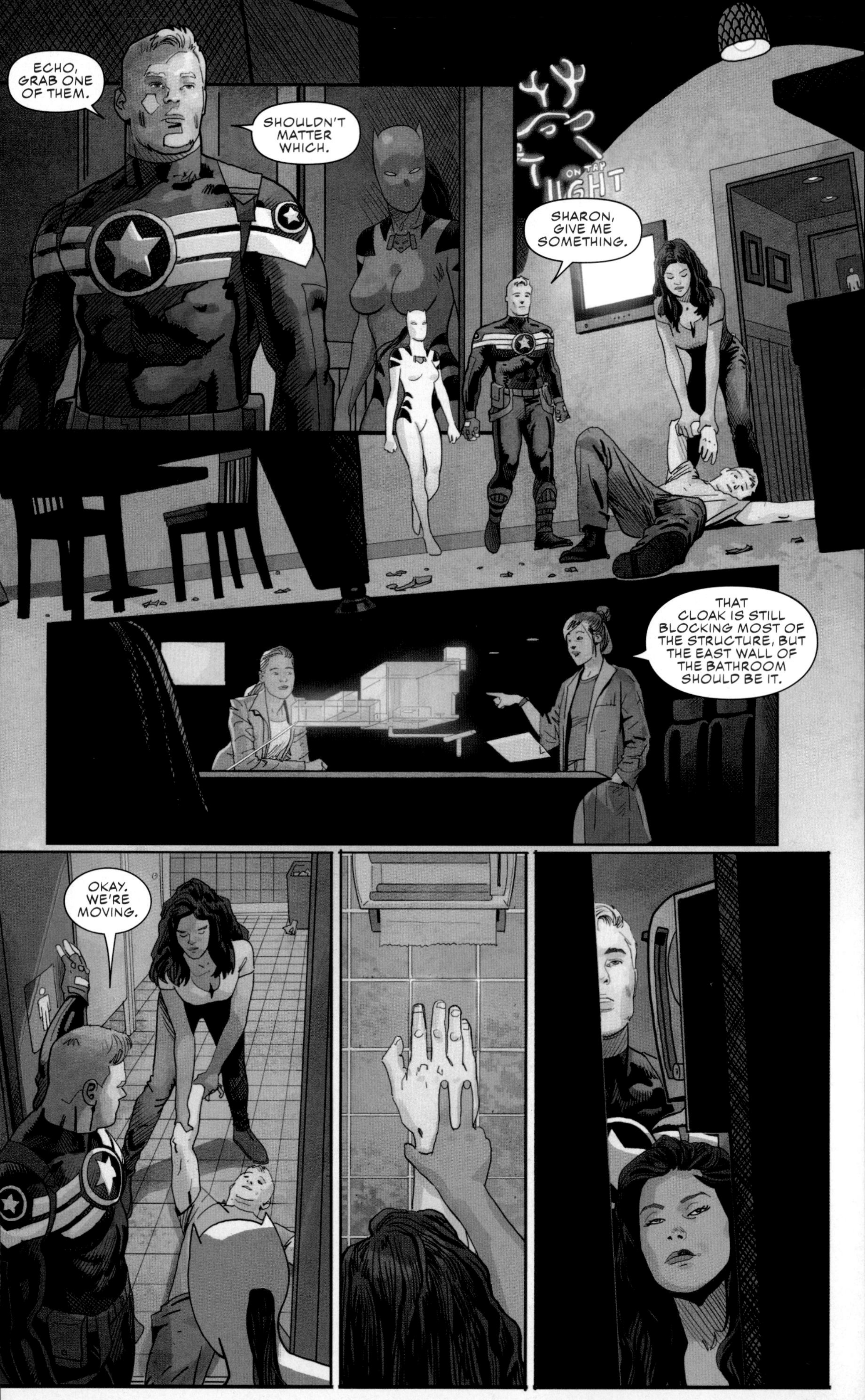
ECHO, GRAB ONE OF THEM.
SHOULDN'T MATTER WHICH.
ON TAP
IGHT
SHARON, GIVE ME SOMETHING.
THAT CLOAK IS STILL BLOCKING MOST OF THE STRUCTURE, BUT THE EAST WALL OF THE BATHROOM SHOULD BE IT.
OKAY. WE'RE MOVING.

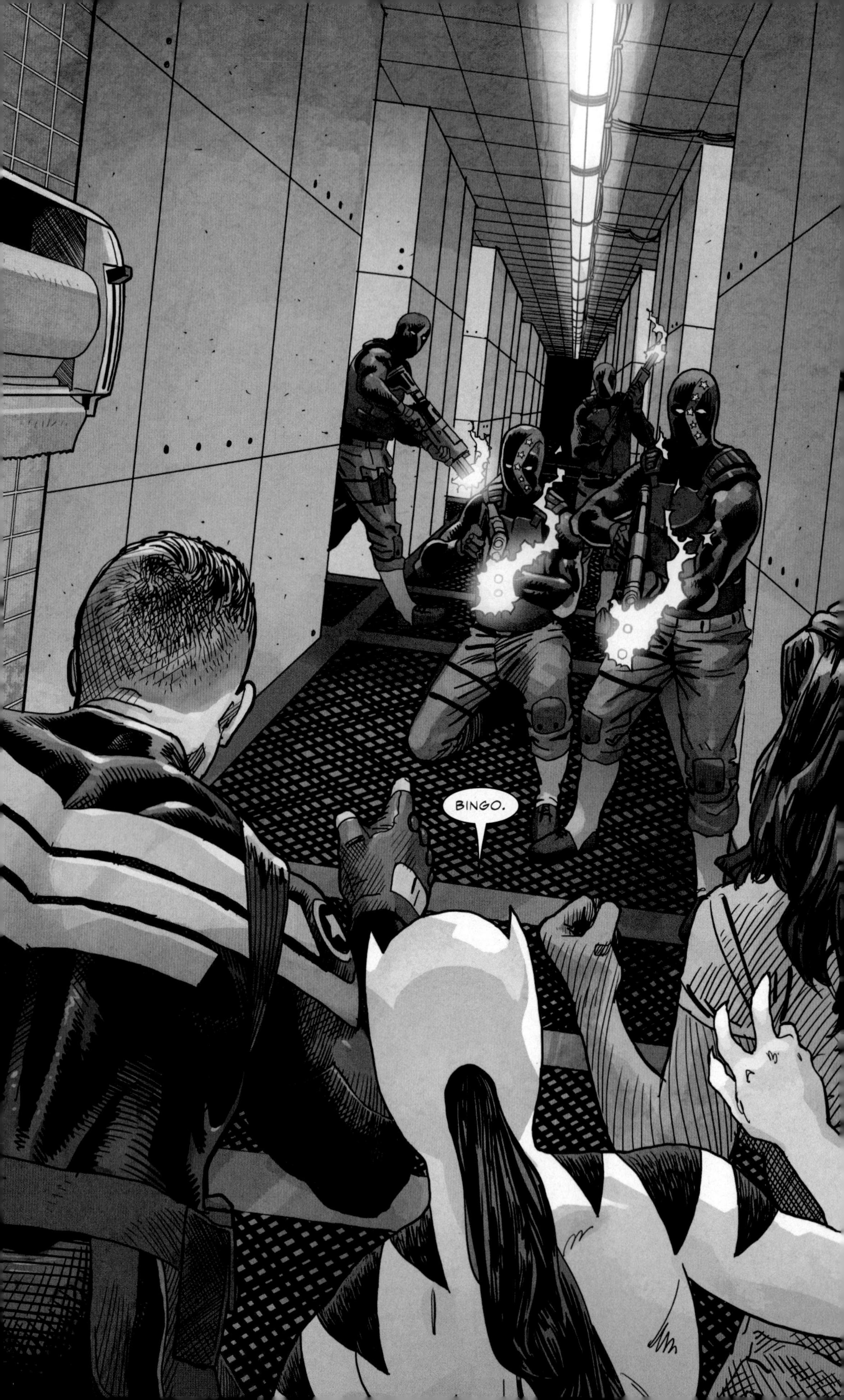
BINGO.

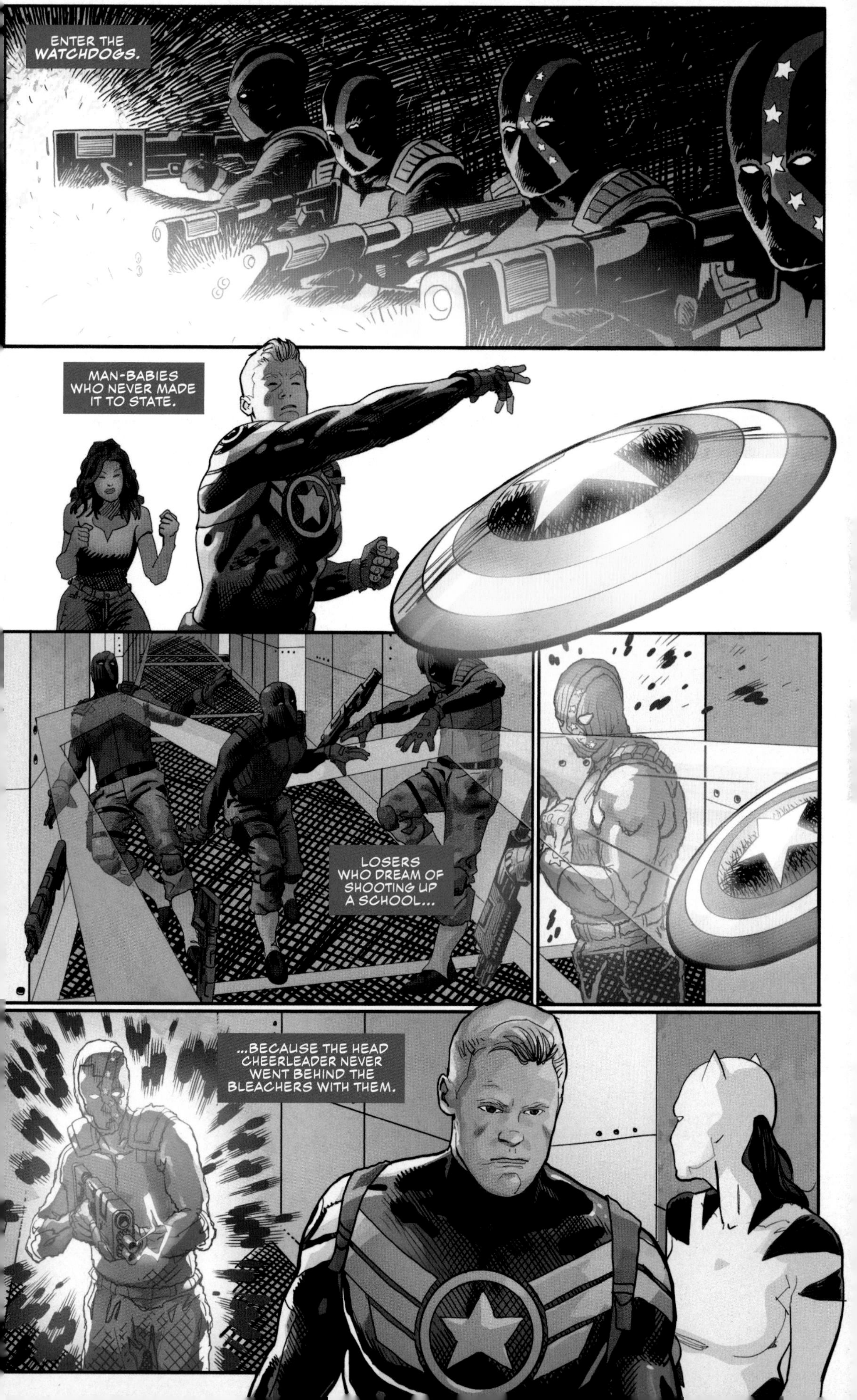

ENTER THE WATCHDOGS.
MAN-BABIES WHO NEVER MADE IT TO STATE.
LOSERS WHO DREAM OF SHOOTING UP A SCHOOL...
...BECAUSE THE HEAD CHEERLEADER NEVER WENT BEHIND THE BLEACHERS WITH THEM.

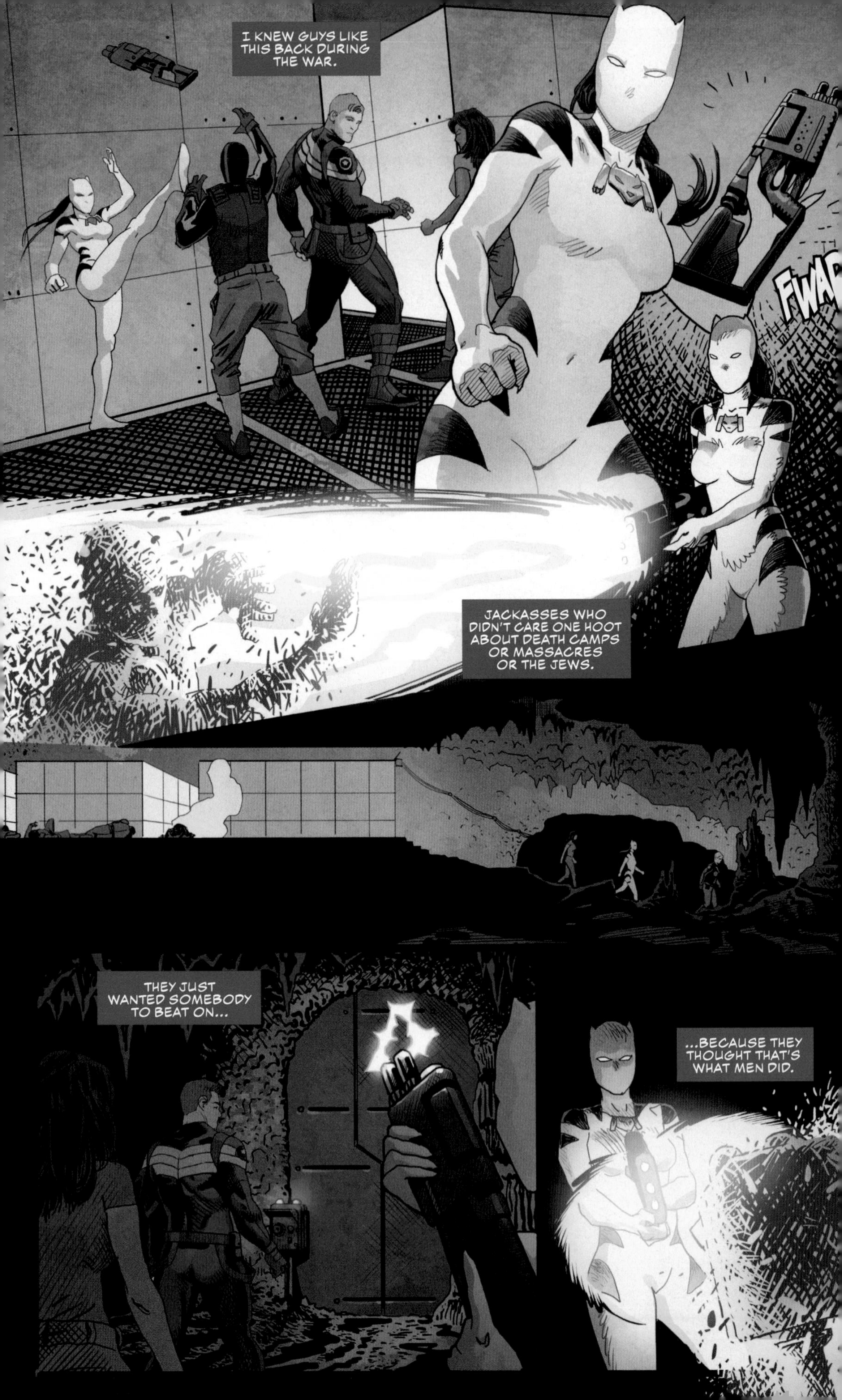
I KNEW GUYS LIKE THIS BACK DURING THE WAR.
FWAP
JACKASSES WHO DIDN'T CARE ONE HOOT ABOUT DEATH CAMPS OR MASSACRES OR THE JEWS.
THEY JUST WANTED SOMEBODY TO BEAT ON...
...BECAUSE THEY THOUGHT THAT'S WHAT MEN DID.

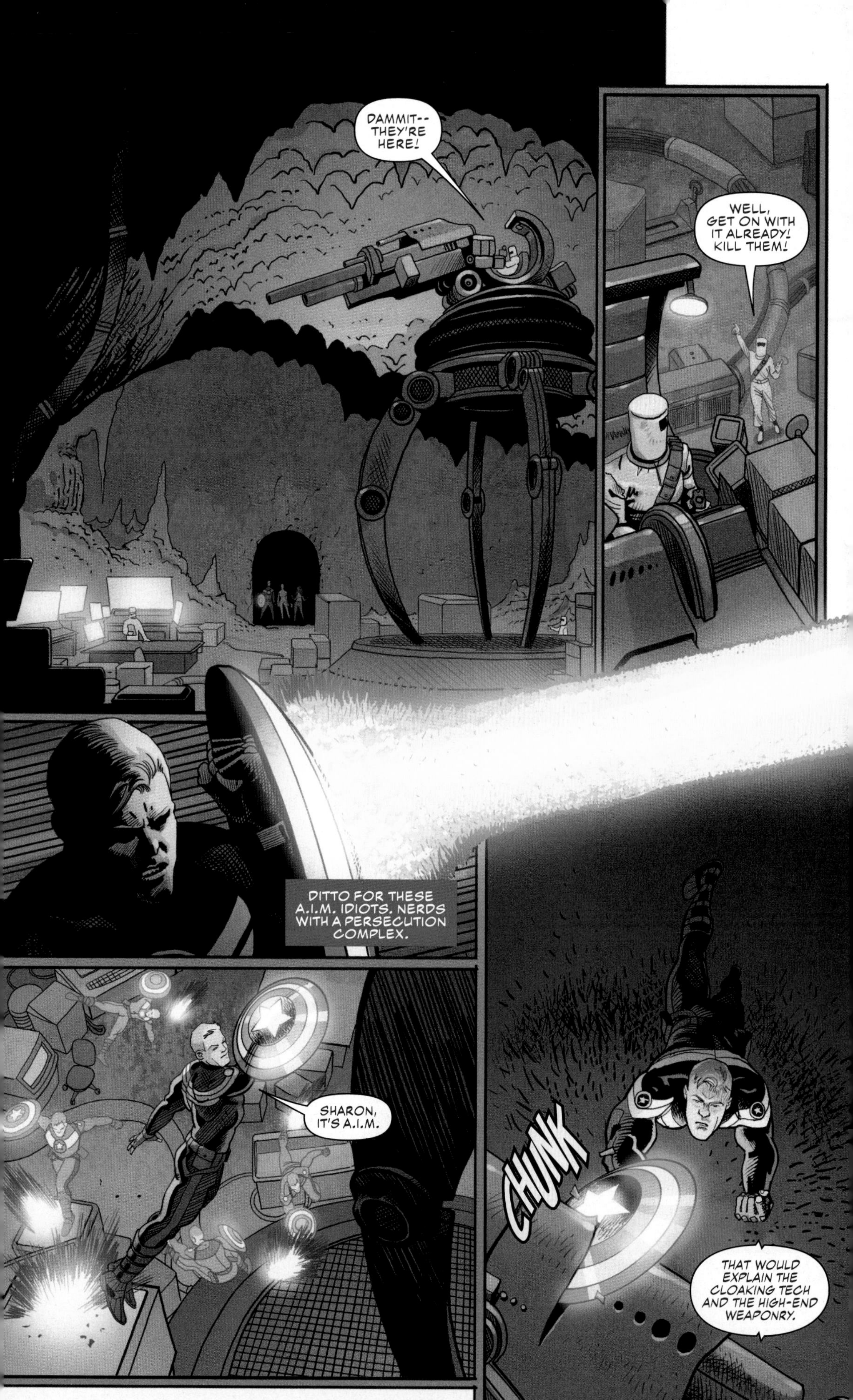
DAMMIT--THEY'RE HERE!
WELL, GET ON WITH IT ALREADY! KILL THEM!
DITTO FOR THESE A.I.M. IDIOTS. NERDS WITH A PERSECUTION COMPLEX.
SHARON, IT'S A.I.M.
CHUNK
THAT WOULD EXPLAIN THE CLOAKING TECH AND THE HIGH-END WEAPONRY.

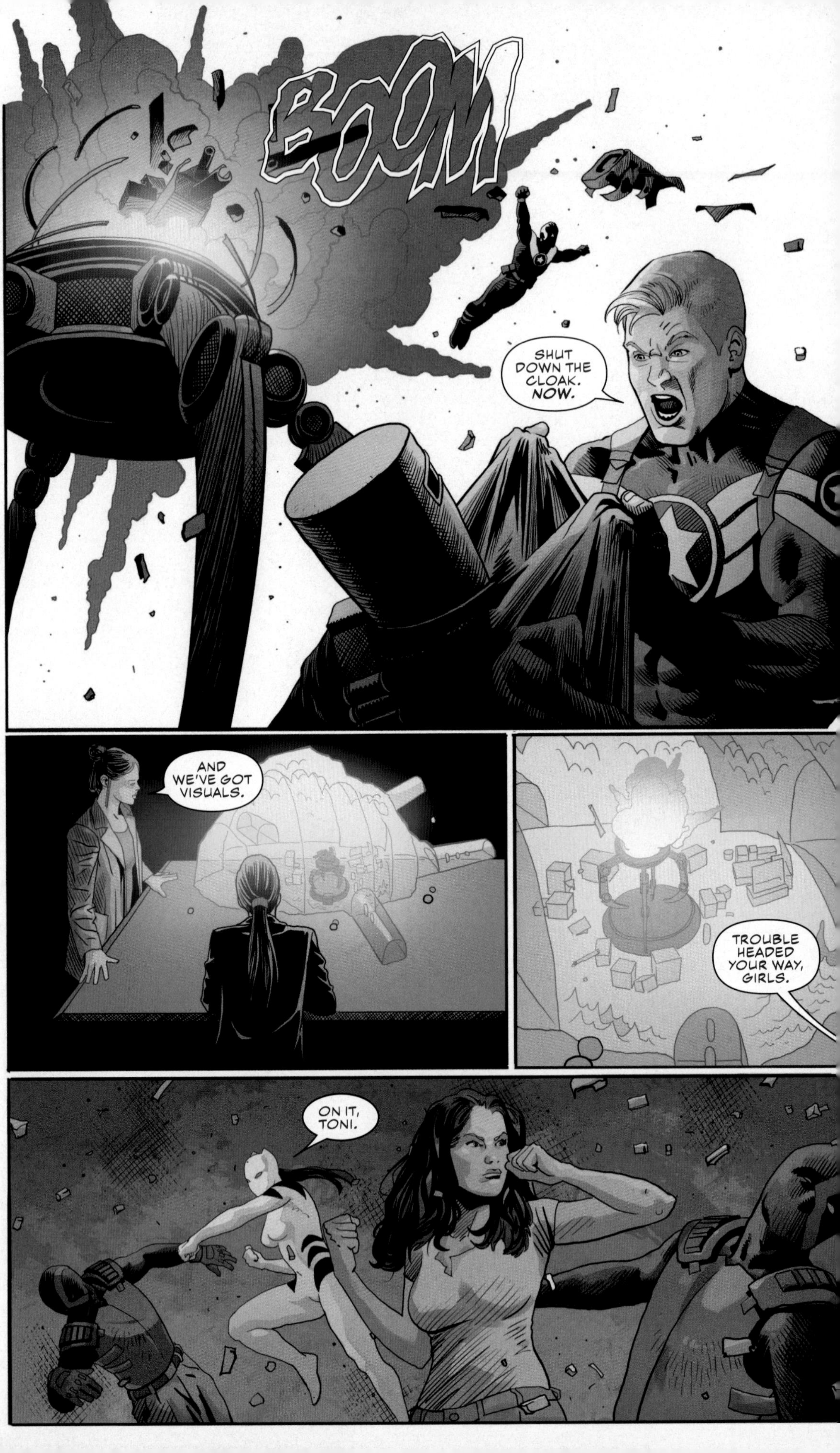
BOOM
SHUT DOWN THE CLOAK. NOW.
AND WE'VE GOT VISUALS.
TROUBLE HEADED YOUR WAY, GIRLS.
ON IT, TONI.

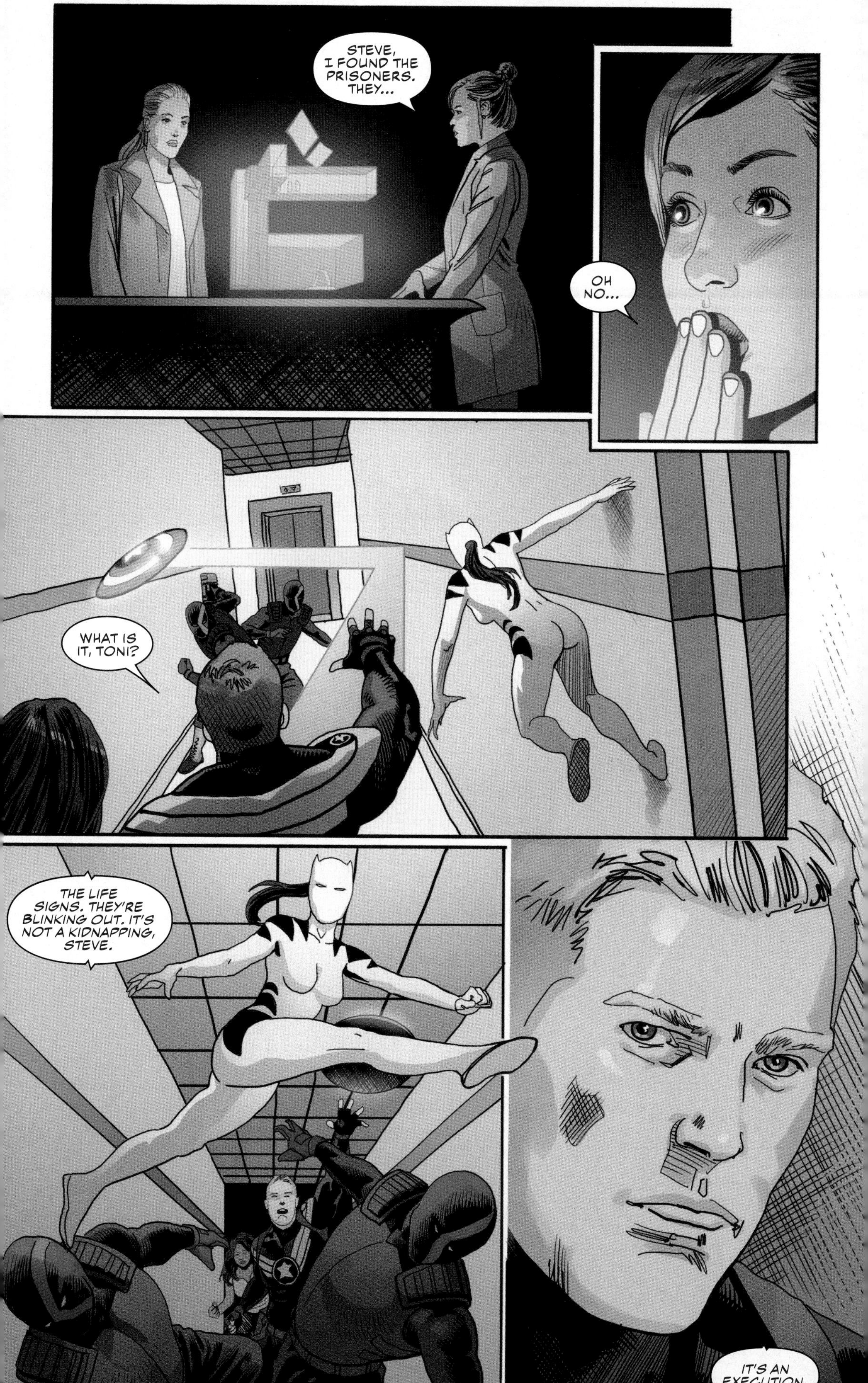
STEVE, I FOUND THE PRISONERS. THEY...
OH NO...
WHAT IS IT, TONI?
THE LIFE SIGNS. THEY'RE BLINKING OUT. IT'S NOT A KIDNAPPING, STEVE.
IT'S AN EXECUTION.

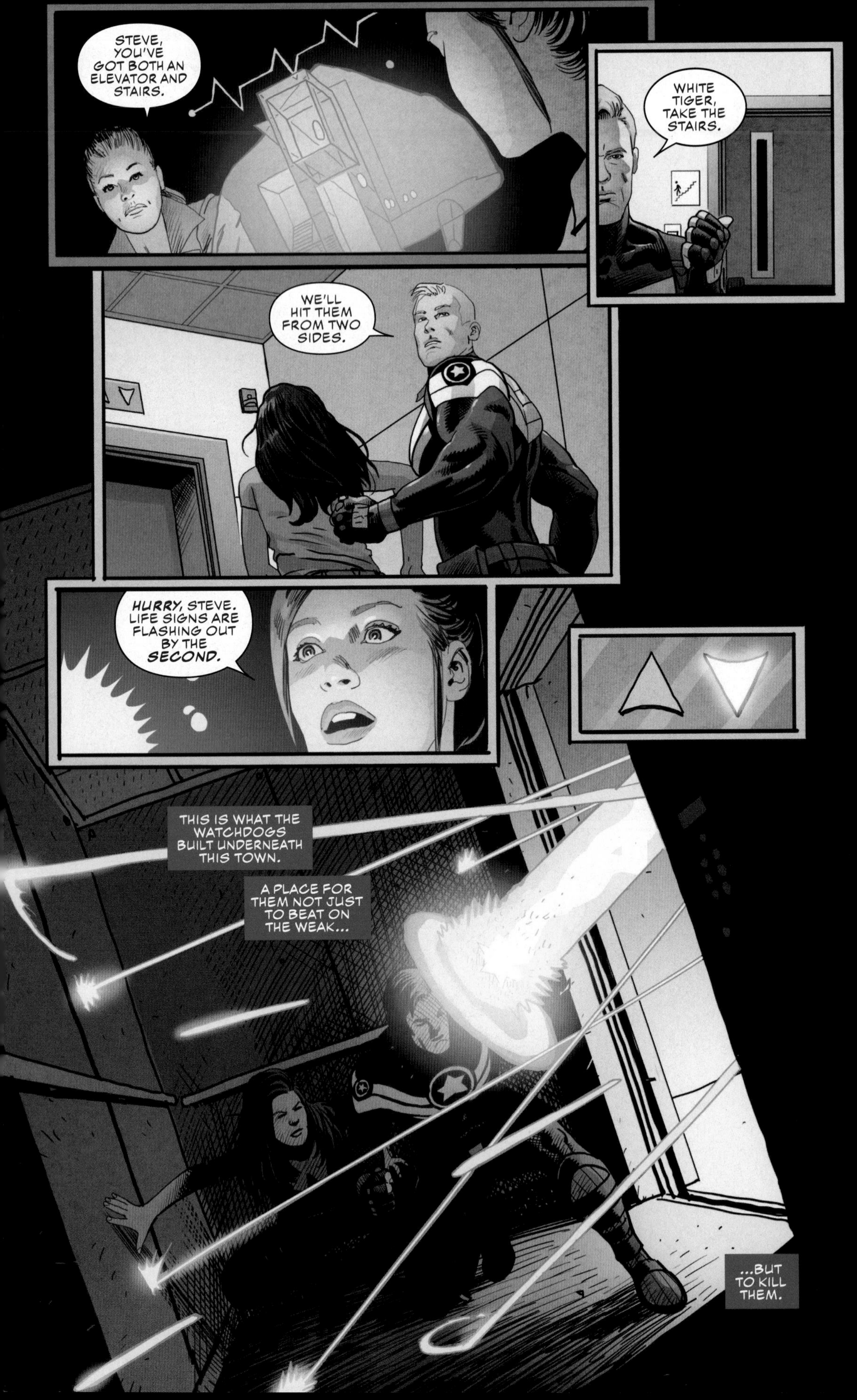

STEVE, YOU'VE GOT BOTH AN ELEVATOR AND STAIRS.
WHITE TIGER, TAKE THE STAIRS.
WE'LL HIT THEM FROM TWO SIDES.
HURRY, STEVE. LIFE SIGNS ARE FLASHING OUT BY THE SECOND.
THIS IS WHAT THE WATCHDOGS BUILT UNDERNEATH THIS TOWN.
A PLACE FOR THEM NOT JUST TO BEAT ON THE WEAK...
...BUT TO KILL THEM.

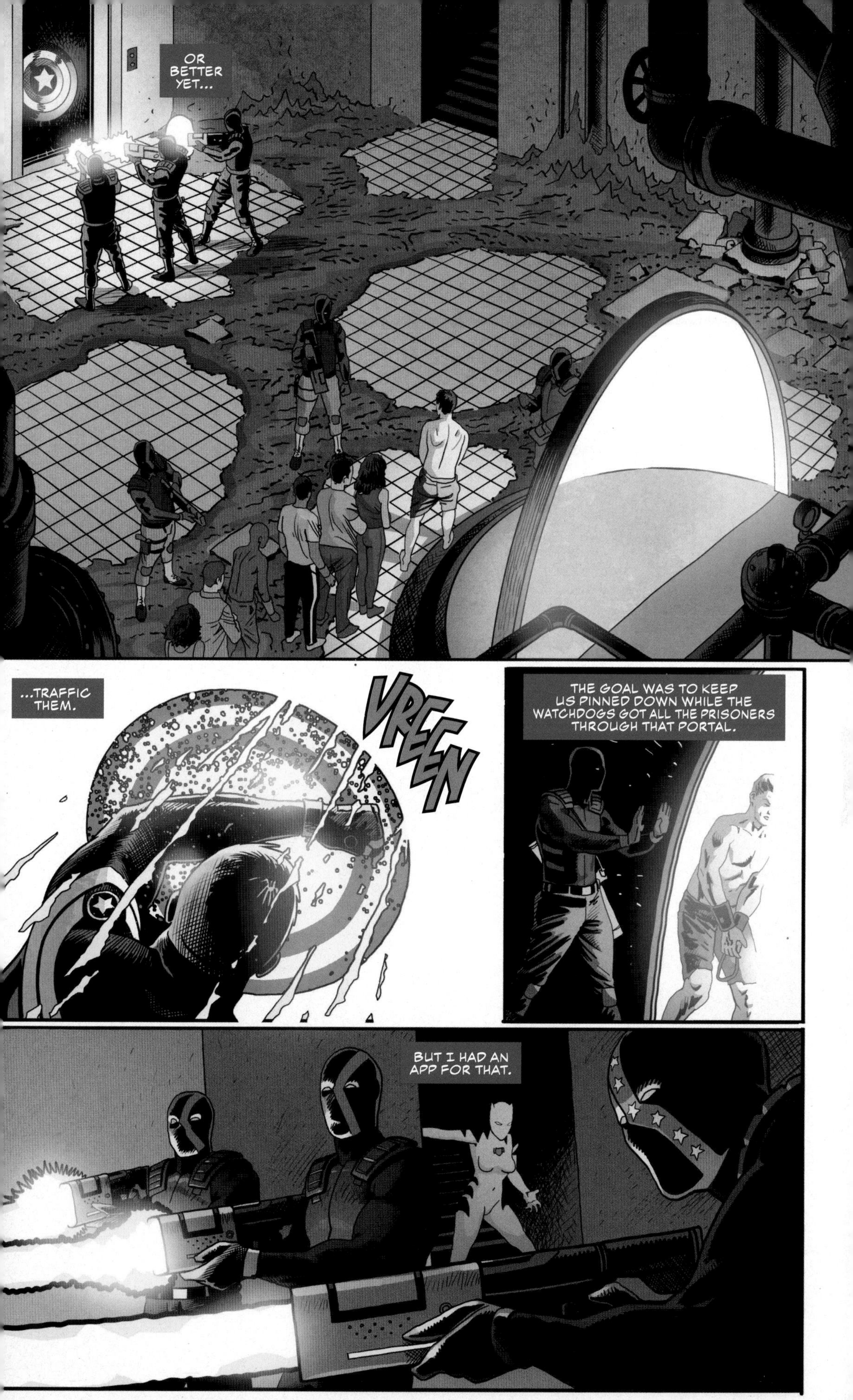

OR BETTER YET...
...TRAFFIC THEM.
VREEN
THE GOAL WAS TO KEEP US PINNED DOWN WHILE THE WATCHDOGS GOT ALL THE PRISONERS THROUGH THAT PORTAL.
BUT I HAD AN APP FOR THAT.

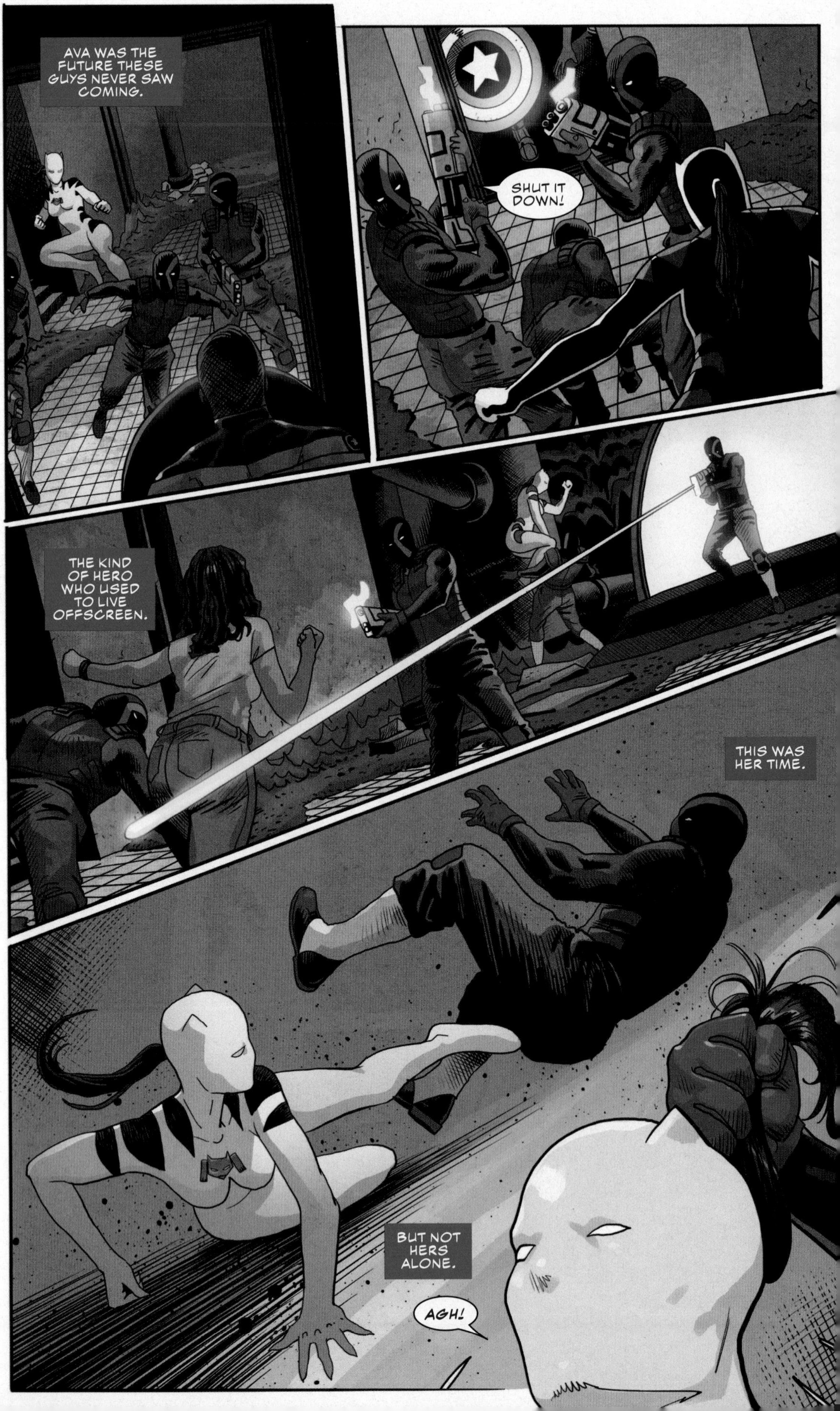
AVA WAS THE FUTURE THESE GUYS NEVER SAW COMING.
SHUT IT DOWN!
THE KIND OF HERO WHO USED TO LIVE OFFSCREEN.
THIS WAS HER TIME.
BUT NOT HERS ALONE.
AGH!

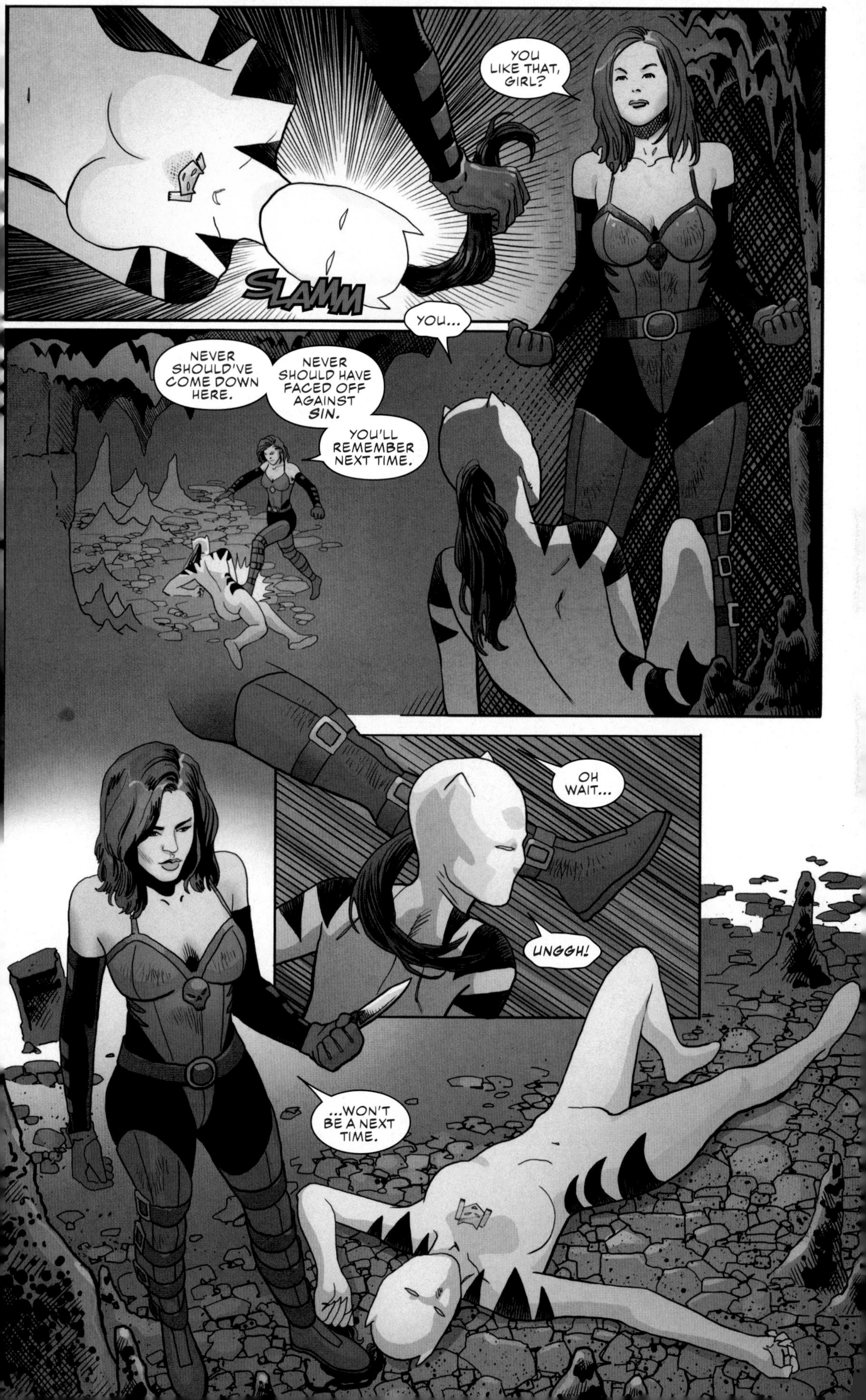
YOU LIKE THAT, GIRL?
SLAMM
YOU...
NEVER SHOULD'VE COME DOWN HERE.
NEVER SHOULD HAVE FACED OFF AGAINST SIN.
YOU'LL REMEMBER NEXT TIME.
OH WAIT...
UNGGH!
...WON'T BE A NEXT TIME.

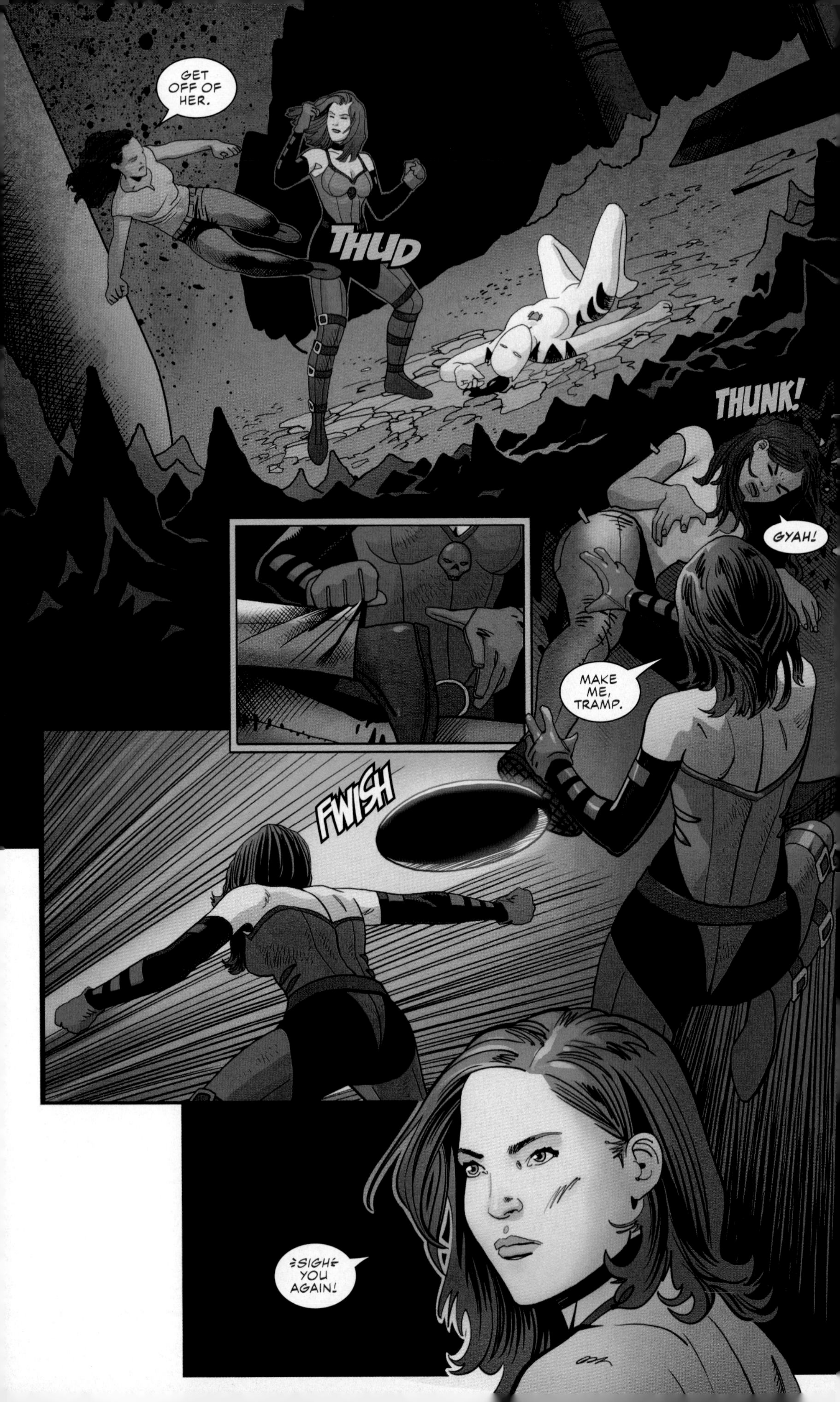
GET OFF OF HER.
THUD
THUNK!
GYAH!
MAKE ME, TRAMP.
FWISH
=SIGH= YOU AGAIN!

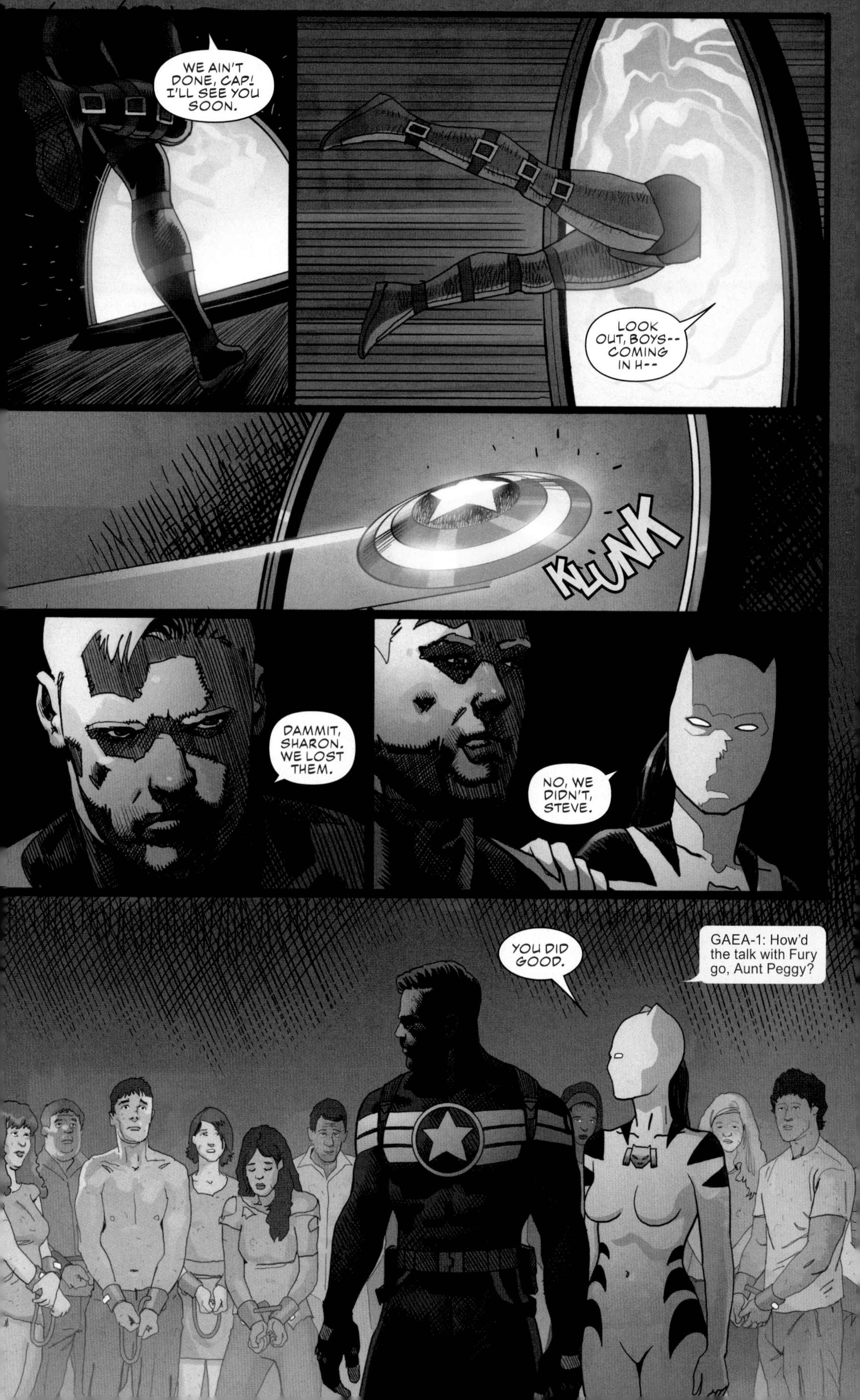
WE AIN'T DONE, CAP! I'LL SEE YOU SOON.
LOOK OUT, BOYS-- COMING IN H--
KLUNK
DAMMIT, SHARON. WE LOST THEM.
NO, WE DIDN'T, STEVE.
YOU DID GOOD.
GAEA-1: How'd the talk with Fury go, Aunt Peggy?

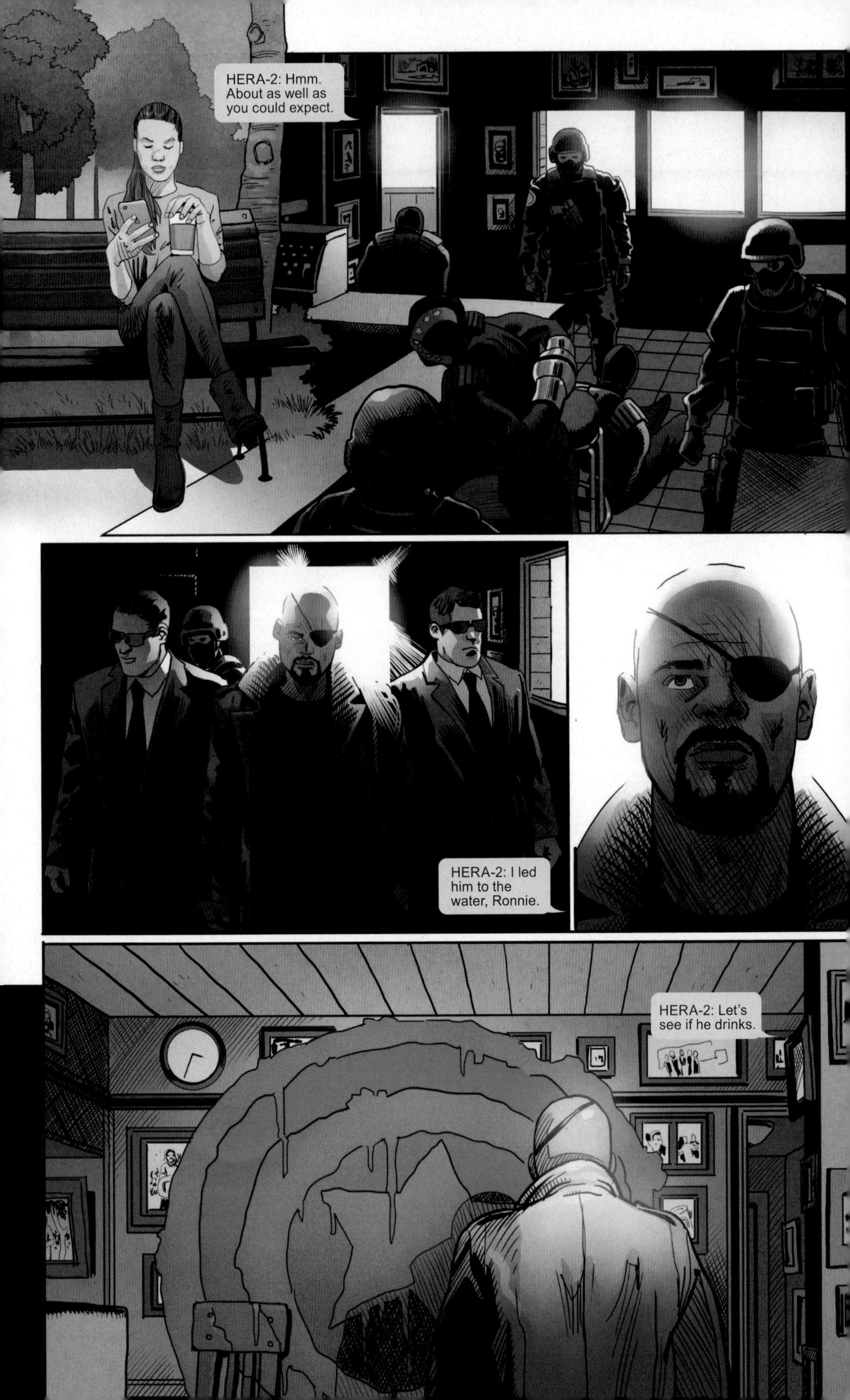
HERA-2: Hmm. About as well as you could expect.
HERA-2: I led him to the water, Ronnie.
HERA-2: Let's see if he drinks.

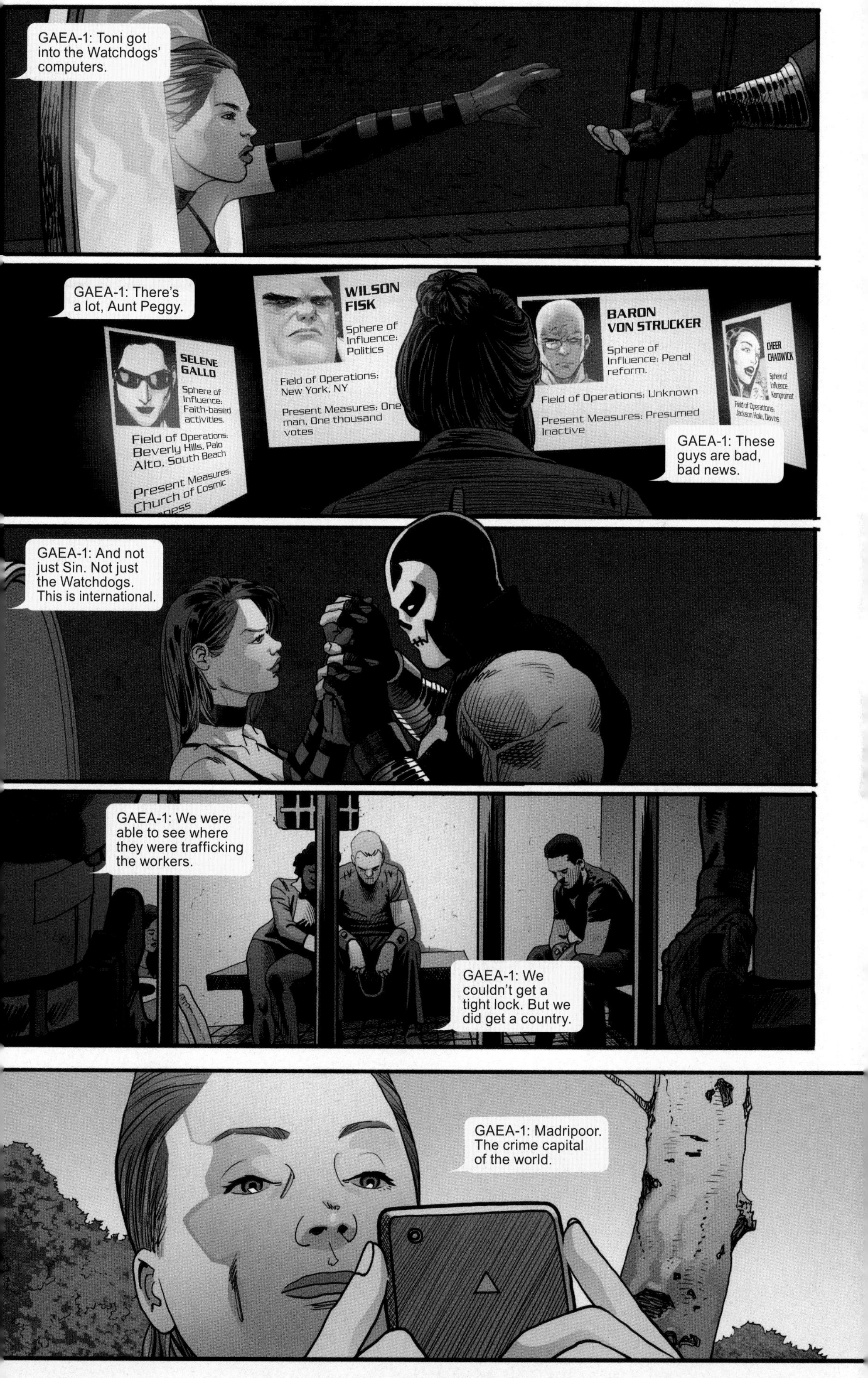

GAEA-1: Toni got into the Watchdogs' computers.
GAEA-1: There's a lot, Aunt Peggy.
SELENE GALLO
Sphere of Influence: Faith-based activities.
Field of Operations: Beverly Hills, Palo Alto, South Beach
Present Measures: Church of Cosmic
WILSON FISK
Sphere of Influence: Politics
Field of Operations: New York, NY
Present Measures: One man, One thousand votes
BARON VON STRUCKER
Sphere of Influence: Penal reform.
Field of Operations: Unknown
Present Measures: Presumed Inactive
CHEER CHADWICK
Sphere of Influence: Kompromat
Field of Operations: Jackson Hole, Davos
GAEA-1: These guys are bad, bad news.
GAEA-1: And not just Sin. Not just the Watchdogs. This is international.
GAEA-1: We were able to see where they were trafficking the workers.
GAEA-1: We couldn't get a tight lock. But we did get a country.
GAEA-1: Madripoor. The crime capital of the world.

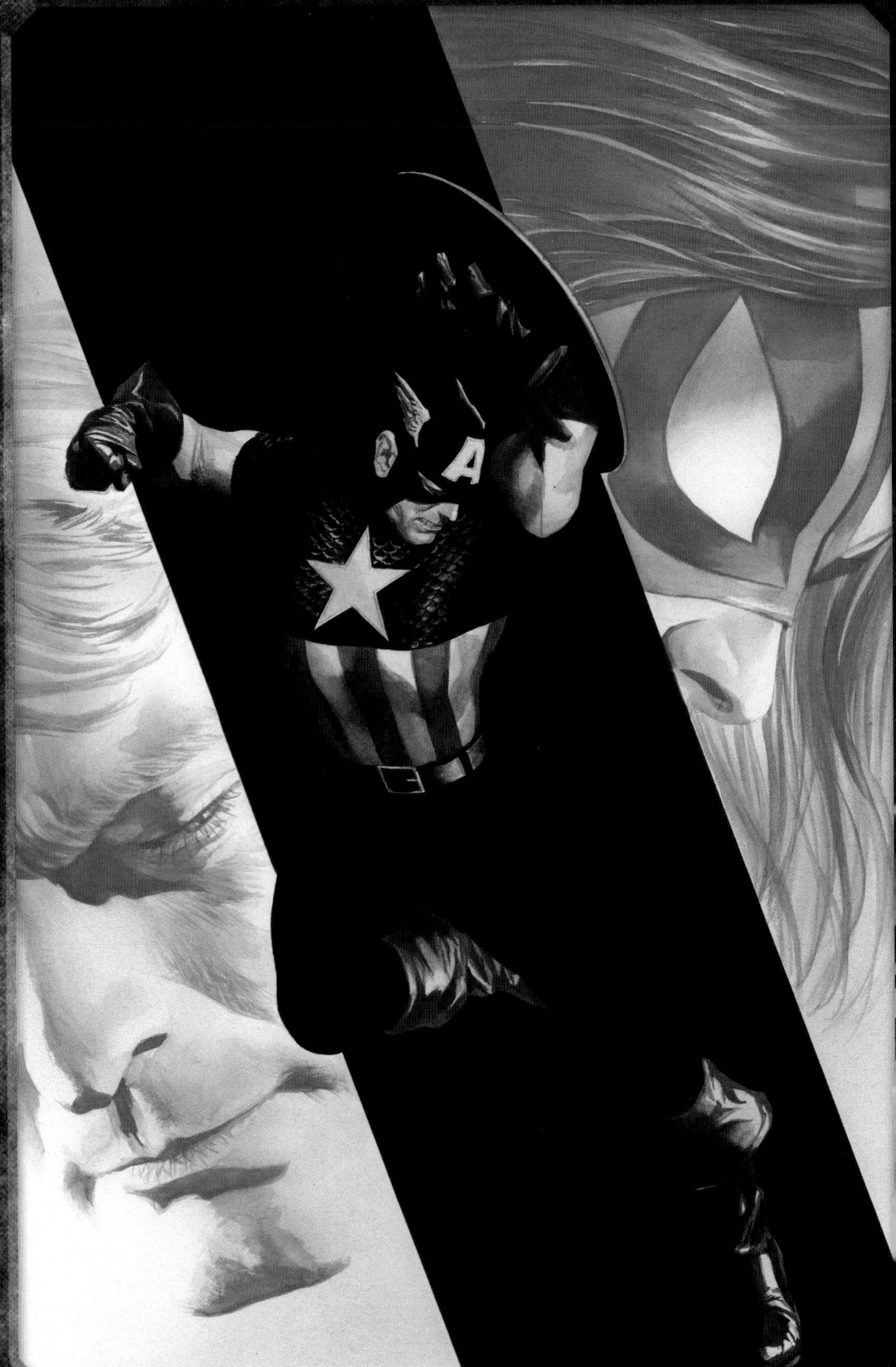

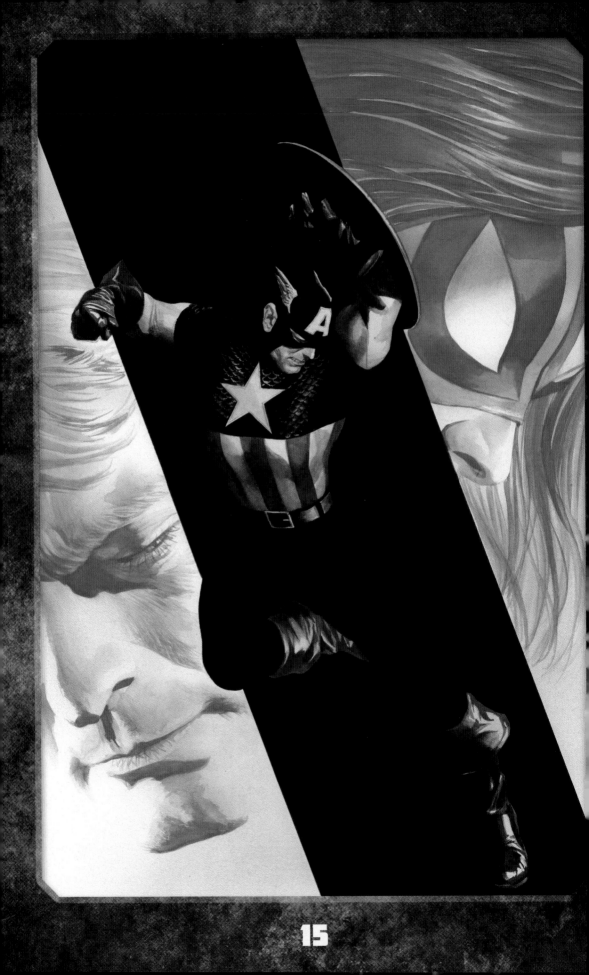

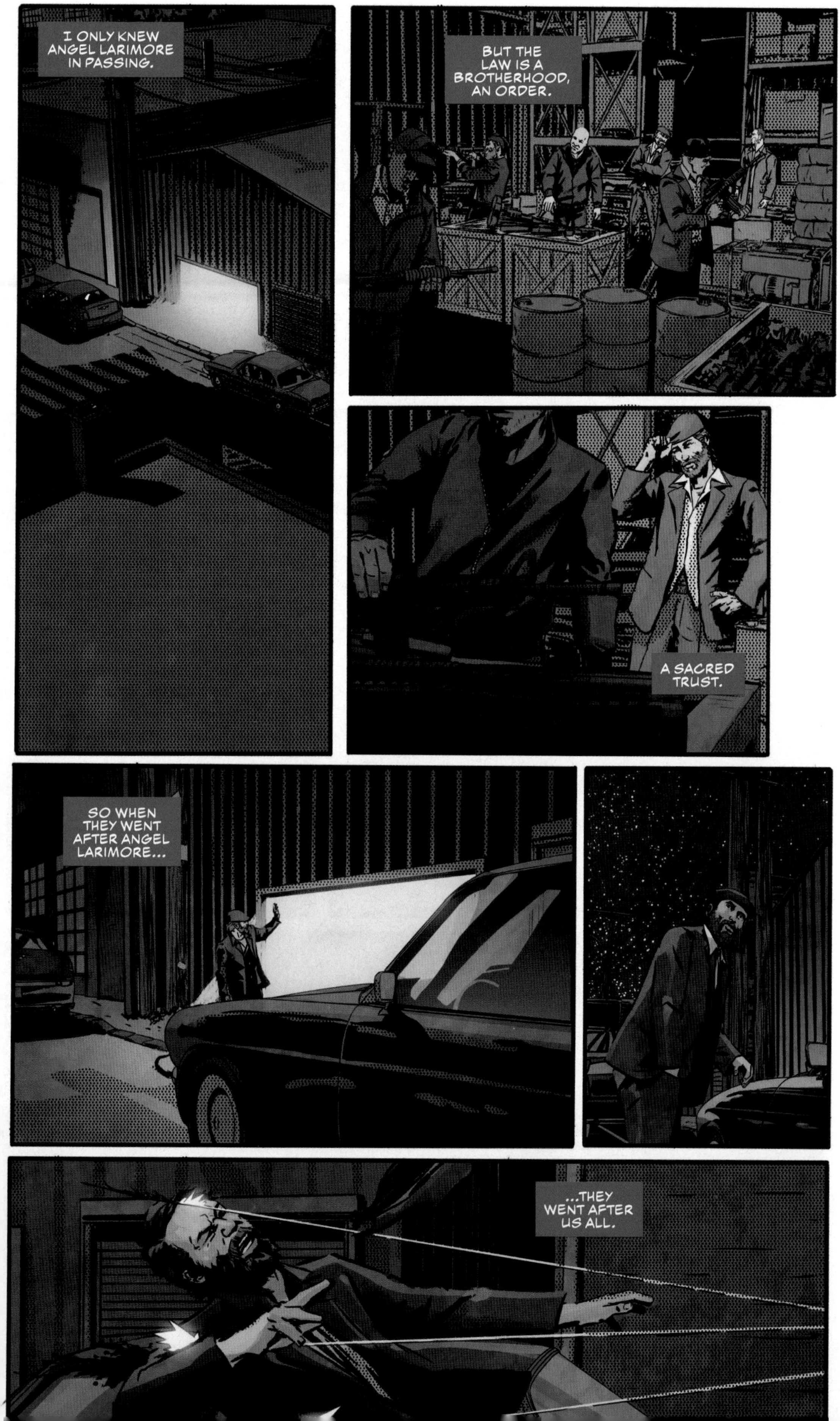
I ONLY KNEW ANGEL LARIMORE IN PASSING.
BUT THE LAW IS A BROTHERHOOD, AN ORDER.
A SACRED TRUST.
SO WHEN THEY WENT AFTER ANGEL LARIMORE...
...THEY WENT AFTER US ALL.

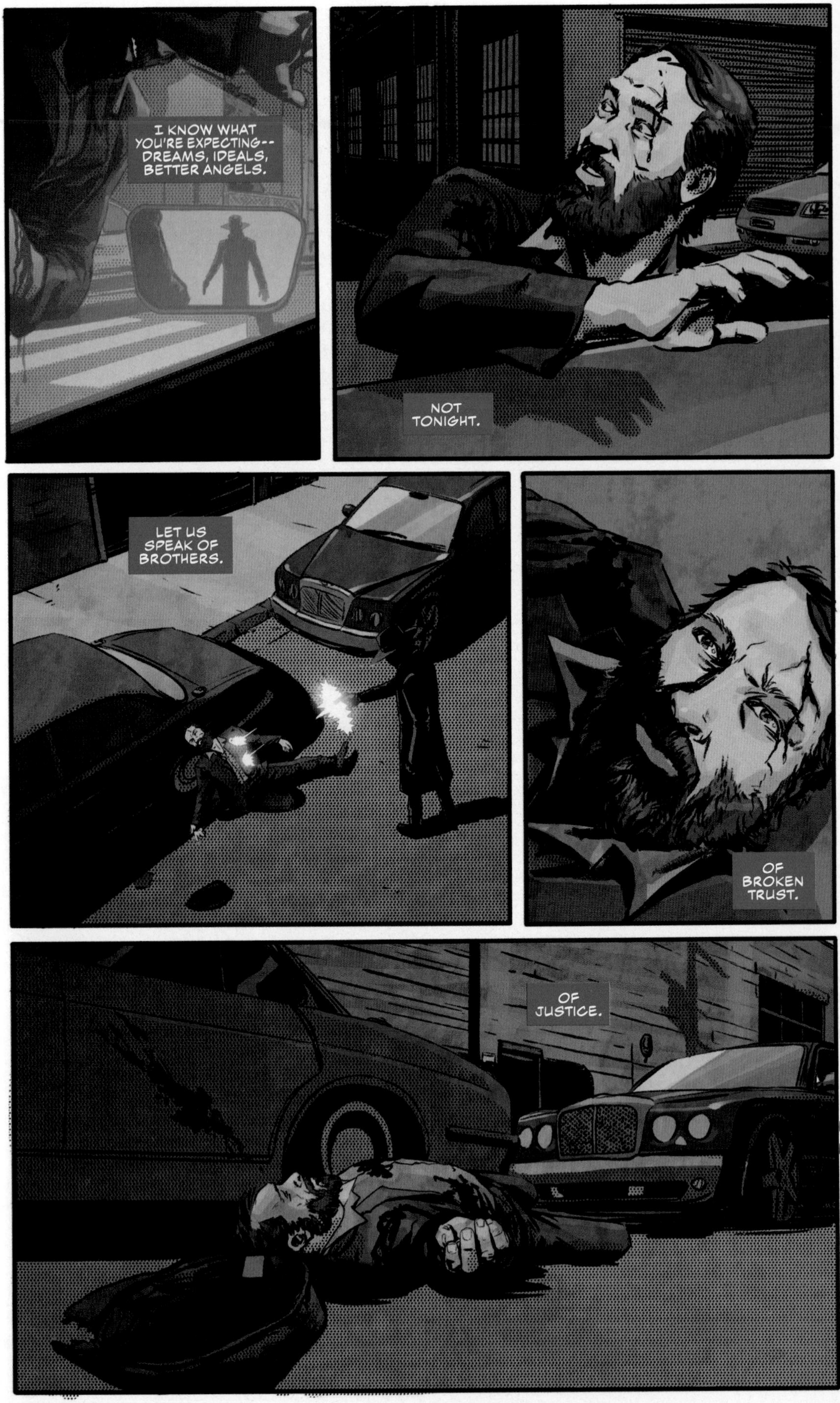
I KNOW WHAT YOU'RE EXPECTING-- DREAMS, IDEALS, BETTER ANGELS.
NOT TONIGHT.
LET US SPEAK OF BROTHERS.
OF BROKEN TRUST.
OF JUSTICE.

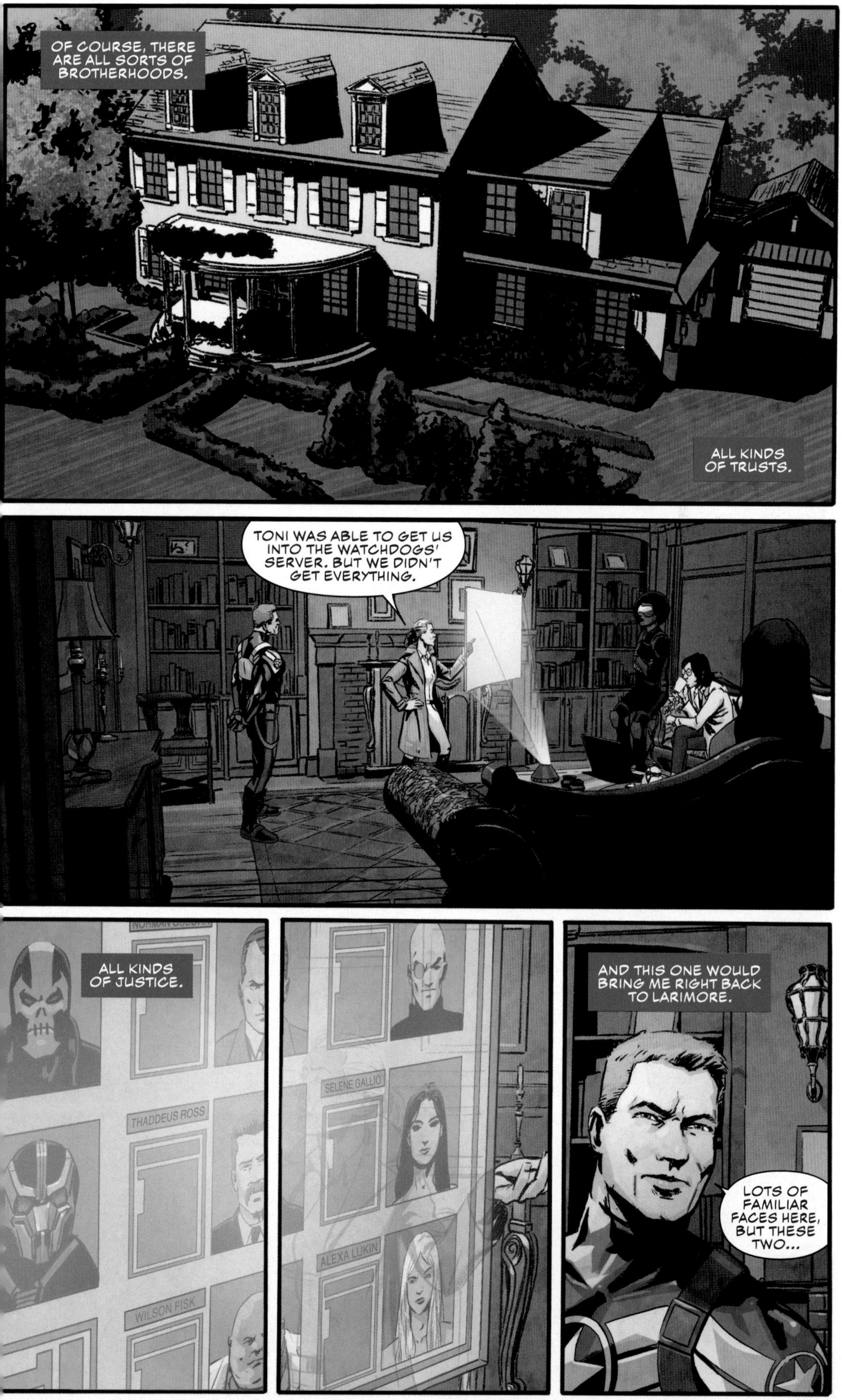

OF COURSE, THERE ARE ALL SORTS OF BROTHERHOODS.
ALL KINDS OF TRUSTS.
TONI WAS ABLE TO GET US INTO THE WATCHDOGS' SERVER. BUT WE DIDN'T GET EVERYTHING.
ALL KINDS OF JUSTICE.
THADDEUS ROSS
WILSON FISK
SELENE GALLIO
ALEXA LUKIN
AND THIS ONE WOULD BRING ME RIGHT BACK TO LARIMORE.
LOTS OF FAMILIAR FACES HERE, BUT THESE TWO...

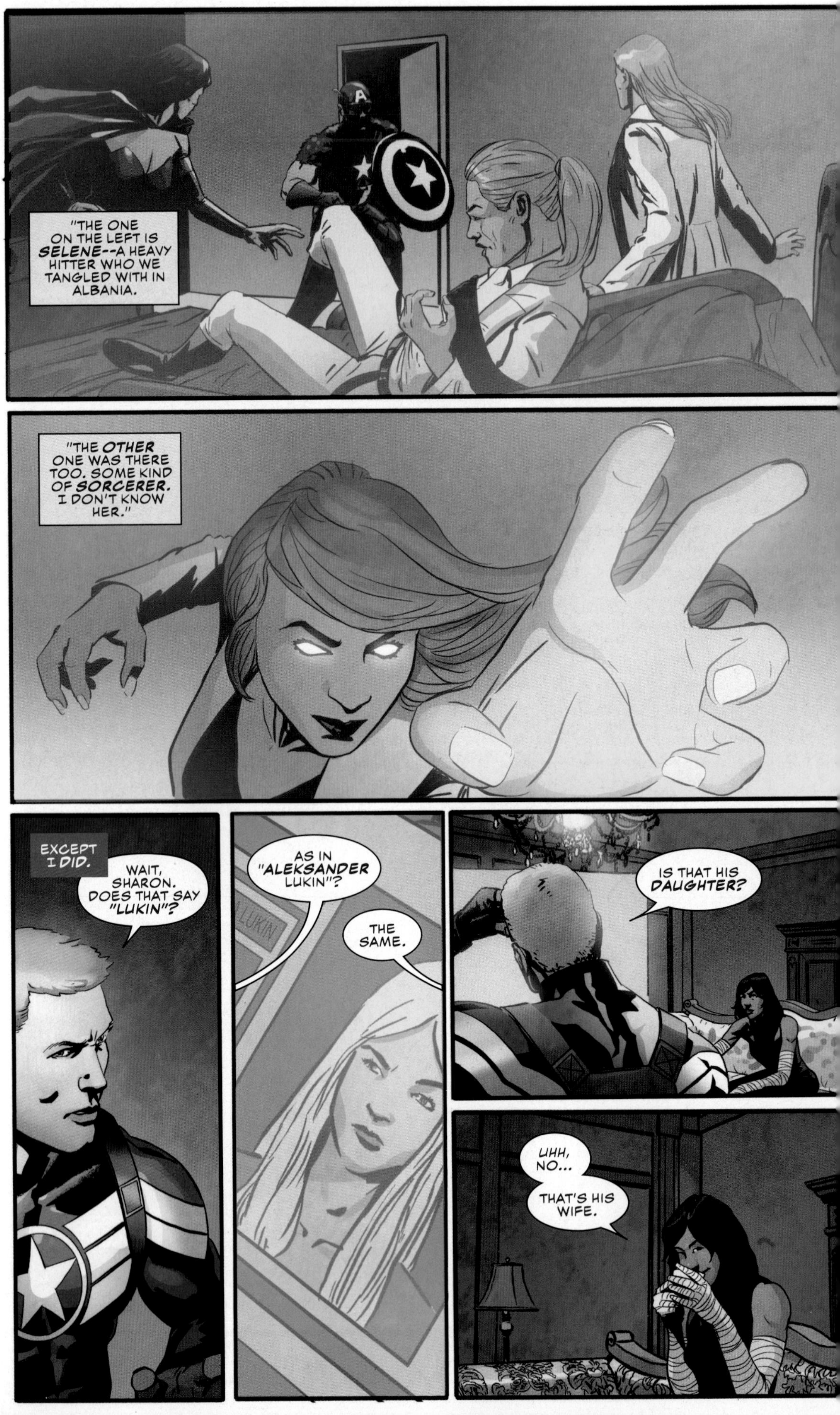
"THE ONE ON THE LEFT IS SELENE--A HEAVY HITTER WHO WE TANGLED WITH IN ALBANIA.
"THE OTHER ONE WAS THERE TOO. SOME KIND OF SORCERER. I DON'T KNOW HER."
EXCEPT I DID.
WAIT, SHARON. DOES THAT SAY "LUKIN"?
AS IN "ALEKSANDER LUKIN"?
THE SAME.
IS THAT HIS DAUGHTER?
UHH, NO...
THAT'S HIS WIFE.

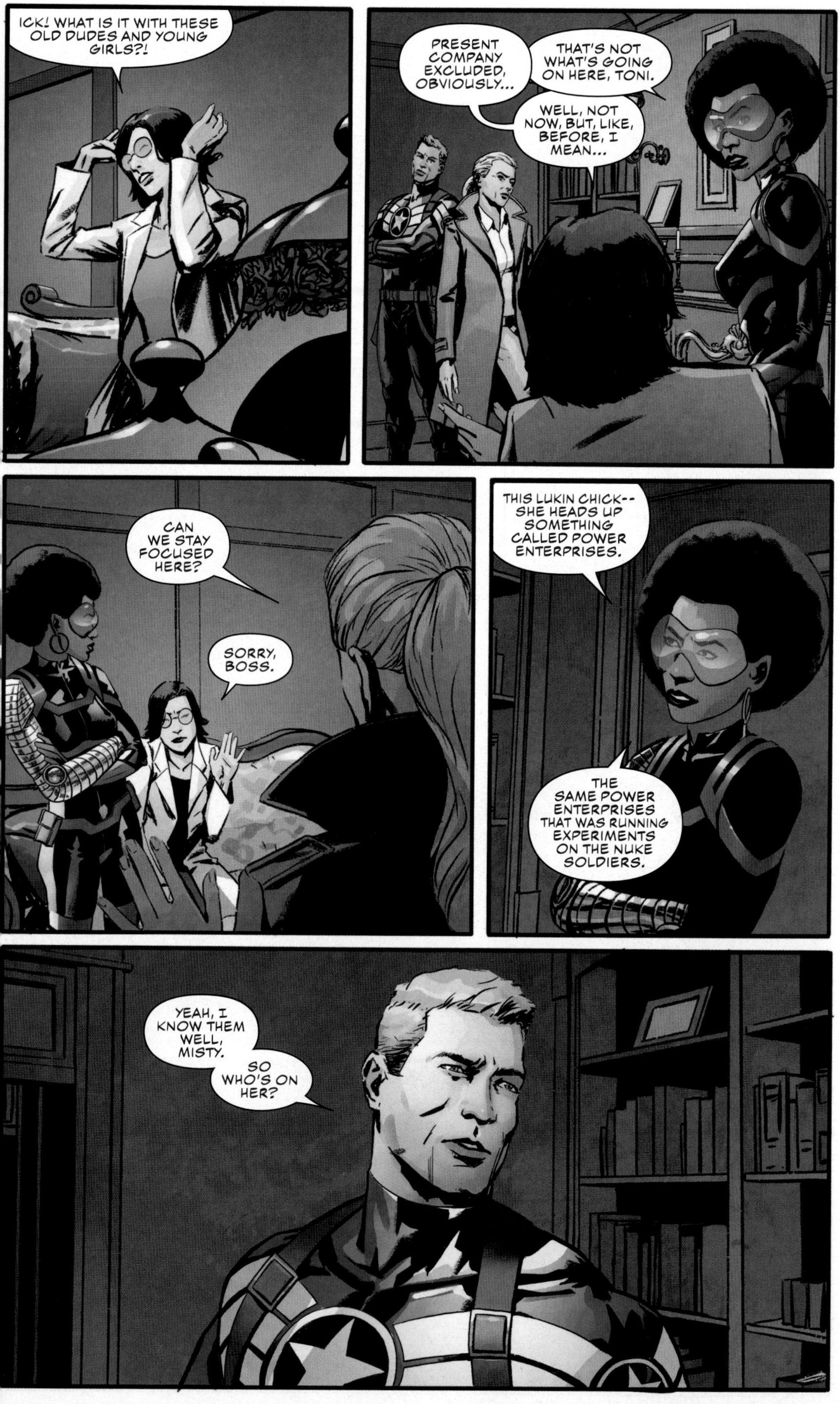
ICK! WHAT IS IT WITH THESE OLD DUDES AND YOUNG GIRLS?!
PRESENT COMPANY EXCLUDED, OBVIOUSLY...
THAT'S NOT WHAT'S GOING ON HERE, TONI.
WELL, NOT NOW, BUT, LIKE, BEFORE, I MEAN...
CAN WE STAY FOCUSED HERE?
SORRY, BOSS.
THIS LUKIN CHICK--SHE HEADS UP SOMETHING CALLED POWER ENTERPRISES.
THE SAME POWER ENTERPRISES THAT WAS RUNNING EXPERIMENTS ON THE NUKE SOLDIERS.
YEAH, I KNOW THEM WELL, MISTY.
SO WHO'S ON HER?

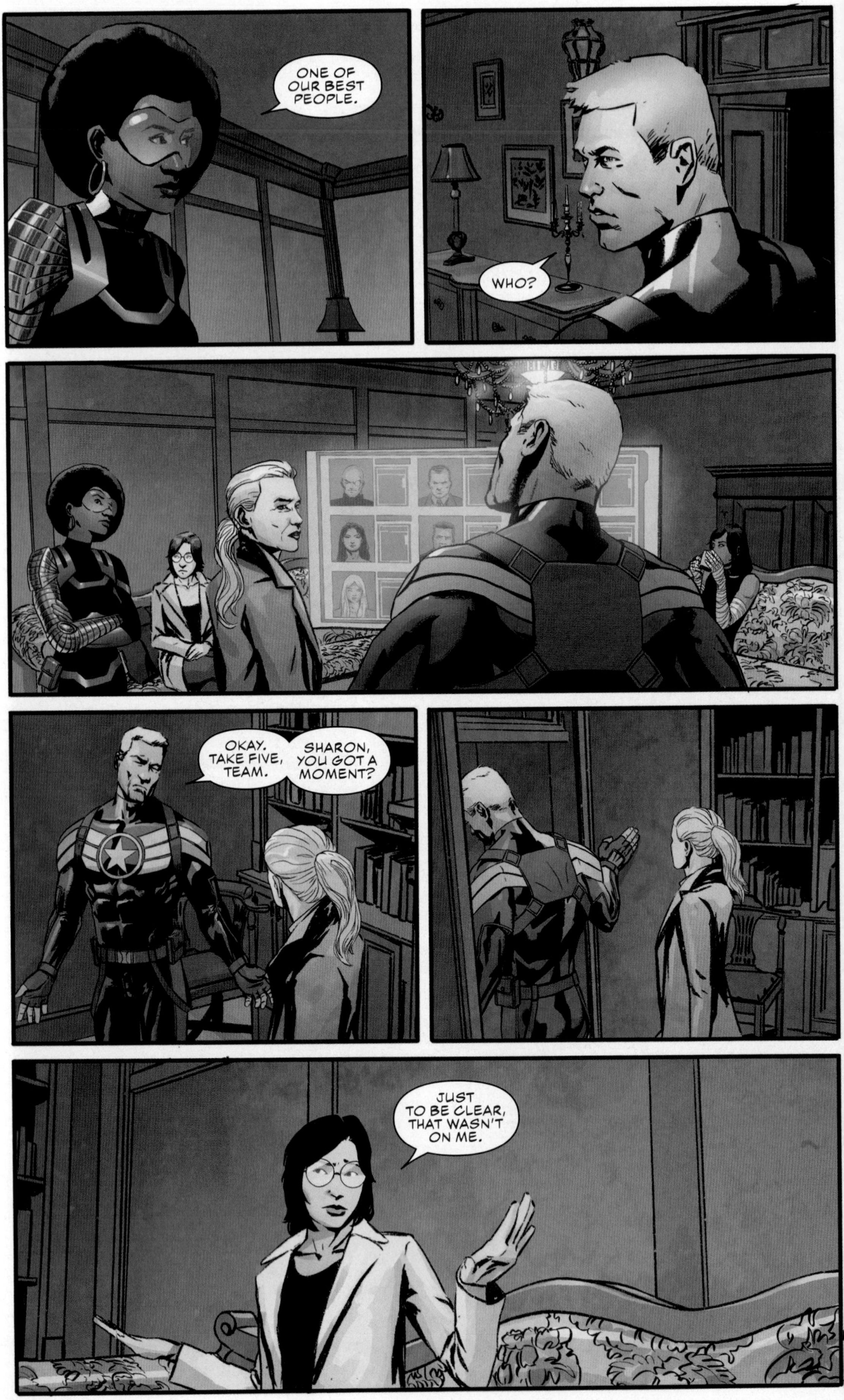
ONE OF OUR BEST PEOPLE.
WHO?
OKAY. TAKE FIVE, TEAM.
SHARON, YOU GOT A MOMENT?
JUST TO BE CLEAR, THAT WASN'T ON ME.

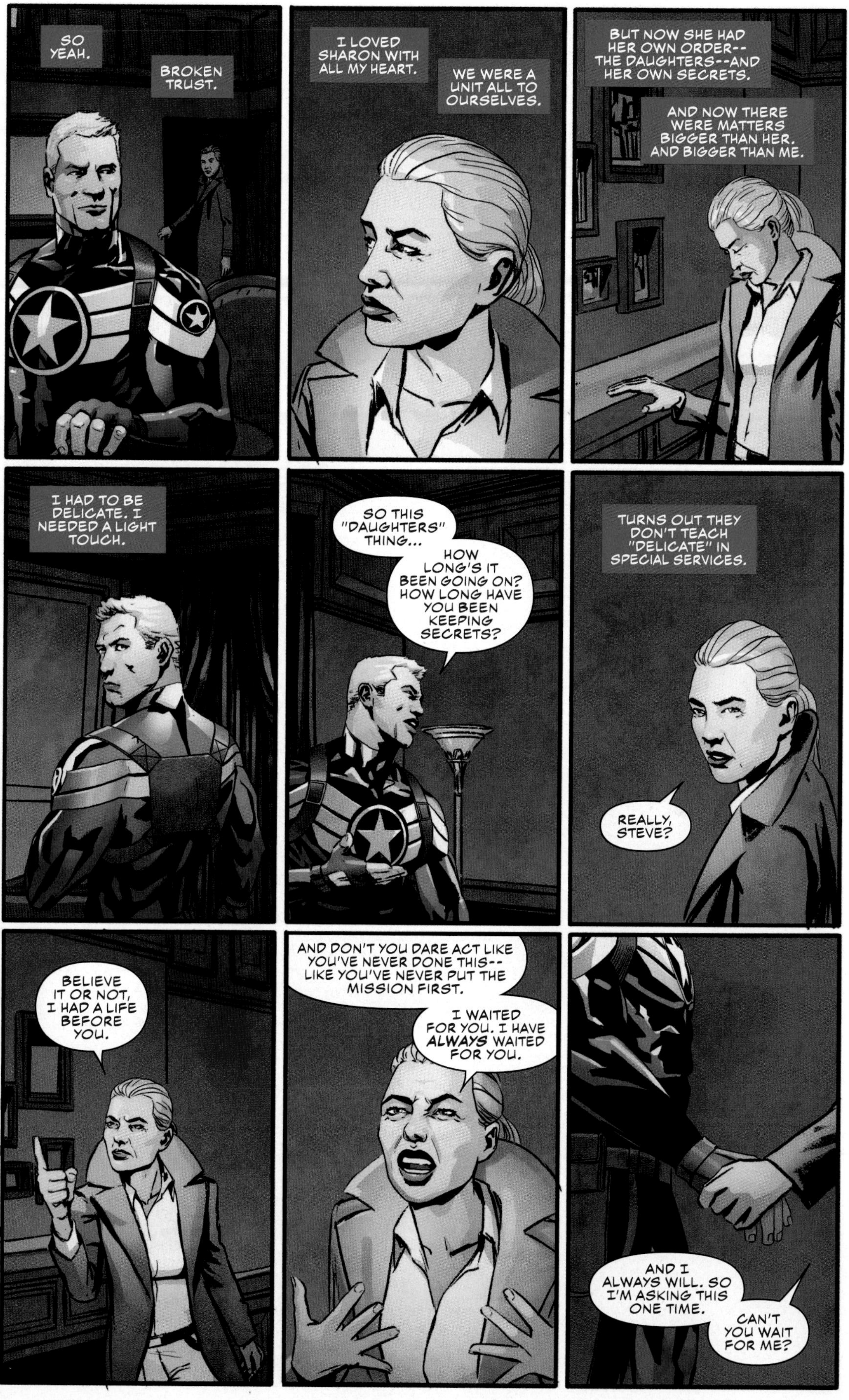
SO YEAH.
BROKEN TRUST.
I LOVED SHARON WITH ALL MY HEART.
WE WERE A UNIT ALL TO OURSELVES.
BUT NOW SHE HAD HER OWN ORDER-- THE DAUGHTERS--AND HER OWN SECRETS.
AND NOW THERE WERE MATTERS BIGGER THAN HER. AND BIGGER THAN ME.
I HAD TO BE DELICATE. I NEEDED A LIGHT TOUCH.
SO THIS "DAUGHTERS" THING...
HOW LONG'S IT BEEN GOING ON? HOW LONG HAVE YOU BEEN KEEPING SECRETS?
TURNS OUT THEY DON'T TEACH "DELICATE" IN SPECIAL SERVICES.
REALLY, STEVE?
BELIEVE IT OR NOT, I HAD A LIFE BEFORE YOU.
AND DON'T YOU DARE ACT LIKE YOU'VE NEVER DONE THIS-- LIKE YOU'VE NEVER PUT THE MISSION FIRST.
I WAITED FOR YOU. I HAVE ALWAYS WAITED FOR YOU.
AND I ALWAYS WILL. SO I'M ASKING THIS ONE TIME.
CAN'T YOU WAIT FOR ME?

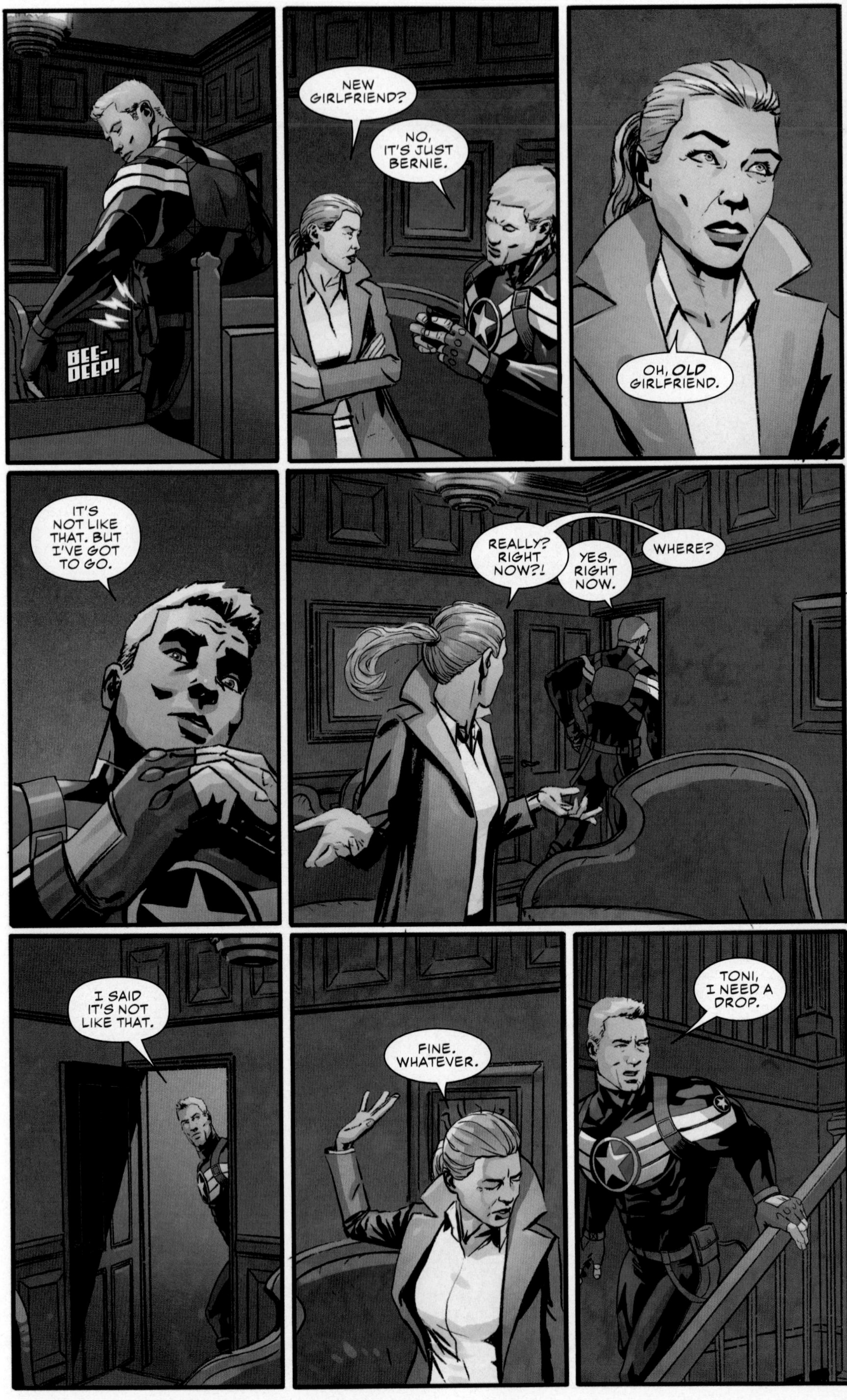
BEE-DEEP!
NEW GIRLFRIEND?
NO, IT'S JUST BERNIE.
OH, OLD GIRLFRIEND.
IT'S NOT LIKE THAT. BUT I'VE GOT TO GO.
REALLY? RIGHT NOW?!
YES, RIGHT NOW.
WHERE?
I SAID IT'S NOT LIKE THAT.
FINE. WHATEVER.
TONI, I NEED A DROP.

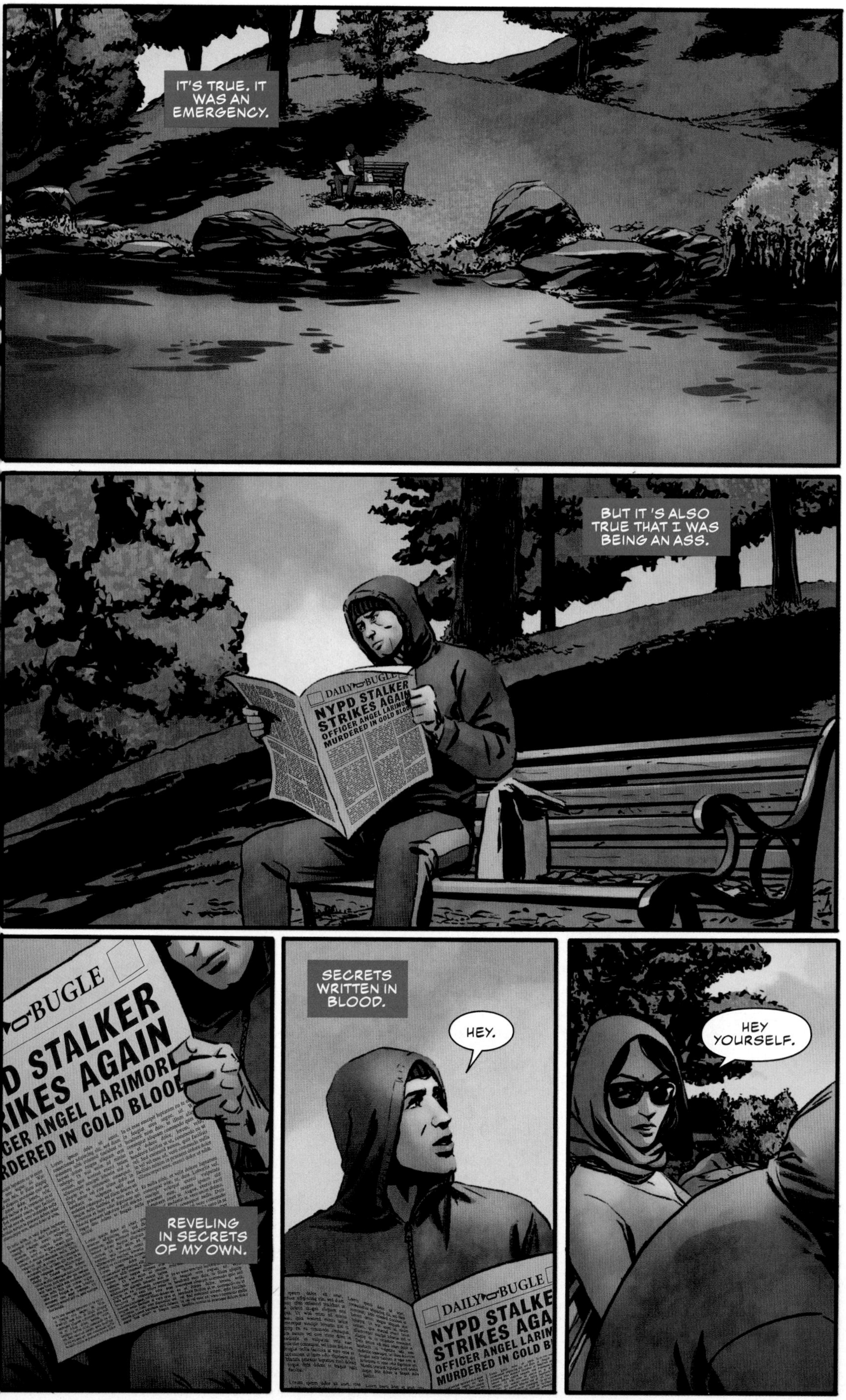
IT'S TRUE. IT WAS AN EMERGENCY.
BUT IT'S ALSO TRUE THAT I WAS BEING AN ASS.
DAILY BUGLE
NYPD STALKER STRIKES AGAIN
OFFICER ANGEL LARIMORE MURDERED IN COLD BLOOD
REVELING IN SECRETS OF MY OWN.
SECRETS WRITTEN IN BLOOD.
HEY.
HEY YOURSELF.

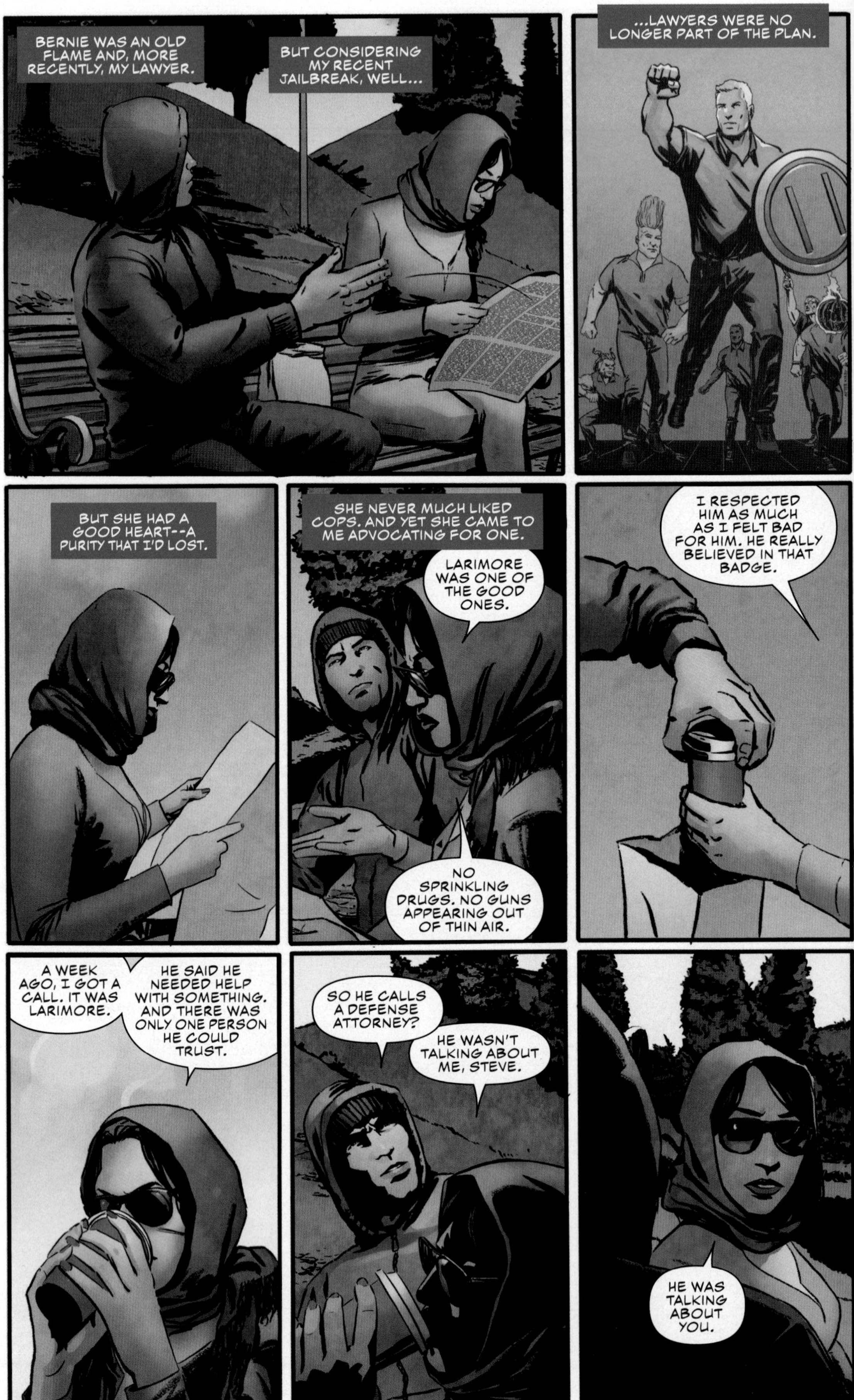
BERNIE WAS AN OLD FLAME AND, MORE RECENTLY, MY LAWYER.
BUT CONSIDERING MY RECENT JAILBREAK, WELL...
...LAWYERS WERE NO LONGER PART OF THE PLAN.
BUT SHE HAD A GOOD HEART--A PURITY THAT I'D LOST.
SHE NEVER MUCH LIKED COPS. AND YET SHE CAME TO ME ADVOCATING FOR ONE.
LARIMORE WAS ONE OF THE GOOD ONES.
NO SPRINKLING DRUGS. NO GUNS APPEARING OUT OF THIN AIR.
I RESPECTED HIM AS MUCH AS I FELT BAD FOR HIM. HE REALLY BELIEVED IN THAT BADGE.
A WEEK AGO, I GOT A CALL. IT WAS LARIMORE.
HE SAID HE NEEDED HELP WITH SOMETHING. AND THERE WAS ONLY ONE PERSON HE COULD TRUST.
SO HE CALLS A DEFENSE ATTORNEY?
HE WASN'T TALKING ABOUT ME, STEVE.
HE WAS TALKING ABOUT YOU.

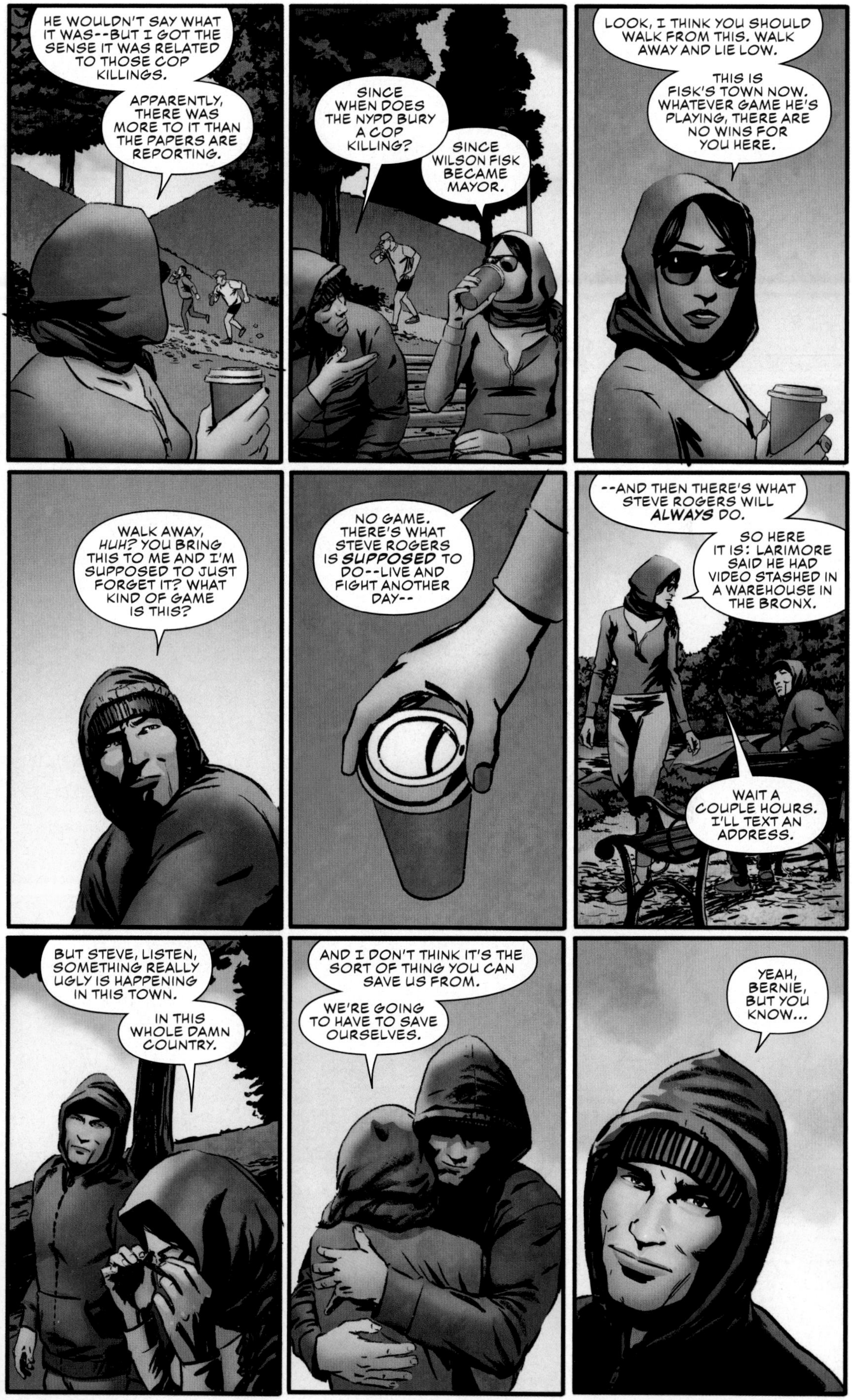
HE WOULDN'T SAY WHAT IT WAS--BUT I GOT THE SENSE IT WAS RELATED TO THOSE COP KILLINGS.
APPARENTLY, THERE WAS MORE TO IT THAN THE PAPERS ARE REPORTING.
SINCE WHEN DOES THE NYPD BURY A COP KILLING?
SINCE WILSON FISK BECAME MAYOR.
LOOK, I THINK YOU SHOULD WALK FROM THIS. WALK AWAY AND LIE LOW.
THIS IS FISK'S TOWN NOW. WHATEVER GAME HE'S PLAYING, THERE ARE NO WINS FOR YOU HERE.
WALK AWAY, HUH? YOU BRING THIS TO ME AND I'M SUPPOSED TO JUST FORGET IT? WHAT KIND OF GAME IS THIS?
NO GAME. THERE'S WHAT STEVE ROGERS IS SUPPOSED TO DO--LIVE AND FIGHT ANOTHER DAY--
--AND THEN THERE'S WHAT STEVE ROGERS WILL ALWAYS DO.
SO HERE IT IS: LARIMORE SAID HE HAD VIDEO STASHED IN A WAREHOUSE IN THE BRONX.
WAIT A COUPLE HOURS. I'LL TEXT AN ADDRESS.
BUT STEVE, LISTEN, SOMETHING REALLY UGLY IS HAPPENING IN THIS TOWN.
IN THIS WHOLE DAMN COUNTRY.
AND I DON'T THINK IT'S THE SORT OF THING YOU CAN SAVE US FROM.
WE'RE GOING TO HAVE TO SAVE OURSELVES.
YEAH, BERNIE, BUT YOU KNOW...

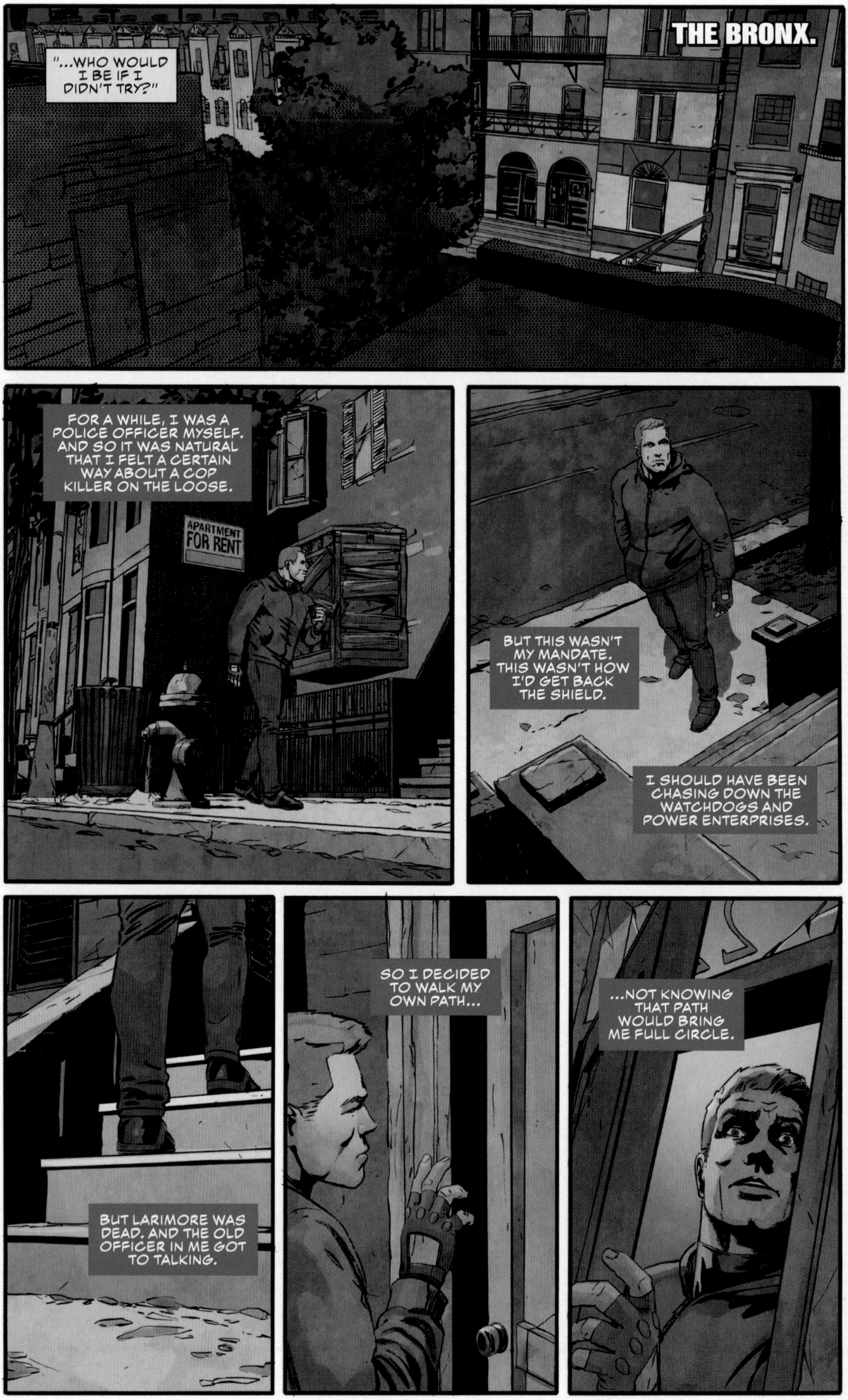
THE BRONX.
"...WHO WOULD I BE IF I DIDN'T TRY?"
FOR A WHILE, I WAS A POLICE OFFICER MYSELF. AND SO IT WAS NATURAL THAT I FELT A CERTAIN WAY ABOUT A COP KILLER ON THE LOOSE.
APARTMENT FOR RENT
BUT THIS WASN'T MY MANDATE. THIS WASN'T HOW I'D GET BACK THE SHIELD.
I SHOULD HAVE BEEN CHASING DOWN THE WATCHDOGS AND POWER ENTERPRISES.
BUT LARIMORE WAS DEAD. AND THE OLD OFFICER IN ME GOT TO TALKING.
SO I DECIDED TO WALK MY OWN PATH...
...NOT KNOWING THAT PATH WOULD BRING ME FULL CIRCLE.

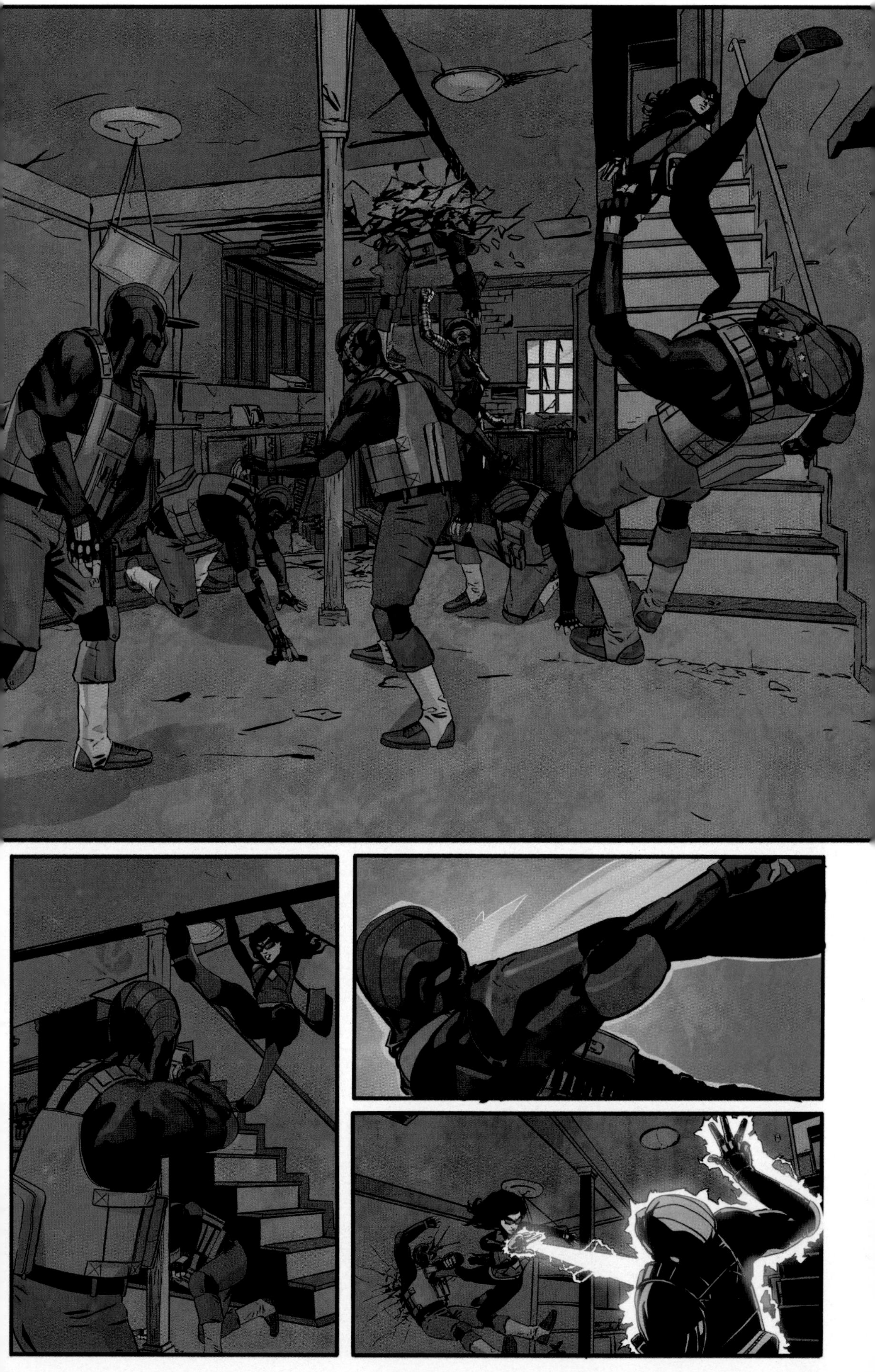

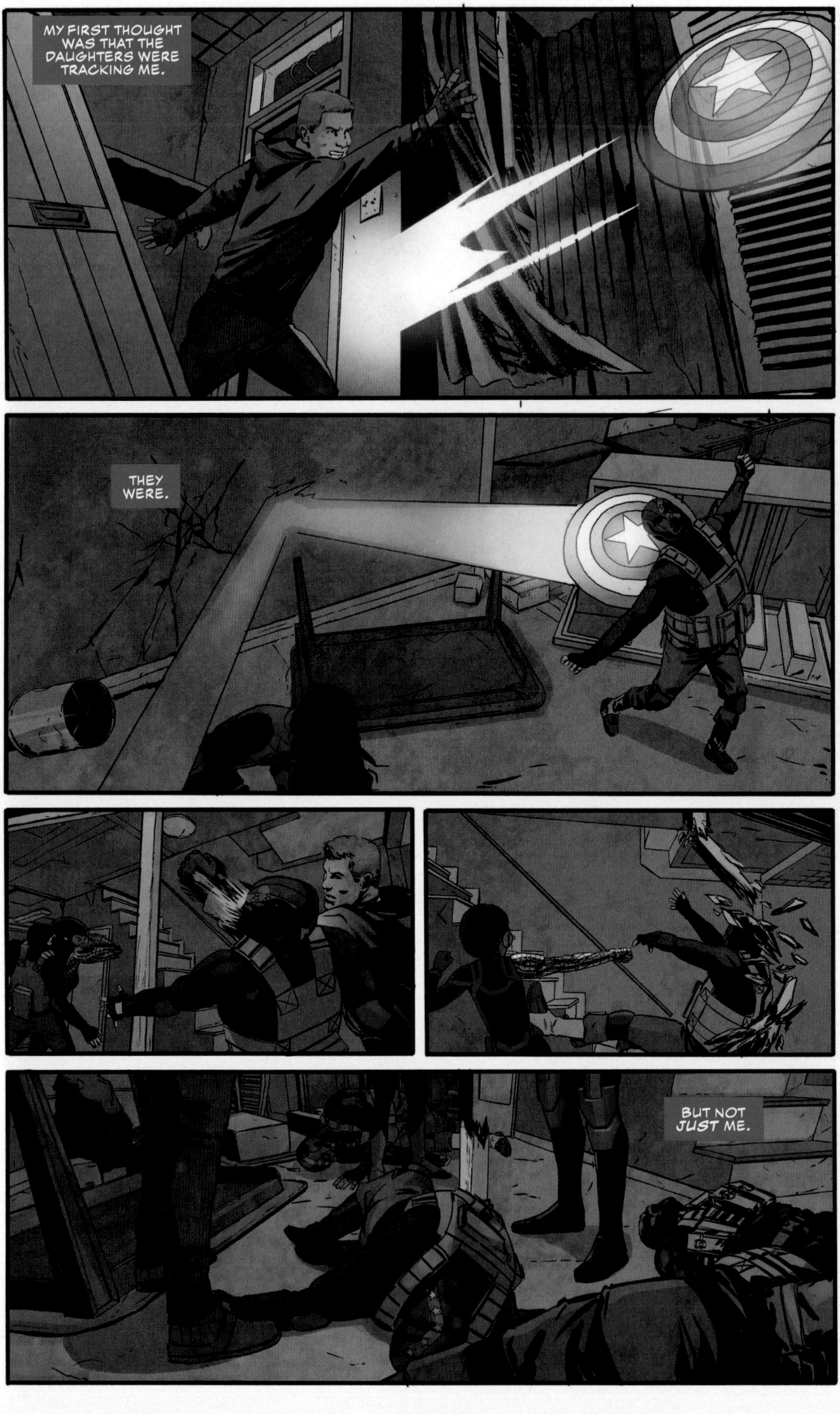
MY FIRST THOUGHT WAS THAT THE DAUGHTERS WERE TRACKING ME.
THEY WERE.
BUT NOT JUST ME.

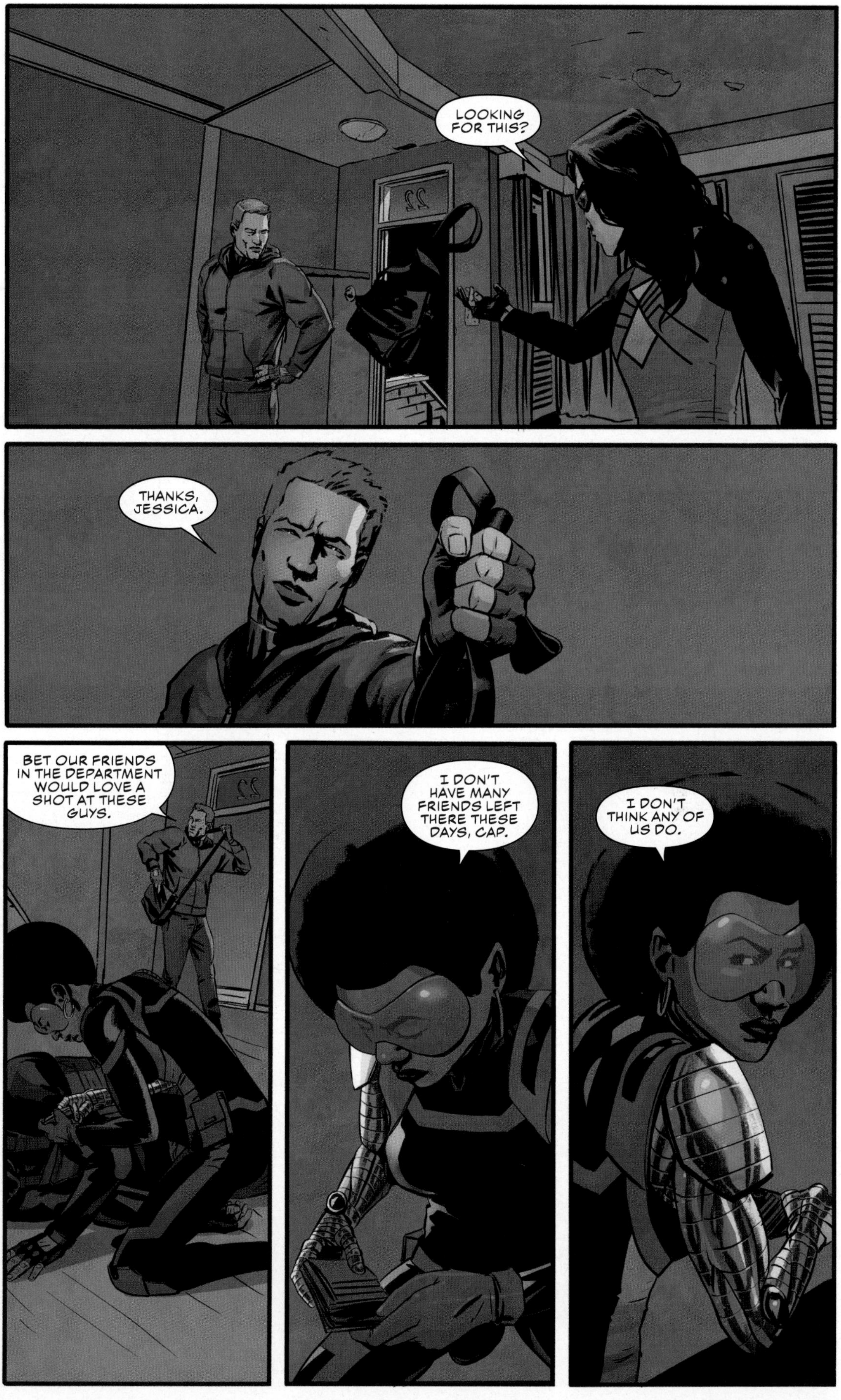
LOOKING FOR THIS?
THANKS, JESSICA.
BET OUR FRIENDS IN THE DEPARTMENT WOULD LOVE A SHOT AT THESE GUYS.
I DON'T HAVE MANY FRIENDS LEFT THERE THESE DAYS, CAP.
I DON'T THINK ANY OF US DO.

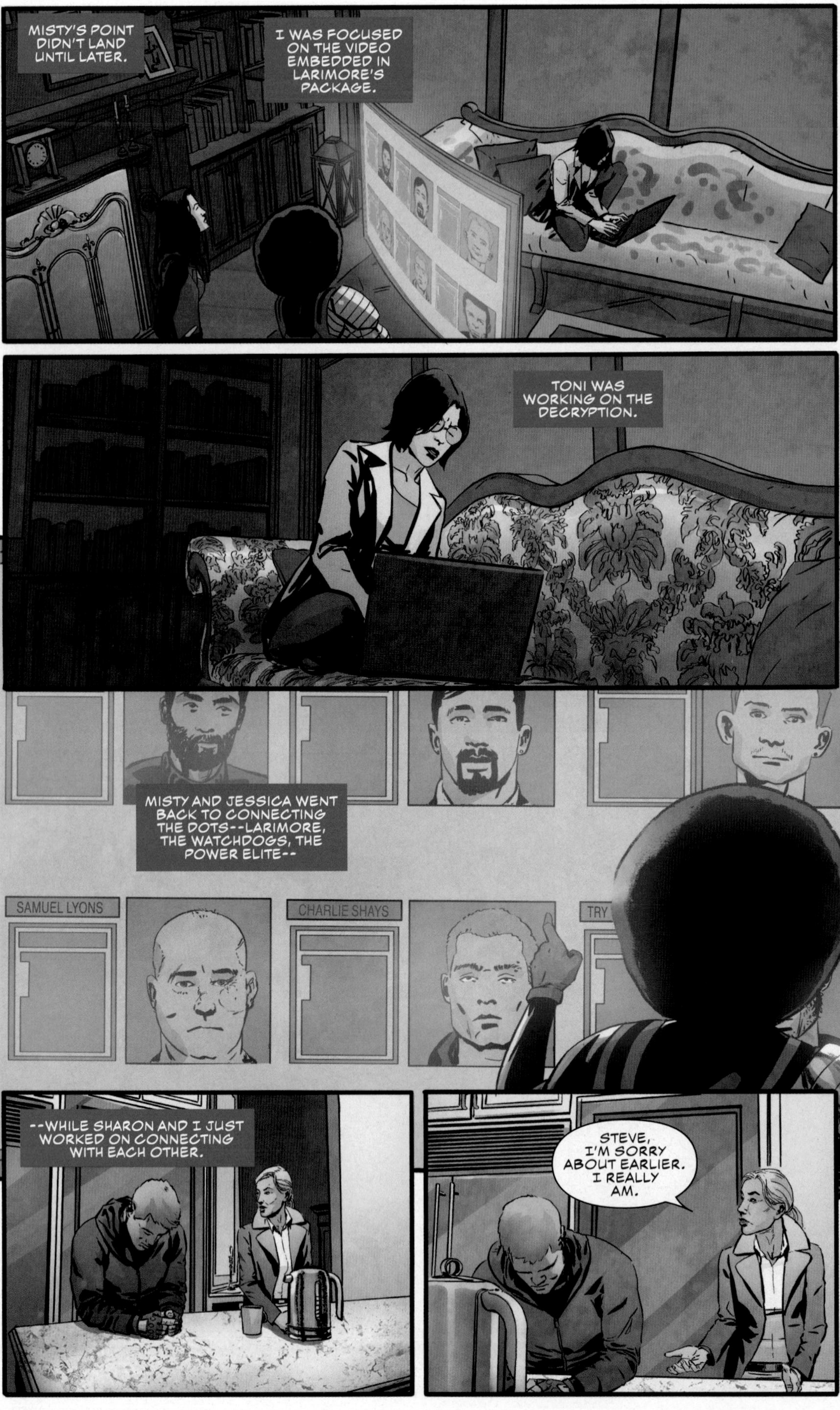
MISTY'S POINT DIDN'T LAND UNTIL LATER.
I WAS FOCUSED ON THE VIDEO EMBEDDED IN LARIMORE'S PACKAGE.
TONI WAS WORKING ON THE DECRYPTION.
MISTY AND JESSICA WENT BACK TO CONNECTING THE DOTS--LARIMORE, THE WATCHDOGS, THE POWER ELITE--
SAMUEL LYONS
CHARLIE SHAYS
--WHILE SHARON AND I JUST WORKED ON CONNECTING WITH EACH OTHER.
STEVE, I'M SORRY ABOUT EARLIER. I REALLY AM.

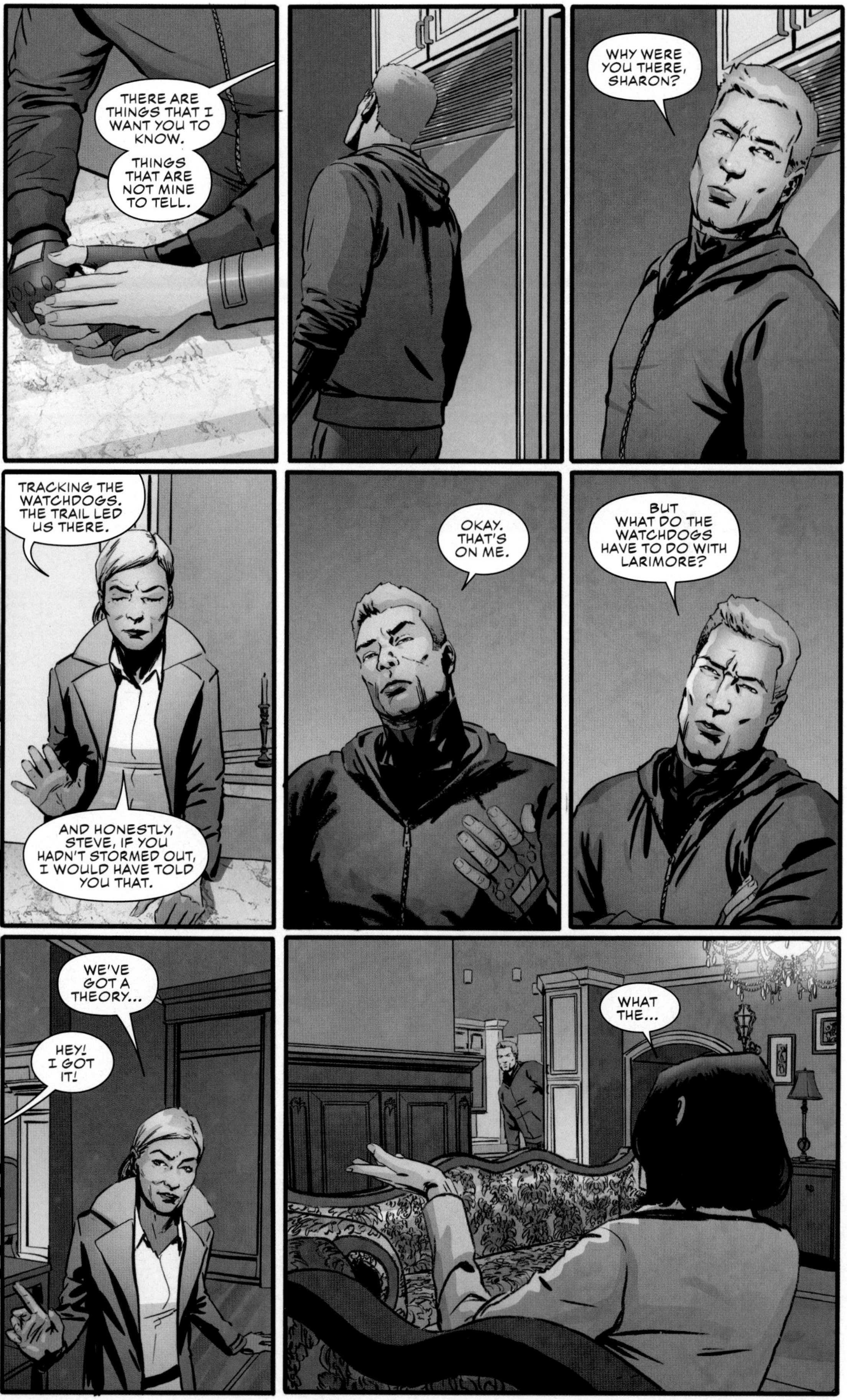
THERE ARE THINGS THAT I WANT YOU TO KNOW.
THINGS THAT ARE NOT MINE TO TELL.
WHY WERE YOU THERE, SHARON?
TRACKING THE WATCHDOGS. THE TRAIL LED US THERE.
AND HONESTLY, STEVE, IF YOU HADN'T STORMED OUT, I WOULD HAVE TOLD YOU THAT.
OKAY. THAT'S ON ME.
BUT WHAT DO THE WATCHDOGS HAVE TO DO WITH LARIMORE?
WE'VE GOT A THEORY...
HEY! I GOT IT!
WHAT THE...

THE VIDEO WAS A COMPOSITE--BODY CAM, SECURITY TAPES, CELL PHONE.

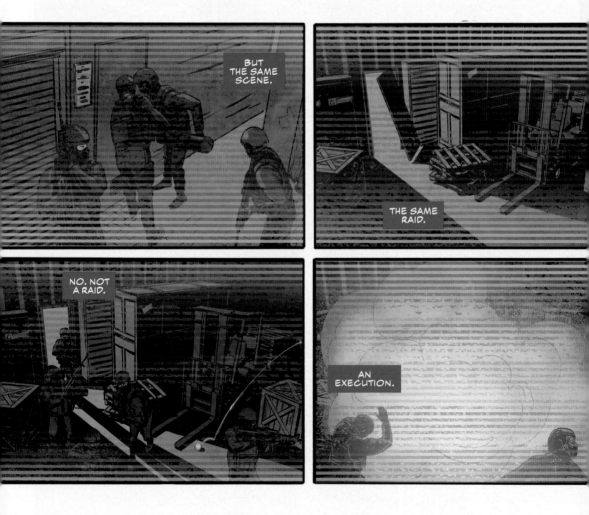

BUT THE SAME SCENE.

THE SAME RAID.

NO. NOT A RAID.

AN EXECUTION.

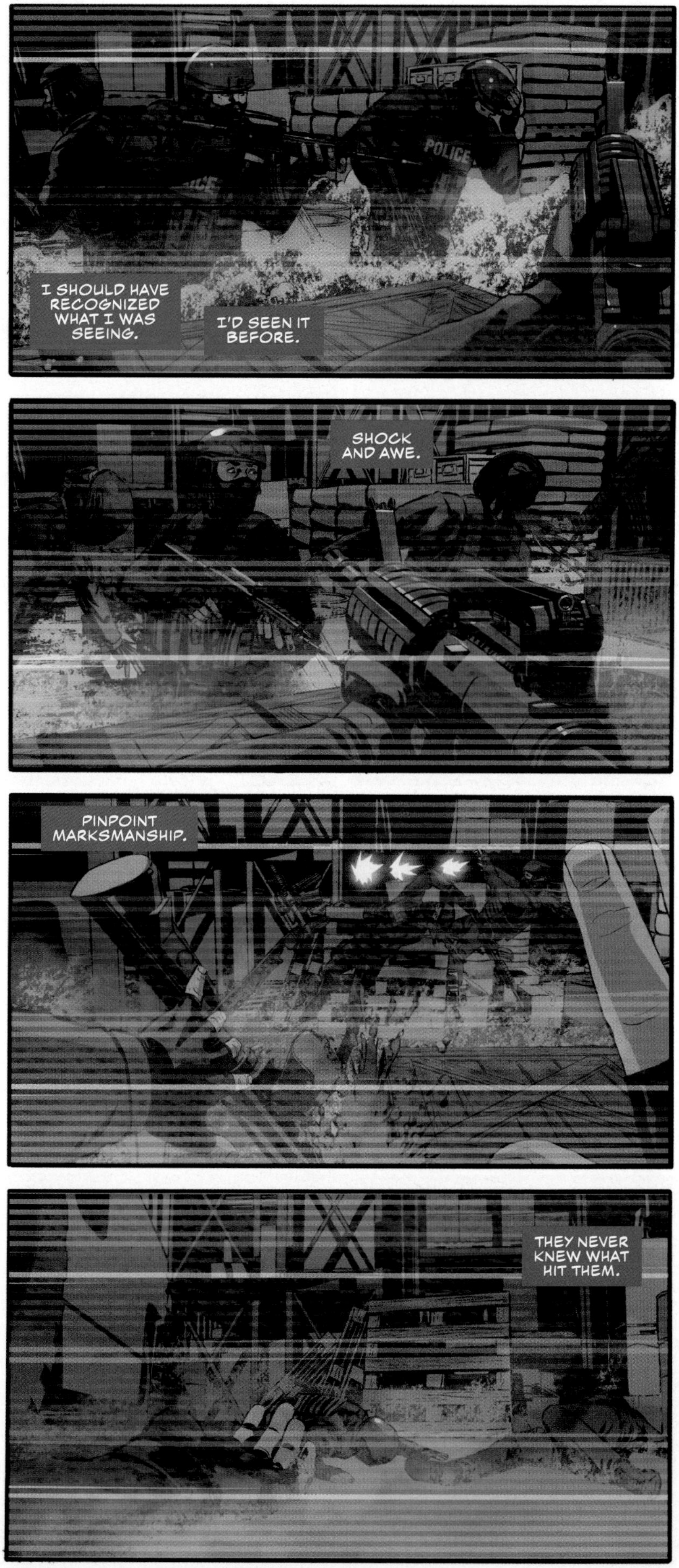
I SHOULD HAVE RECOGNIZED WHAT I WAS SEEING.
I'D SEEN IT BEFORE.
POLICE
SHOCK AND AWE.
PINPOINT MARKSMANSHIP.
THEY NEVER KNEW WHAT HIT THEM.

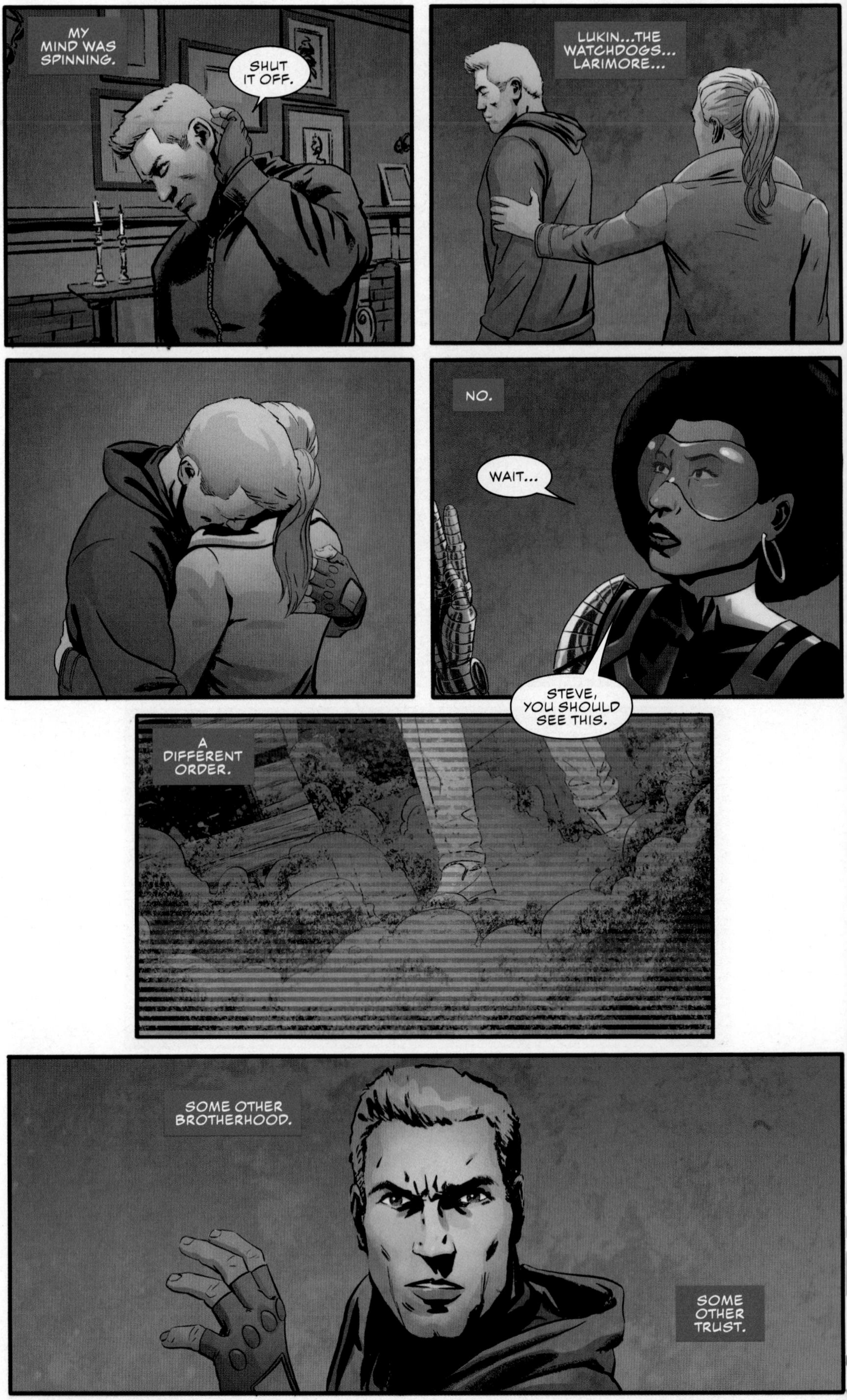
MY MIND WAS SPINNING.
SHUT IT OFF.
LUKIN...THE WATCHDOGS... LARIMORE...
NO.
WAIT...
STEVE, YOU SHOULD SEE THIS.
A DIFFERENT ORDER.
SOME OTHER BROTHERHOOD.
SOME OTHER TRUST.

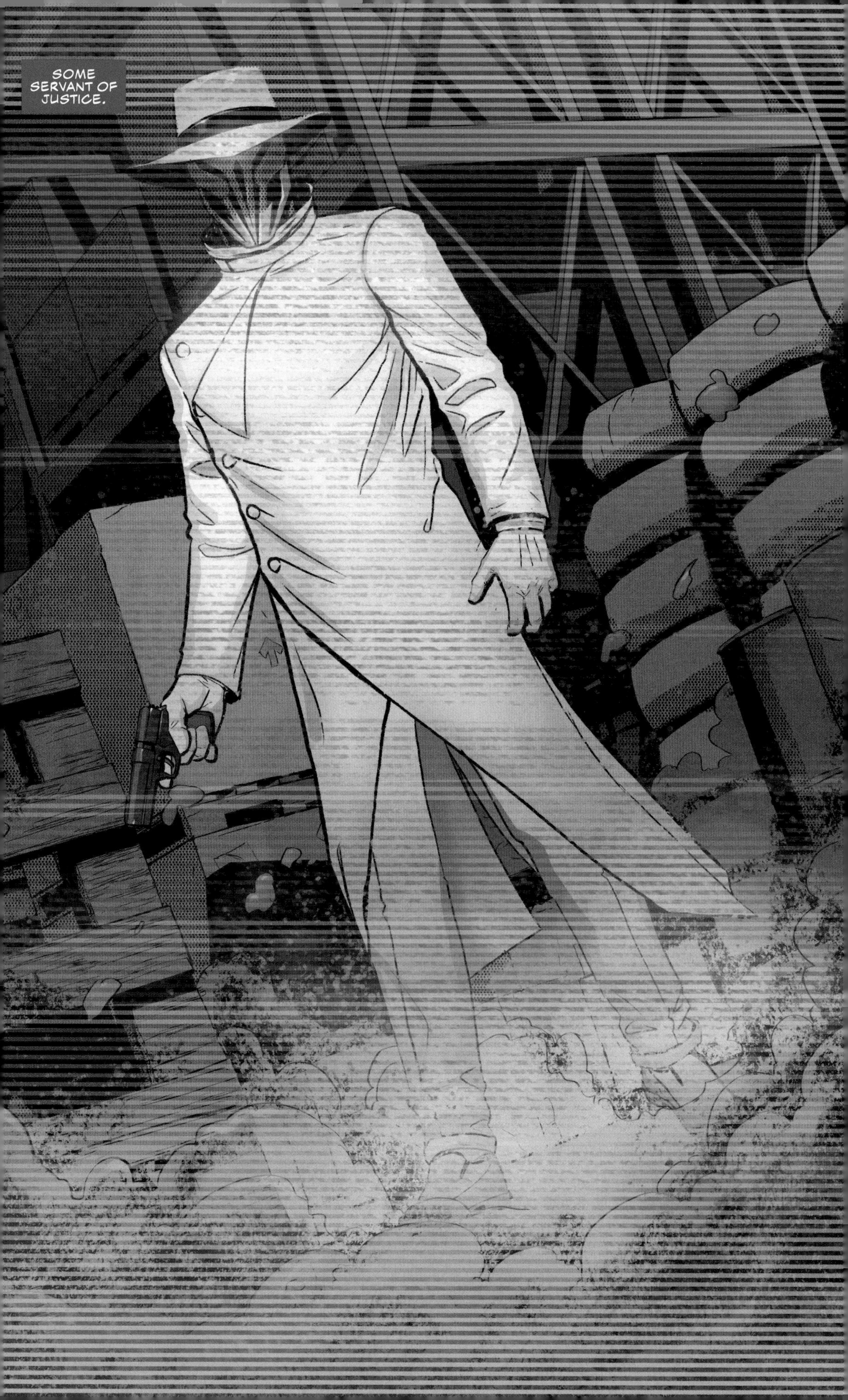
SOME SERVANT OF JUSTICE.

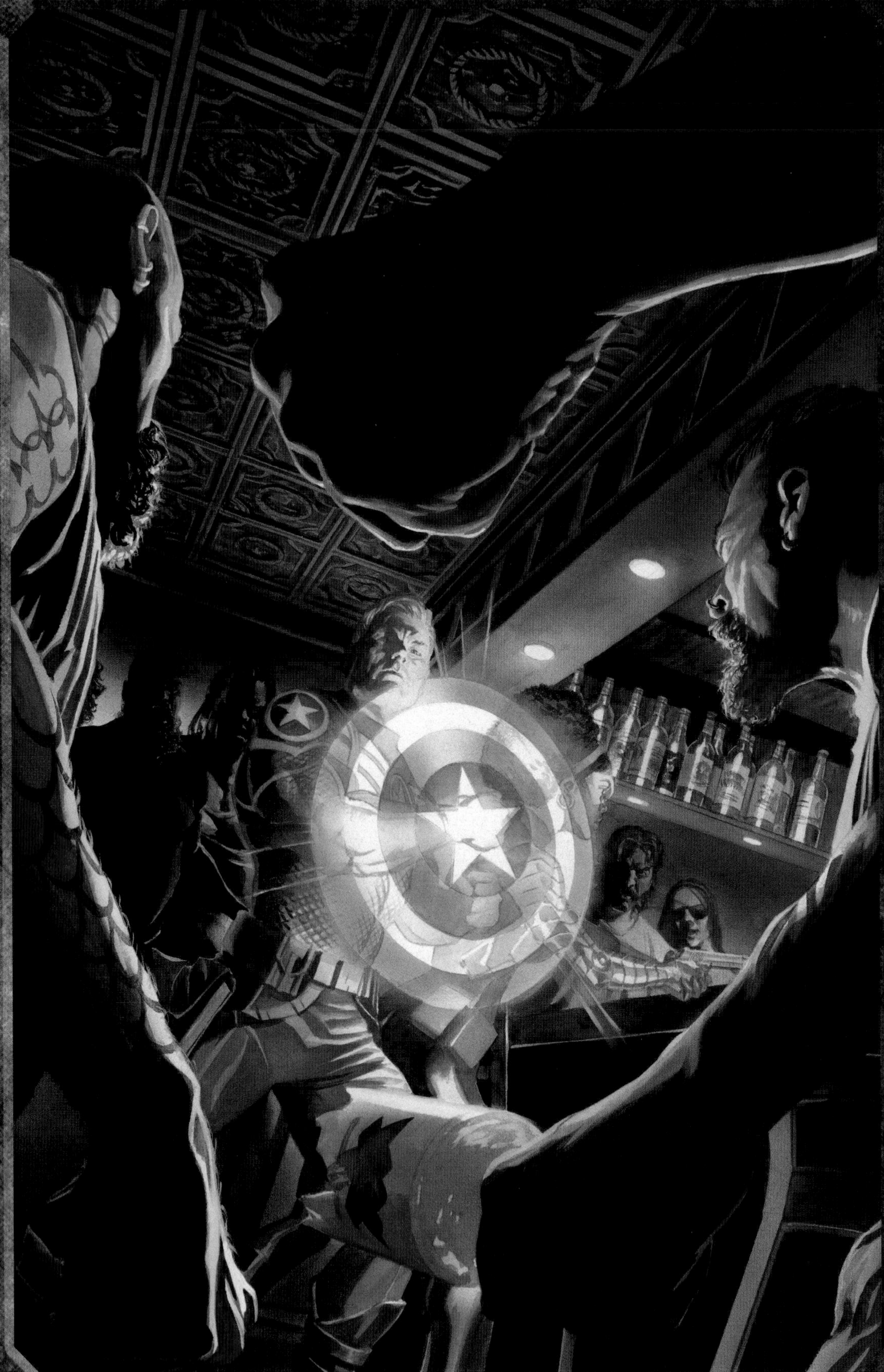

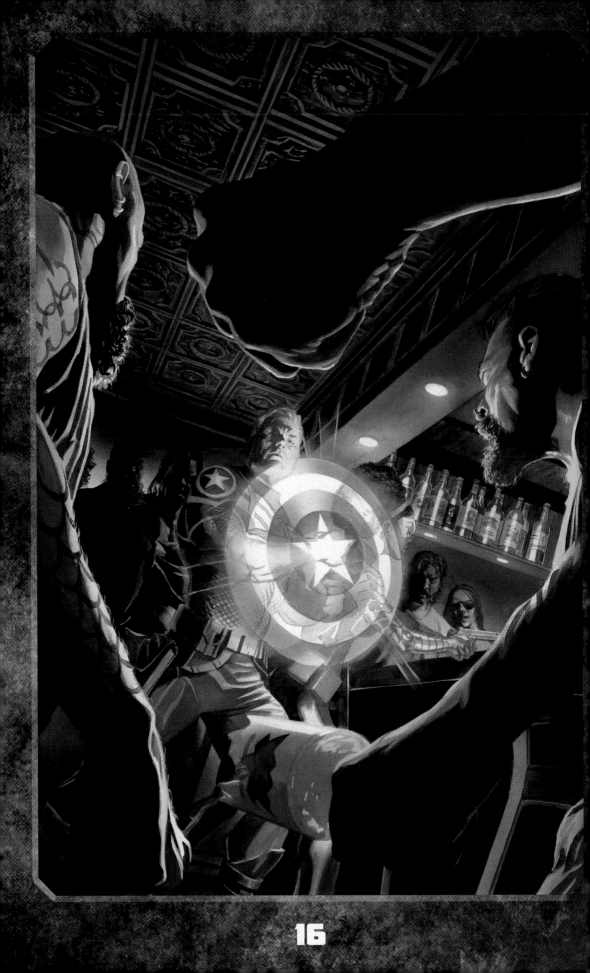

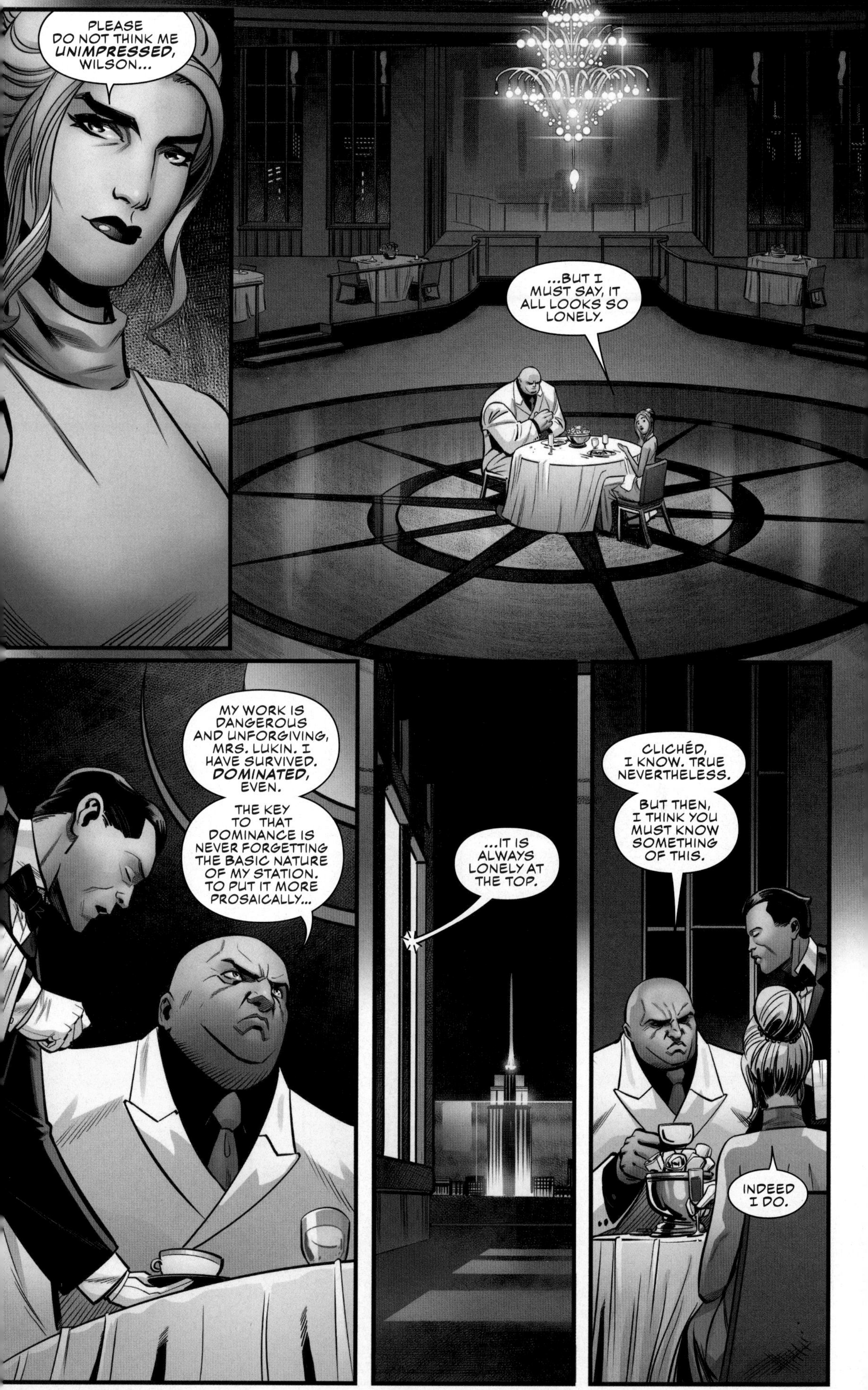
PLEASE DO NOT THINK ME *UNIMPRESSED*, WILSON...
...BUT I MUST SAY, IT ALL LOOKS SO LONELY.
MY WORK IS DANGEROUS AND UNFORGIVING, MRS. LUKIN. I HAVE SURVIVED. *DOMINATED*, EVEN.
THE KEY TO THAT DOMINANCE IS NEVER FORGETTING THE BASIC NATURE OF MY STATION. TO PUT IT MORE PROSAICALLY...
...IT IS ALWAYS LONELY AT THE TOP.
CLICHÉD, I KNOW. TRUE NEVERTHELESS.
BUT THEN, I THINK YOU MUST KNOW SOMETHING OF THIS.
INDEED I DO.

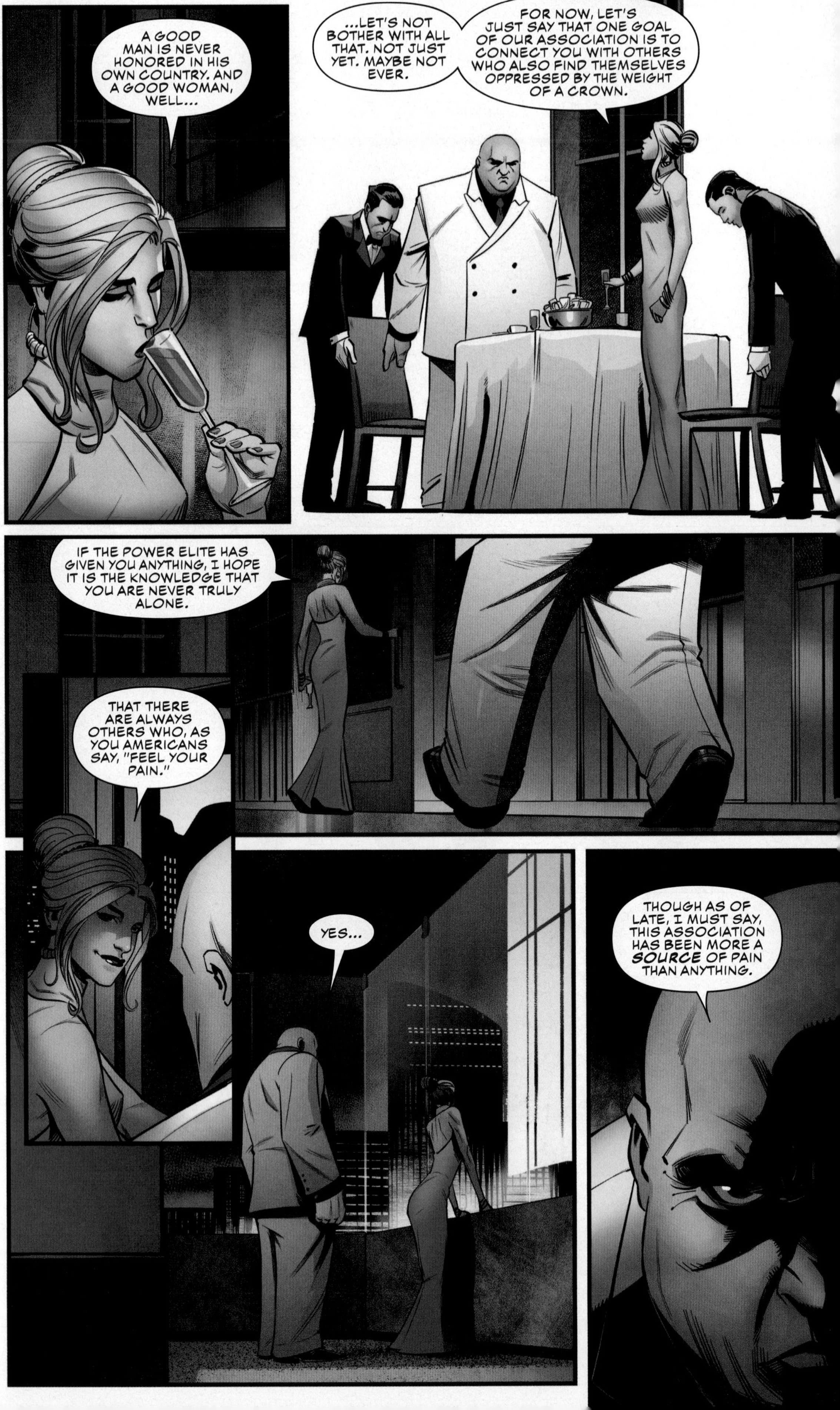
A GOOD MAN IS NEVER HONORED IN HIS OWN COUNTRY. AND A GOOD WOMAN, WELL...
...LET'S NOT BOTHER WITH ALL THAT. NOT JUST YET. MAYBE NOT EVER.
FOR NOW, LET'S JUST SAY THAT ONE GOAL OF OUR ASSOCIATION IS TO CONNECT YOU WITH OTHERS WHO ALSO FIND THEMSELVES OPPRESSED BY THE WEIGHT OF A CROWN.
IF THE POWER ELITE HAS GIVEN YOU ANYTHING, I HOPE IT IS THE KNOWLEDGE THAT YOU ARE NEVER TRULY ALONE.
THAT THERE ARE ALWAYS OTHERS WHO, AS YOU AMERICANS SAY, "FEEL YOUR PAIN."
YES...
THOUGH AS OF LATE, I MUST SAY, THIS ASSOCIATION HAS BEEN MORE A SOURCE OF PAIN THAN ANYTHING.

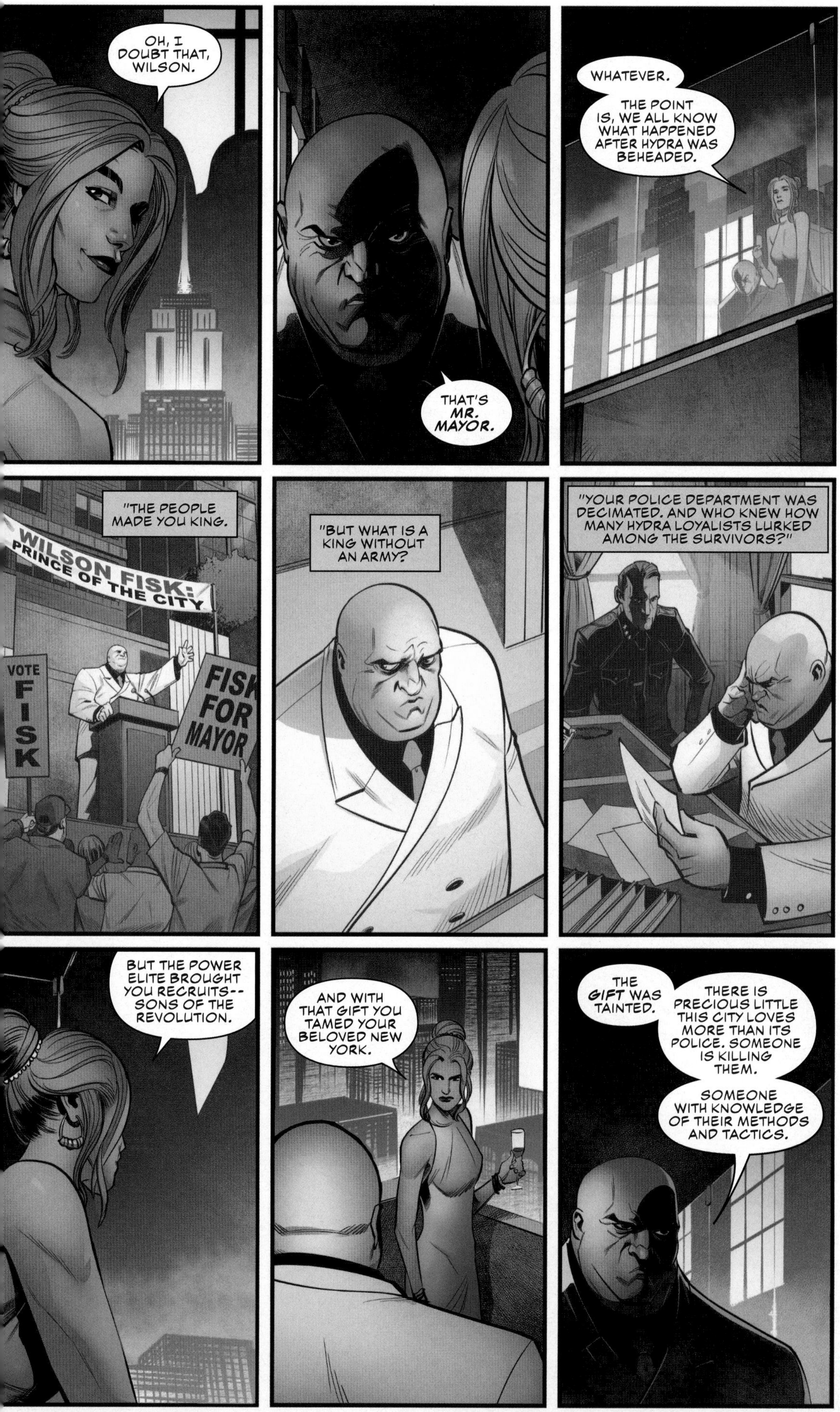

OH, I DOUBT THAT, WILSON.
THAT'S MR. MAYOR.
WHATEVER.
THE POINT IS, WE ALL KNOW WHAT HAPPENED AFTER HYDRA WAS BEHEADED.
"THE PEOPLE MADE YOU KING.
WILSON FISK: PRINCE OF THE CITY
VOTE FISK
FISK FOR MAYOR
"BUT WHAT IS A KING WITHOUT AN ARMY?
"YOUR POLICE DEPARTMENT WAS DECIMATED. AND WHO KNEW HOW MANY HYDRA LOYALISTS LURKED AMONG THE SURVIVORS?"
BUT THE POWER ELITE BROUGHT YOU RECRUITS-- SONS OF THE REVOLUTION.
AND WITH THAT GIFT YOU TAMED YOUR BELOVED NEW YORK.
THE GIFT WAS TAINTED.
THERE IS PRECIOUS LITTLE THIS CITY LOVES MORE THAN ITS POLICE. SOMEONE IS KILLING THEM.
SOMEONE WITH KNOWLEDGE OF THEIR METHODS AND TACTICS.

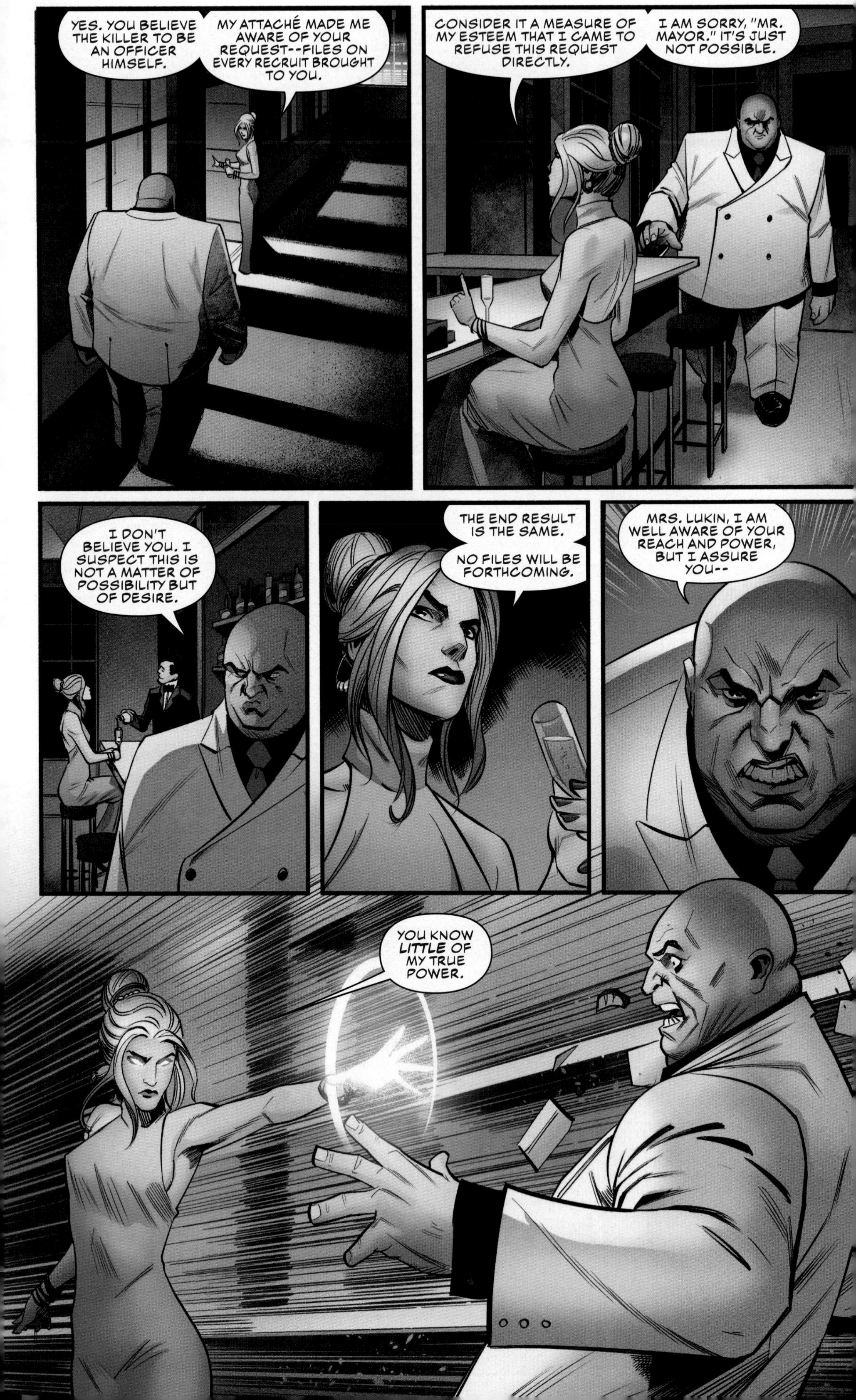
YES. YOU BELIEVE THE KILLER TO BE AN OFFICER HIMSELF.
MY ATTACHÉ MADE ME AWARE OF YOUR REQUEST--FILES ON EVERY RECRUIT BROUGHT TO YOU.
CONSIDER IT A MEASURE OF MY ESTEEM THAT I CAME TO REFUSE THIS REQUEST DIRECTLY.
I AM SORRY, "MR. MAYOR." IT'S JUST NOT POSSIBLE.
I DON'T BELIEVE YOU. I SUSPECT THIS IS NOT A MATTER OF POSSIBILITY BUT OF DESIRE.
THE END RESULT IS THE SAME.
NO FILES WILL BE FORTHCOMING.
MRS. LUKIN, I AM WELL AWARE OF YOUR REACH AND POWER, BUT I ASSURE YOU--
YOU KNOW LITTLE OF MY TRUE POWER.

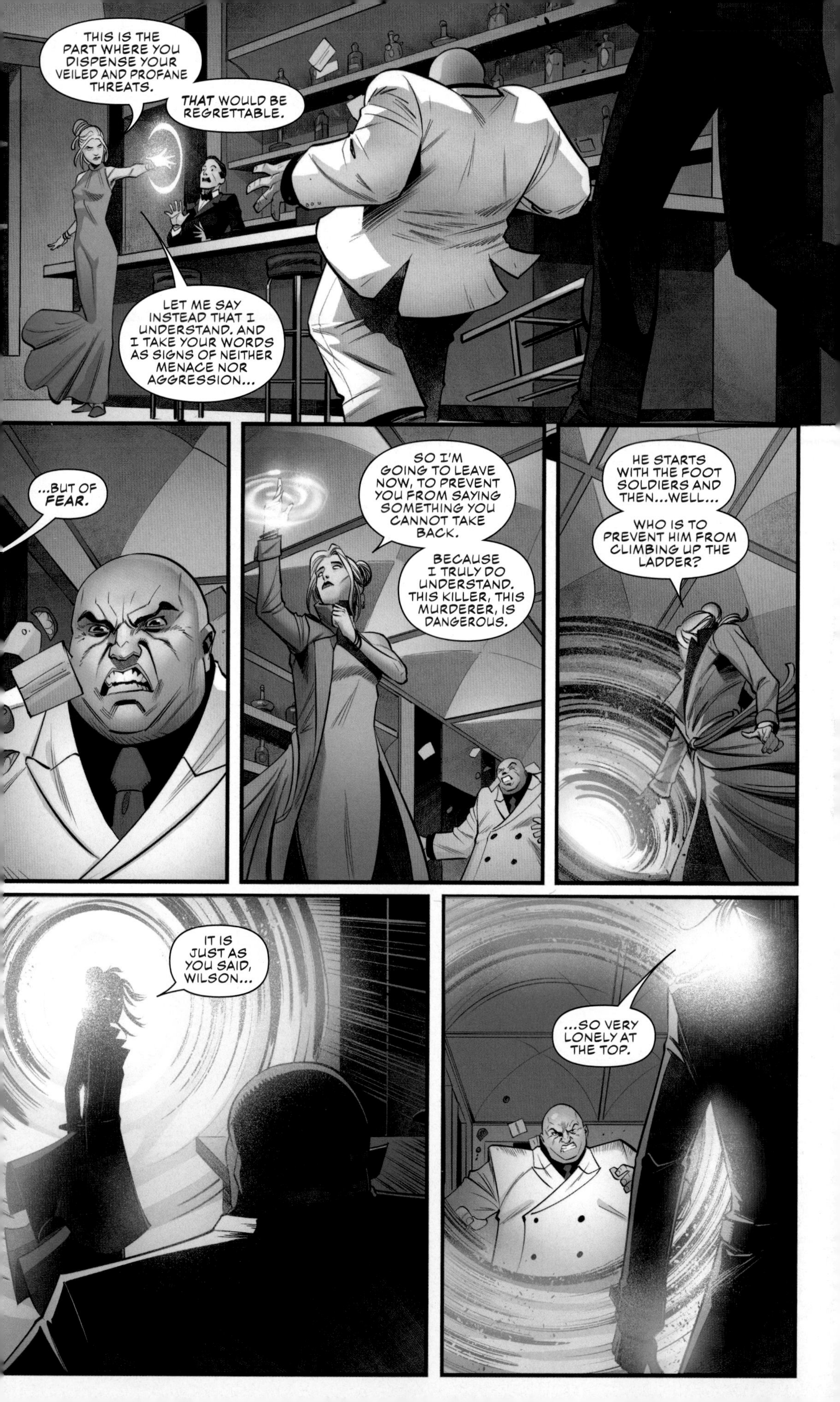
THIS IS THE PART WHERE YOU DISPENSE YOUR VEILED AND PROFANE THREATS.
THAT WOULD BE REGRETTABLE.
LET ME SAY INSTEAD THAT I UNDERSTAND. AND I TAKE YOUR WORDS AS SIGNS OF NEITHER MENACE NOR AGGRESSION...
...BUT OF FEAR.
SO I'M GOING TO LEAVE NOW, TO PREVENT YOU FROM SAYING SOMETHING YOU CANNOT TAKE BACK.
BECAUSE I TRULY DO UNDERSTAND. THIS KILLER, THIS MURDERER, IS DANGEROUS.
HE STARTS WITH THE FOOT SOLDIERS AND THEN...WELL...
WHO IS TO PREVENT HIM FROM CLIMBING UP THE LADDER?
IT IS JUST AS YOU SAID, WILSON...
...SO VERY LONELY AT THE TOP.

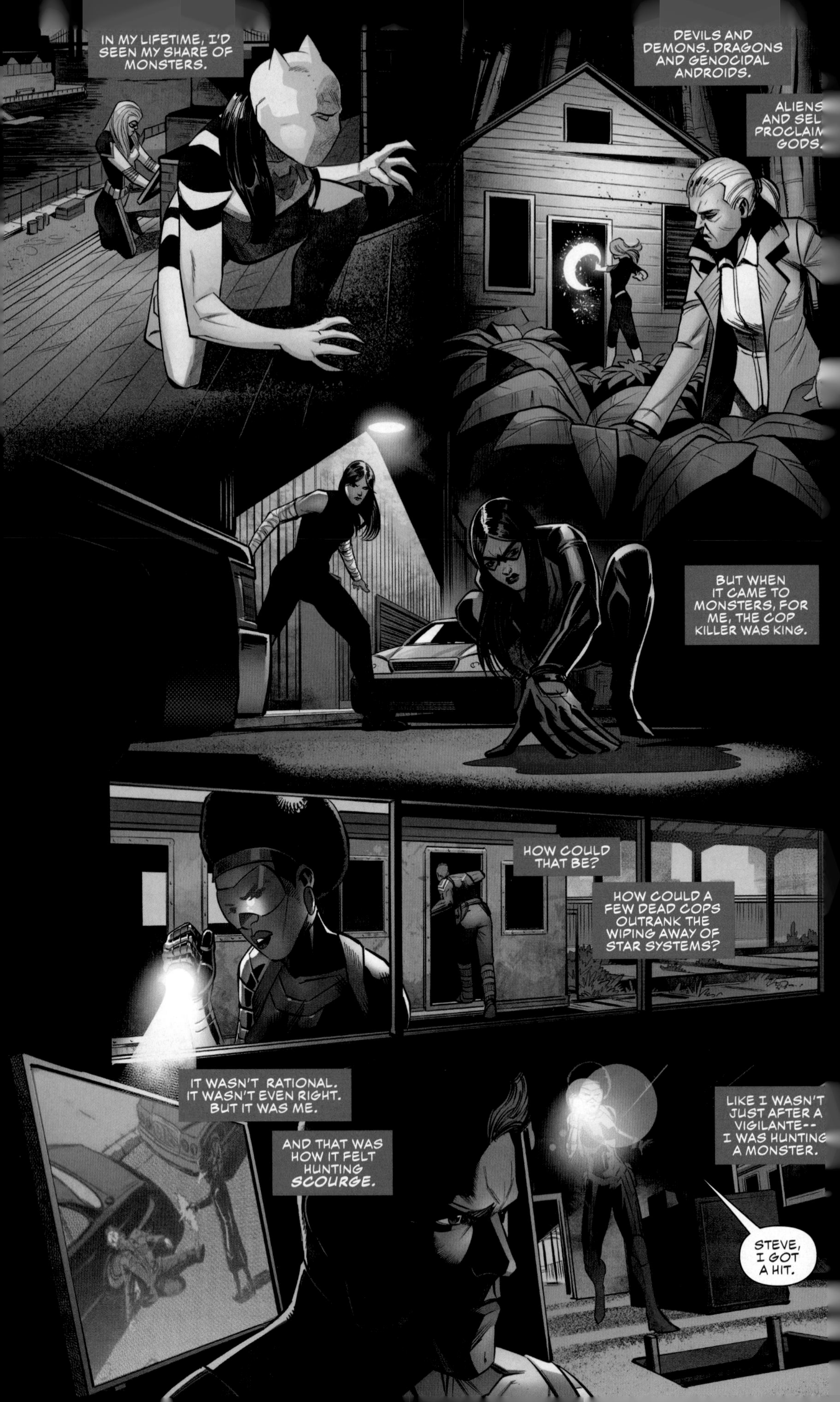
IN MY LIFETIME, I'D SEEN MY SHARE OF MONSTERS.
DEVILS AND DEMONS. DRAGONS AND GENOCIDAL ANDROIDS.
ALIENS AND SEL PROCLAIM GODS.
BUT WHEN IT CAME TO MONSTERS, FOR ME, THE COP KILLER WAS KING.
HOW COULD THAT BE?
HOW COULD A FEW DEAD COPS OUTRANK THE WIPING AWAY OF STAR SYSTEMS?
IT WASN'T RATIONAL. IT WASN'T EVEN RIGHT. BUT IT WAS ME.
AND THAT WAS HOW IT FELT HUNTING SCOURGE.
LIKE I WASN'T JUST AFTER A VIGILANTE-- I WAS HUNTING A MONSTER.
STEVE, I GOT A HIT.

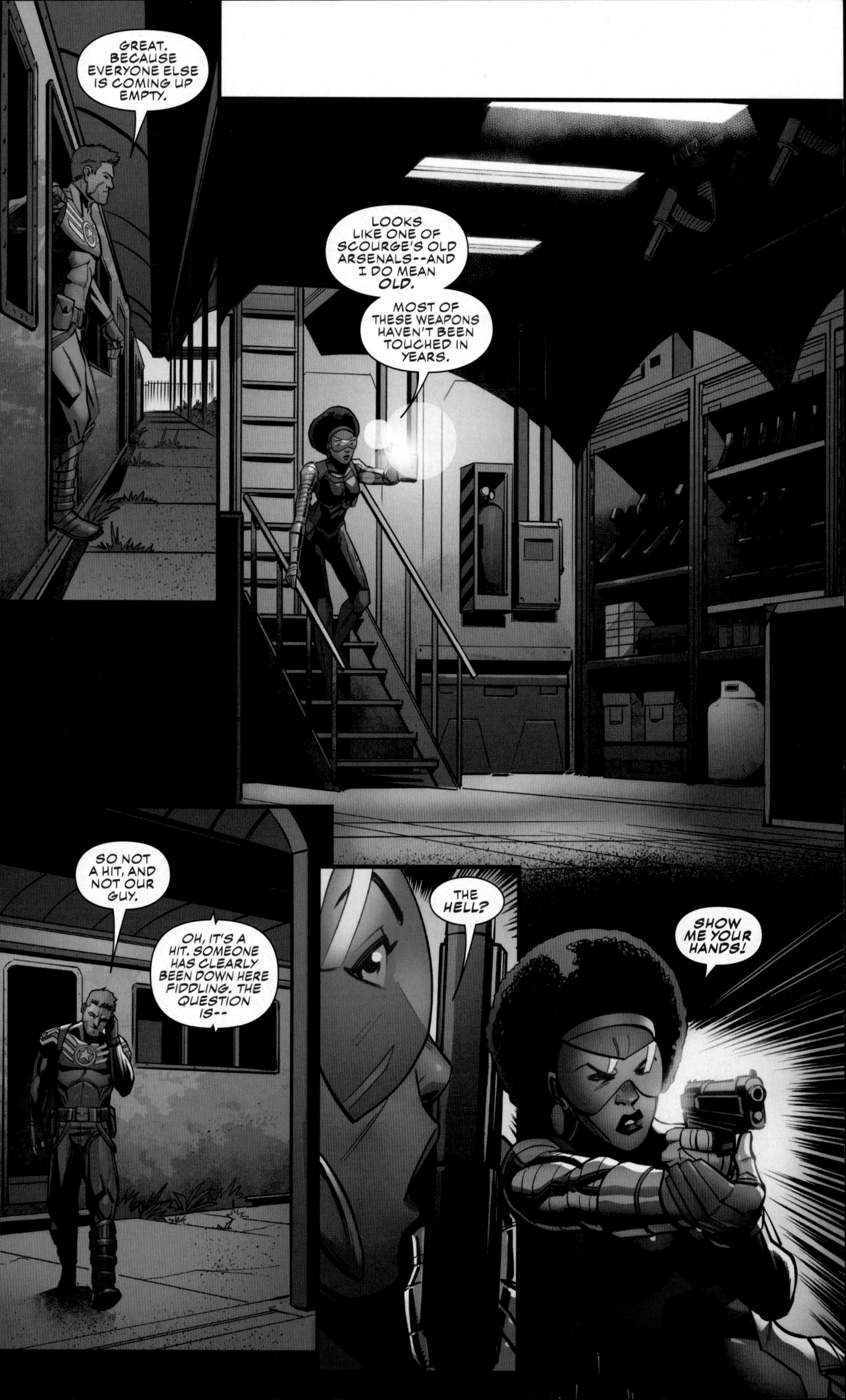
GREAT. BECAUSE EVERYONE ELSE IS COMING UP EMPTY.
LOOKS LIKE ONE OF SCOURGE'S OLD ARSENALS--AND I DO MEAN OLD.
MOST OF THESE WEAPONS HAVEN'T BEEN TOUCHED IN YEARS.
SO NOT A HIT, AND NOT OUR GUY.
OH, IT'S A HIT. SOMEONE HAS CLEARLY BEEN DOWN HERE FIDDLING. THE QUESTION IS--
THE HELL?
SHOW ME YOUR HANDS!

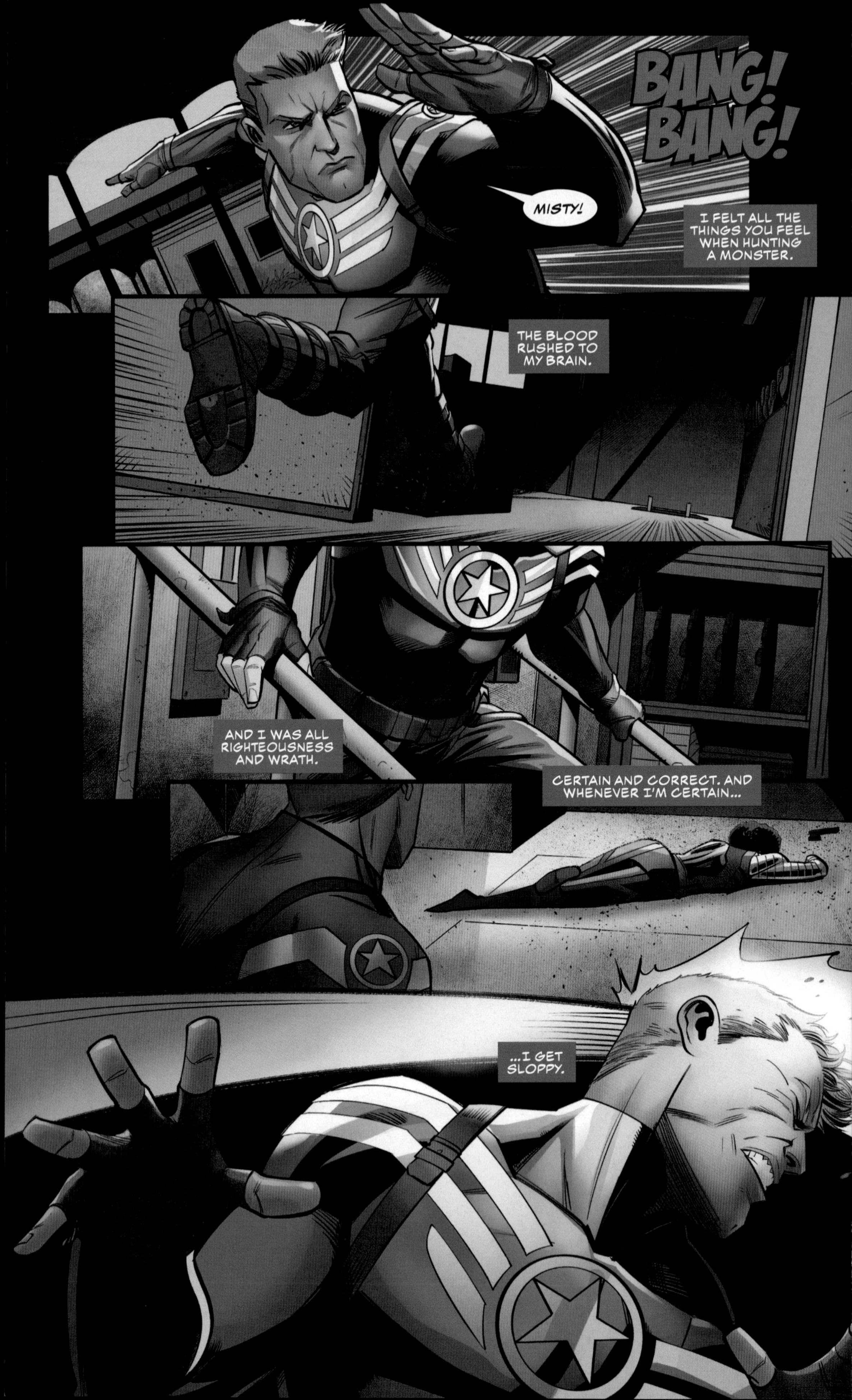
BANG! BANG!
MISTY!
I FELT ALL THE THINGS YOU FEEL WHEN HUNTING A MONSTER.
THE BLOOD RUSHED TO MY BRAIN.
AND I WAS ALL RIGHTEOUSNESS AND WRATH.
CERTAIN AND CORRECT. AND WHENEVER I'M CERTAIN...
...I GET SLOPPY.

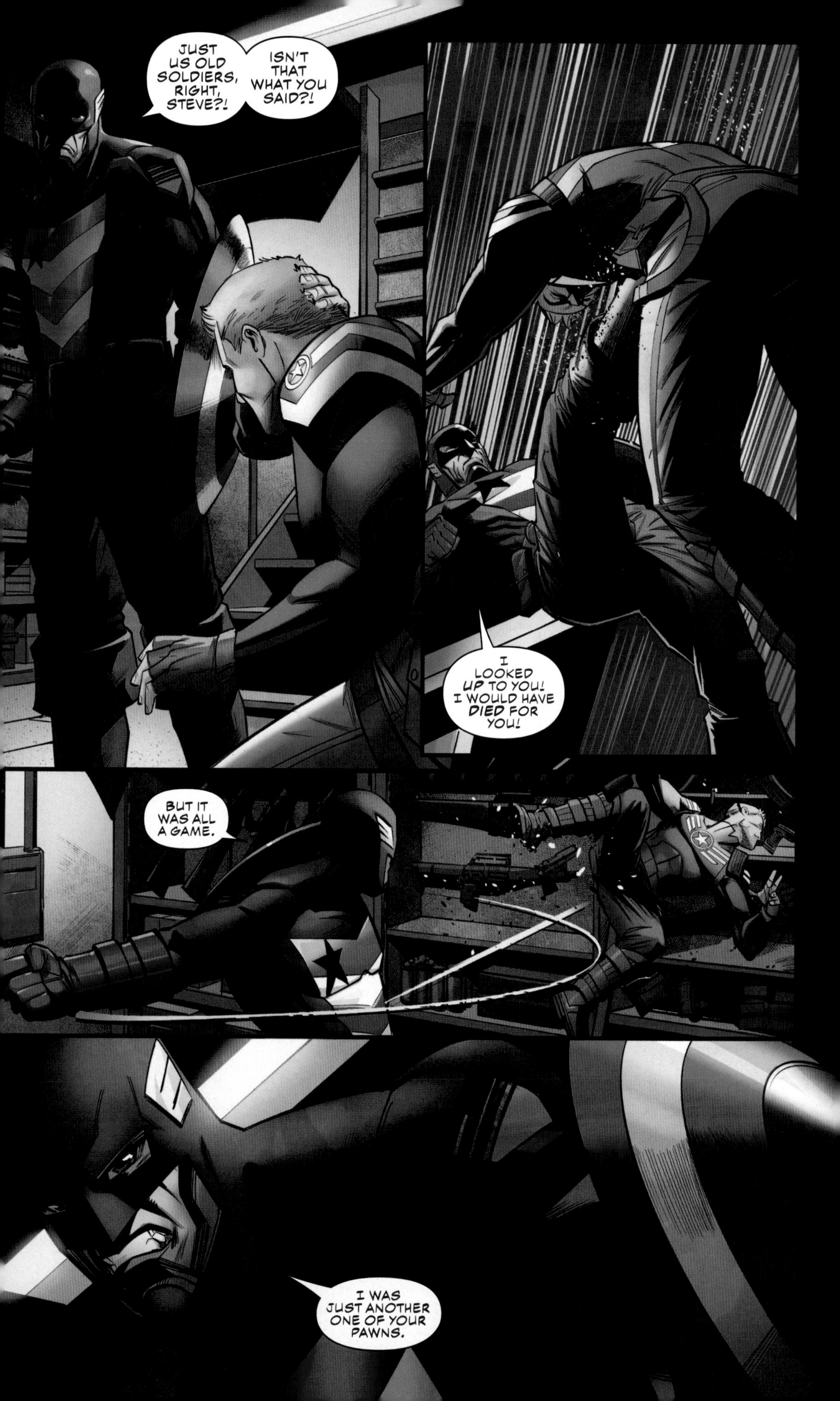
JUST US OLD SOLDIERS, RIGHT, STEVE?!
ISN'T THAT WHAT YOU SAID?!
I LOOKED UP TO YOU! I WOULD HAVE DIED FOR YOU!
BUT IT WAS ALL A GAME.
I WAS JUST ANOTHER ONE OF YOUR PAWNS.

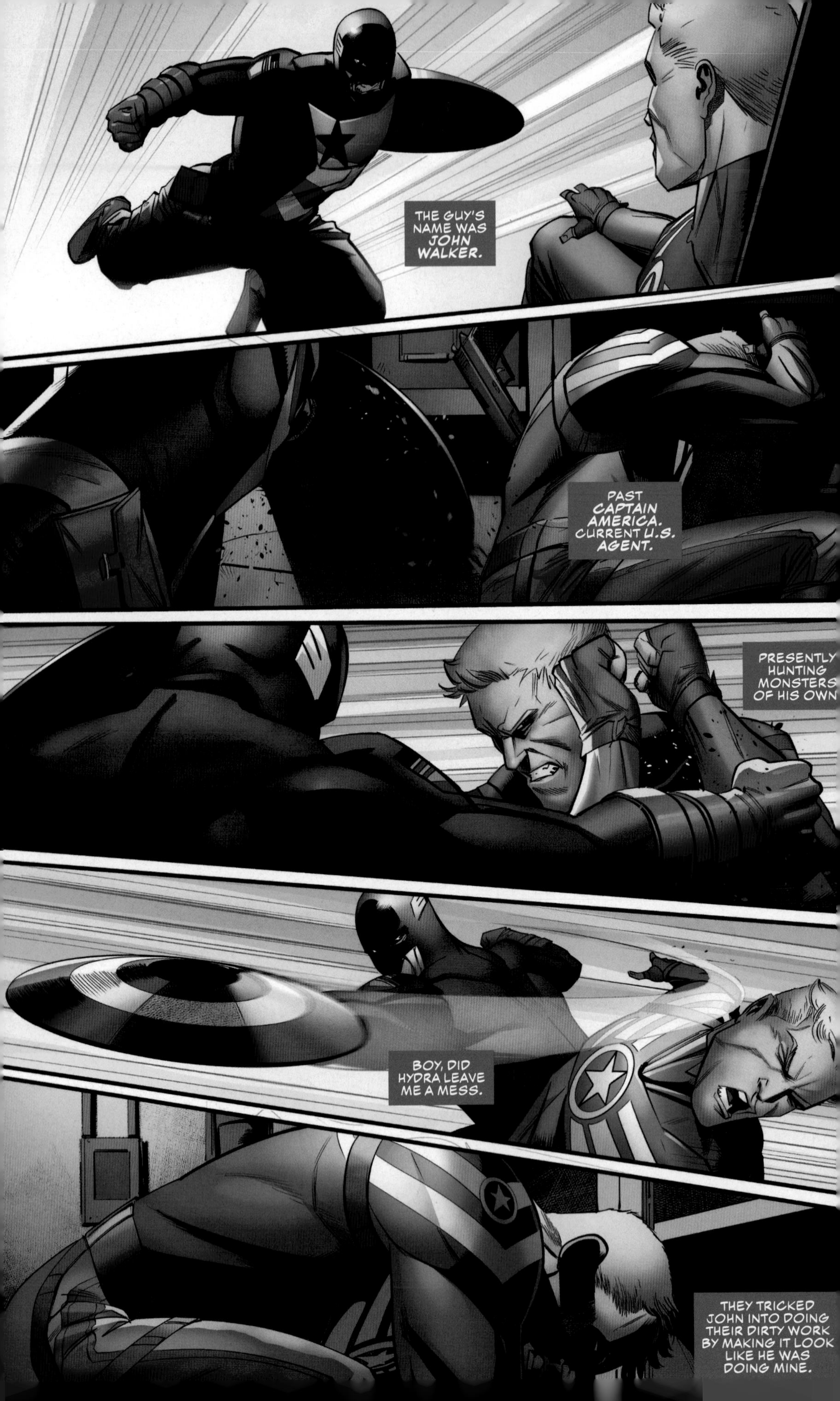
THE GUY'S NAME WAS JOHN WALKER.
PAST CAPTAIN AMERICA. CURRENT U.S. AGENT.
PRESENTLY HUNTING MONSTERS OF HIS OWN
BOY, DID HYDRA LEAVE ME A MESS.
THEY TRICKED JOHN INTO DOING THEIR DIRTY WORK BY MAKING IT LOOK LIKE HE WAS DOING MINE.

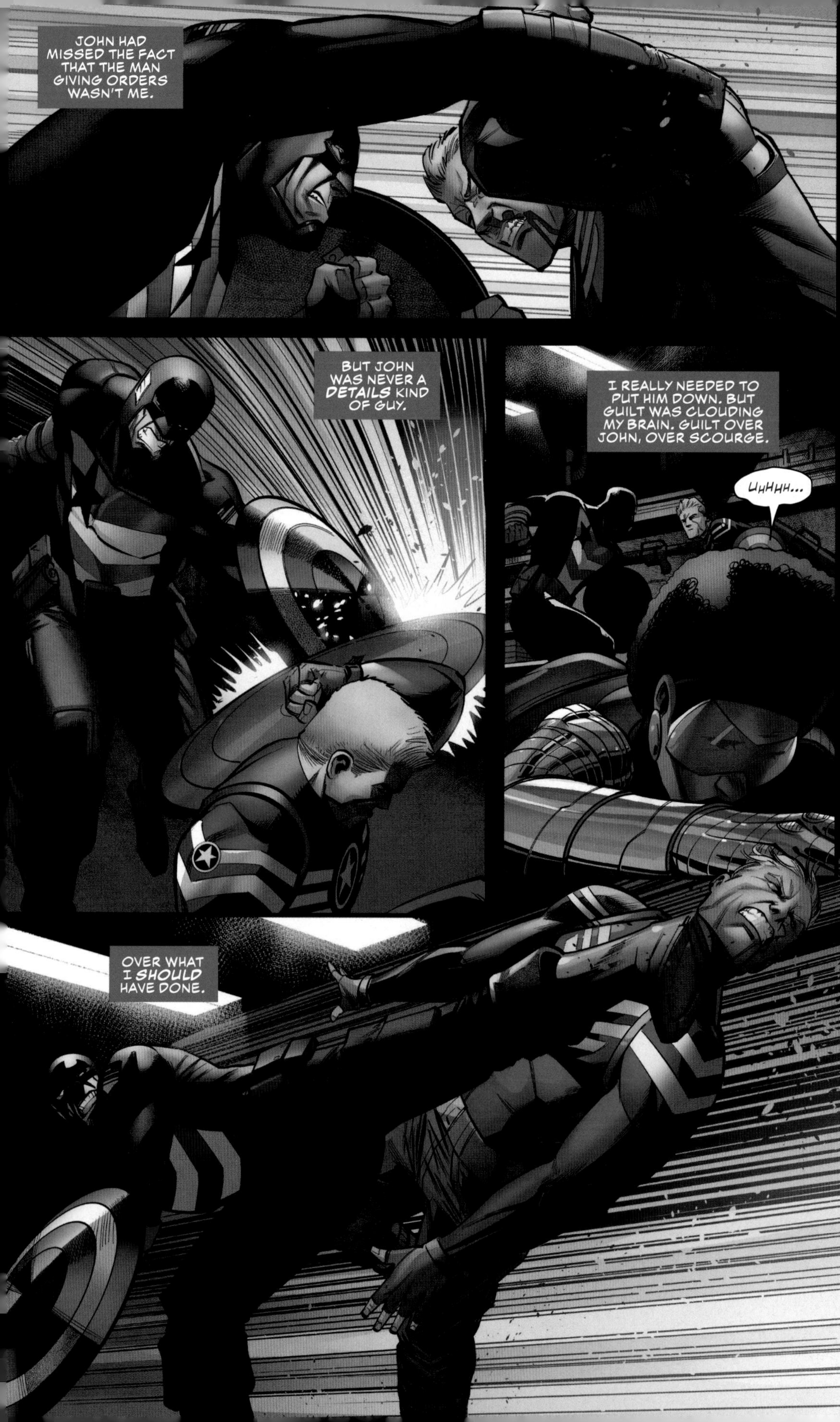

JOHN HAD MISSED THE FACT THAT THE MAN GIVING ORDERS WASN'T ME.
BUT JOHN WAS NEVER A *DETAILS* KIND OF GUY.
I REALLY NEEDED TO PUT HIM DOWN. BUT GUILT WAS CLOUDING MY BRAIN. GUILT OVER JOHN, OVER SCOURGE.
UHHHH...
OVER WHAT I *SHOULD* HAVE DONE.

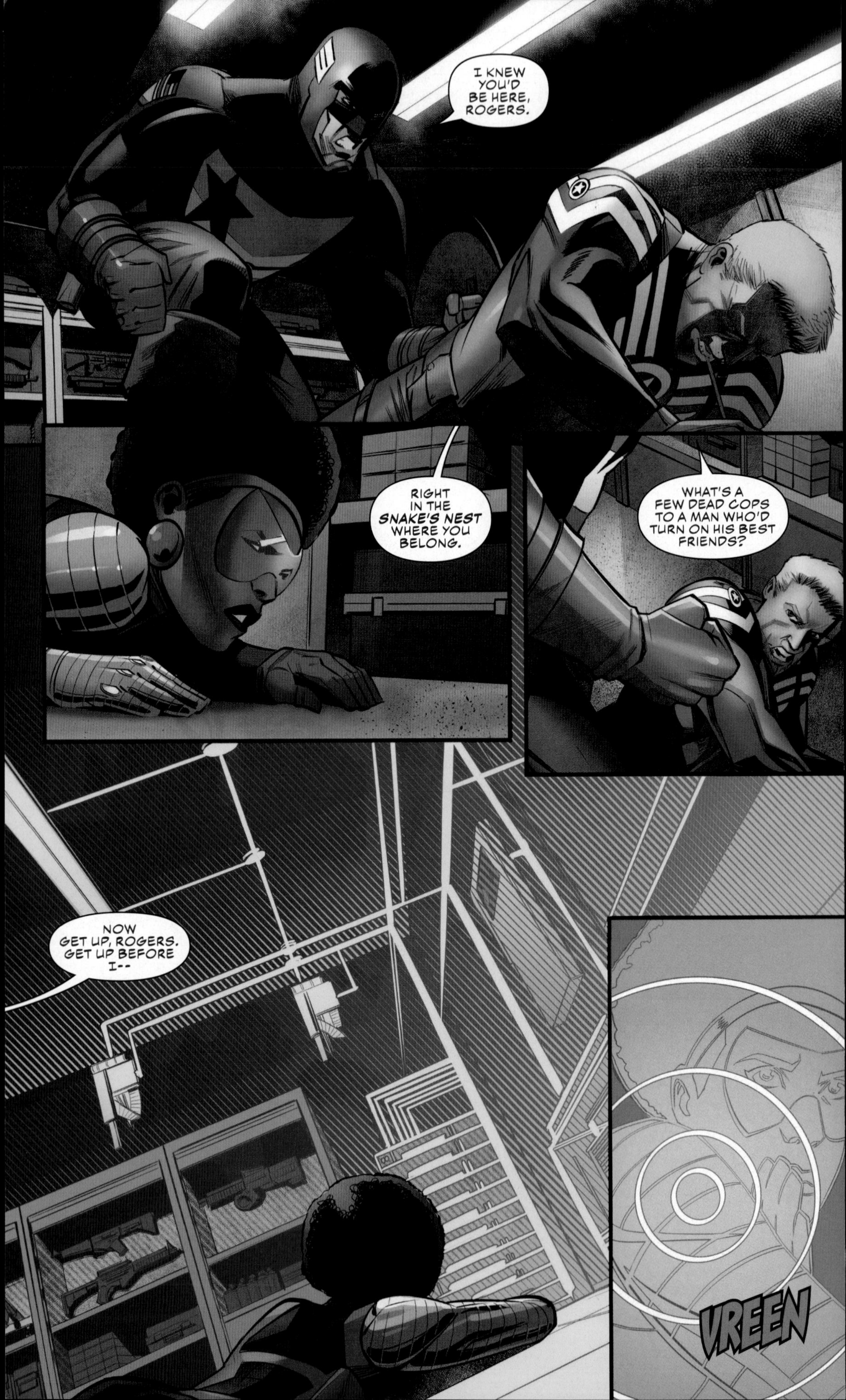
I KNEW YOU'D BE HERE, ROGERS.
RIGHT IN THE SNAKE'S NEST WHERE YOU BELONG.
WHAT'S A FEW DEAD COPS TO A MAN WHO'D TURN ON HIS BEST FRIENDS?
NOW GET UP, ROGERS. GET UP BEFORE I--
VREEN

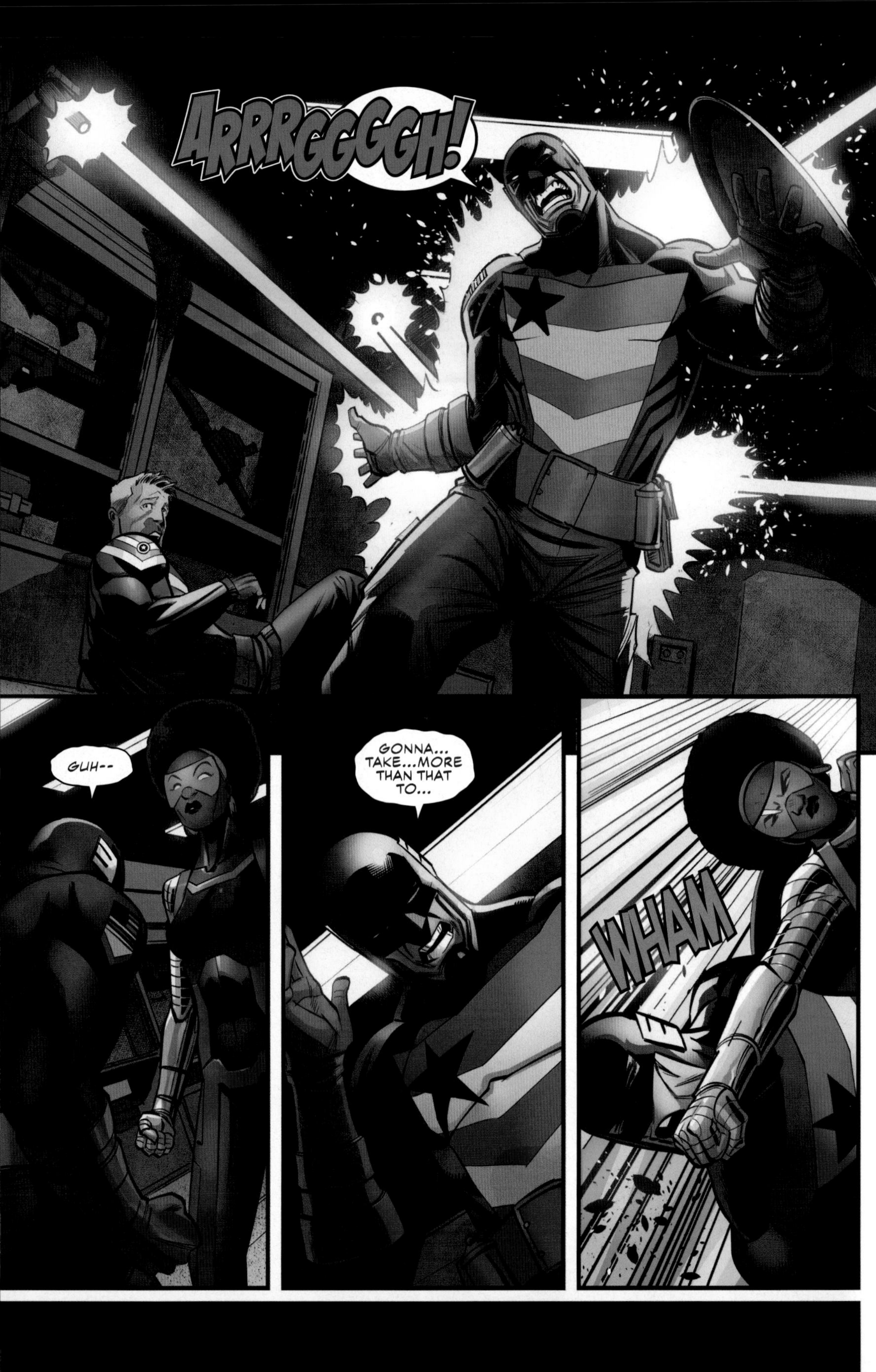
ARRRGGGGH!
GUH--
GONNA... TAKE...MORE THAN THAT TO...
WHAM

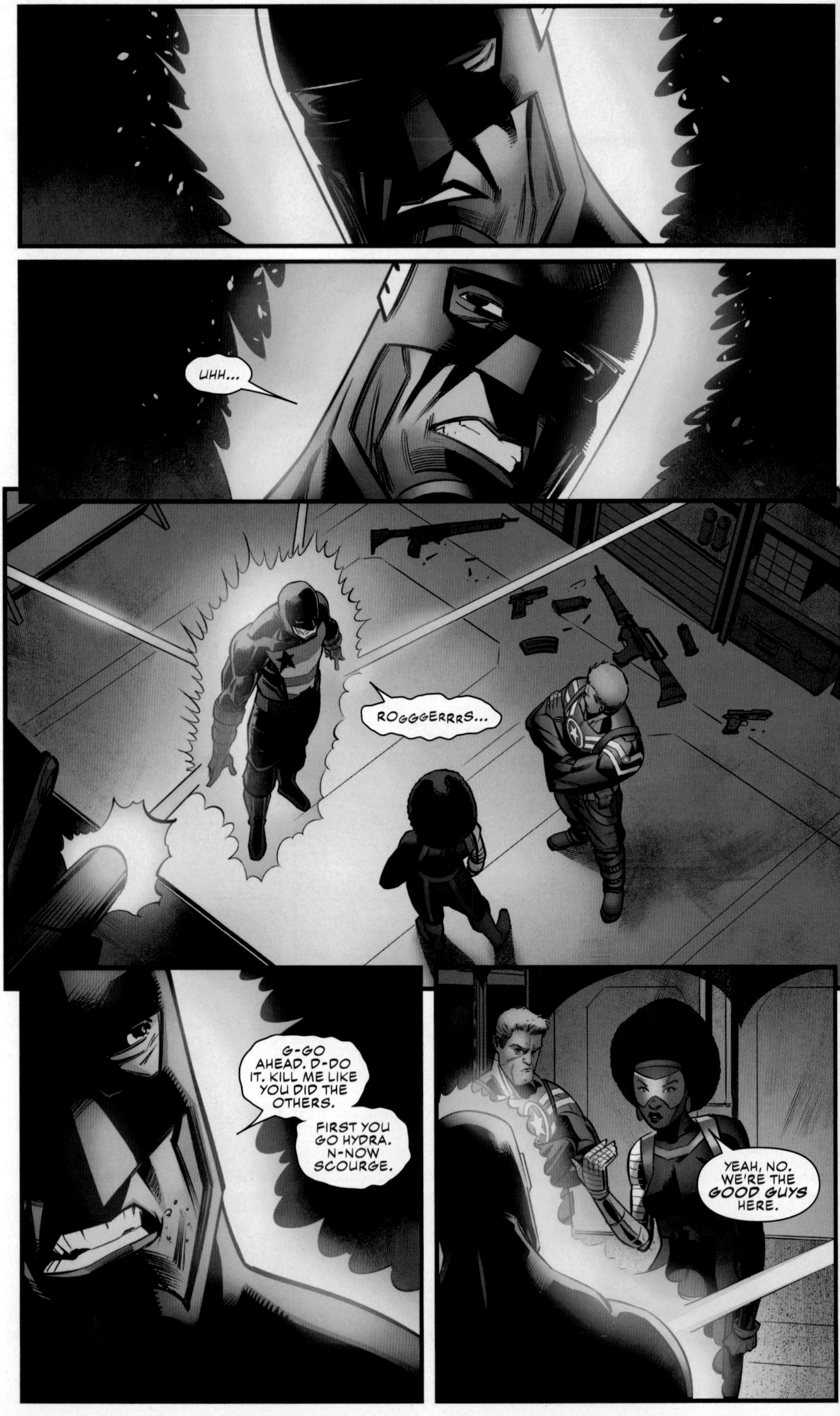
UHH...
ROGGGERRRS...
G-GO AHEAD. D-DO IT. KILL ME LIKE YOU DID THE OTHERS.
FIRST YOU GO HYDRA. N-NOW SCOURGE.
YEAH, NO. WE'RE THE GOOD GUYS HERE.

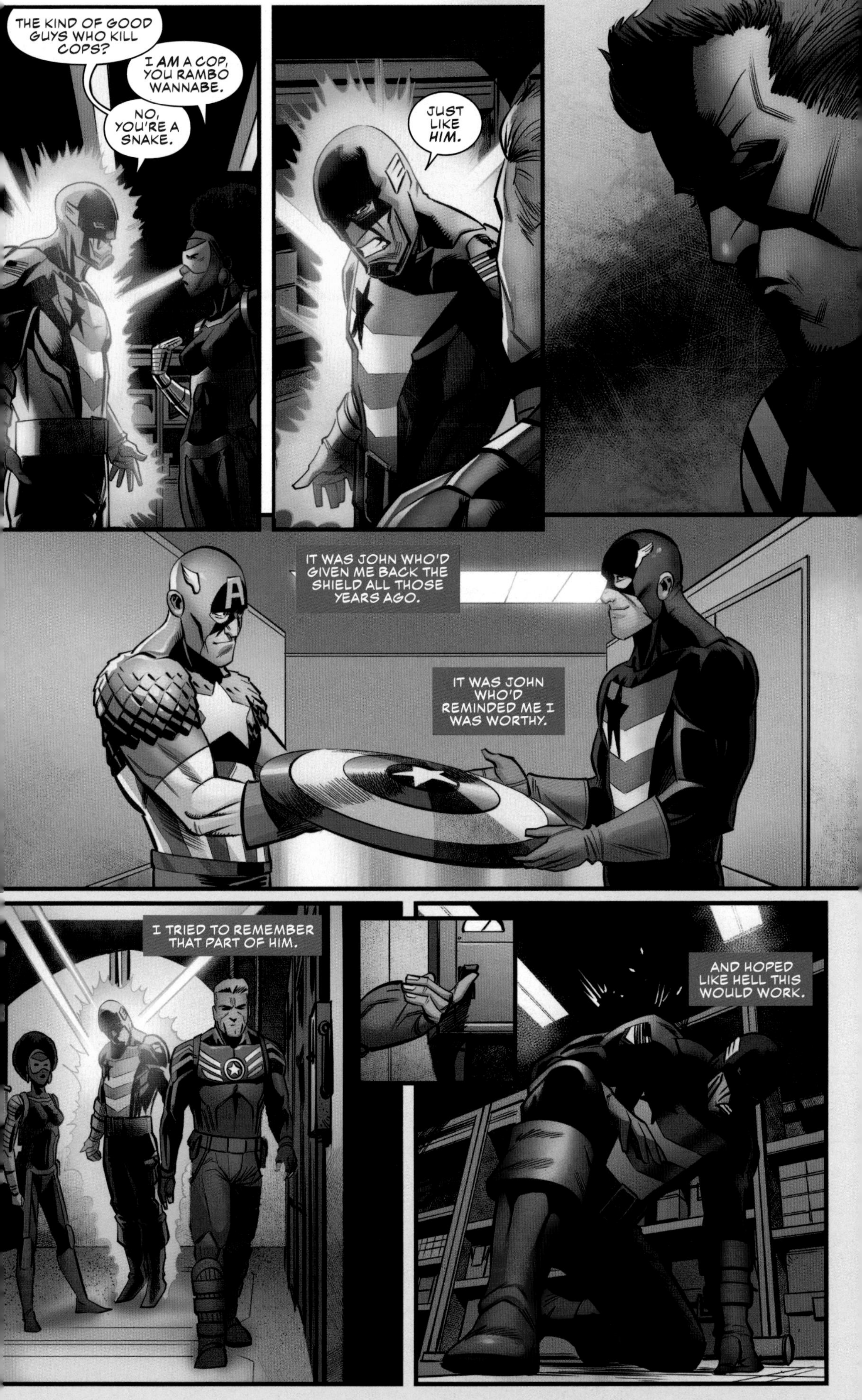
THE KIND OF GOOD GUYS WHO KILL COPS?
I AM A COP, YOU RAMBO WANNABE.
NO, YOU'RE A SNAKE.
JUST LIKE HIM.
IT WAS JOHN WHO'D GIVEN ME BACK THE SHIELD ALL THOSE YEARS AGO.
IT WAS JOHN WHO'D REMINDED ME I WAS WORTHY.
I TRIED TO REMEMBER THAT PART OF HIM.
AND HOPED LIKE HELL THIS WOULD WORK.

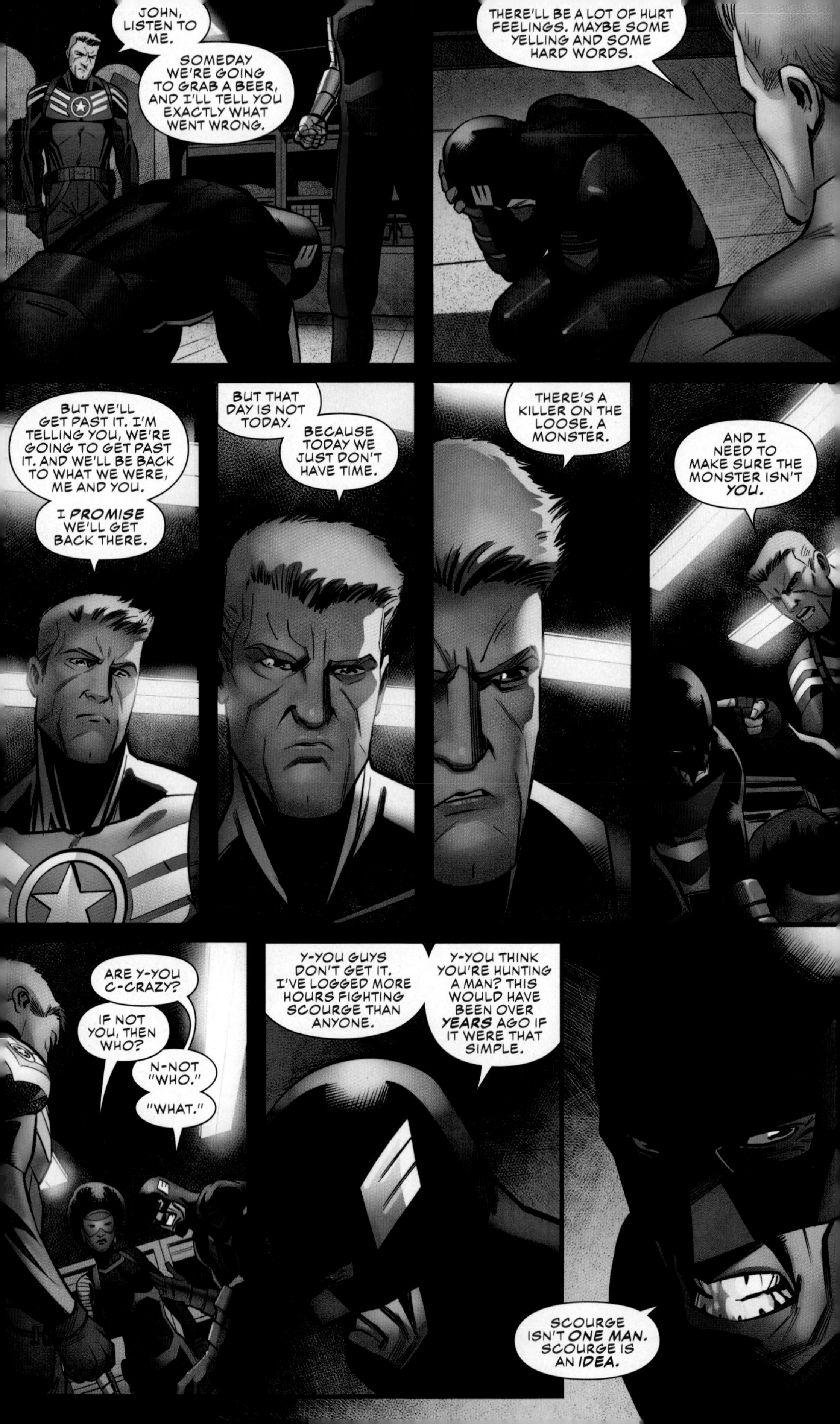

JOHN, LISTEN TO ME.
SOMEDAY WE'RE GOING TO GRAB A BEER, AND I'LL TELL YOU EXACTLY WHAT WENT WRONG.
THERE'LL BE A LOT OF HURT FEELINGS. MAYBE SOME YELLING AND SOME HARD WORDS.
BUT WE'LL GET PAST IT. I'M TELLING YOU, WE'RE GOING TO GET PAST IT. AND WE'LL BE BACK TO WHAT WE WERE, ME AND YOU.
I PROMISE WE'LL GET BACK THERE.
BUT THAT DAY IS NOT TODAY.
BECAUSE TODAY WE JUST DON'T HAVE TIME.
THERE'S A KILLER ON THE LOOSE. A MONSTER.
AND I NEED TO MAKE SURE THE MONSTER ISN'T YOU.
ARE Y-YOU C-CRAZY?
IF NOT YOU, THEN WHO?
N-NOT "WHO."
"WHAT."
Y-YOU GUYS DON'T GET IT. I'VE LOGGED MORE HOURS FIGHTING SCOURGE THAN ANYONE.
Y-YOU THINK YOU'RE HUNTING A MAN? THIS WOULD HAVE BEEN OVER YEARS AGO IF IT WERE THAT SIMPLE.
SCOURGE ISN'T ONE MAN. SCOURGE IS AN IDEA.

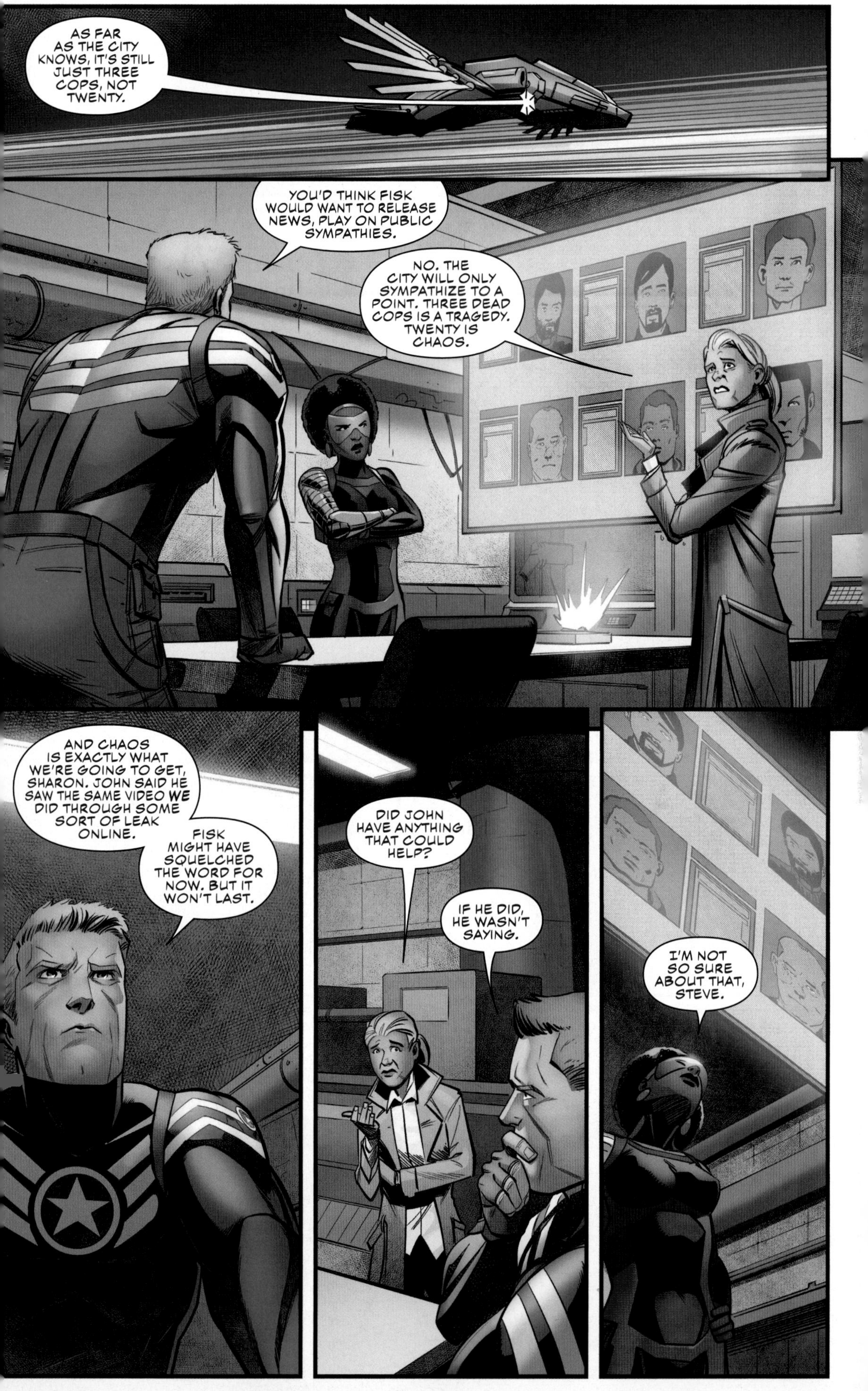
AS FAR AS THE CITY KNOWS, IT'S STILL JUST THREE COPS, NOT TWENTY.
YOU'D THINK FISK WOULD WANT TO RELEASE NEWS, PLAY ON PUBLIC SYMPATHIES.
NO. THE CITY WILL ONLY SYMPATHIZE TO A POINT. THREE DEAD COPS IS A TRAGEDY. TWENTY IS CHAOS.
AND CHAOS IS EXACTLY WHAT WE'RE GOING TO GET, SHARON. JOHN SAID HE SAW THE SAME VIDEO WE DID THROUGH SOME SORT OF LEAK ONLINE.
FISK MIGHT HAVE SQUELCHED THE WORD FOR NOW. BUT IT WON'T LAST.
DID JOHN HAVE ANYTHING THAT COULD HELP?
IF HE DID, HE WASN'T SAYING.
I'M NOT SO SURE ABOUT THAT, STEVE.

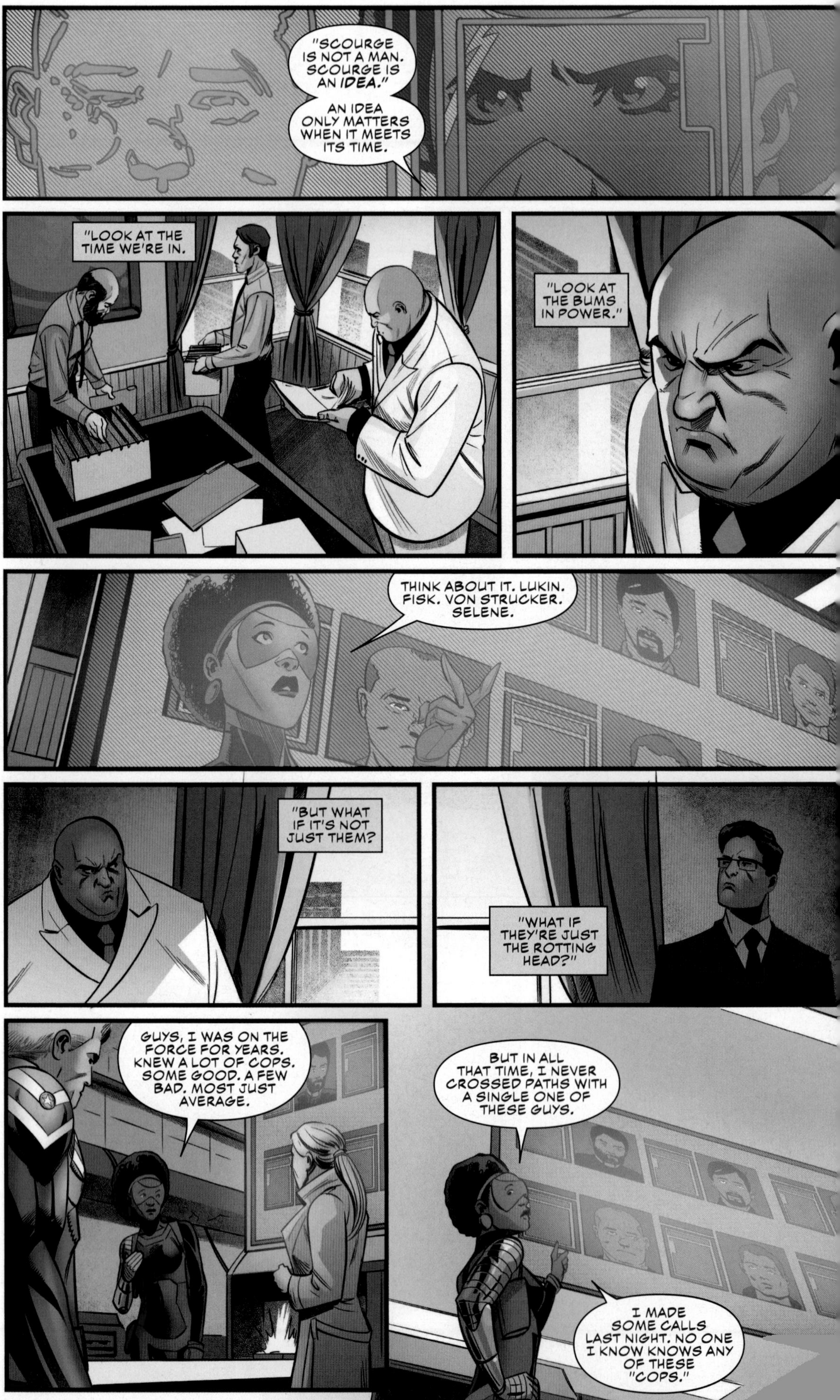
"SCOURGE IS NOT A MAN. SCOURGE IS AN *IDEA.*"
AN IDEA ONLY MATTERS WHEN IT MEETS ITS TIME.
"LOOK AT THE TIME WE'RE IN.
"LOOK AT THE BUMS IN POWER."
THINK ABOUT IT. LUKIN. FISK. VON STRUCKER. SELENE.
"BUT WHAT IF IT'S NOT JUST THEM?
"WHAT IF THEY'RE JUST THE ROTTING HEAD?"
GUYS, I WAS ON THE FORCE FOR YEARS. KNEW A LOT OF COPS. SOME GOOD. A FEW BAD. MOST JUST AVERAGE.
BUT IN ALL THAT TIME, I NEVER CROSSED PATHS WITH A SINGLE ONE OF THESE GUYS.
I MADE SOME CALLS LAST NIGHT. NO ONE I KNOW KNOWS ANY OF THESE "COPS."

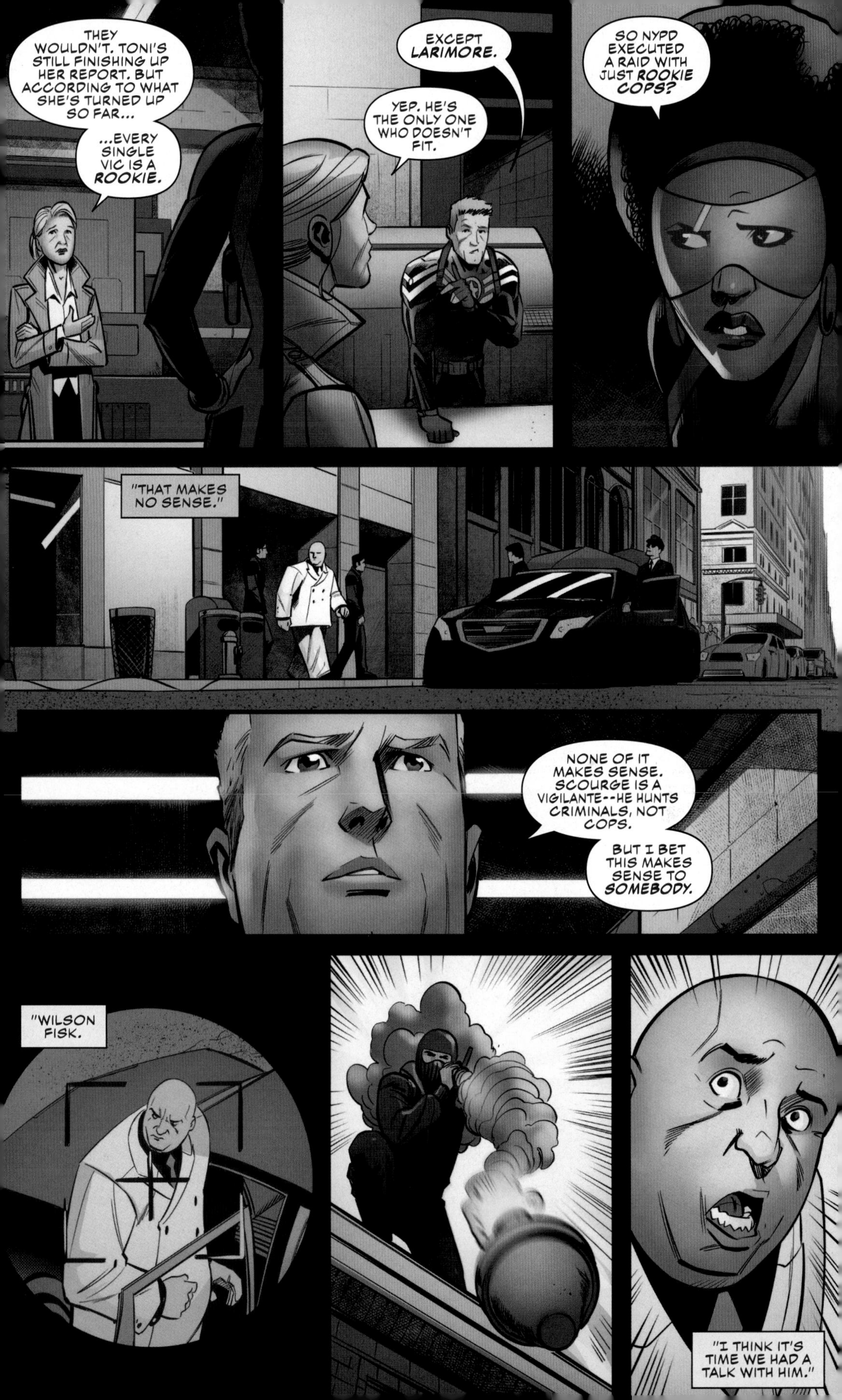
THEY WOULDN'T. TONI'S STILL FINISHING UP HER REPORT. BUT ACCORDING TO WHAT SHE'S TURNED UP SO FAR...
...EVERY SINGLE VIC IS A ROOKIE.
EXCEPT LARIMORE.
YEP. HE'S THE ONLY ONE WHO DOESN'T FIT.
SO NYPD EXECUTED A RAID WITH JUST ROOKIE COPS?
"THAT MAKES NO SENSE."
NONE OF IT MAKES SENSE. SCOURGE IS A VIGILANTE--HE HUNTS CRIMINALS, NOT COPS.
BUT I BET THIS MAKES SENSE TO SOMEBODY.
"WILSON FISK.
"I THINK IT'S TIME WE HAD A TALK WITH HIM."

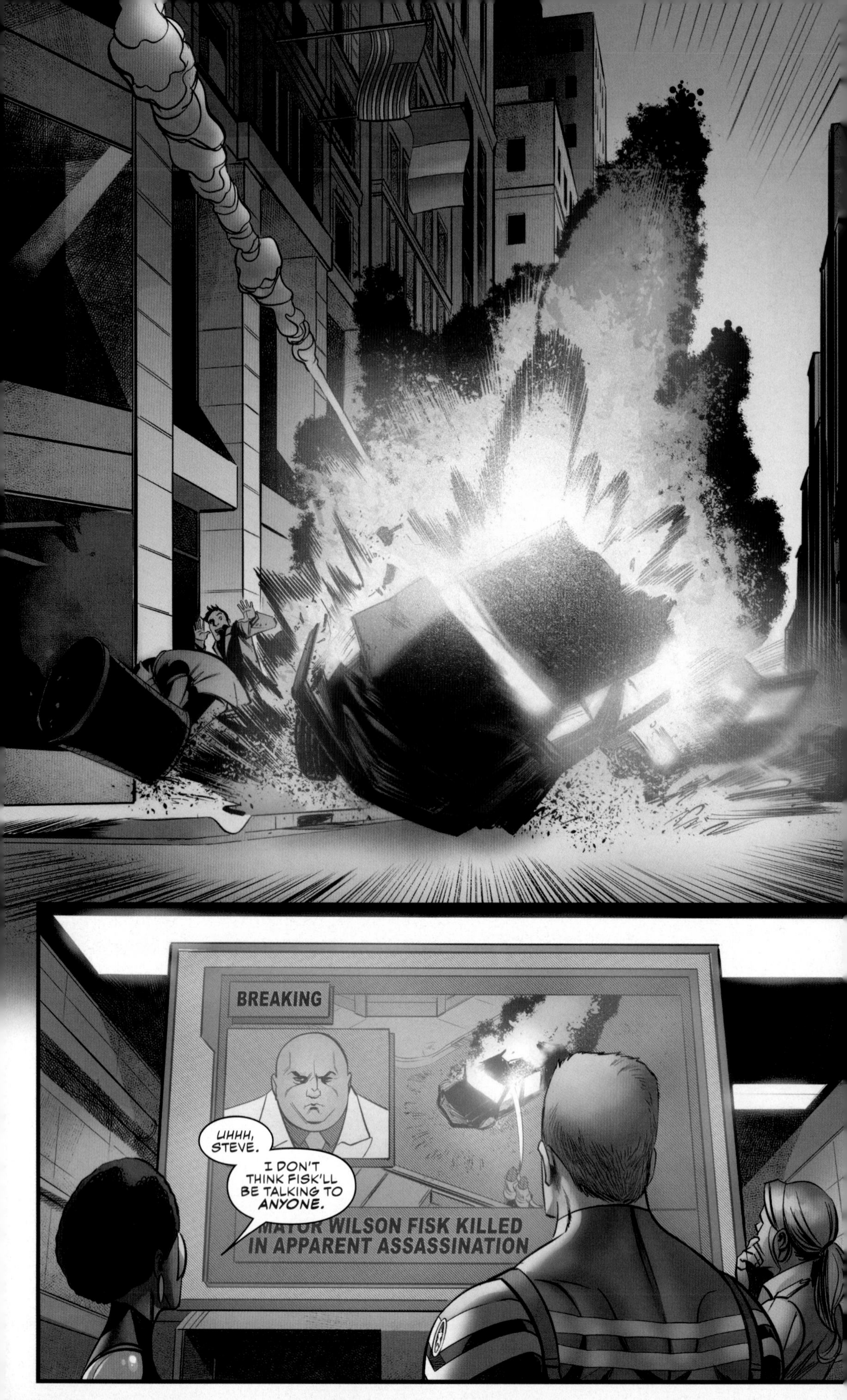
BREAKING
UHHH, STEVE.
I DON'T THINK FISK'LL BE TALKING TO *ANYONE.*
MAYOR WILSON FISK KILLED IN APPARENT ASSASSINATION

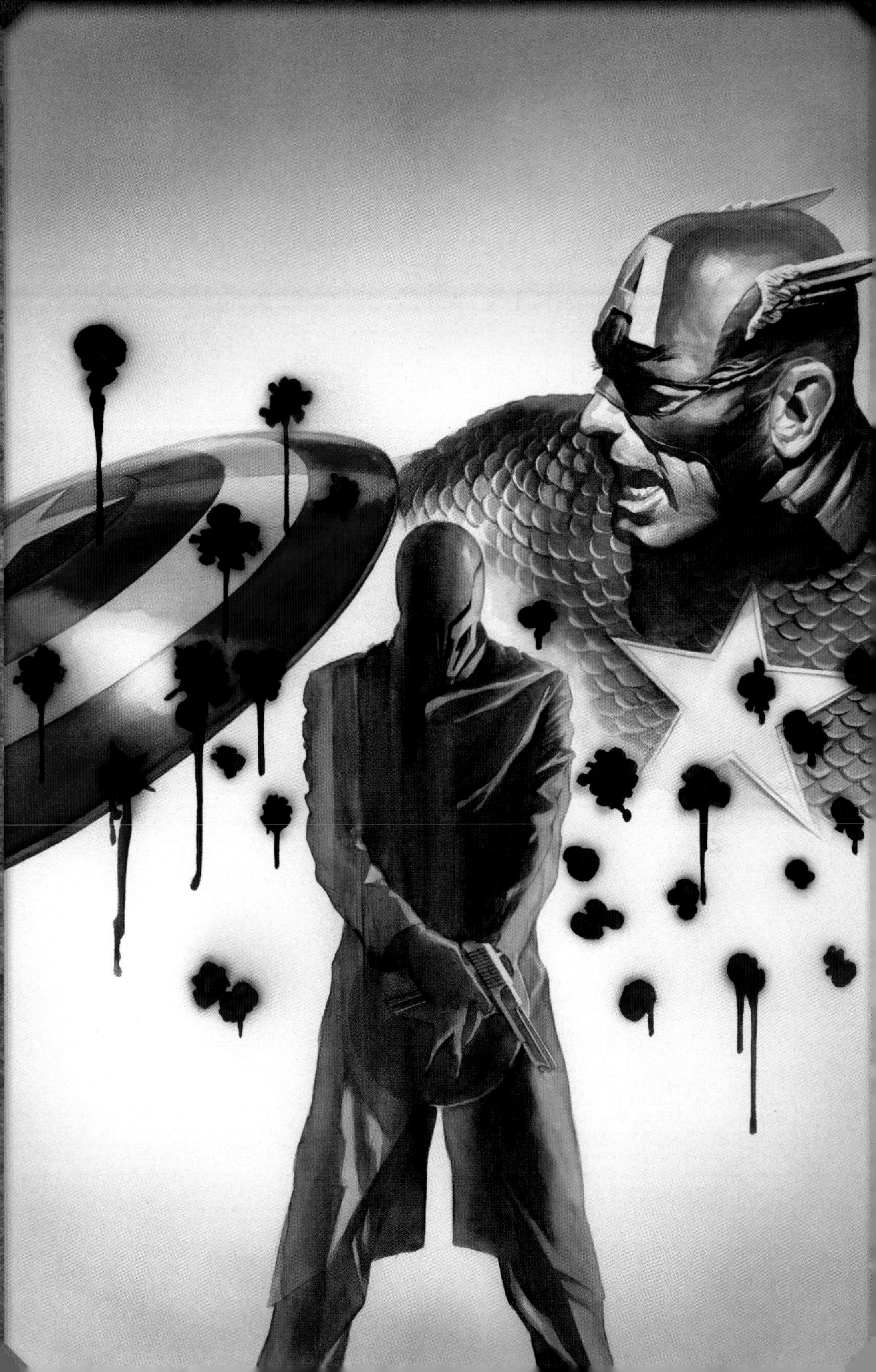

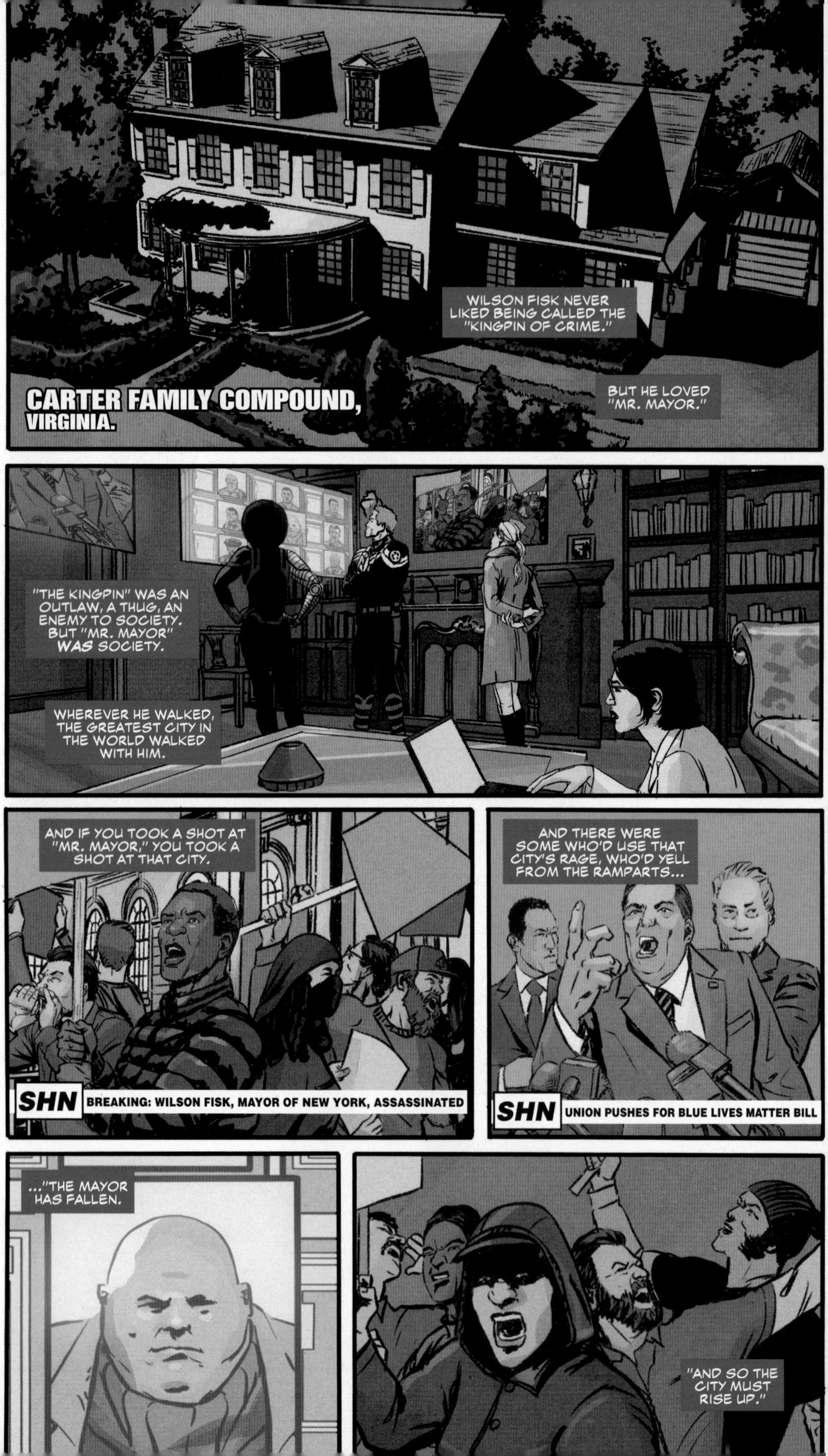
WILSON FISK NEVER LIKED BEING CALLED THE "KINGPIN OF CRIME."
BUT HE LOVED "MR. MAYOR."
CARTER FAMILY COMPOUND, VIRGINIA.
"THE KINGPIN" WAS AN OUTLAW, A THUG, AN ENEMY TO SOCIETY. BUT "MR. MAYOR" WAS SOCIETY.
WHEREVER HE WALKED, THE GREATEST CITY IN THE WORLD WALKED WITH HIM.
AND IF YOU TOOK A SHOT AT "MR. MAYOR," YOU TOOK A SHOT AT THAT CITY.
SHN
BREAKING: WILSON FISK, MAYOR OF NEW YORK, ASSASSINATED
AND THERE WERE SOME WHO'D USE THAT CITY'S RAGE, WHO'D YELL FROM THE RAMPARTS...
SHN
UNION PUSHES FOR BLUE LIVES MATTER BILL
..."THE MAYOR HAS FALLEN.
"AND SO THE CITY MUST RISE UP."

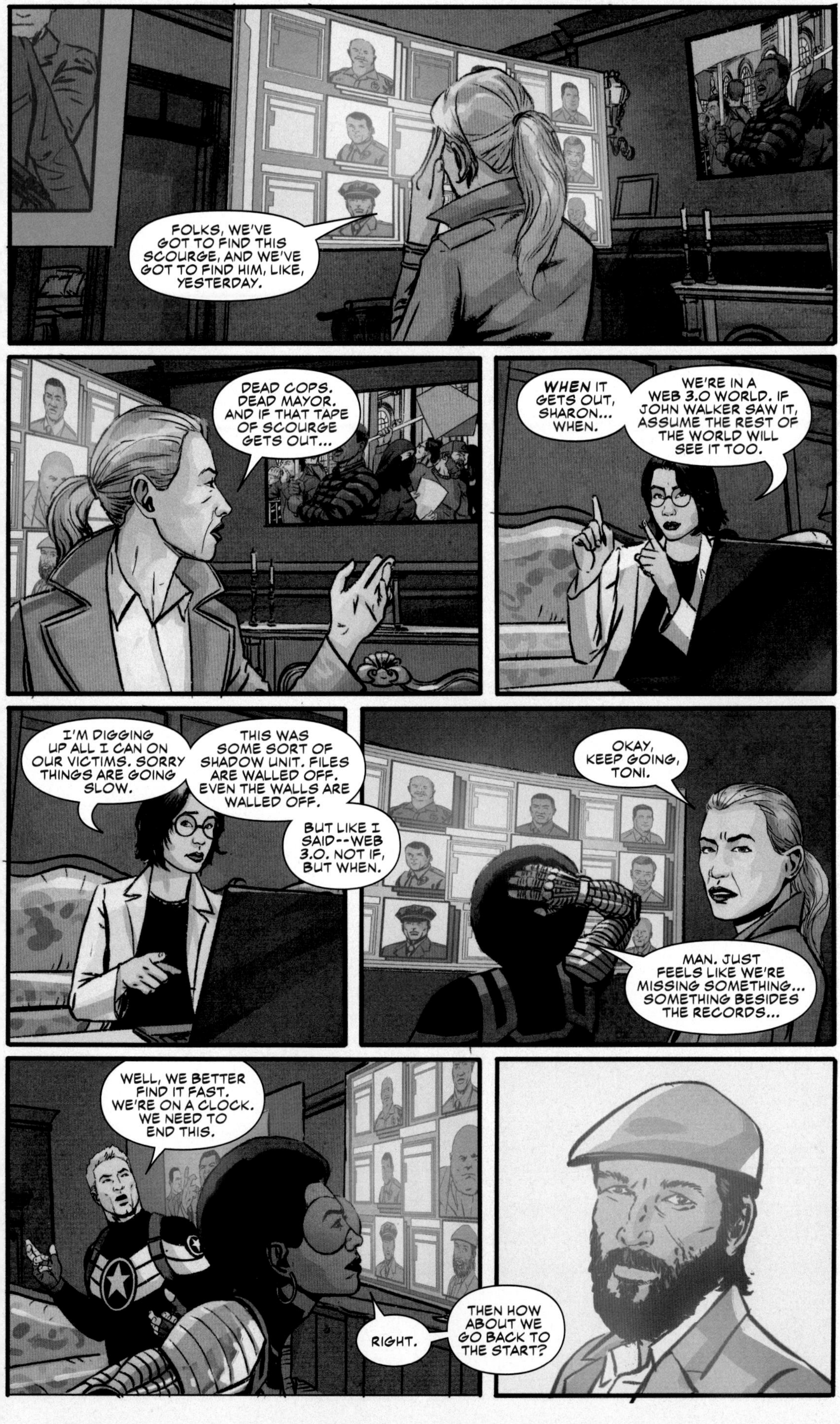
FOLKS, WE'VE GOT TO FIND THIS SCOURGE, AND WE'VE GOT TO FIND HIM, LIKE, YESTERDAY.
DEAD COPS. DEAD MAYOR. AND IF THAT TAPE OF SCOURGE GETS OUT...
WHEN IT GETS OUT, SHARON... WHEN.
WE'RE IN A WEB 3.0 WORLD. IF JOHN WALKER SAW IT, ASSUME THE REST OF THE WORLD WILL SEE IT TOO.
I'M DIGGING UP ALL I CAN ON OUR VICTIMS. SORRY THINGS ARE GOING SLOW.
THIS WAS SOME SORT OF SHADOW UNIT. FILES ARE WALLED OFF. EVEN THE WALLS ARE WALLED OFF.
BUT LIKE I SAID--WEB 3.0. NOT IF, BUT WHEN.
OKAY, KEEP GOING, TONI.
MAN. JUST FEELS LIKE WE'RE MISSING SOMETHING... SOMETHING BESIDES THE RECORDS...
WELL, WE BETTER FIND IT FAST. WE'RE ON A CLOCK. WE NEED TO END THIS.
RIGHT.
THEN HOW ABOUT WE GO BACK TO THE START?

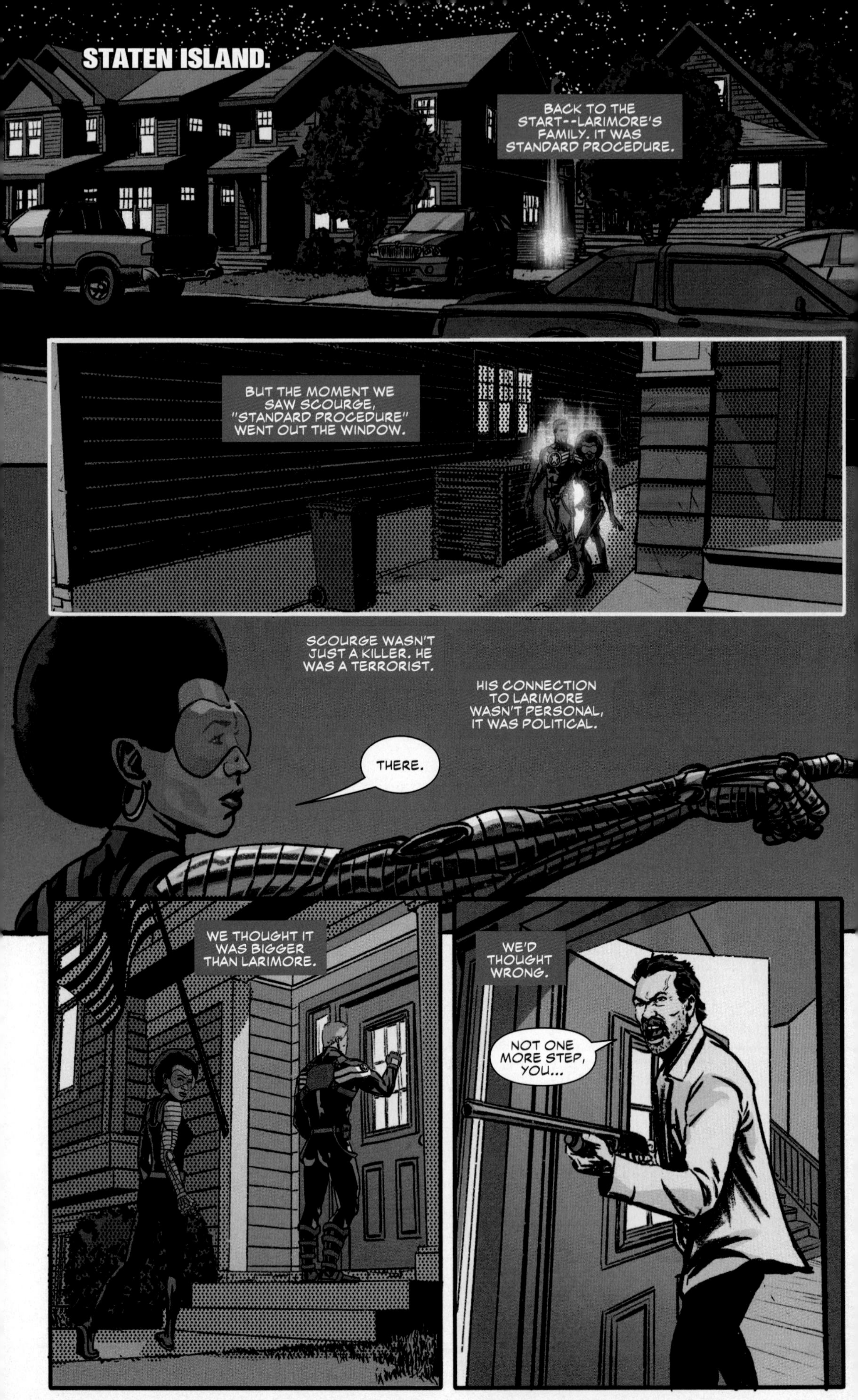
STATEN ISLAND.
BACK TO THE START--LARIMORE'S FAMILY. IT WAS STANDARD PROCEDURE.
BUT THE MOMENT WE SAW SCOURGE, "STANDARD PROCEDURE" WENT OUT THE WINDOW.
SCOURGE WASN'T JUST A KILLER. HE WAS A TERRORIST.
HIS CONNECTION TO LARIMORE WASN'T PERSONAL, IT WAS POLITICAL.
THERE.
WE THOUGHT IT WAS BIGGER THAN LARIMORE.
WE'D THOUGHT WRONG.
NOT ONE MORE STEP, YOU...

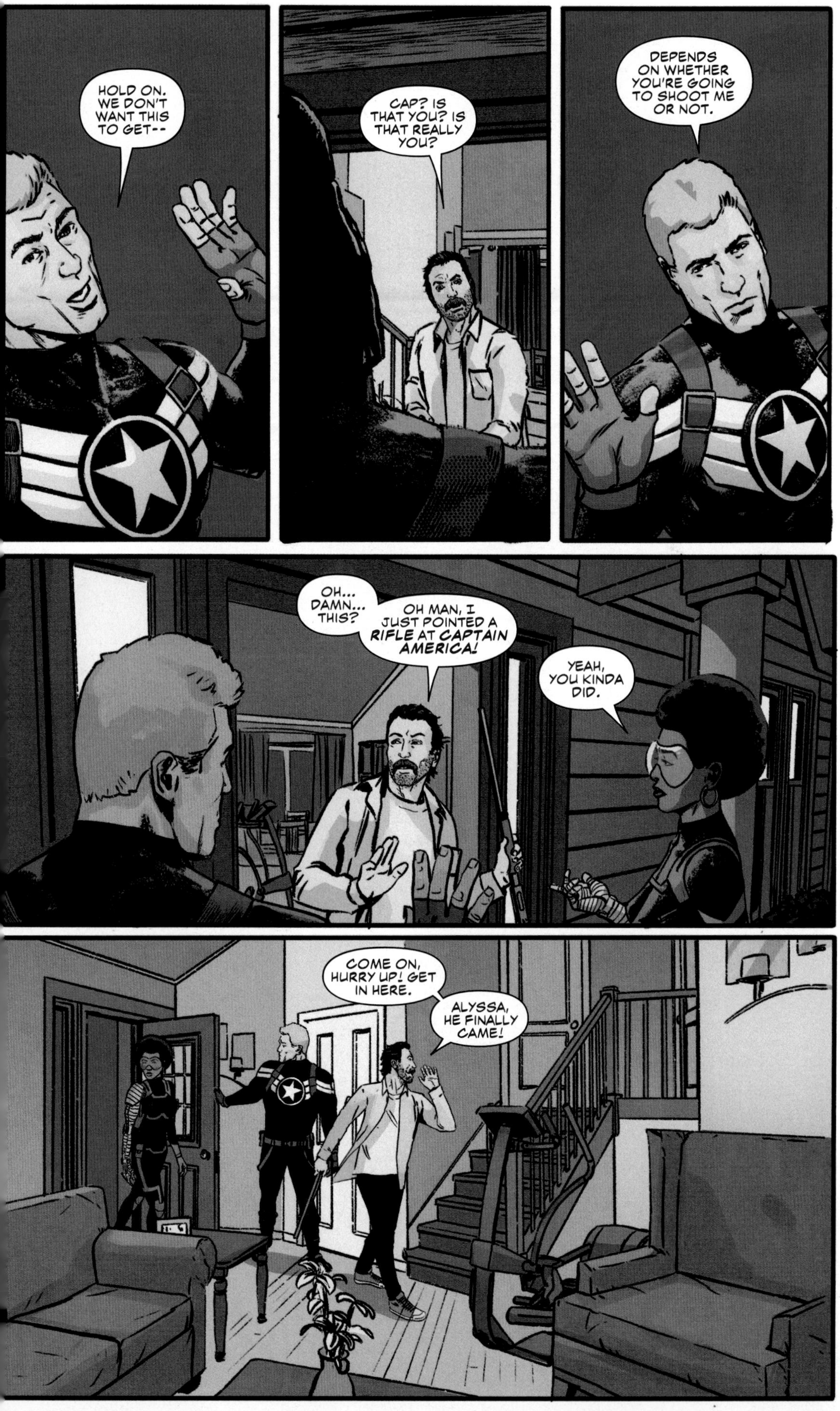
HOLD ON. WE DON'T WANT THIS TO GET--
CAP? IS THAT YOU? IS THAT REALLY YOU?
DEPENDS ON WHETHER YOU'RE GOING TO SHOOT ME OR NOT.
OH... DAMN... THIS?
OH MAN, I JUST POINTED A RIFLE AT CAPTAIN AMERICA!
YEAH, YOU KINDA DID.
COME ON, HURRY UP! GET IN HERE.
ALYSSA, HE FINALLY CAME!

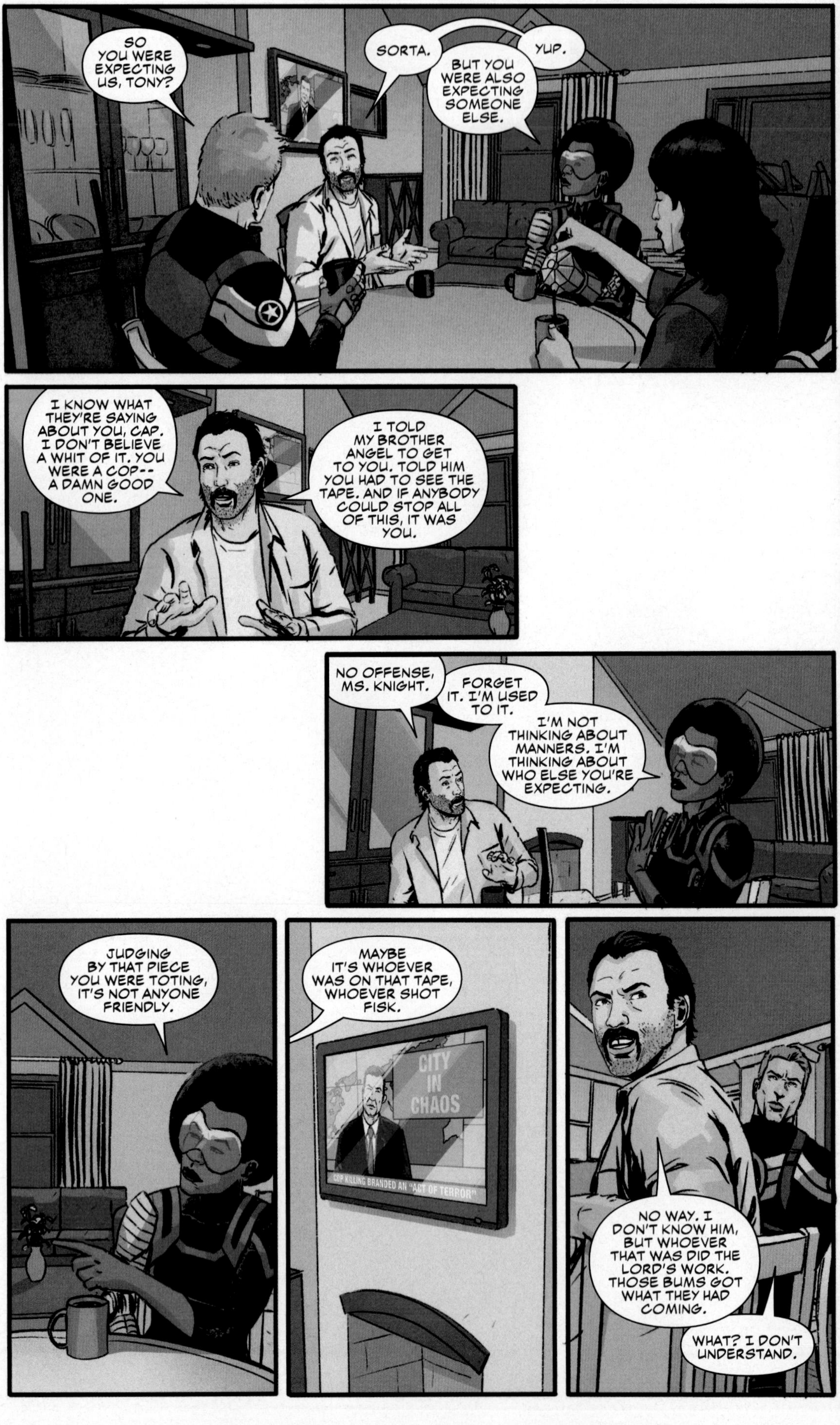
SO YOU WERE EXPECTING US, TONY?
SORTA.
YUP.
BUT YOU WERE ALSO EXPECTING SOMEONE ELSE.
I KNOW WHAT THEY'RE SAYING ABOUT YOU, CAP. I DON'T BELIEVE A WHIT OF IT. YOU WERE A COP-- A DAMN GOOD ONE.
I TOLD MY BROTHER ANGEL TO GET TO YOU. TOLD HIM YOU HAD TO SEE THE TAPE. AND IF ANYBODY COULD STOP ALL OF THIS, IT WAS YOU.
NO OFFENSE, MS. KNIGHT.
FORGET IT. I'M USED TO IT.
I'M NOT THINKING ABOUT MANNERS. I'M THINKING ABOUT WHO ELSE YOU'RE EXPECTING.
JUDGING BY THAT PIECE YOU WERE TOTING, IT'S NOT ANYONE FRIENDLY.
MAYBE IT'S WHOEVER WAS ON THAT TAPE, WHOEVER SHOT FISK.
CITY IN CHAOS
COP KILLING BRANDED AN "ACT OF TERROR"
NO WAY. I DON'T KNOW HIM, BUT WHOEVER THAT WAS DID THE LORD'S WORK. THOSE BUMS GOT WHAT THEY HAD COMING.
WHAT? I DON'T UNDERSTAND.

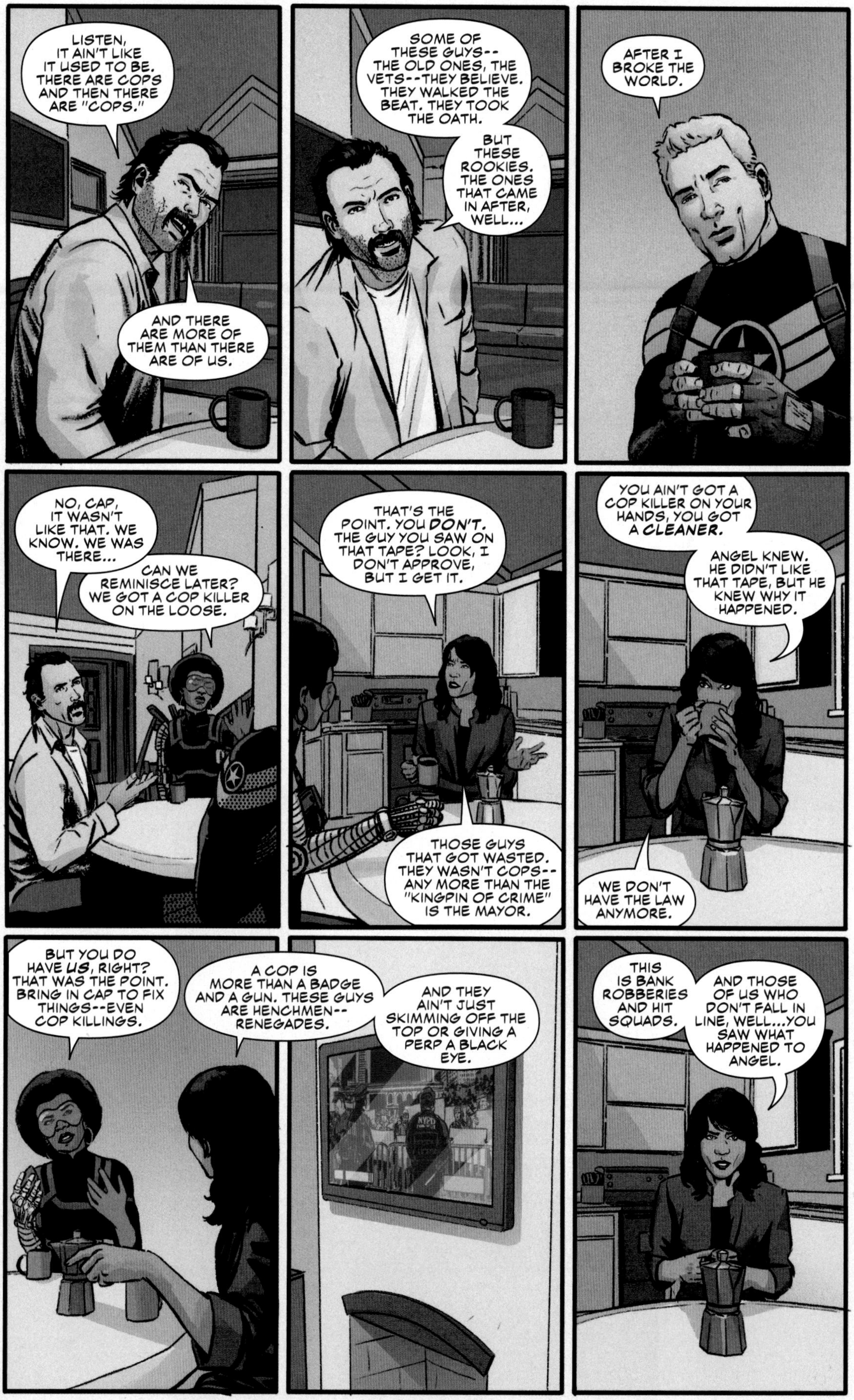
LISTEN, IT AIN'T LIKE IT USED TO BE. THERE ARE COPS AND THEN THERE ARE "COPS."
AND THERE ARE MORE OF THEM THAN THERE ARE OF US.
SOME OF THESE GUYS-- THE OLD ONES, THE VETS--THEY BELIEVE. THEY WALKED THE BEAT. THEY TOOK THE OATH.
BUT THESE ROOKIES. THE ONES THAT CAME IN AFTER, WELL...
AFTER I BROKE THE WORLD.
NO, CAP, IT WASN'T LIKE THAT. WE KNOW. WE WAS THERE...
CAN WE REMINISCE LATER? WE GOT A COP KILLER ON THE LOOSE.
THAT'S THE POINT. YOU ***DON'T.*** THE GUY YOU SAW ON THAT TAPE? LOOK, I DON'T APPROVE, BUT I GET IT.
THOSE GUYS THAT GOT WASTED. THEY WASN'T COPS-- ANY MORE THAN THE "KINGPIN OF CRIME" IS THE MAYOR.
YOU AIN'T GOT A COP KILLER ON YOUR HANDS, YOU GOT A ***CLEANER.***
ANGEL KNEW. HE DIDN'T LIKE THAT TAPE, BUT HE KNEW WHY IT HAPPENED.
WE DON'T HAVE THE LAW ANYMORE.
BUT YOU DO HAVE ***US***, RIGHT? THAT WAS THE POINT. BRING IN CAP TO FIX THINGS--EVEN COP KILLINGS.
A COP IS MORE THAN A BADGE AND A GUN. THESE GUYS ARE HENCHMEN-- RENEGADES.
AND THEY AIN'T JUST SKIMMING OFF THE TOP OR GIVING A PERP A BLACK EYE.
THIS IS BANK ROBBERIES AND HIT SQUADS.
AND THOSE OF US WHO DON'T FALL IN LINE, WELL...YOU SAW WHAT HAPPENED TO ANGEL.

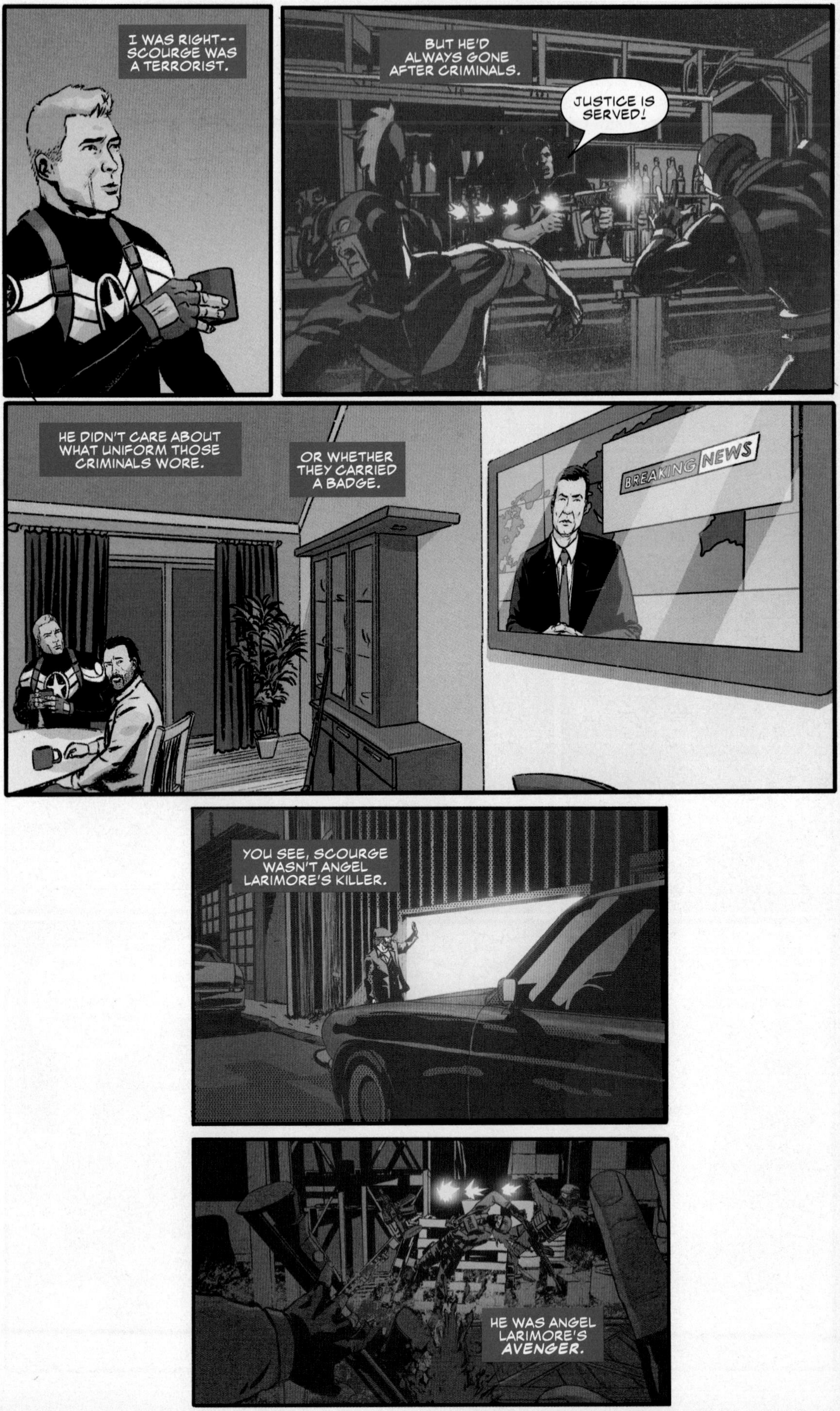
I WAS RIGHT--
SCOURGE WAS
A TERRORIST.
BUT HE'D
ALWAYS GONE
AFTER CRIMINALS.
JUSTICE IS
SERVED!
HE DIDN'T CARE ABOUT
WHAT UNIFORM THOSE
CRIMINALS WORE.
OR WHETHER
THEY CARRIED
A BADGE.
BREAKING NEWS
YOU SEE, SCOURGE
WASN'T ANGEL
LARIMORE'S KILLER.
HE WAS ANGEL
LARIMORE'S
AVENGER.

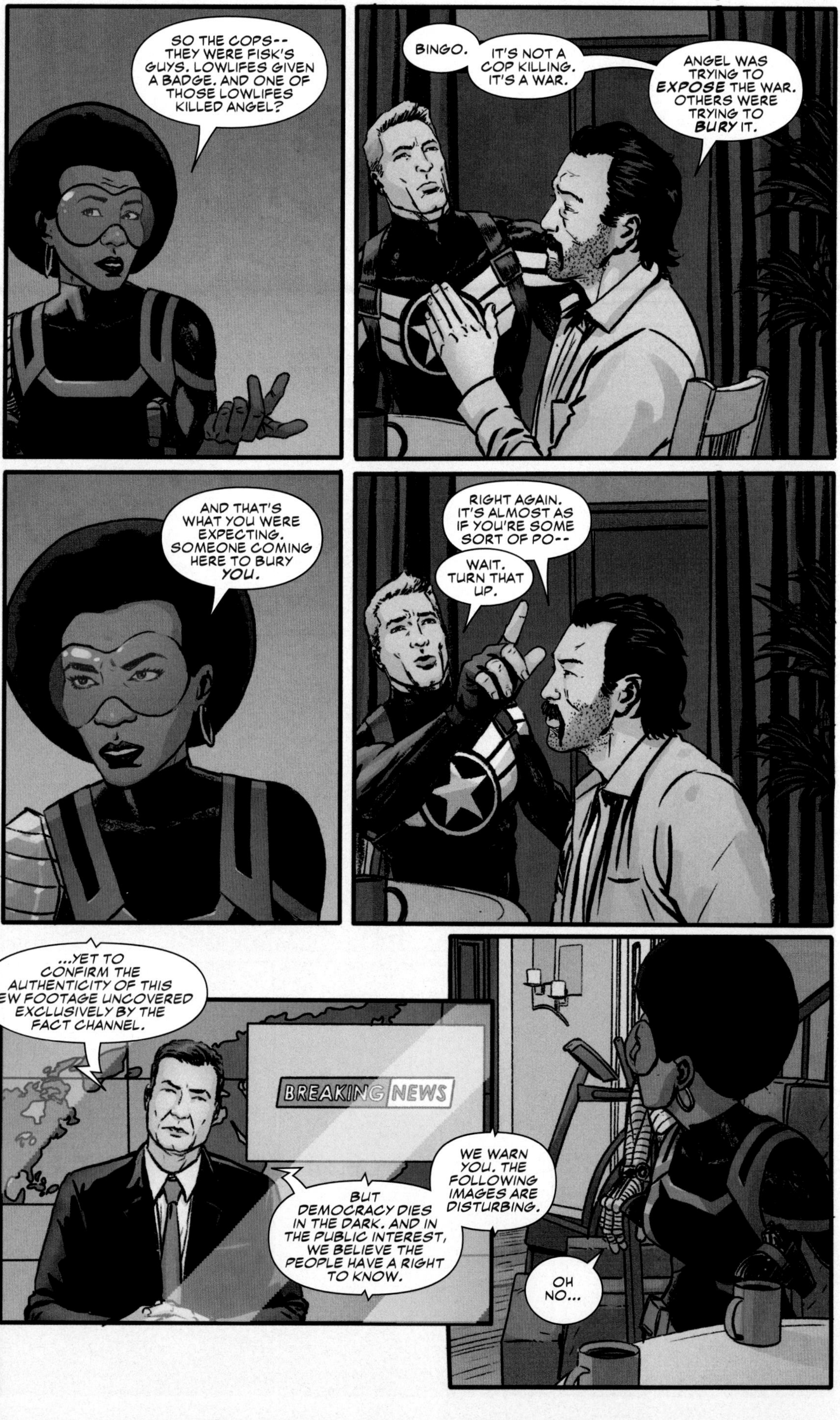
SO THE COPS--
THEY WERE FISK'S GUYS. LOWLIFES GIVEN A BADGE. AND ONE OF THOSE LOWLIFES KILLED ANGEL?
BINGO.
IT'S NOT A COP KILLING. IT'S A WAR.
ANGEL WAS TRYING TO EXPOSE THE WAR. OTHERS WERE TRYING TO BURY IT.
AND THAT'S WHAT YOU WERE EXPECTING. SOMEONE COMING HERE TO BURY YOU.
RIGHT AGAIN. IT'S ALMOST AS IF YOU'RE SOME SORT OF PO--
WAIT. TURN THAT UP.
...YET TO CONFIRM THE AUTHENTICITY OF THIS EW FOOTAGE UNCOVERED EXCLUSIVELY BY THE FACT CHANNEL.
BREAKING NEWS
BUT DEMOCRACY DIES IN THE DARK. AND IN THE PUBLIC INTEREST, WE BELIEVE THE PEOPLE HAVE A RIGHT TO KNOW.
WE WARN YOU. THE FOLLOWING IMAGES ARE DISTURBING.
OH NO...

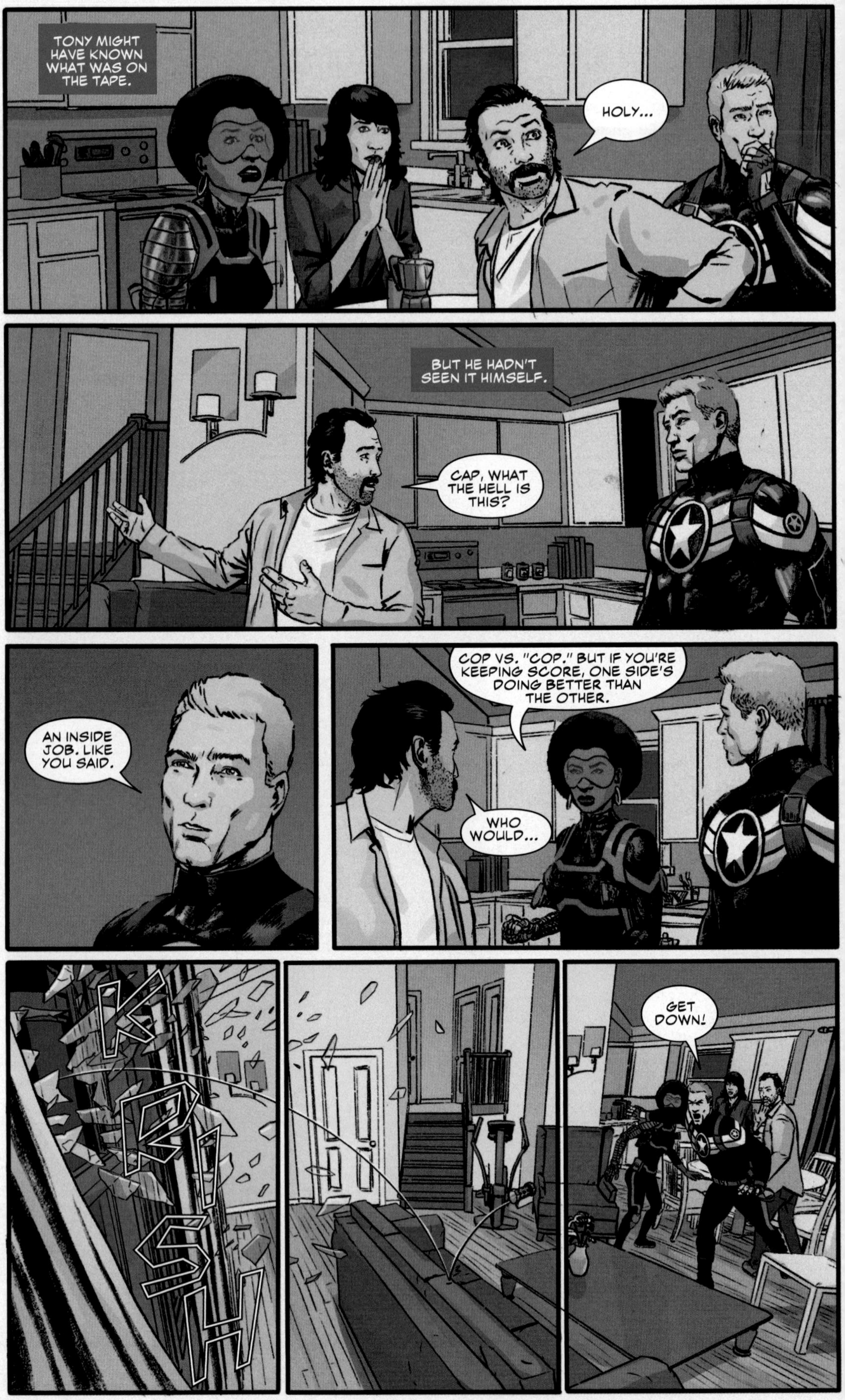
TONY MIGHT HAVE KNOWN WHAT WAS ON THE TAPE.
HOLY...
BUT HE HADN'T SEEN IT HIMSELF.
CAP, WHAT THE HELL IS THIS?
AN INSIDE JOB. LIKE YOU SAID.
COP VS. "COP." BUT IF YOU'RE KEEPING SCORE, ONE SIDE'S DOING BETTER THAN THE OTHER.
WHO WOULD...
KRASH
GET DOWN!

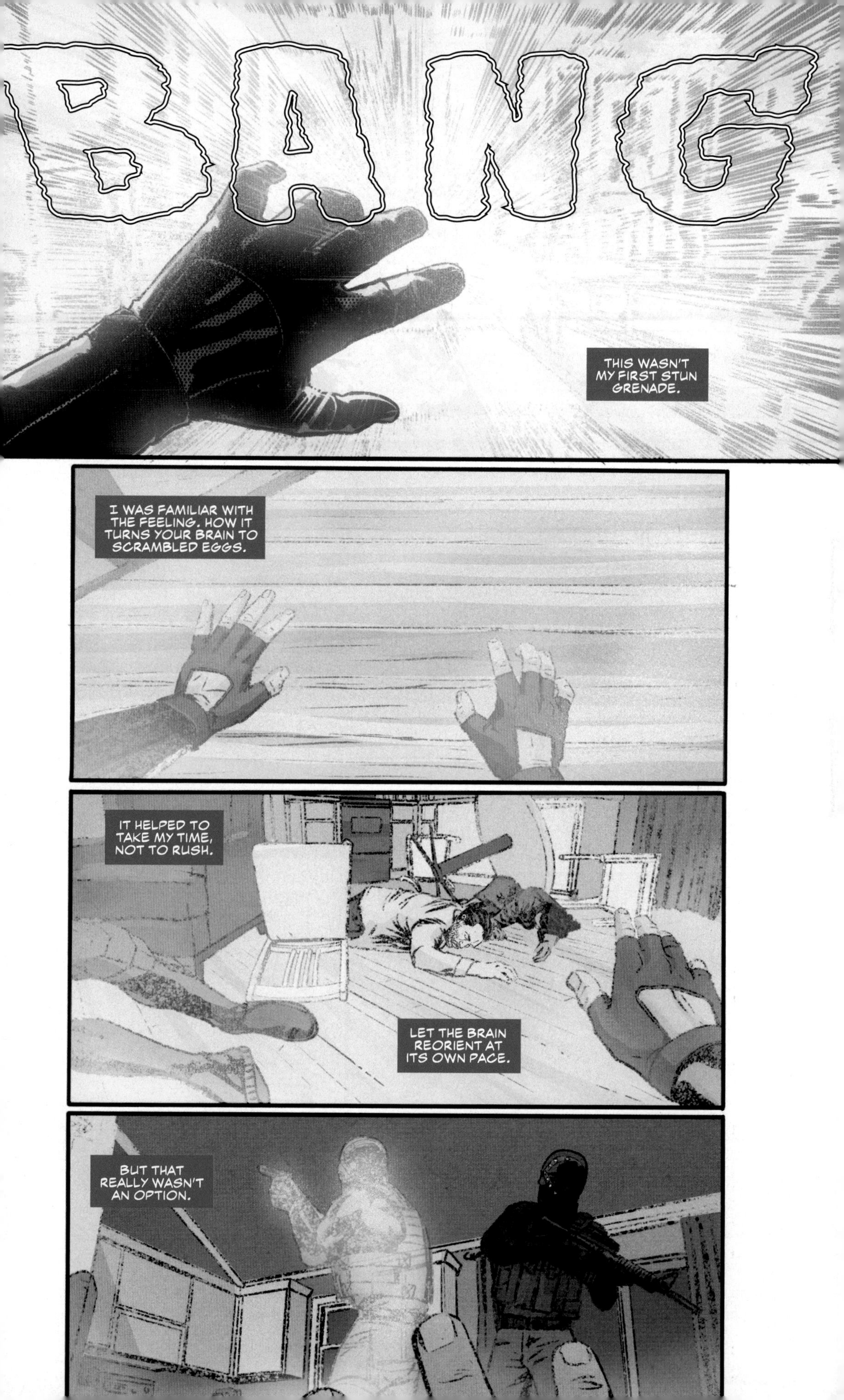
BANG
THIS WASN'T MY FIRST STUN GRENADE.
I WAS FAMILIAR WITH THE FEELING. HOW IT TURNS YOUR BRAIN TO SCRAMBLED EGGS.
IT HELPED TO TAKE MY TIME, NOT TO RUSH.
LET THE BRAIN REORIENT AT ITS OWN PACE.
BUT THAT REALLY WASN'T AN OPTION.

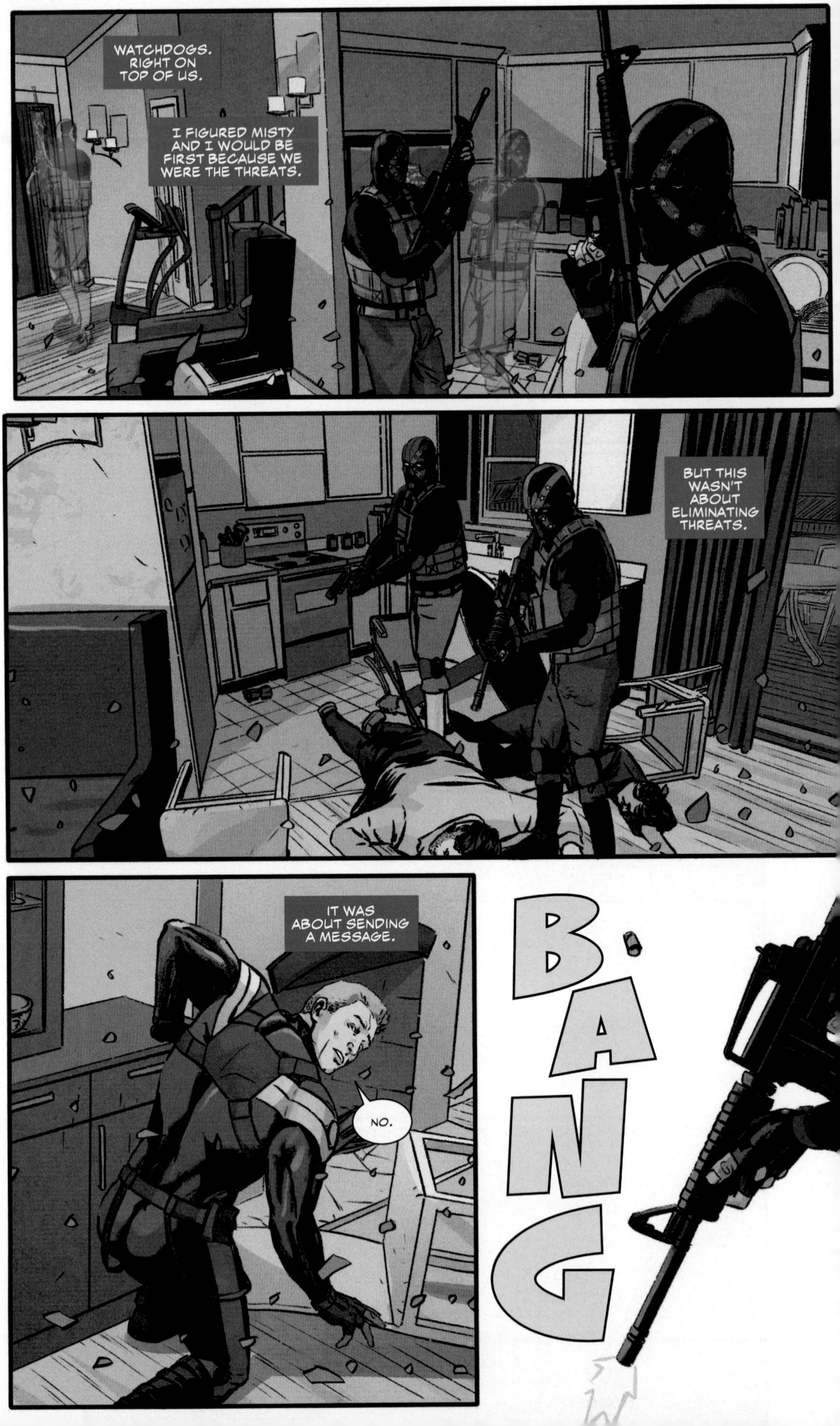
WATCHDOGS. RIGHT ON TOP OF US.
I FIGURED MISTY AND I WOULD BE FIRST BECAUSE WE WERE THE THREATS.
BUT THIS WASN'T ABOUT ELIMINATING THREATS.
IT WAS ABOUT SENDING A MESSAGE.
NO.
BANG

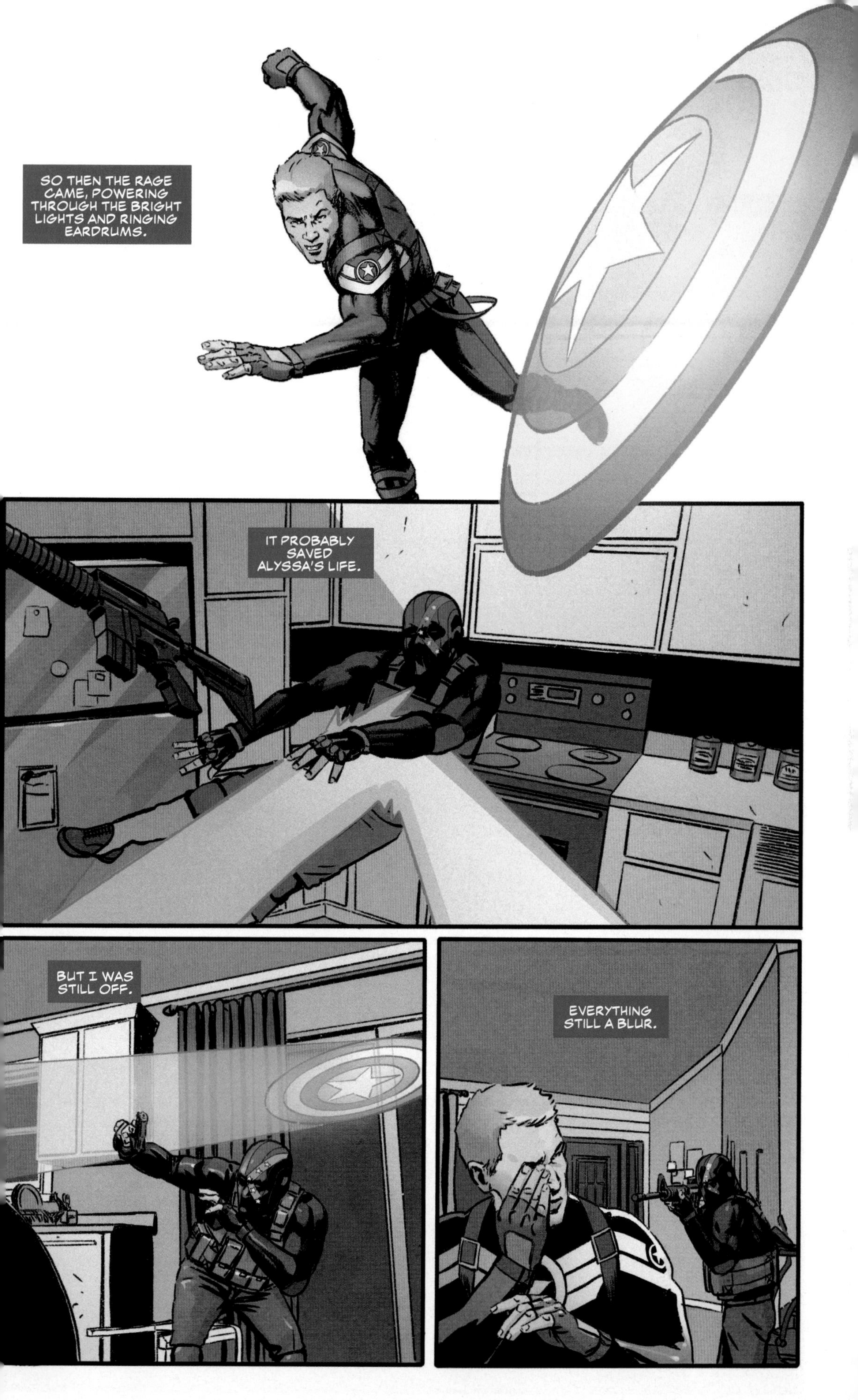

SO THEN THE RAGE CAME, POWERING THROUGH THE BRIGHT LIGHTS AND RINGING EARDRUMS.
IT PROBABLY SAVED ALYSSA'S LIFE.
BUT I WAS STILL OFF.
EVERYTHING STILL A BLUR.

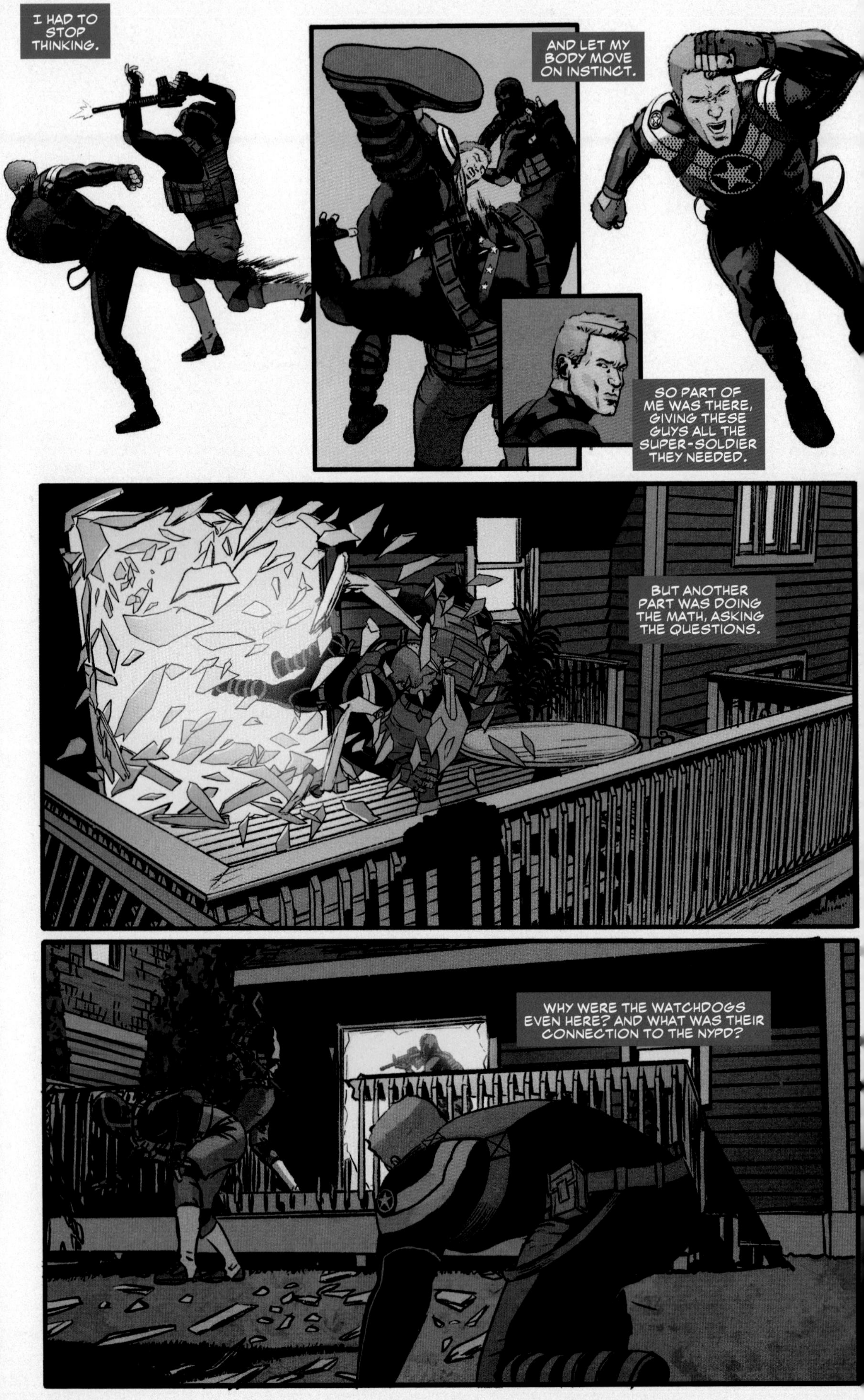
I HAD TO STOP THINKING.
AND LET MY BODY MOVE ON INSTINCT.
SO PART OF ME WAS THERE, GIVING THESE GUYS ALL THE SUPER-SOLDIER THEY NEEDED.
BUT ANOTHER PART WAS DOING THE MATH, ASKING THE QUESTIONS.
WHY WERE THE WATCHDOGS EVEN HERE? AND WHAT WAS THEIR CONNECTION TO THE NYPD?

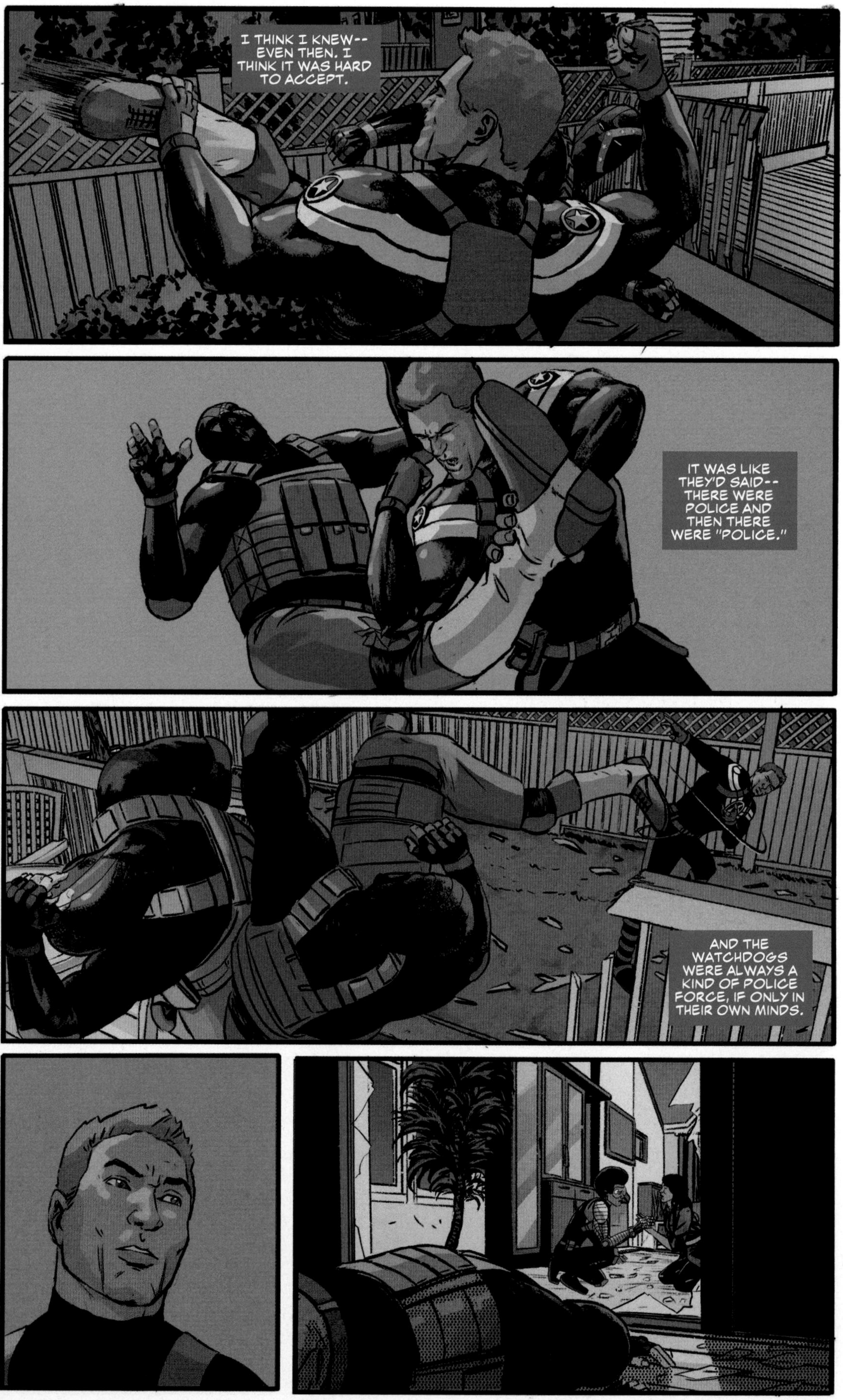
I THINK I KNEW-- EVEN THEN. I THINK IT WAS HARD TO ACCEPT.
IT WAS LIKE THEY'D SAID-- THERE WERE POLICE AND THEN THERE WERE "POLICE."
AND THE WATCHDOGS WERE ALWAYS A KIND OF POLICE FORCE, IF ONLY IN THEIR OWN MINDS.

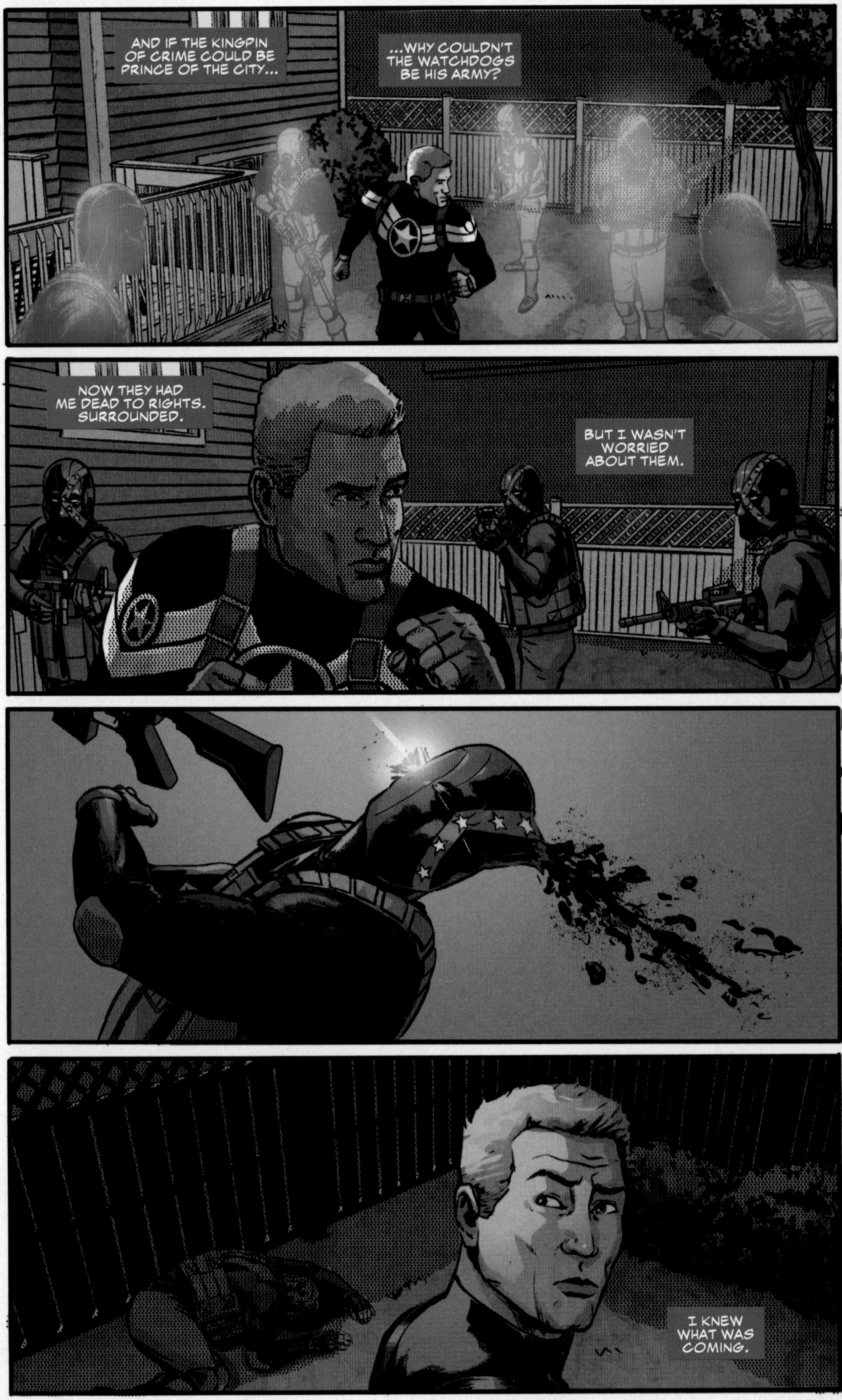
AND IF THE KINGPIN OF CRIME COULD BE PRINCE OF THE CITY...
...WHY COULDN'T THE WATCHDOGS BE HIS ARMY?
NOW THEY HAD ME DEAD TO RIGHTS. SURROUNDED.
BUT I WASN'T WORRIED ABOUT THEM.
I KNEW WHAT WAS COMING.

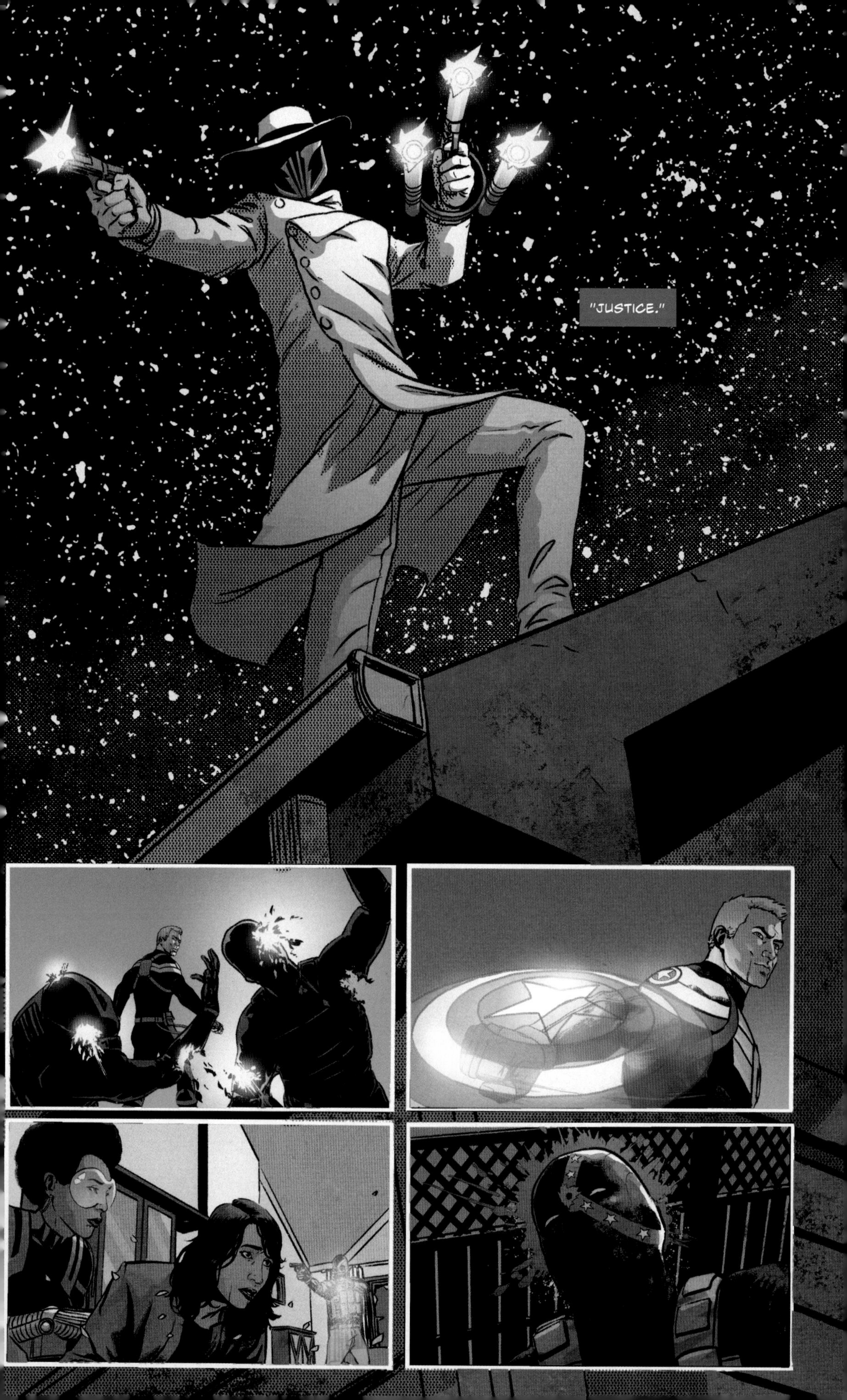
"JUSTICE."

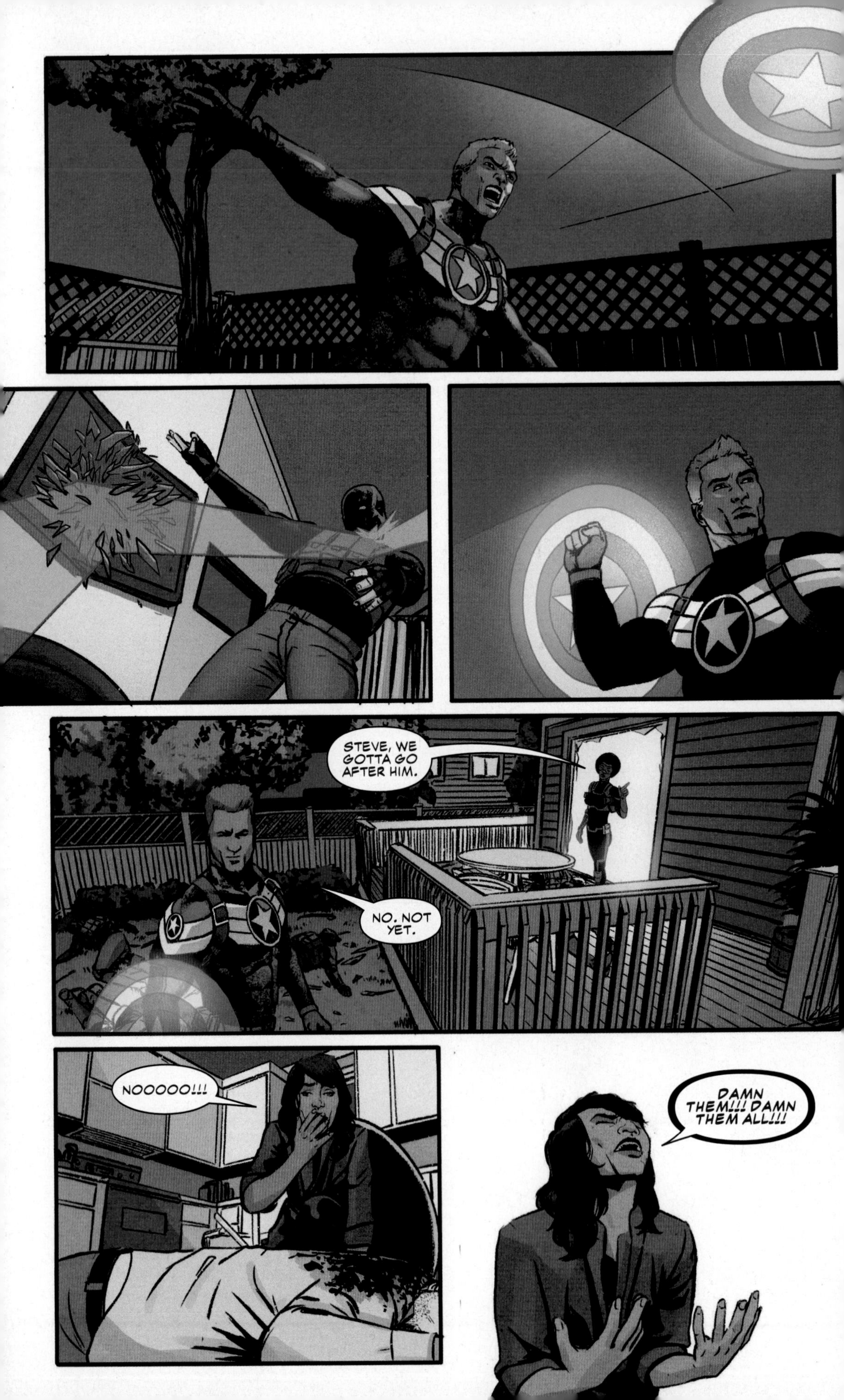
STEVE, WE GOTTA GO AFTER HIM.
NO. NOT YET.
NOOOOO!!!
DAMN THEM!!! DAMN THEM ALL!!!

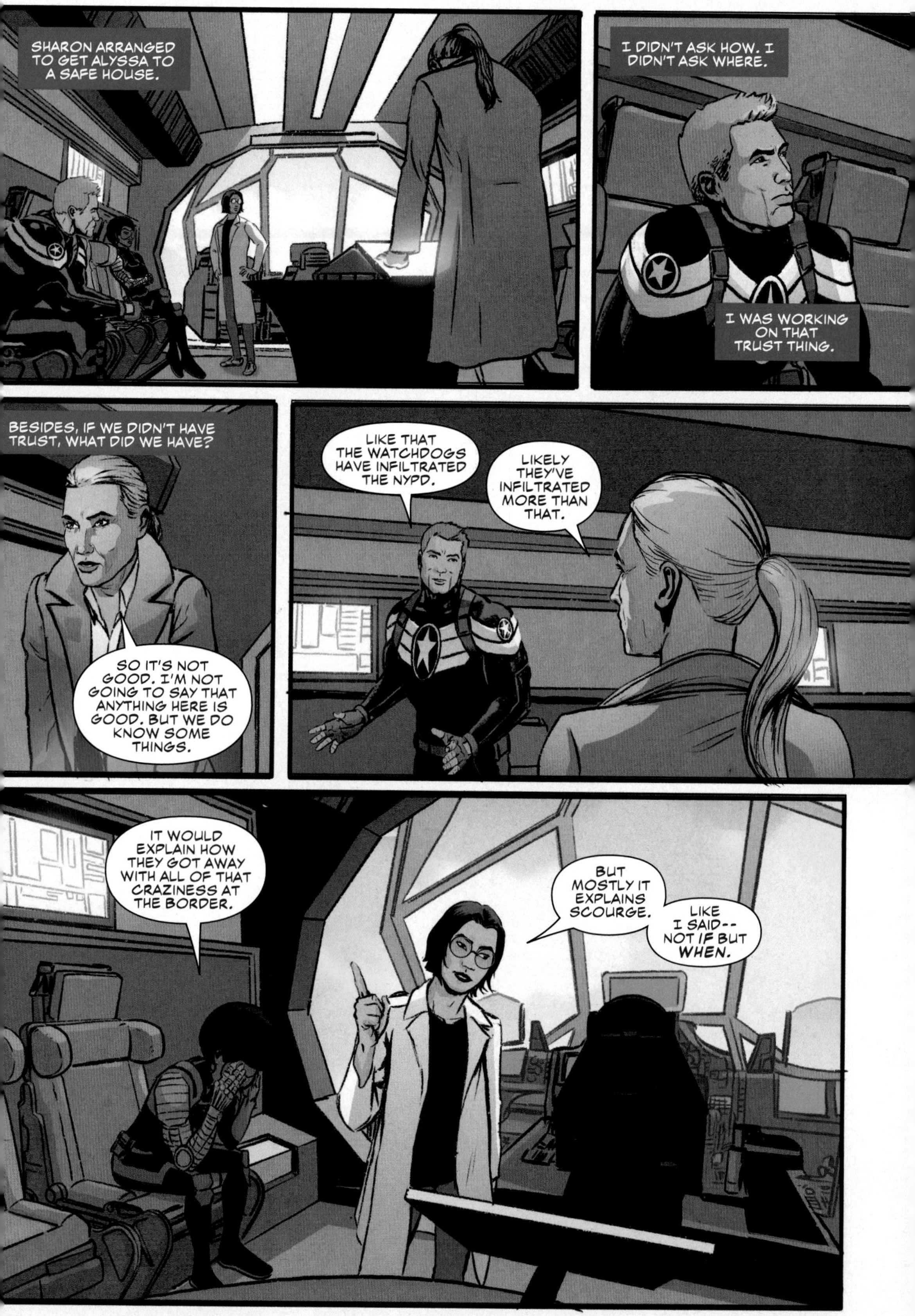

SHARON ARRANGED TO GET ALYSSA TO A SAFE HOUSE.
I DIDN'T ASK HOW. I DIDN'T ASK WHERE.
I WAS WORKING ON THAT TRUST THING.
BESIDES, IF WE DIDN'T HAVE TRUST, WHAT DID WE HAVE?
SO IT'S NOT GOOD. I'M NOT GOING TO SAY THAT ANYTHING HERE IS GOOD. BUT WE DO KNOW SOME THINGS.
LIKE THAT THE WATCHDOGS HAVE INFILTRATED THE NYPD.
LIKELY THEY'VE INFILTRATED MORE THAN THAT.
IT WOULD EXPLAIN HOW THEY GOT AWAY WITH ALL OF THAT CRAZINESS AT THE BORDER.
BUT MOSTLY IT EXPLAINS SCOURGE.
LIKE I SAID-- NOT *IF* BUT **WHEN.**

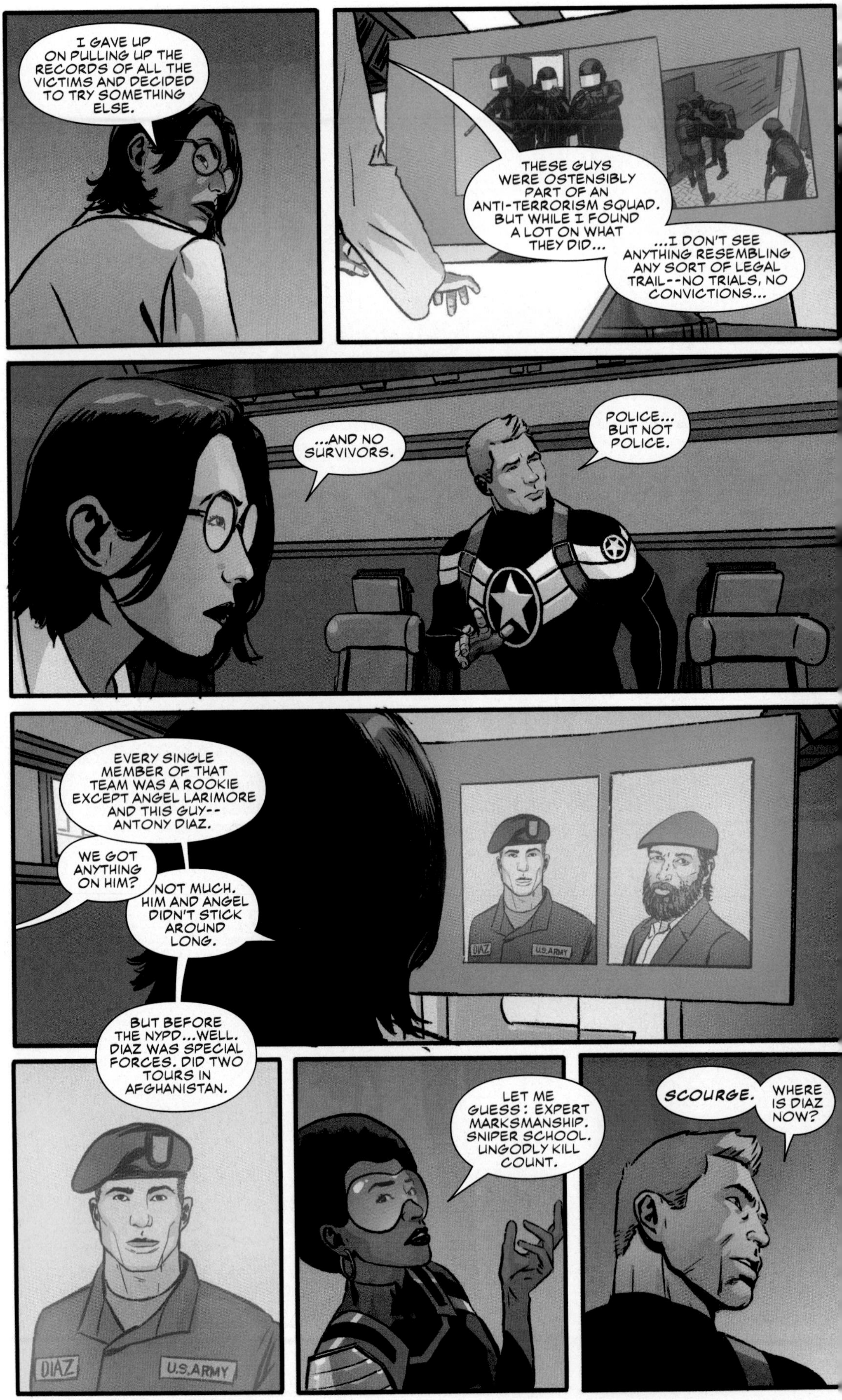
I GAVE UP ON PULLING UP THE RECORDS OF ALL THE VICTIMS AND DECIDED TO TRY SOMETHING ELSE.
THESE GUYS WERE OSTENSIBLY PART OF AN ANTI-TERRORISM SQUAD. BUT WHILE I FOUND A LOT ON WHAT THEY DID...
...I DON'T SEE ANYTHING RESEMBLING ANY SORT OF LEGAL TRAIL--NO TRIALS, NO CONVICTIONS...
...AND NO SURVIVORS.
POLICE... BUT NOT POLICE.
EVERY SINGLE MEMBER OF THAT TEAM WAS A ROOKIE EXCEPT ANGEL LARIMORE AND THIS GUY--ANTONY DIAZ.
WE GOT ANYTHING ON HIM?
NOT MUCH. HIM AND ANGEL DIDN'T STICK AROUND LONG.
DIAZ
U.S.ARMY
BUT BEFORE THE NYPD...WELL. DIAZ WAS SPECIAL FORCES. DID TWO TOURS IN AFGHANISTAN.
DIAZ
U.S.ARMY
LET ME GUESS: EXPERT MARKSMANSHIP. SNIPER SCHOOL. UNGODLY KILL COUNT.
SCOURGE.
WHERE IS DIAZ NOW?

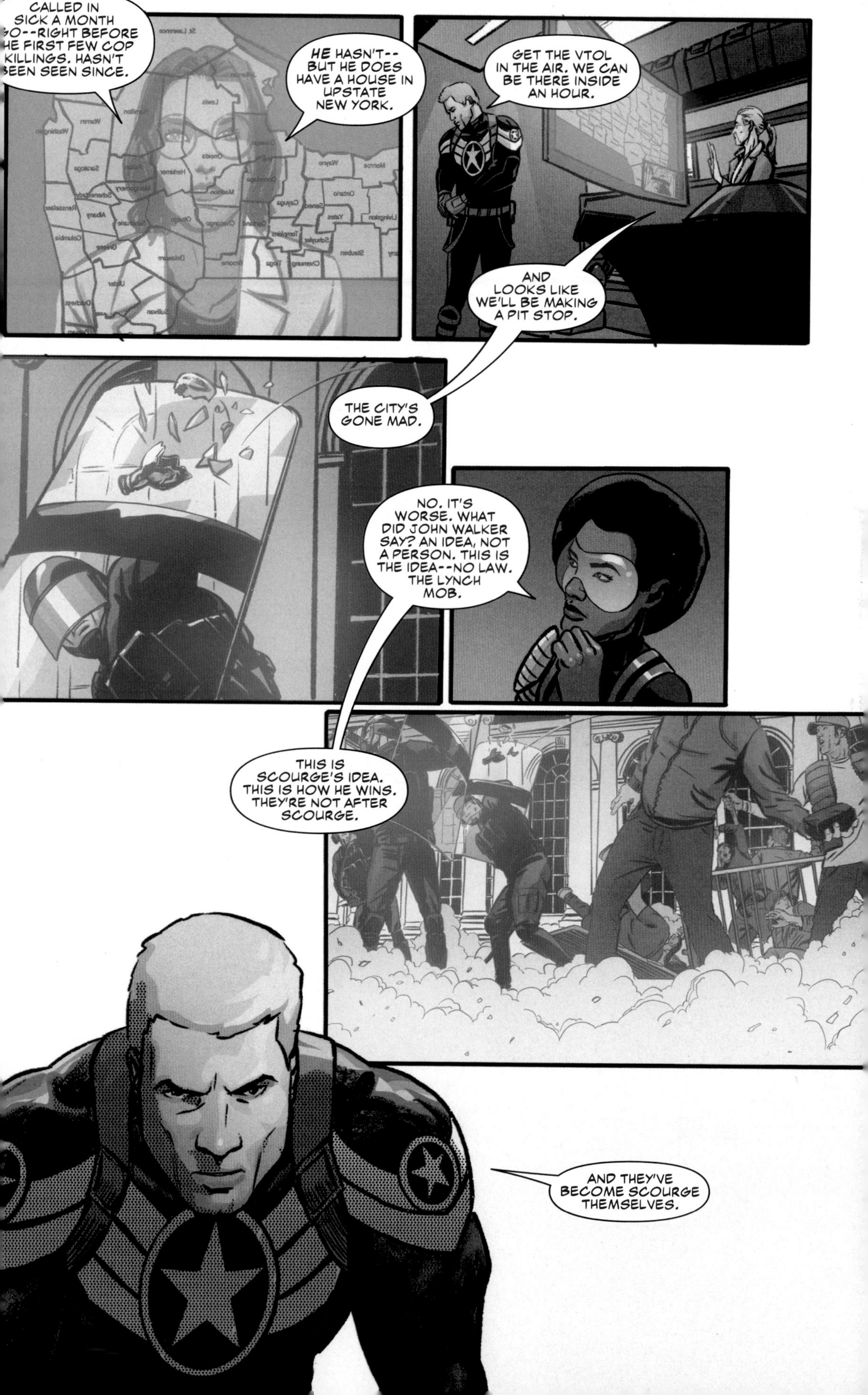
CALLED IN SICK A MONTH AGO--RIGHT BEFORE THE FIRST FEW COP KILLINGS. HASN'T BEEN SEEN SINCE.
HE HASN'T--BUT HE DOES HAVE A HOUSE IN UPSTATE NEW YORK.
GET THE VTOL IN THE AIR. WE CAN BE THERE INSIDE AN HOUR.
AND LOOKS LIKE WE'LL BE MAKING A PIT STOP.
THE CITY'S GONE MAD.
NO. IT'S WORSE. WHAT DID JOHN WALKER SAY? AN IDEA, NOT A PERSON. THIS IS THE IDEA--NO LAW. THE LYNCH MOB.
THIS IS SCOURGE'S IDEA. THIS IS HOW HE WINS. THEY'RE NOT AFTER SCOURGE.
AND THEY'VE BECOME SCOURGE THEMSELVES.

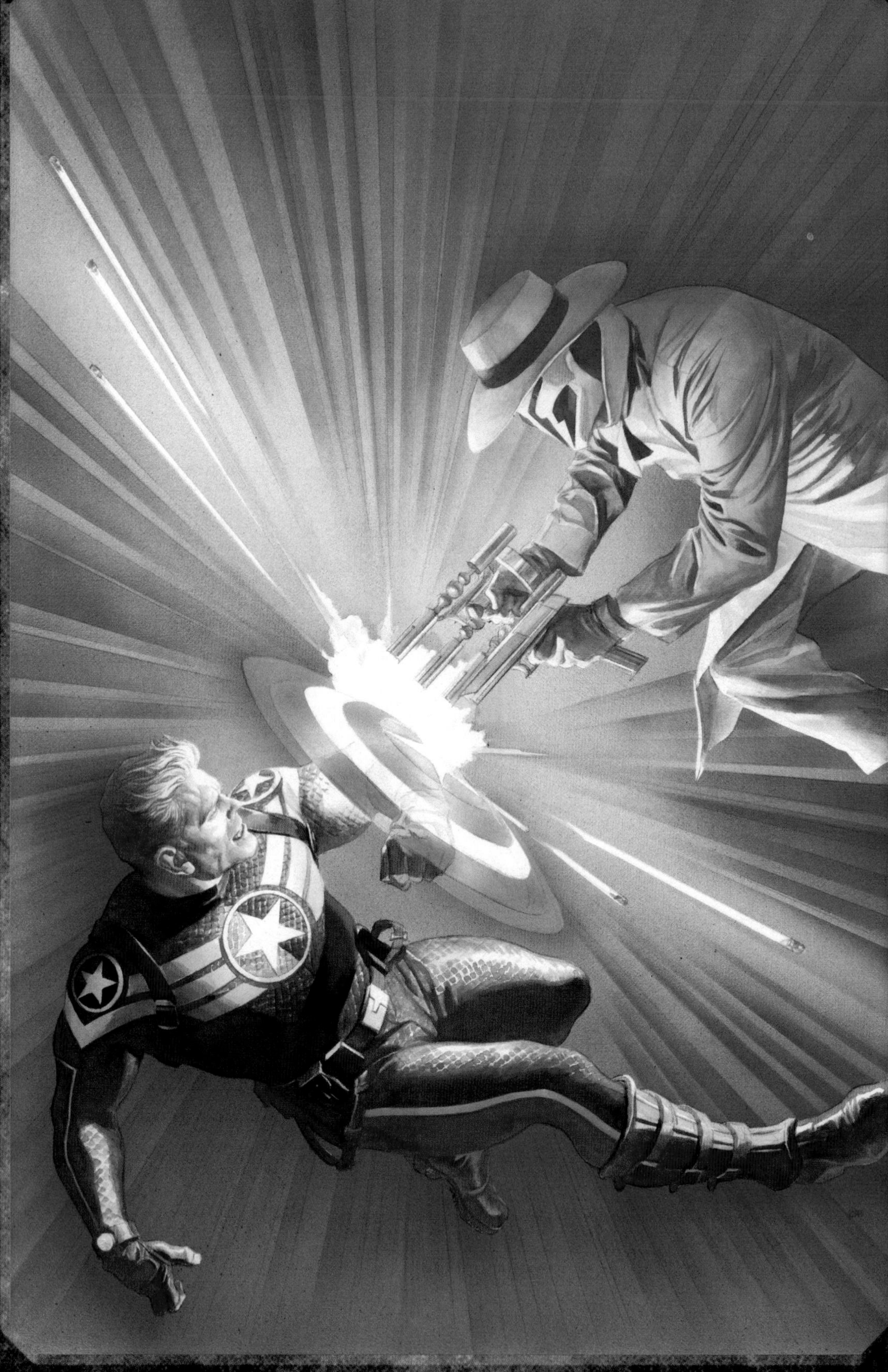

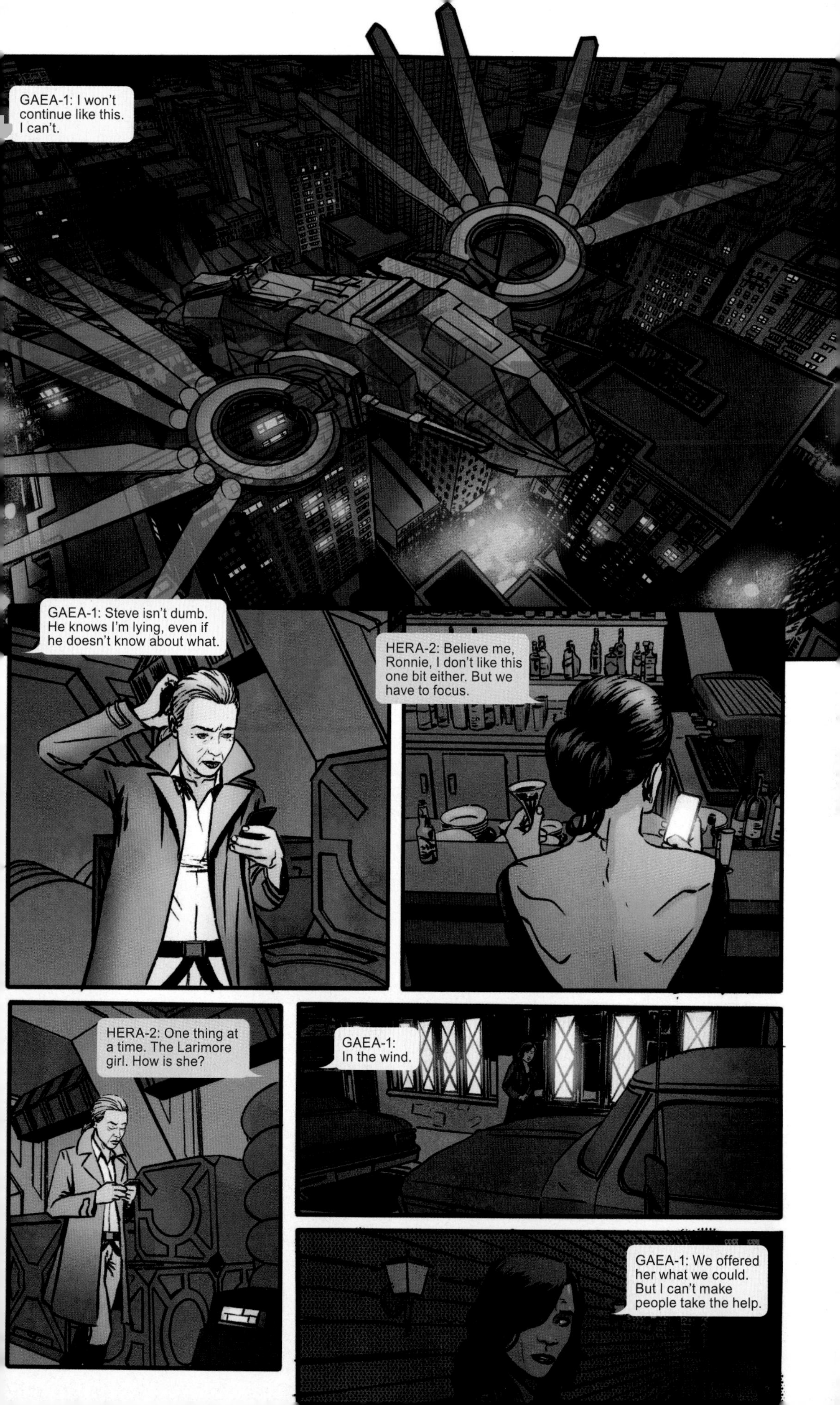
GAEA-1: I won't continue like this. I can't.
GAEA-1: Steve isn't dumb. He knows I'm lying, even if he doesn't know about what.
HERA-2: Believe me, Ronnie, I don't like this one bit either. But we have to focus.
HERA-2: One thing at a time. The Larimore girl. How is she?
GAEA-1: In the wind.
GAEA-1: We offered her what we could. But I can't make people take the help.

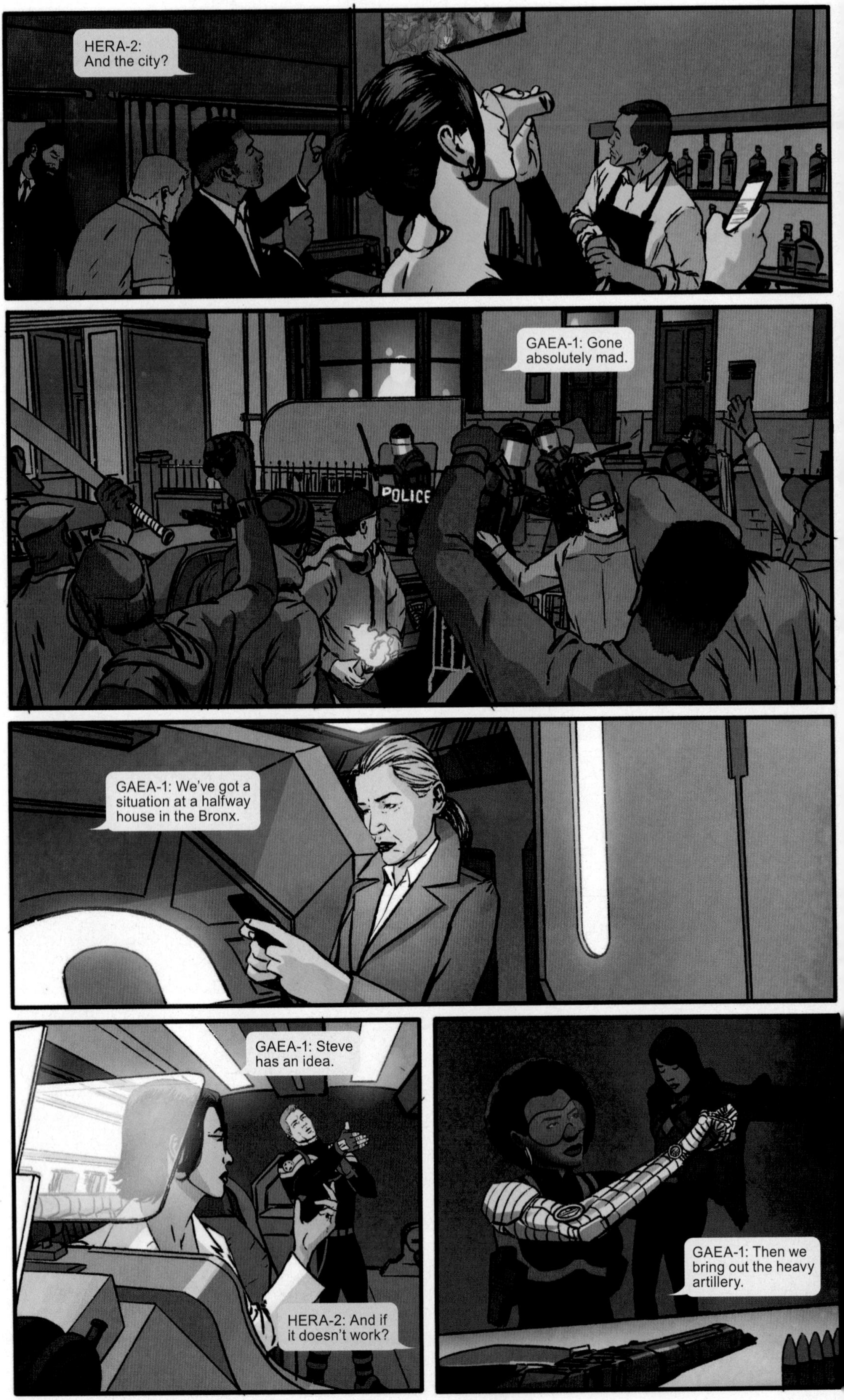

HERA-2: And the city?
GAEA-1: Gone absolutely mad.
POLICE
GAEA-1: We've got a situation at a halfway house in the Bronx.
GAEA-1: Steve has an idea.
HERA-2: And if it doesn't work?
GAEA-1: Then we bring out the heavy artillery.

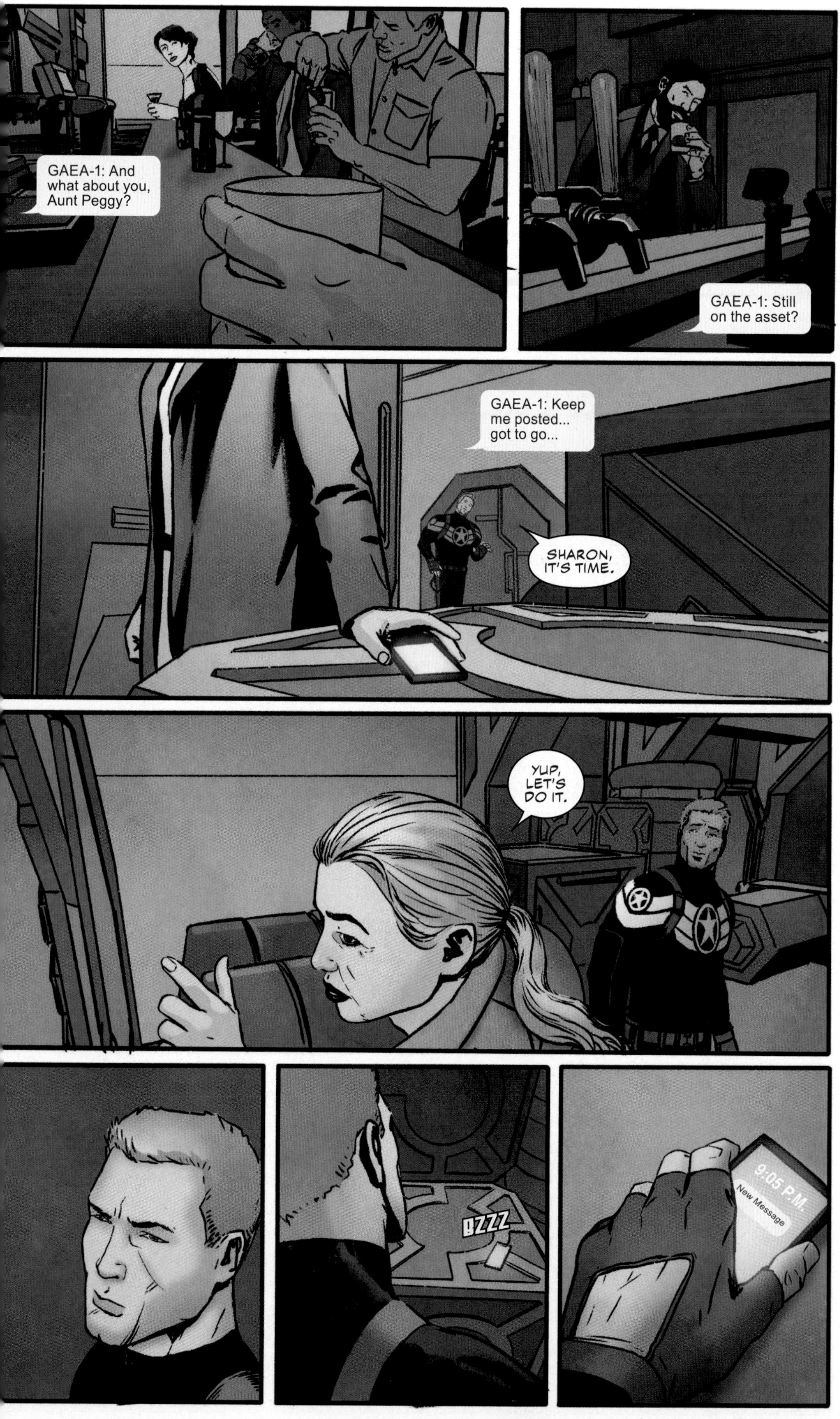
GAEA-1: And what about you, Aunt Peggy?
GAEA-1: Still on the asset?
GAEA-1: Keep me posted... got to go...
SHARON, IT'S TIME.
YUP, LET'S DO IT.
BZZZ
9:05 P.M.
New Message

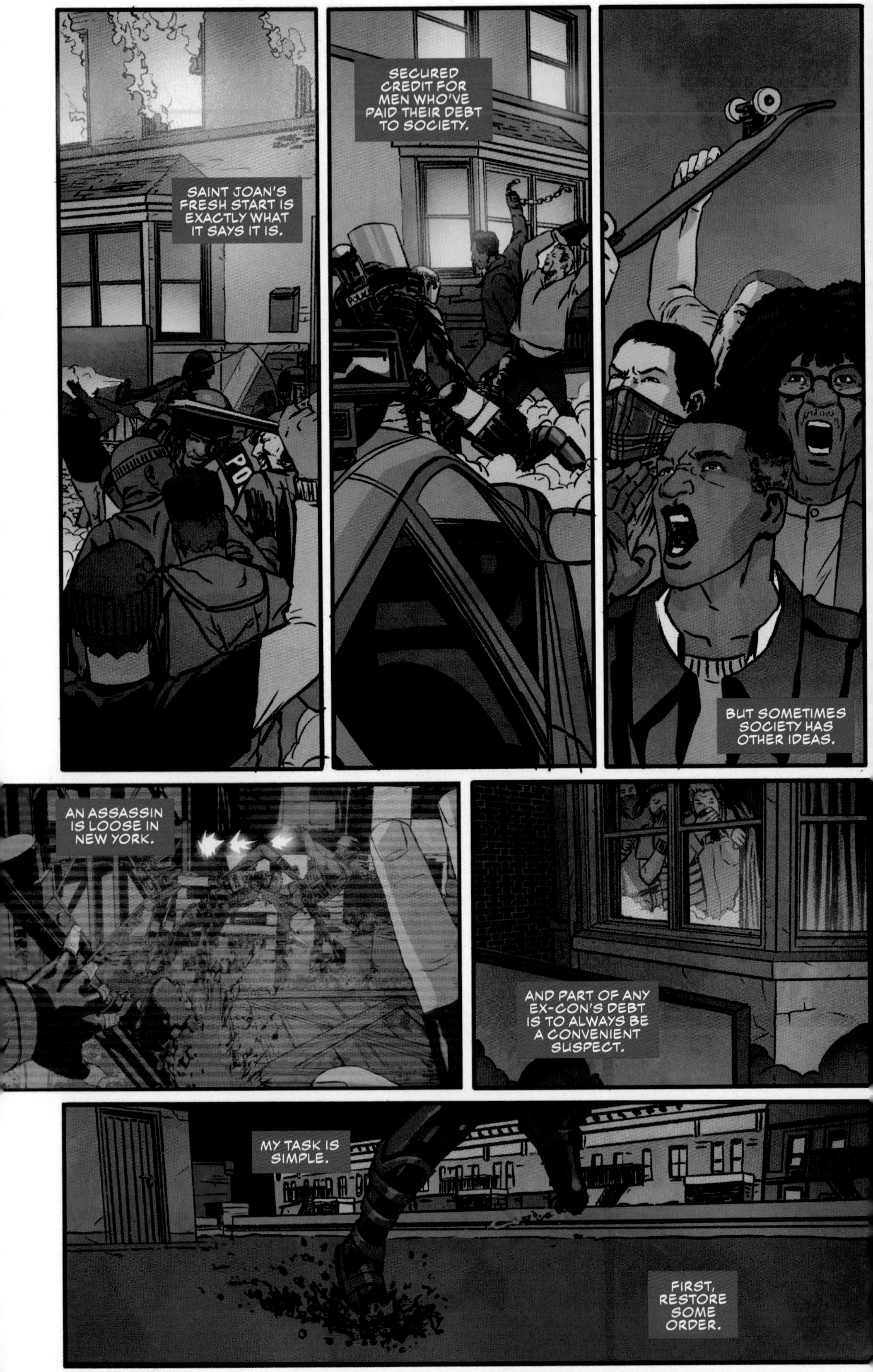
SAINT JOAN'S FRESH START IS EXACTLY WHAT IT SAYS IT IS.
SECURED CREDIT FOR MEN WHO'VE PAID THEIR DEBT TO SOCIETY.
BUT SOMETIMES SOCIETY HAS OTHER IDEAS.
AN ASSASSIN IS LOOSE IN NEW YORK.
AND PART OF ANY EX-CON'S DEBT IS TO ALWAYS BE A CONVENIENT SUSPECT.
MY TASK IS SIMPLE.
FIRST, RESTORE SOME ORDER.

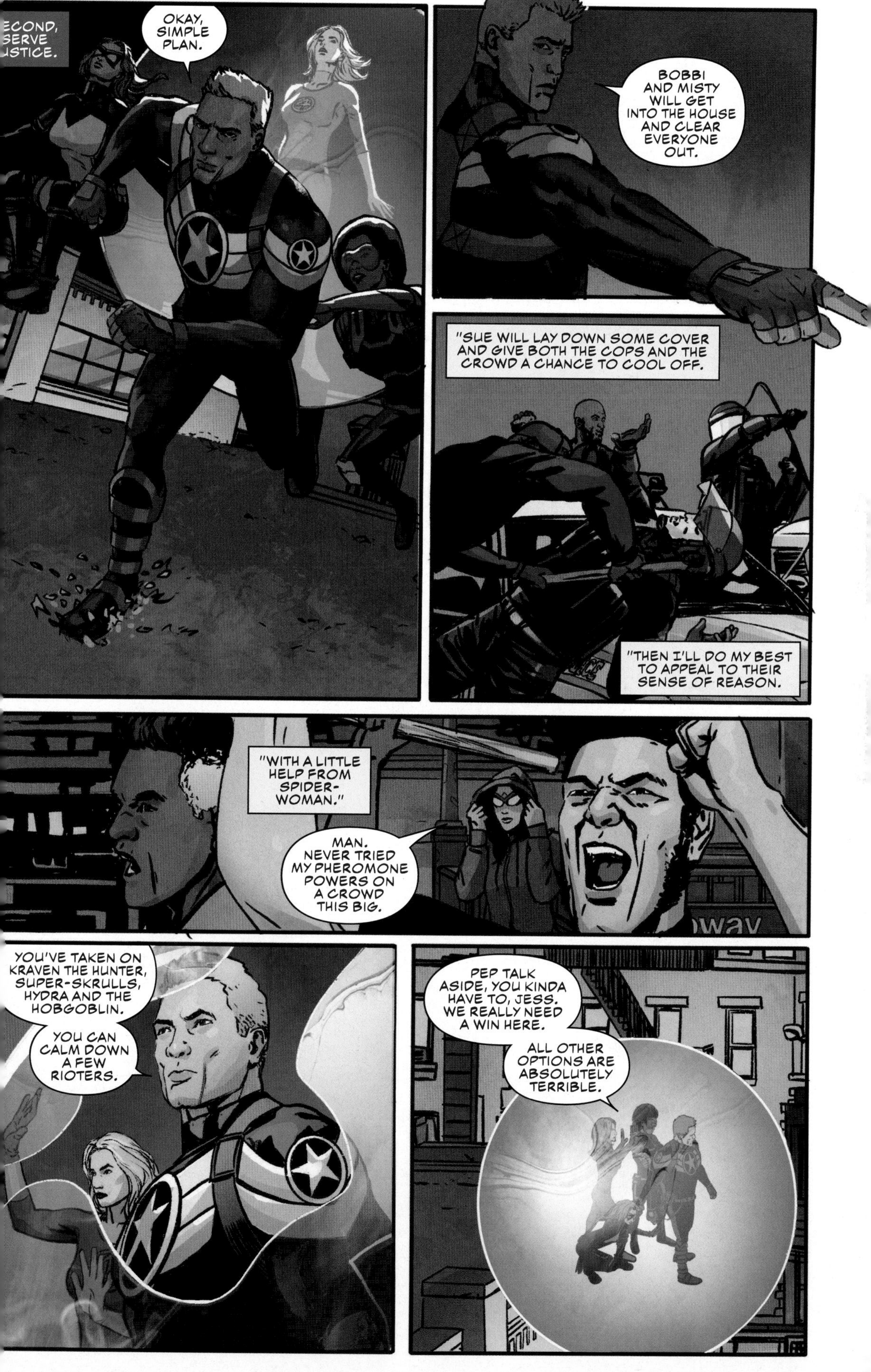
ECOND,
SERVE
USTICE.
OKAY, SIMPLE PLAN.
BOBBI AND MISTY WILL GET INTO THE HOUSE AND CLEAR EVERYONE OUT.
"SUE WILL LAY DOWN SOME COVER AND GIVE BOTH THE COPS AND THE CROWD A CHANCE TO COOL OFF.
"THEN I'LL DO MY BEST TO APPEAL TO THEIR SENSE OF REASON.
"WITH A LITTLE HELP FROM SPIDER-WOMAN."
MAN. NEVER TRIED MY PHEROMONE POWERS ON A CROWD THIS BIG.
YOU'VE TAKEN ON KRAVEN THE HUNTER, SUPER-SKRULLS, HYDRA AND THE HOBGOBLIN.
YOU CAN CALM DOWN A FEW RIOTERS.
PEP TALK ASIDE, YOU KINDA HAVE TO, JESS. WE REALLY NEED A WIN HERE.
ALL OTHER OPTIONS ARE ABSOLUTELY TERRIBLE.

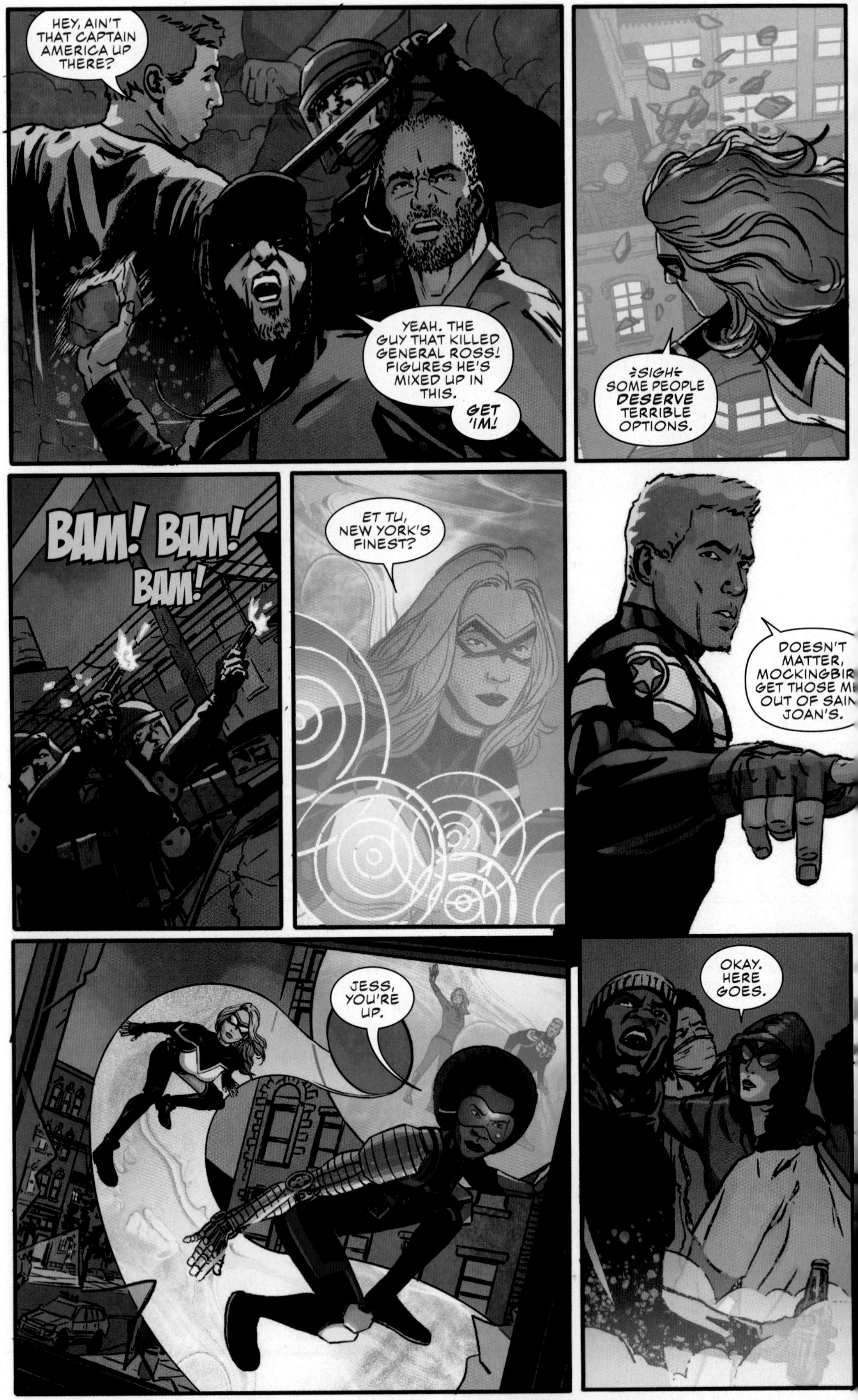
HEY, AIN'T THAT CAPTAIN AMERICA UP THERE?
YEAH. THE GUY THAT KILLED GENERAL ROSS! FIGURES HE'S MIXED UP IN THIS.
GET 'IM!
SIGH SOME PEOPLE DESERVE TERRIBLE OPTIONS.
BAM! BAM! BAM!
ET TU, NEW YORK'S FINEST?
DOESN'T MATTER, MOCKINGBIR GET THOSE ME OUT OF SAIN JOAN'S.
JESS, YOU'RE UP.
OKAY. HERE GOES.

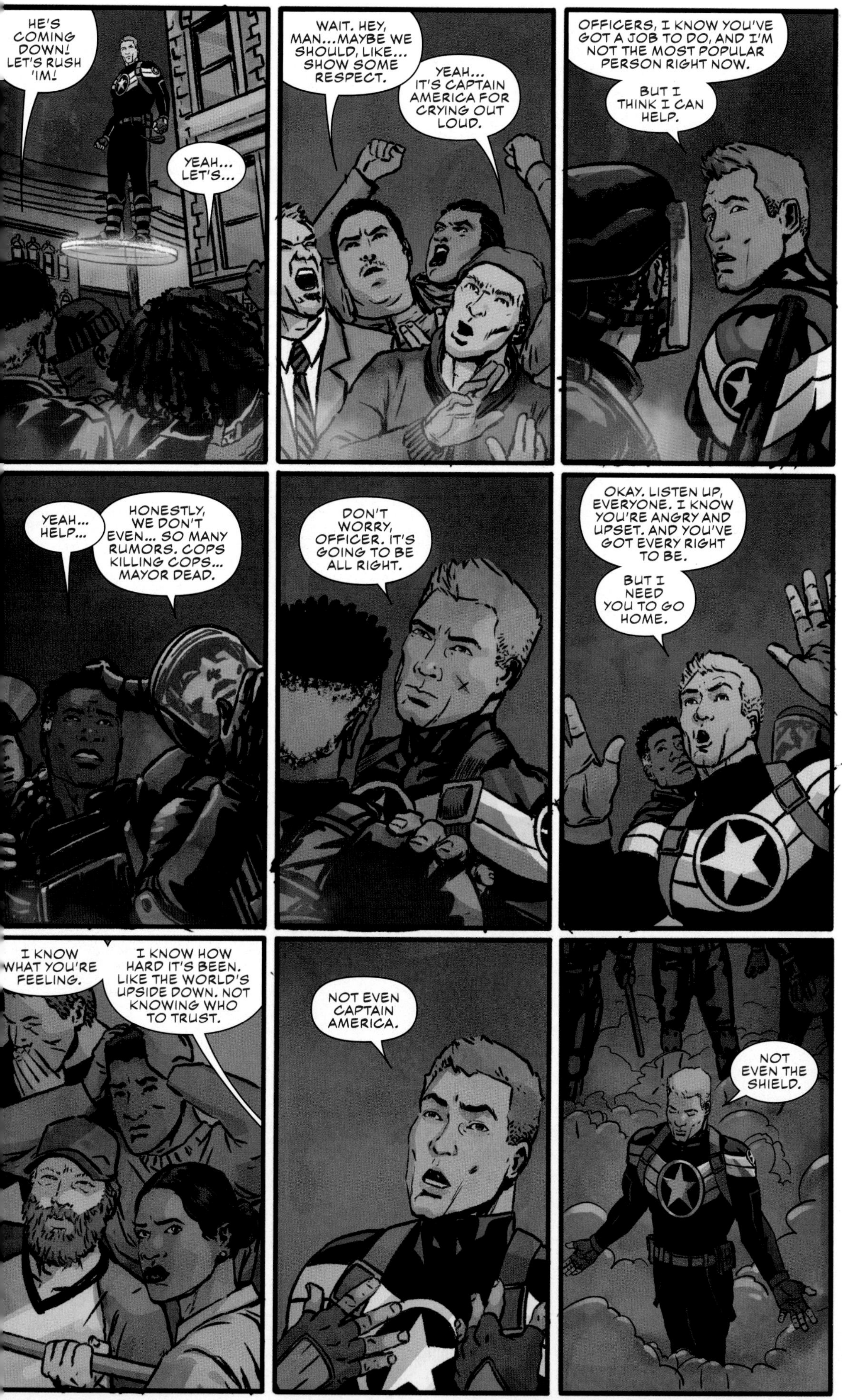
HE'S COMING DOWN! LET'S RUSH 'IM!
YEAH... LET'S...
WAIT. HEY, MAN...MAYBE WE SHOULD, LIKE... SHOW SOME RESPECT.
YEAH... IT'S CAPTAIN AMERICA FOR CRYING OUT LOUD.
OFFICERS, I KNOW YOU'VE GOT A JOB TO DO, AND I'M NOT THE MOST POPULAR PERSON RIGHT NOW.
BUT I THINK I CAN HELP.
YEAH... HELP...
HONESTLY, WE DON'T EVEN... SO MANY RUMORS. COPS KILLING COPS... MAYOR DEAD.
DON'T WORRY, OFFICER. IT'S GOING TO BE ALL RIGHT.
OKAY. LISTEN UP, EVERYONE. I KNOW YOU'RE ANGRY AND UPSET. AND YOU'VE GOT EVERY RIGHT TO BE.
BUT I NEED YOU TO GO HOME.
I KNOW WHAT YOU'RE FEELING.
I KNOW HOW HARD IT'S BEEN. LIKE THE WORLD'S UPSIDE DOWN. NOT KNOWING WHO TO TRUST.
NOT EVEN CAPTAIN AMERICA.
NOT EVEN THE SHIELD.

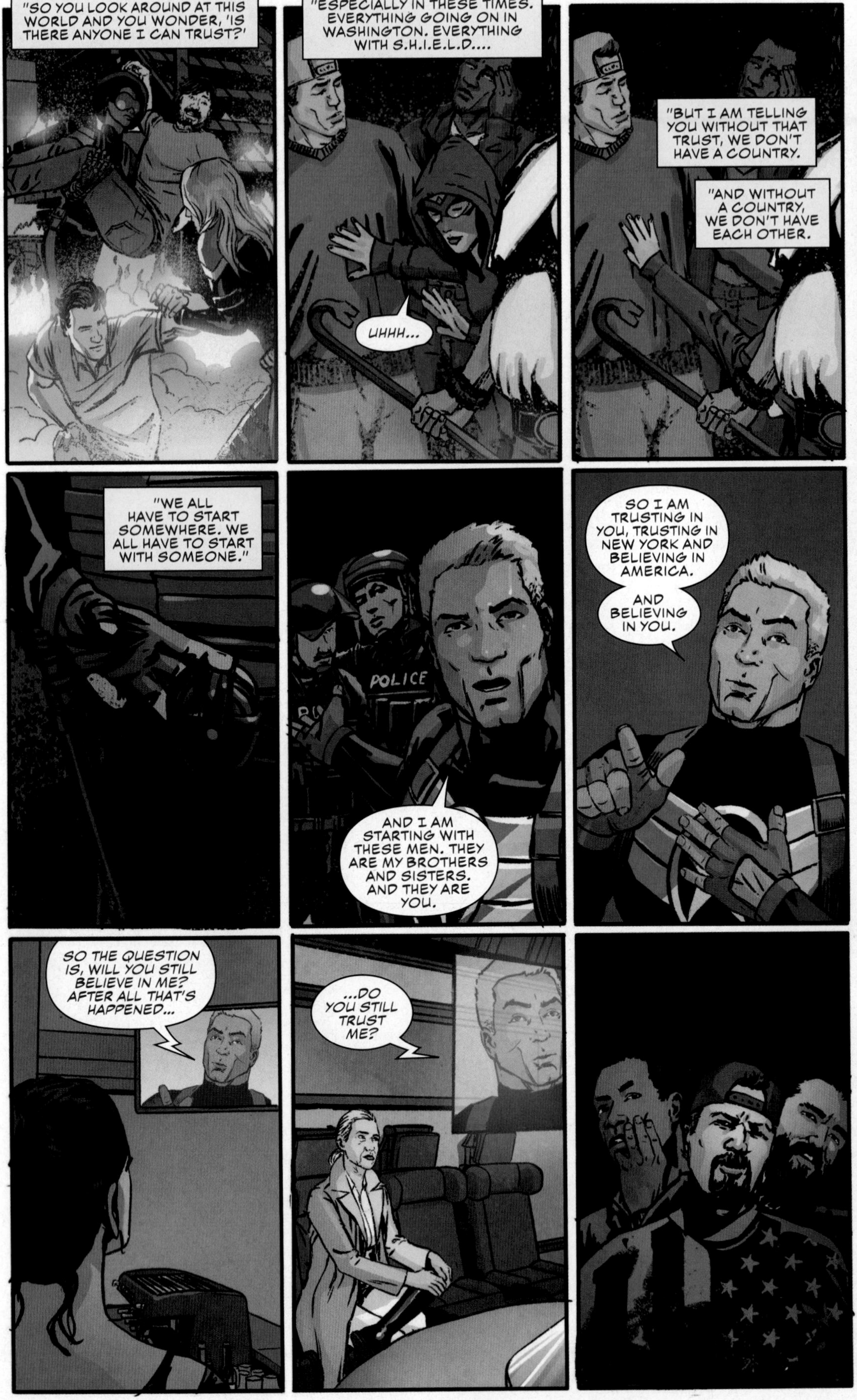
"SO YOU LOOK AROUND AT THIS WORLD AND YOU WONDER, 'IS THERE ANYONE I CAN TRUST?'
"ESPECIALLY IN THESE TIMES. EVERYTHING GOING ON IN WASHINGTON. EVERYTHING WITH S.H.I.E.L.D....
UHHH...
"BUT I AM TELLING YOU WITHOUT THAT TRUST, WE DON'T HAVE A COUNTRY.
"AND WITHOUT A COUNTRY, WE DON'T HAVE EACH OTHER.
"WE ALL HAVE TO START SOMEWHERE. WE ALL HAVE TO START WITH SOMEONE."
POLICE
AND I AM STARTING WITH THESE MEN. THEY ARE MY BROTHERS AND SISTERS. AND THEY ARE YOU.
SO I AM TRUSTING IN YOU, TRUSTING IN NEW YORK AND BELIEVING IN AMERICA.
AND BELIEVING IN YOU.
SO THE QUESTION IS, WILL YOU STILL BELIEVE IN ME? AFTER ALL THAT'S HAPPENED...
...DO YOU STILL TRUST ME?

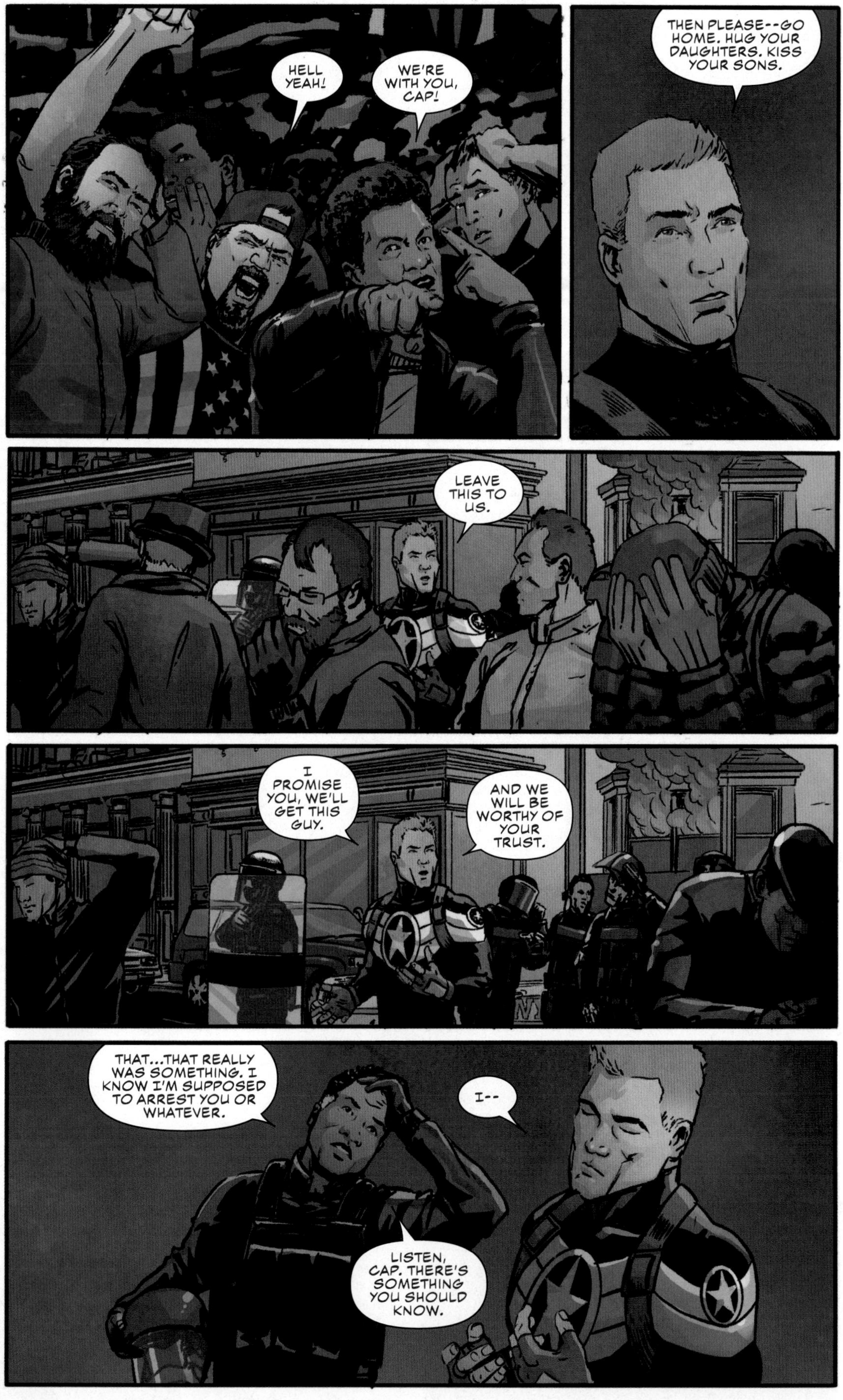
HELL YEAH!
WE'RE WITH YOU, CAP!
THEN PLEASE--GO HOME. HUG YOUR DAUGHTERS. KISS YOUR SONS.
LEAVE THIS TO US.
I PROMISE YOU, WE'LL GET THIS GUY.
AND WE WILL BE WORTHY OF YOUR TRUST.
THAT...THAT REALLY WAS SOMETHING. I KNOW I'M SUPPOSED TO ARREST YOU OR WHATEVER.
I--
LISTEN, CAP. THERE'S SOMETHING YOU SHOULD KNOW.

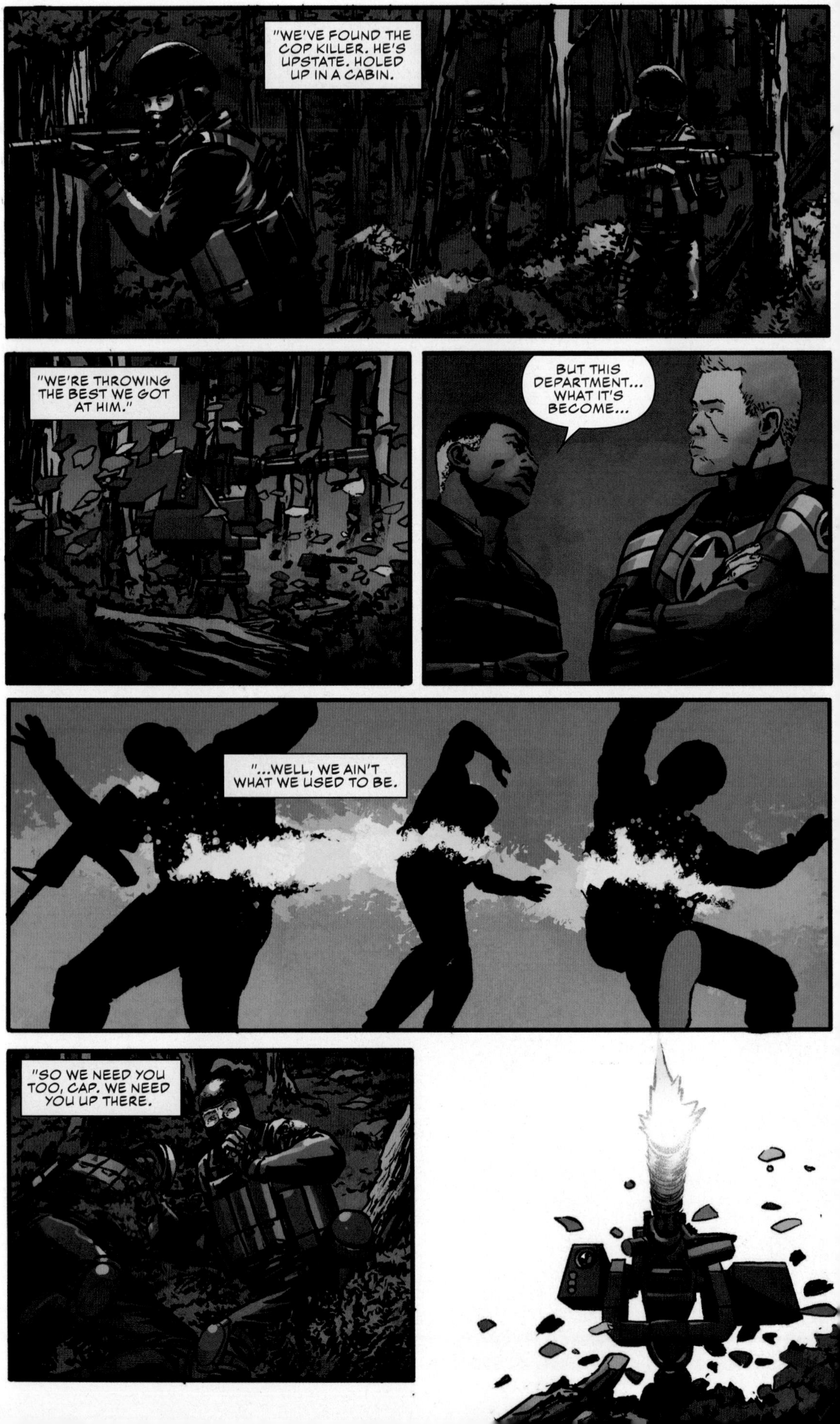
"WE'VE FOUND THE COP KILLER. HE'S UPSTATE. HOLED UP IN A CABIN.
"WE'RE THROWING THE BEST WE GOT AT HIM."
BUT THIS DEPARTMENT... WHAT IT'S BECOME...
"...WELL, WE AIN'T WHAT WE USED TO BE.
"SO WE NEED YOU TOO, CAP. WE NEED YOU UP THERE.

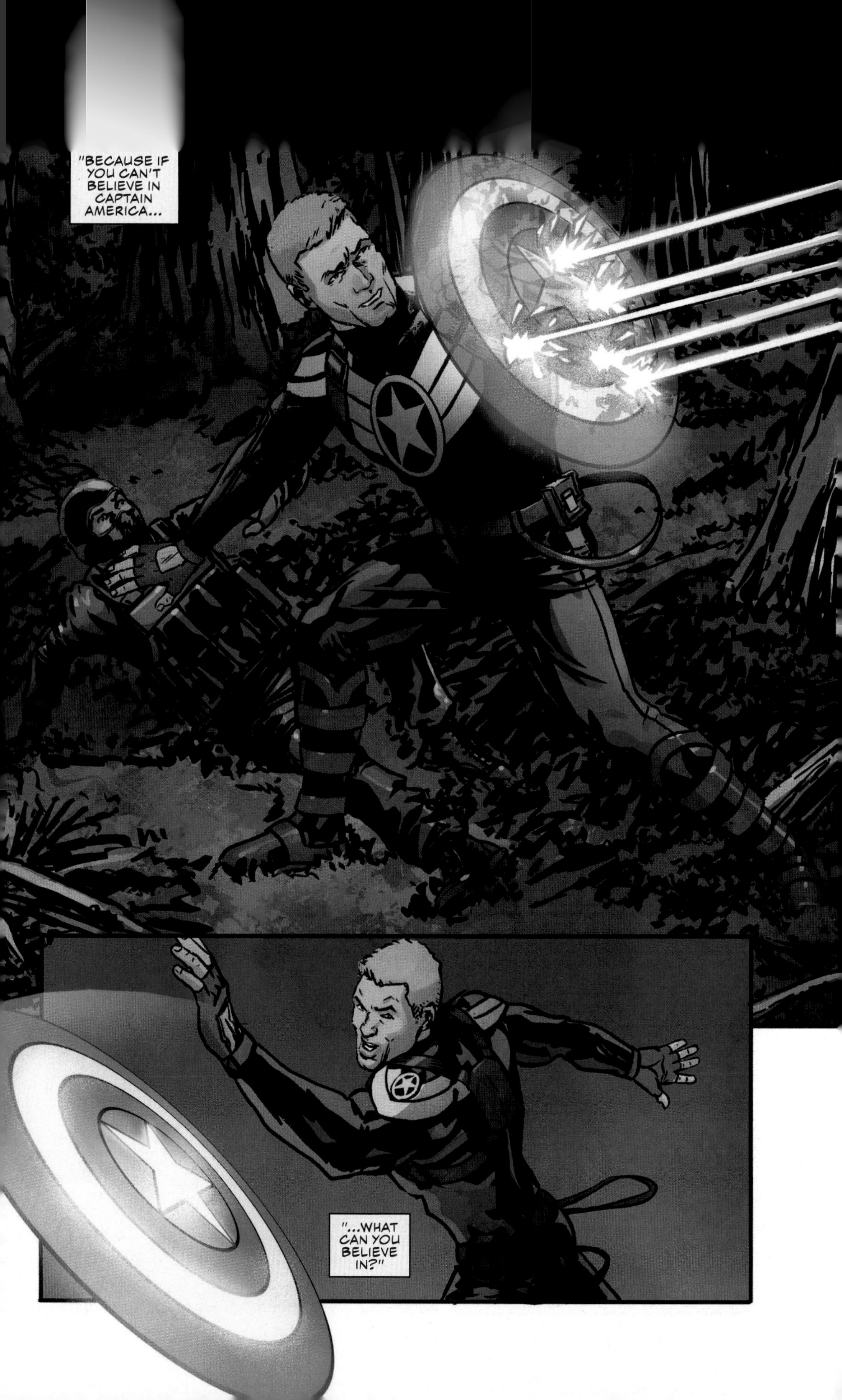
"BECAUSE IF YOU CAN'T BELIEVE IN CAPTAIN AMERICA...
"...WHAT CAN YOU BELIEVE IN?"

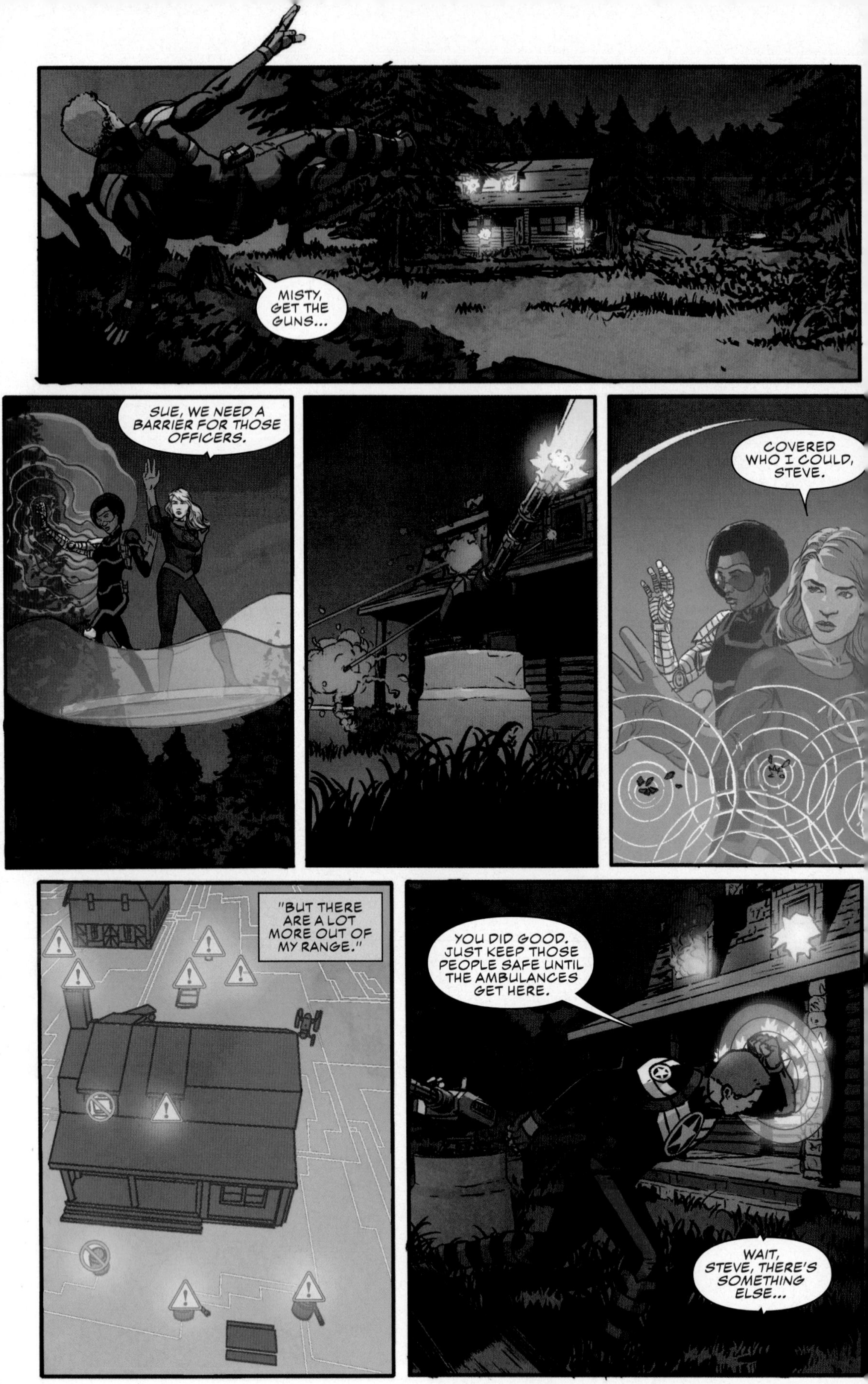

MISTY, GET THE GUNS...
SUE, WE NEED A BARRIER FOR THOSE OFFICERS.
COVERED WHO I COULD, STEVE.
"BUT THERE ARE A LOT MORE OUT OF MY RANGE."
YOU DID GOOD. JUST KEEP THOSE PEOPLE SAFE UNTIL THE AMBULANCES GET HERE.
WAIT, STEVE, THERE'S SOMETHING ELSE...

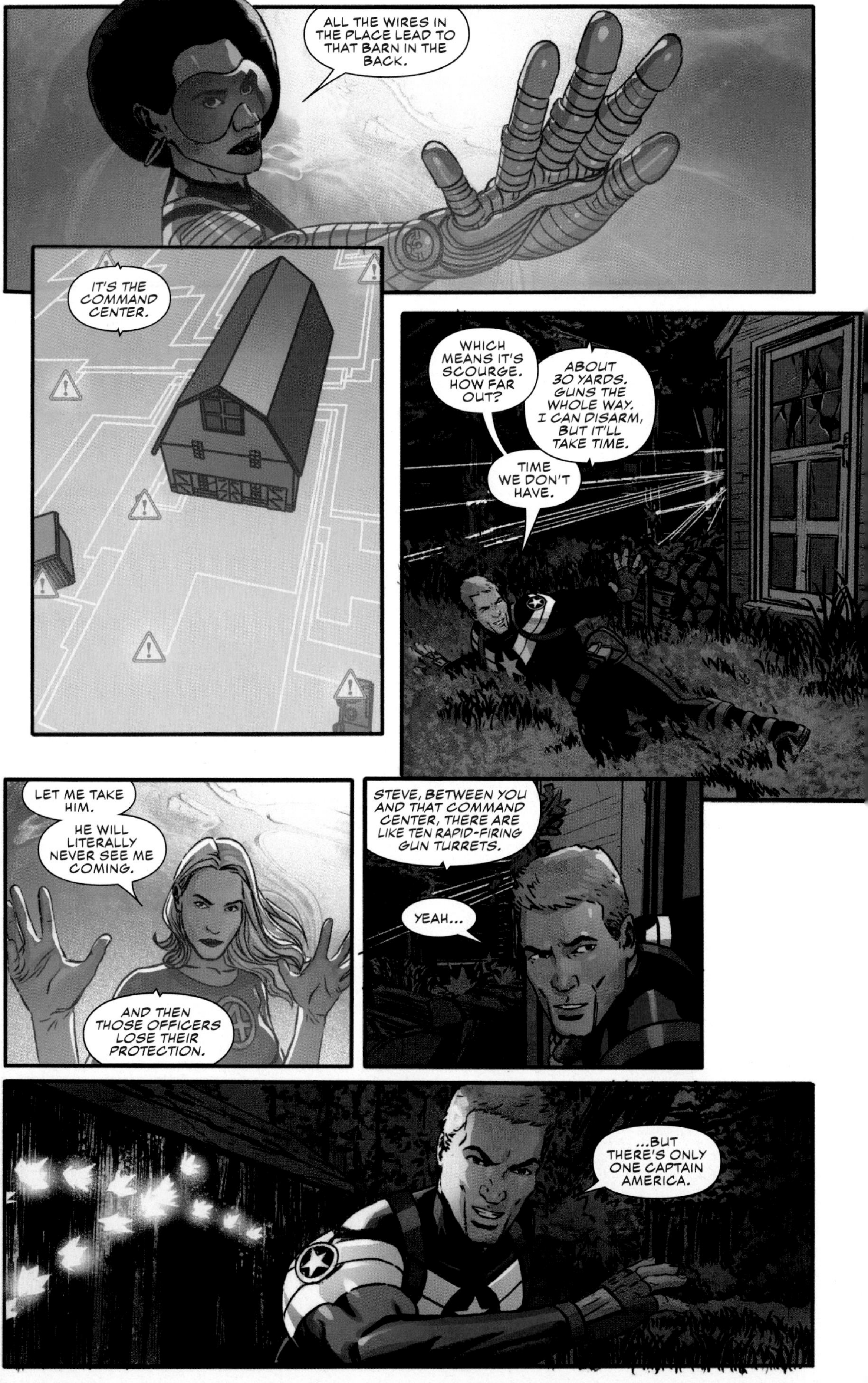
ALL THE WIRES IN THE PLACE LEAD TO THAT BARN IN THE BACK.
IT'S THE COMMAND CENTER.
WHICH MEANS IT'S SCOURGE. HOW FAR OUT?
ABOUT 30 YARDS. GUNS THE WHOLE WAY. I CAN DISARM, BUT IT'LL TAKE TIME.
TIME WE DON'T HAVE.
LET ME TAKE HIM.
HE WILL LITERALLY NEVER SEE ME COMING.
AND THEN THOSE OFFICERS LOSE THEIR PROTECTION.
STEVE, BETWEEN YOU AND THAT COMMAND CENTER, THERE ARE LIKE TEN RAPID-FIRING GUN TURRETS.
YEAH...
...BUT THERE'S ONLY ONE CAPTAIN AMERICA.

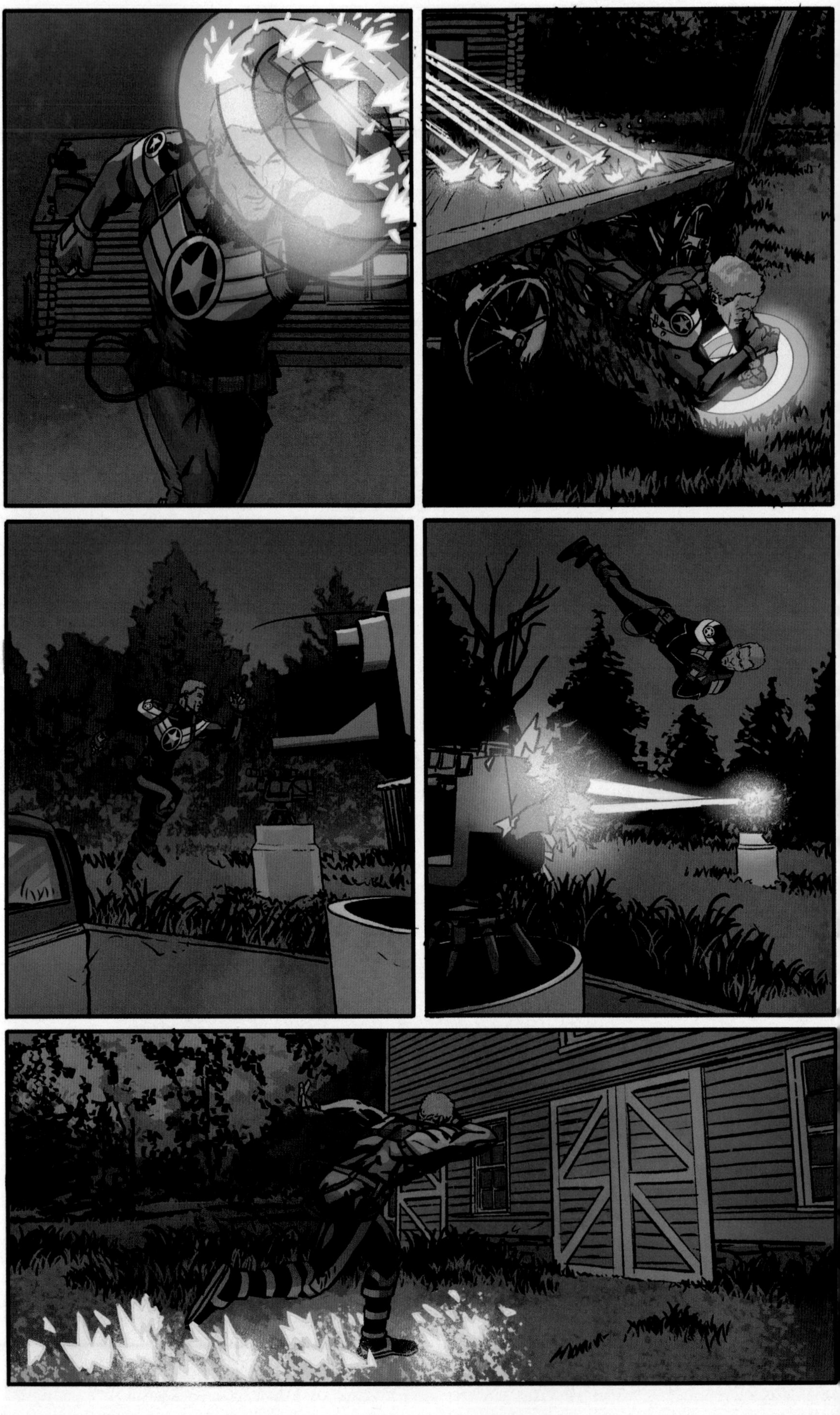

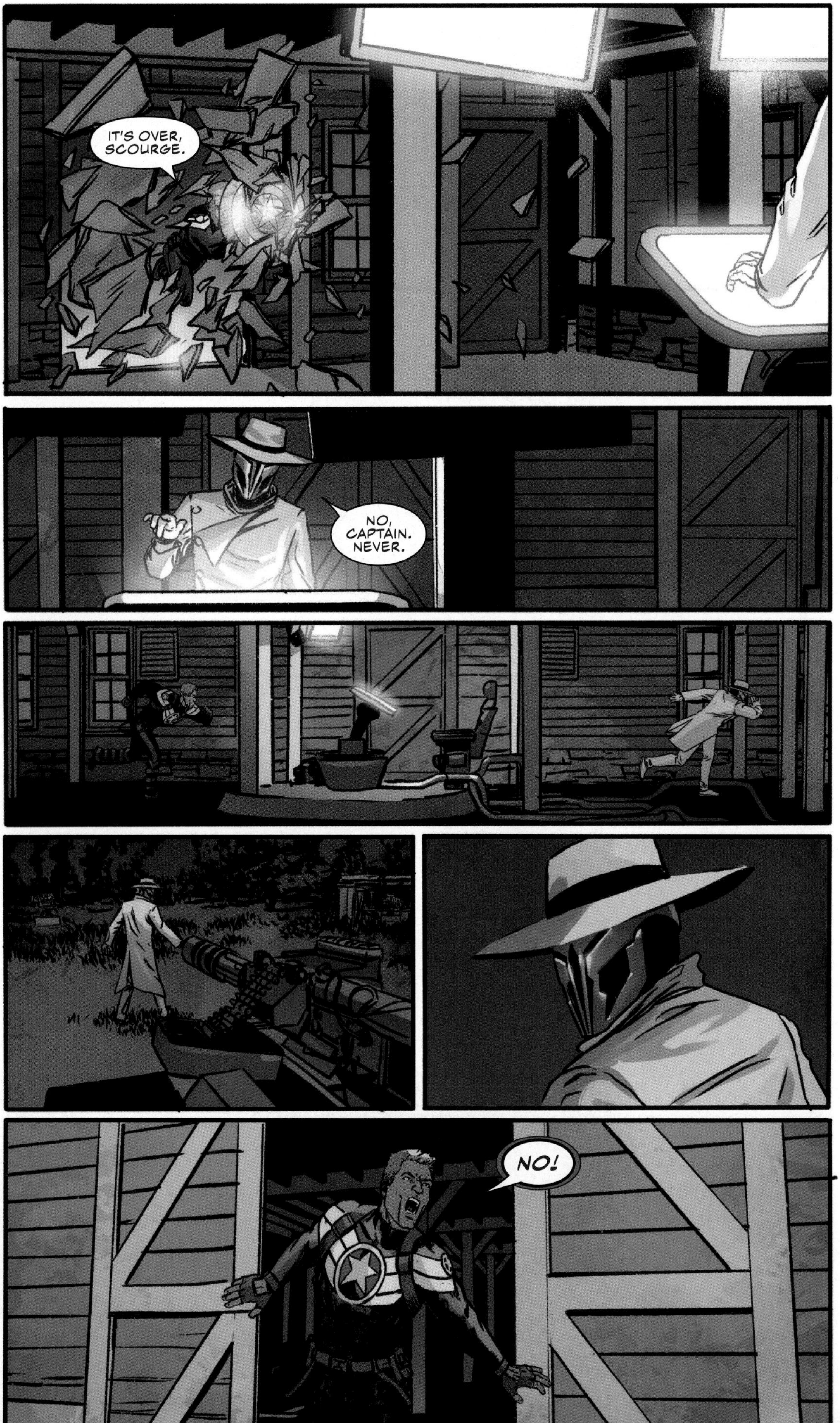
IT'S OVER, SCOURGE.
NO, CAPTAIN. NEVER.
NO!

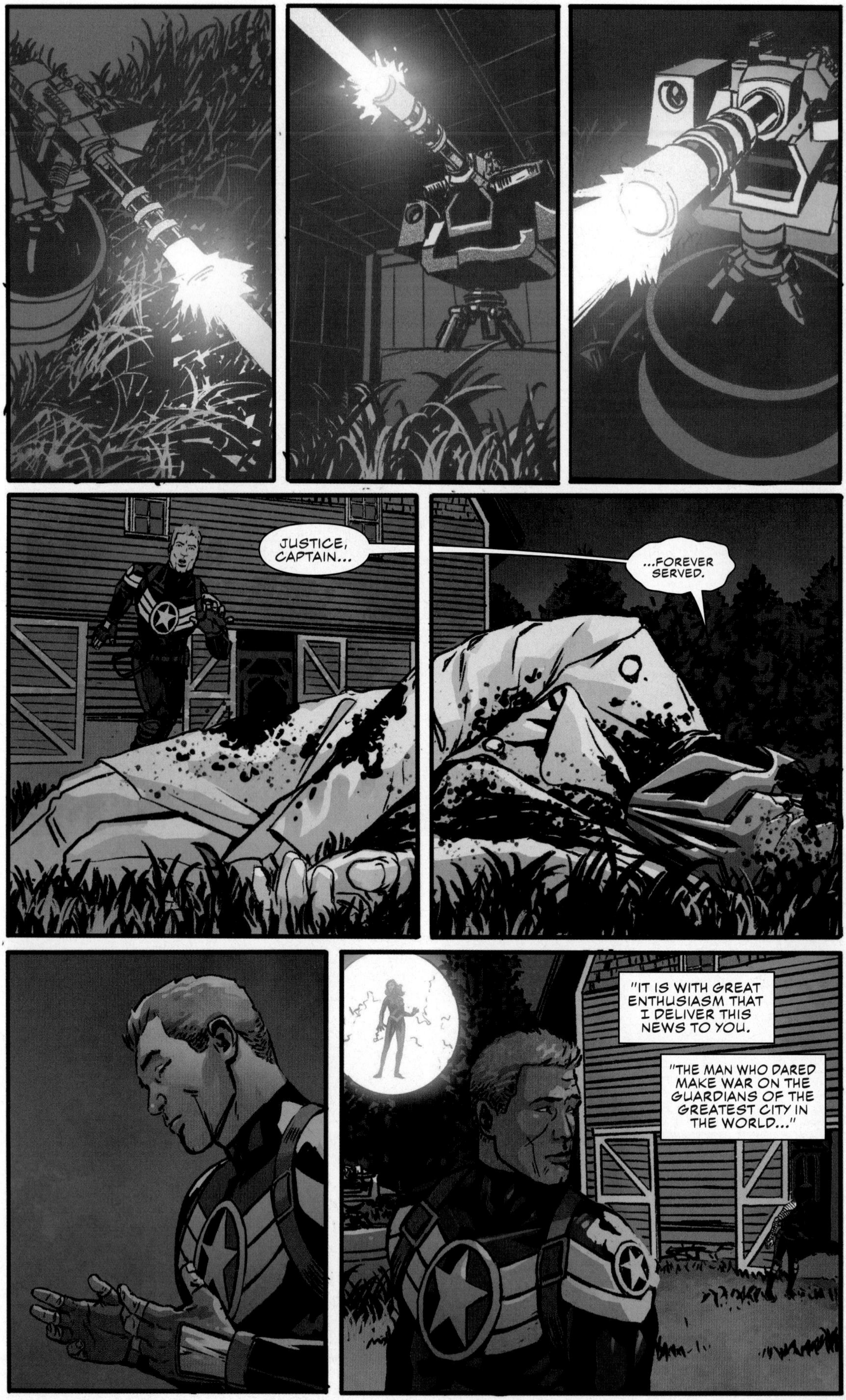
JUSTICE, CAPTAIN...
...FOREVER SERVED.
"IT IS WITH GREAT ENTHUSIASM THAT I DELIVER THIS NEWS TO YOU.
"THE MAN WHO DARED MAKE WAR ON THE GUARDIANS OF THE GREATEST CITY IN THE WORLD..."

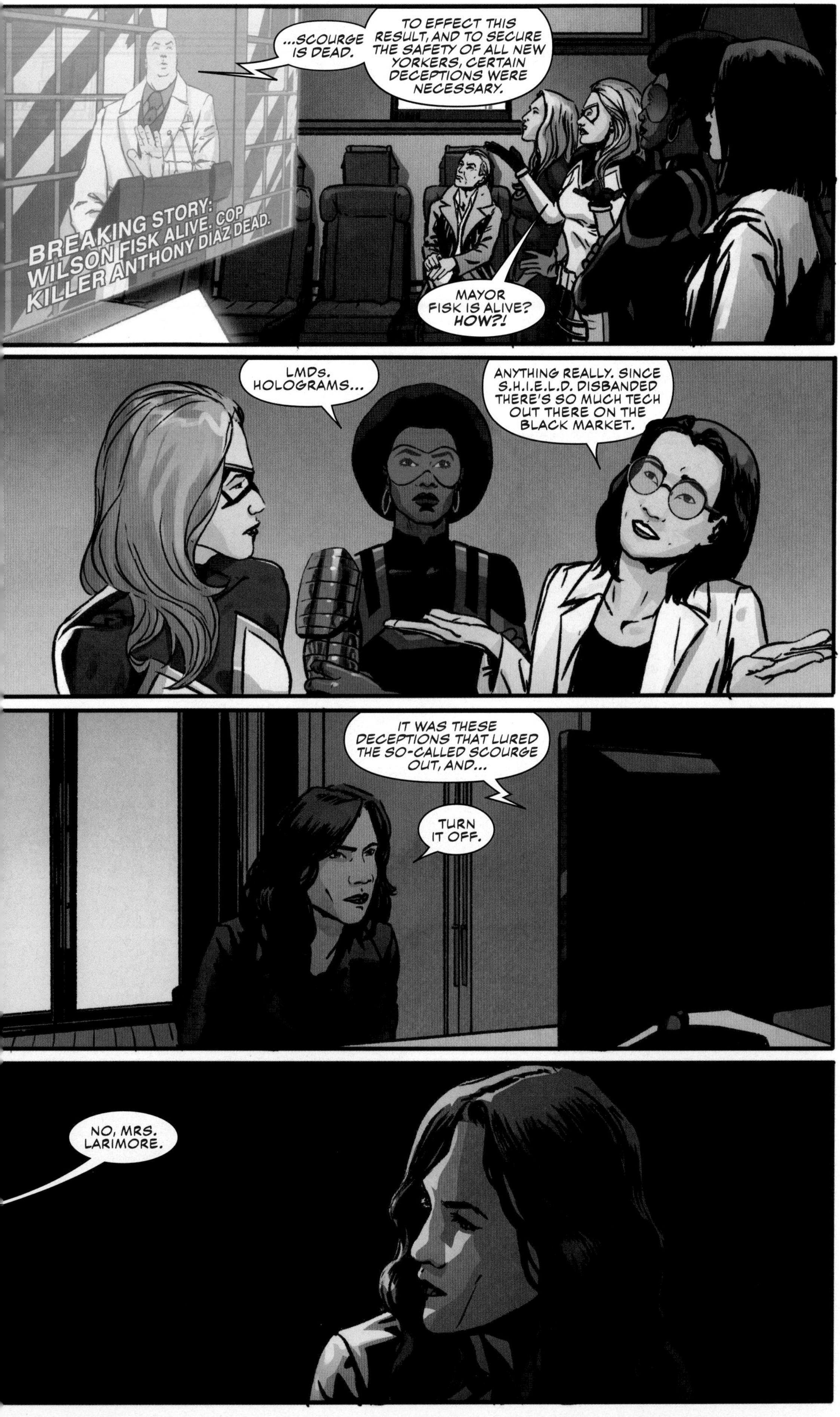
...SCOURGE IS DEAD.
TO EFFECT THIS RESULT, AND TO SECURE THE SAFETY OF ALL NEW YORKERS, CERTAIN DECEPTIONS WERE NECESSARY.
BREAKING STORY: WILSON FISK ALIVE. COP KILLER ANTHONY DIAZ DEAD.
MAYOR FISK IS ALIVE? HOW?!
LMDs. HOLOGRAMS...
ANYTHING REALLY. SINCE S.H.I.E.L.D. DISBANDED THERE'S SO MUCH TECH OUT THERE ON THE BLACK MARKET.
IT WAS THESE DECEPTIONS THAT LURED THE SO-CALLED SCOURGE OUT, AND...
TURN IT OFF.
NO, MRS. LARIMORE.

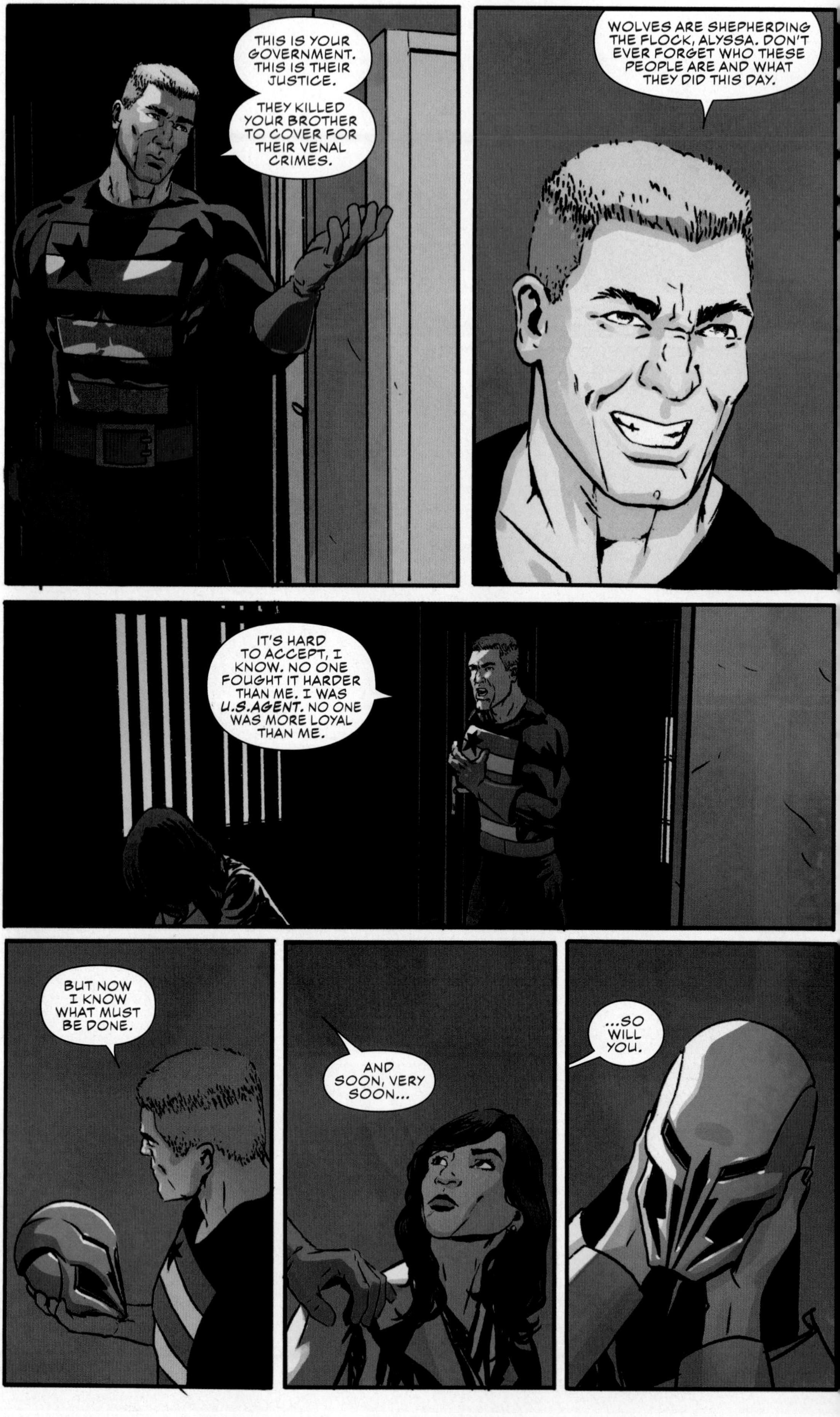

THIS IS YOUR GOVERNMENT. THIS IS THEIR JUSTICE.
THEY KILLED YOUR BROTHER TO COVER FOR THEIR VENAL CRIMES.
WOLVES ARE SHEPHERDING THE FLOCK, ALYSSA. DON'T EVER FORGET WHO THESE PEOPLE ARE AND WHAT THEY DID THIS DAY.
IT'S HARD TO ACCEPT, I KNOW. NO ONE FOUGHT IT HARDER THAN ME. I WAS *U.S.AGENT*. NO ONE WAS MORE LOYAL THAN ME.
BUT NOW I KNOW WHAT MUST BE DONE.
AND SOON, VERY SOON...
...SO WILL YOU.

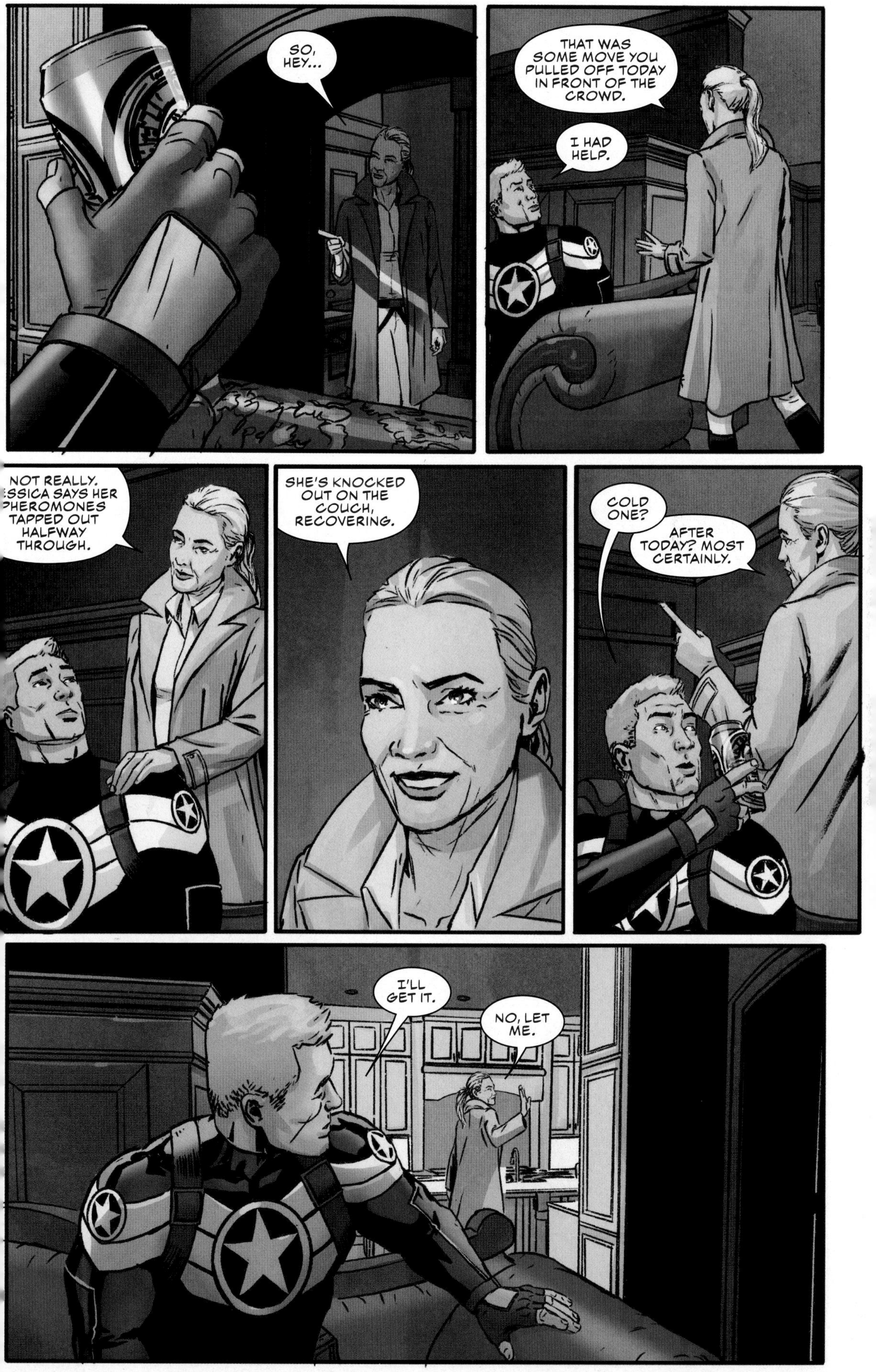
SO, HEY...
THAT WAS SOME MOVE YOU PULLED OFF TODAY IN FRONT OF THE CROWD.
I HAD HELP.
NOT REALLY. ESSICA SAYS HER PHEROMONES TAPPED OUT HALFWAY THROUGH.
SHE'S KNOCKED OUT ON THE COUCH, RECOVERING.
COLD ONE?
AFTER TODAY? MOST CERTAINLY.
I'LL GET IT.
NO, LET ME.

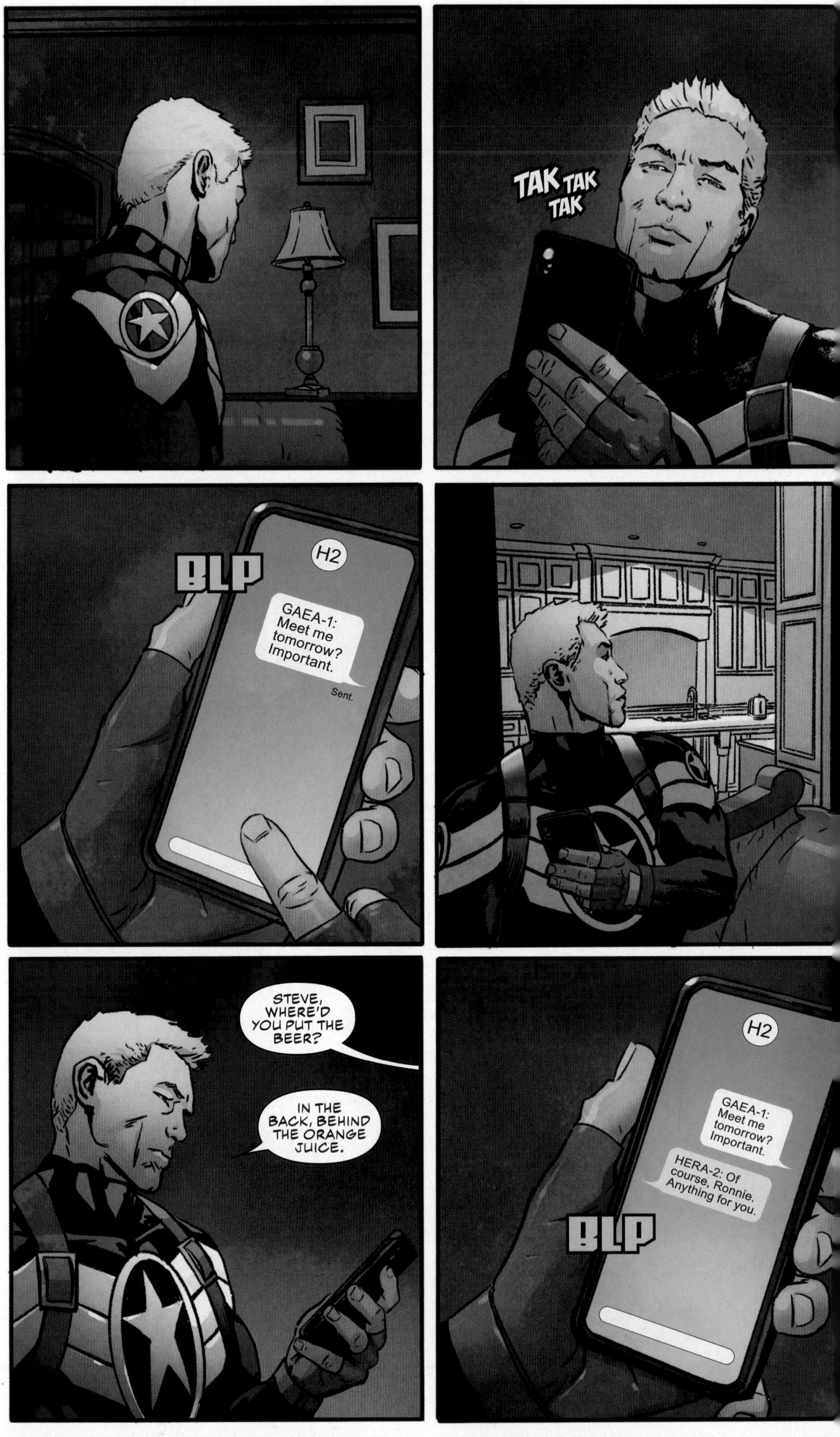
TAK TAK TAK
BLP
H2
GAEA-1: Meet me tomorrow? Important.
Sent.
STEVE, WHERE'D YOU PUT THE BEER?
IN THE BACK, BEHIND THE ORANGE JUICE.
H2
GAEA-1: Meet me tomorrow? Important.
HERA-2: Of course, Ronnie. Anything for you.
BLP

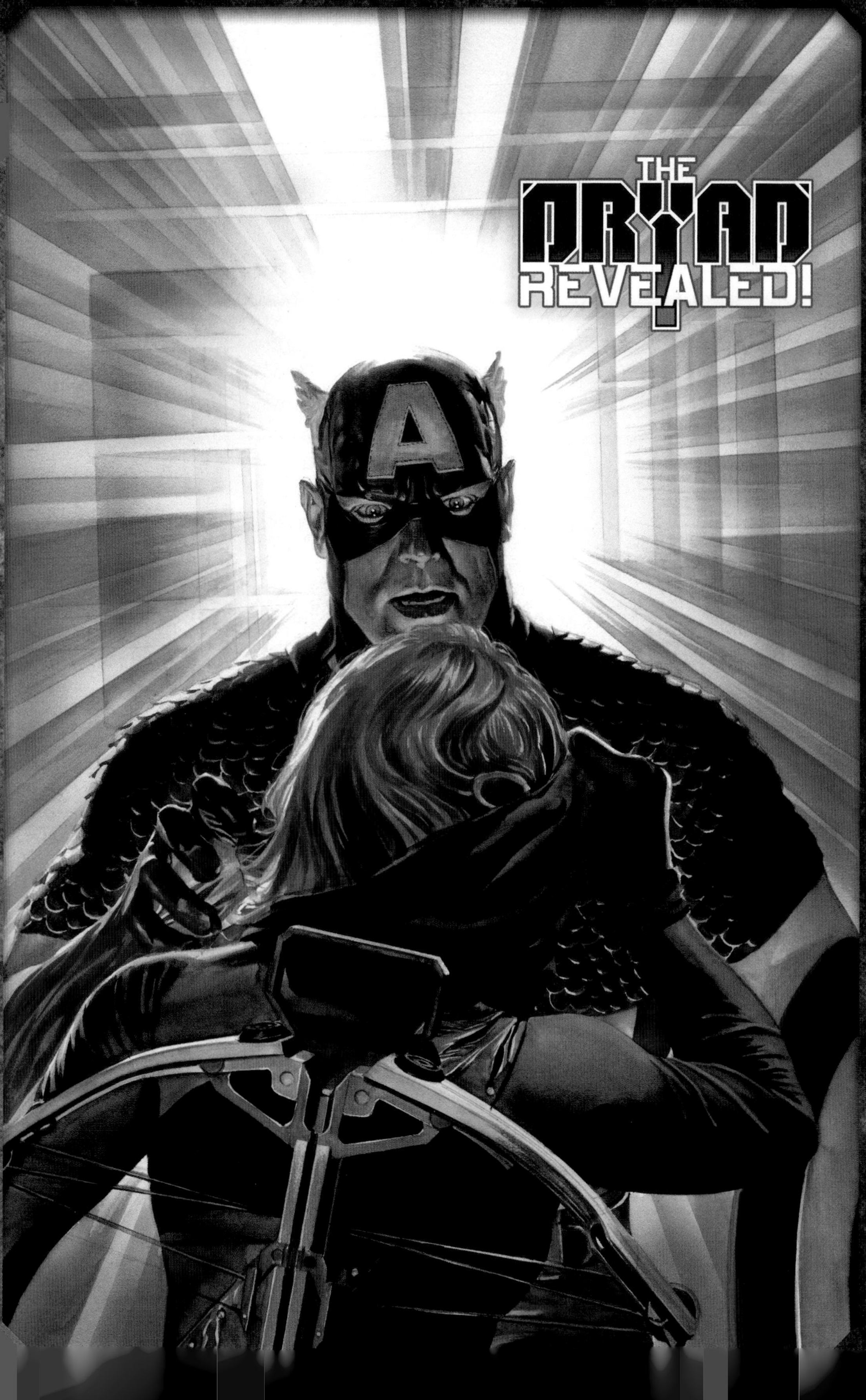
THE
DRYAD
REVEALED!

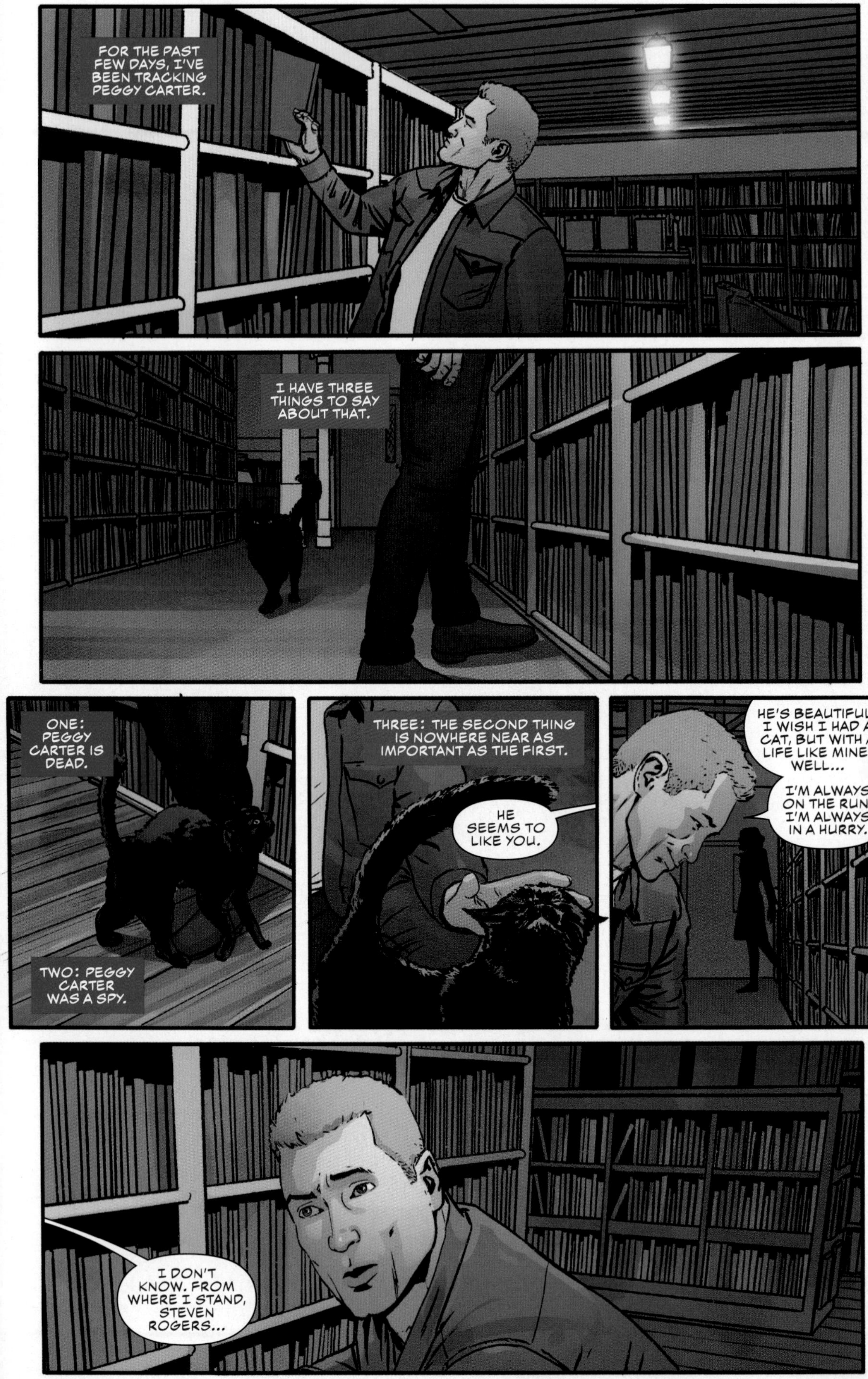
FOR THE PAST FEW DAYS, I'VE BEEN TRACKING PEGGY CARTER.
I HAVE THREE THINGS TO SAY ABOUT THAT.
ONE: PEGGY CARTER IS DEAD.
TWO: PEGGY CARTER WAS A SPY.
THREE: THE SECOND THING IS NOWHERE NEAR AS IMPORTANT AS THE FIRST.
HE SEEMS TO LIKE YOU.
HE'S BEAUTIFUL. I WISH I HAD A CAT, BUT WITH A LIFE LIKE MINE, WELL...
I'M ALWAYS ON THE RUN. I'M ALWAYS IN A HURRY.
I DON'T KNOW. FROM WHERE I STAND, STEVEN ROGERS...

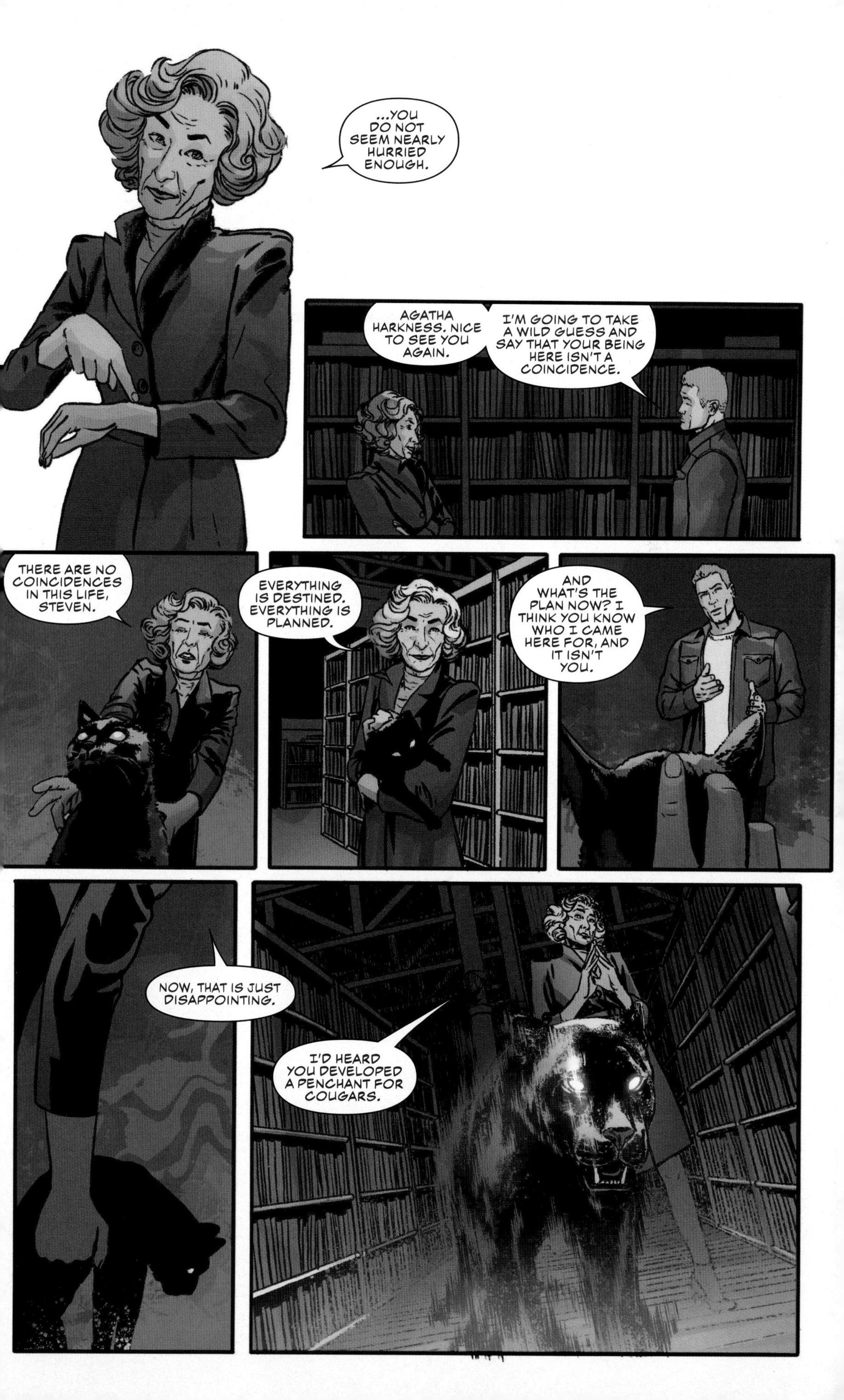
...YOU DO NOT SEEM NEARLY HURRIED ENOUGH.
AGATHA HARKNESS. NICE TO SEE YOU AGAIN.
I'M GOING TO TAKE A WILD GUESS AND SAY THAT YOUR BEING HERE ISN'T A COINCIDENCE.
THERE ARE NO COINCIDENCES IN THIS LIFE, STEVEN.
EVERYTHING IS DESTINED. EVERYTHING IS PLANNED.
AND WHAT'S THE PLAN NOW? I THINK YOU KNOW WHO I CAME HERE FOR, AND IT ISN'T YOU.
NOW, THAT IS JUST DISAPPOINTING.
I'D HEARD YOU DEVELOPED A PENCHANT FOR COUGARS.

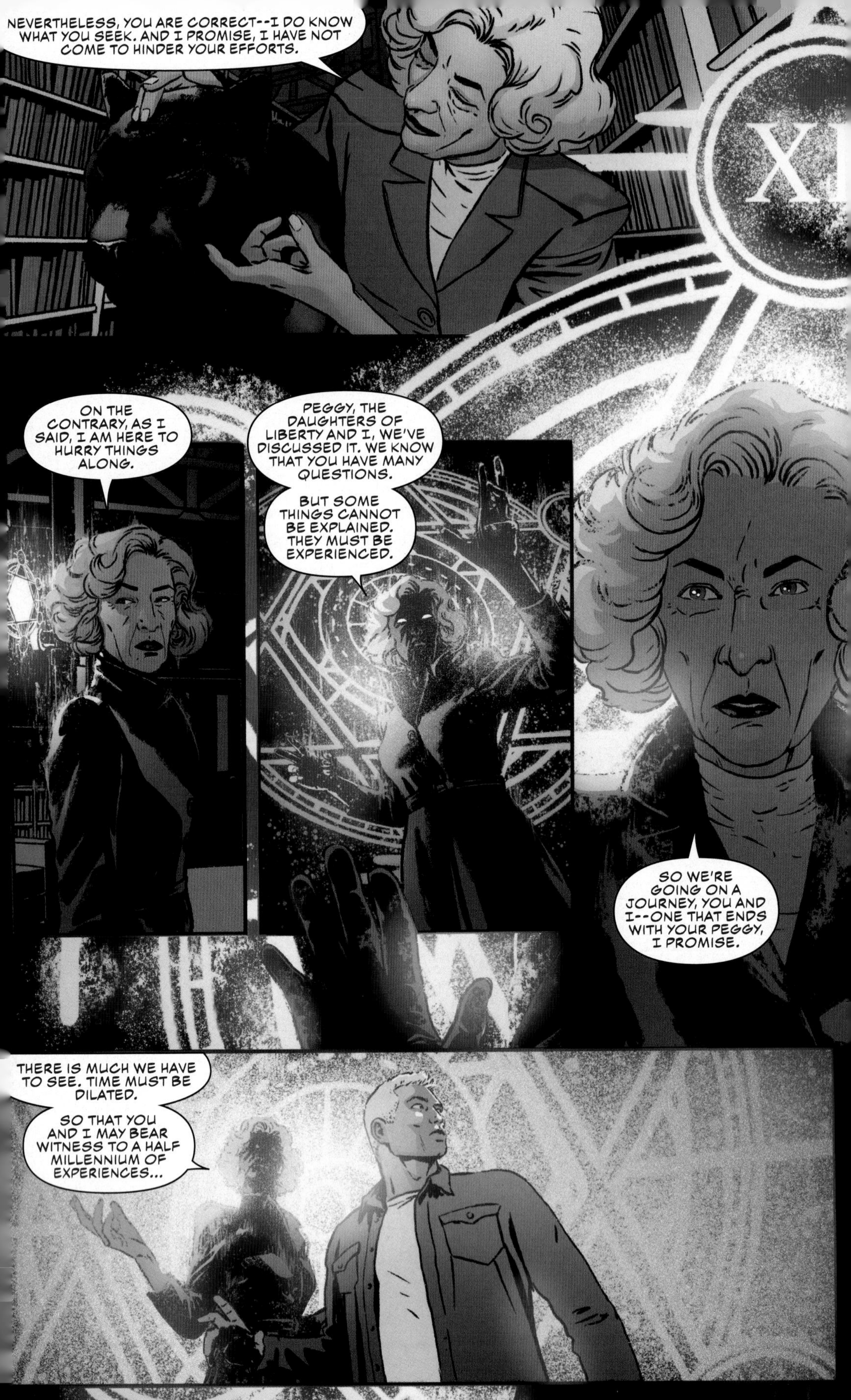
NEVERTHELESS, YOU ARE CORRECT--I DO KNOW WHAT YOU SEEK. AND I PROMISE, I HAVE NOT COME TO HINDER YOUR EFFORTS.
ON THE CONTRARY, AS I SAID, I AM HERE TO HURRY THINGS ALONG.
PEGGY, THE DAUGHTERS OF LIBERTY AND I, WE'VE DISCUSSED IT. WE KNOW THAT YOU HAVE MANY QUESTIONS.
BUT SOME THINGS CANNOT BE EXPLAINED. THEY MUST BE EXPERIENCED.
SO WE'RE GOING ON A JOURNEY, YOU AND I--ONE THAT ENDS WITH YOUR PEGGY, I PROMISE.
THERE IS MUCH WE HAVE TO SEE. TIME MUST BE DILATED.
SO THAT YOU AND I MAY BEAR WITNESS TO A HALF MILLENNIUM OF EXPERIENCES...

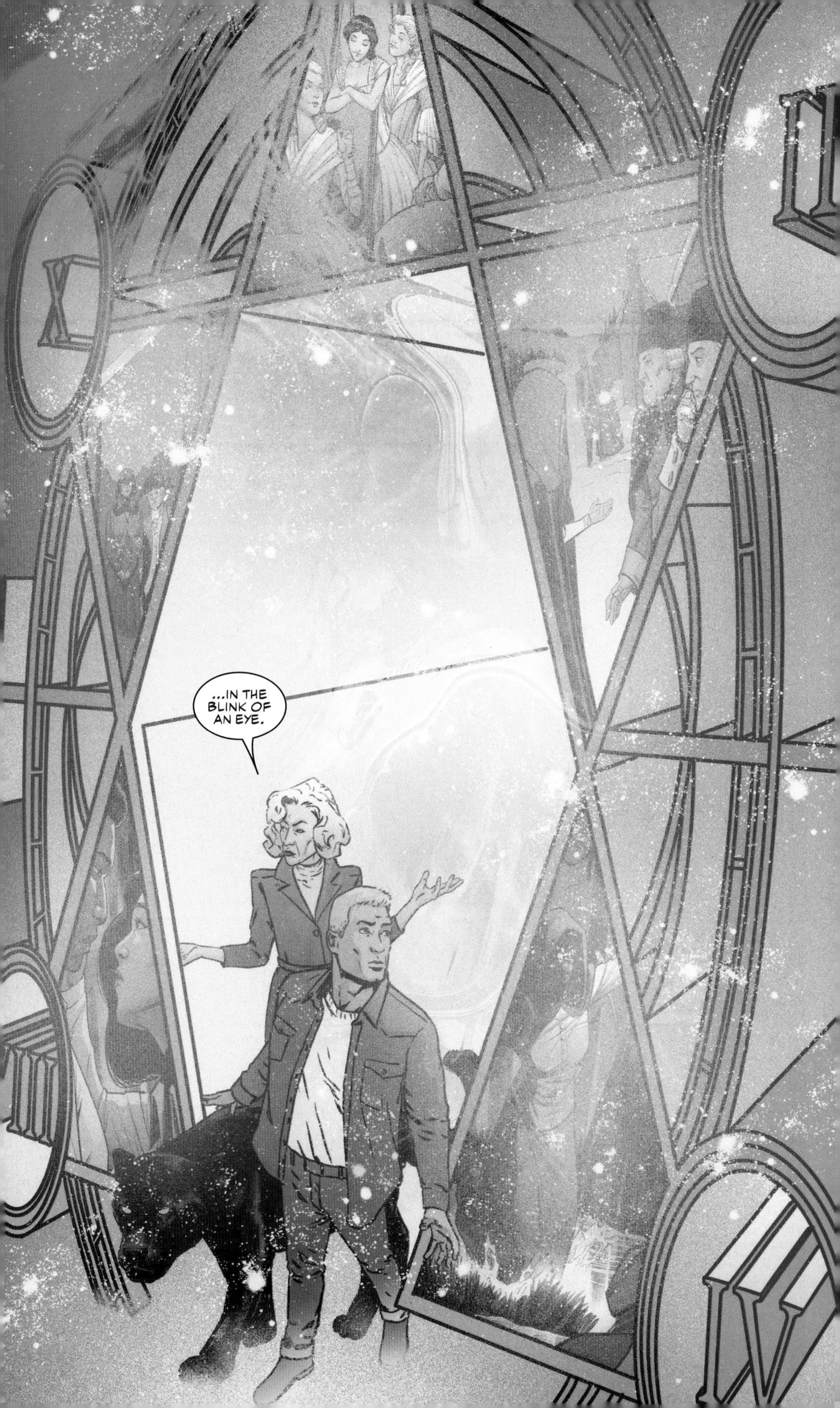
...IN THE BLINK OF AN EYE.

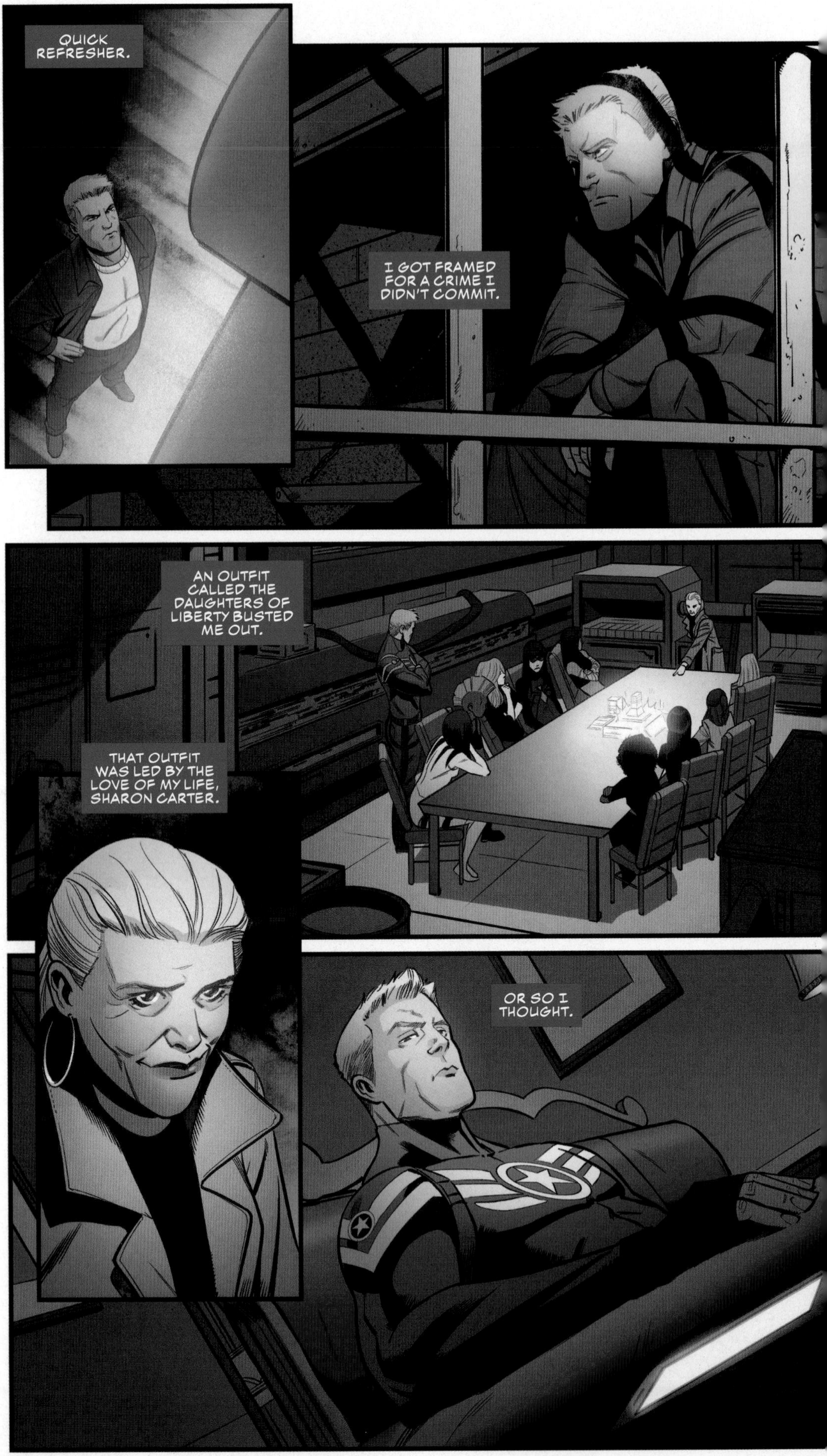
QUICK REFRESHER.
I GOT FRAMED FOR A CRIME I DIDN'T COMMIT.
AN OUTFIT CALLED THE DAUGHTERS OF LIBERTY BUSTED ME OUT.
THAT OUTFIT WAS LED BY THE LOVE OF MY LIFE, SHARON CARTER.
OR SO I THOUGHT.

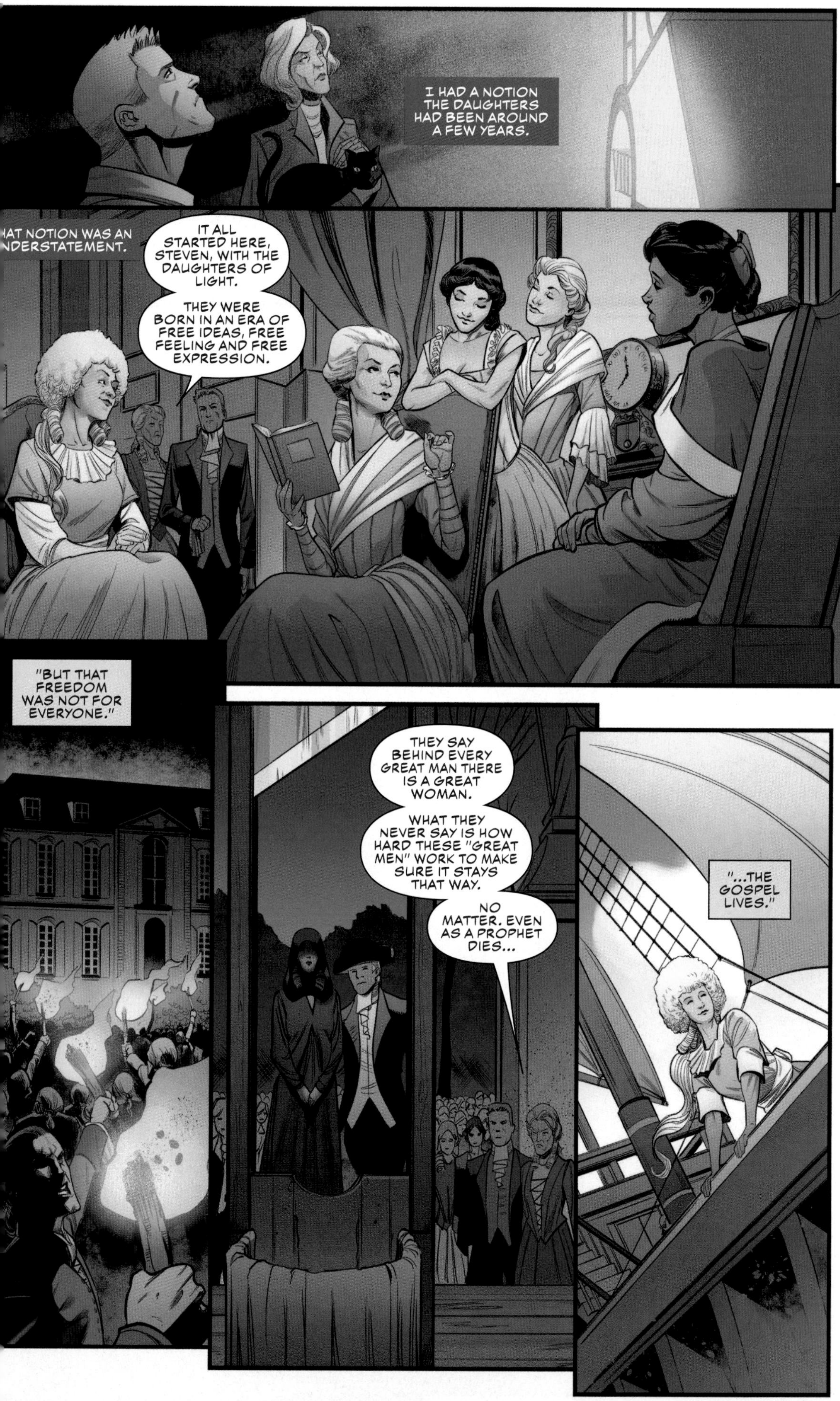
I HAD A NOTION THE DAUGHTERS HAD BEEN AROUND A FEW YEARS.
AT NOTION WAS AN NDERSTATEMENT.
IT ALL STARTED HERE, STEVEN, WITH THE DAUGHTERS OF LIGHT.
THEY WERE BORN IN AN ERA OF FREE IDEAS, FREE FEELING AND FREE EXPRESSION.
"BUT THAT FREEDOM WAS NOT FOR EVERYONE."
THEY SAY BEHIND EVERY GREAT MAN THERE IS A GREAT WOMAN.
WHAT THEY NEVER SAY IS HOW HARD THESE "GREAT MEN" WORK TO MAKE SURE IT STAYS THAT WAY.
NO MATTER. EVEN AS A PROPHET DIES...
"...THE GOSPEL LIVES."

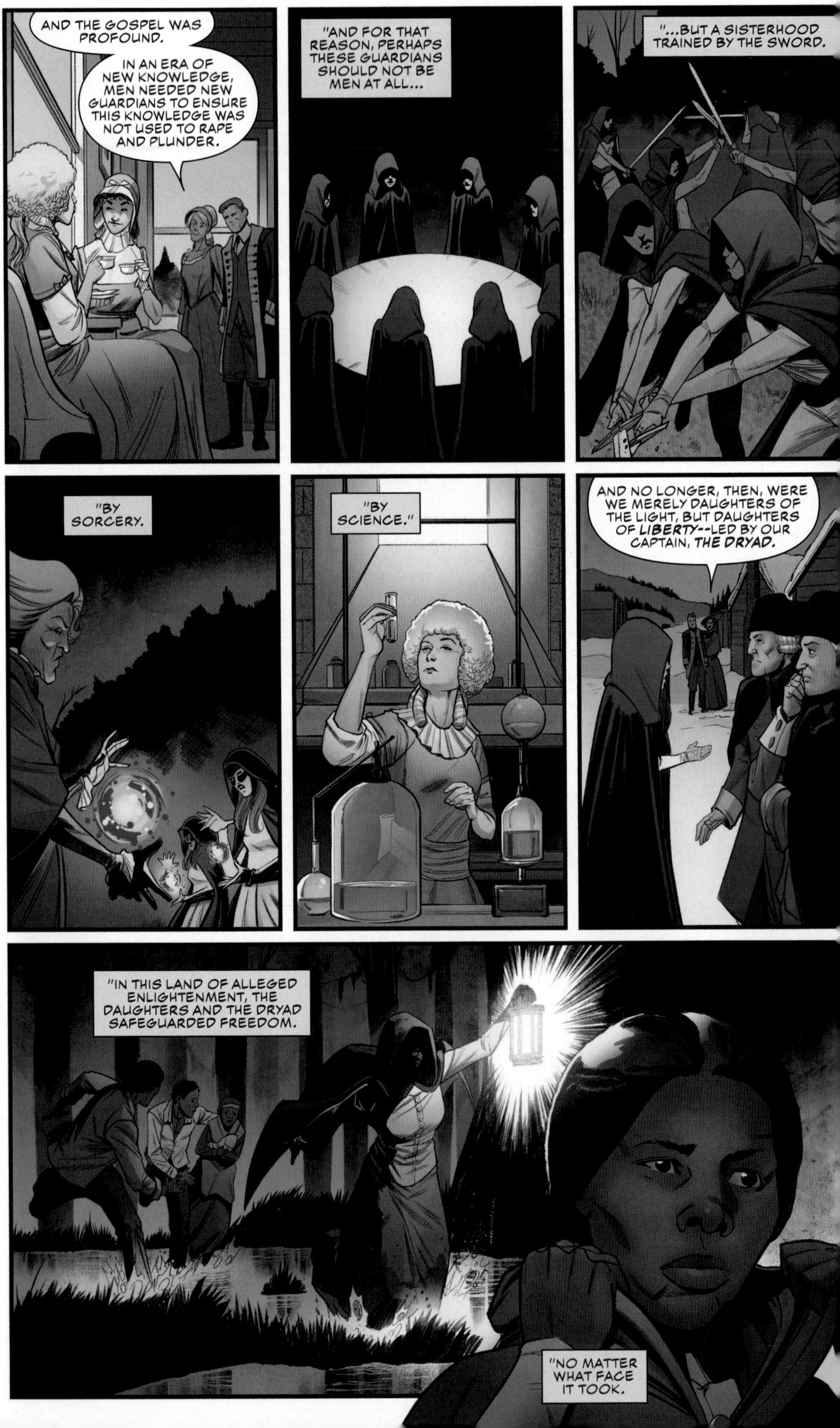
AND THE GOSPEL WAS PROFOUND.
IN AN ERA OF NEW KNOWLEDGE, MEN NEEDED NEW GUARDIANS TO ENSURE THIS KNOWLEDGE WAS NOT USED TO RAPE AND PLUNDER.
"AND FOR THAT REASON, PERHAPS THESE GUARDIANS SHOULD NOT BE MEN AT ALL...
"...BUT A SISTERHOOD TRAINED BY THE SWORD.
"BY SORCERY.
"BY SCIENCE."
AND NO LONGER, THEN, WERE WE MERELY DAUGHTERS OF THE LIGHT, BUT DAUGHTERS OF LIBERTY--LED BY OUR CAPTAIN, THE DRYAD.
"IN THIS LAND OF ALLEGED ENLIGHTENMENT, THE DAUGHTERS AND THE DRYAD SAFEGUARDED FREEDOM.
"NO MATTER WHAT FACE IT TOOK.

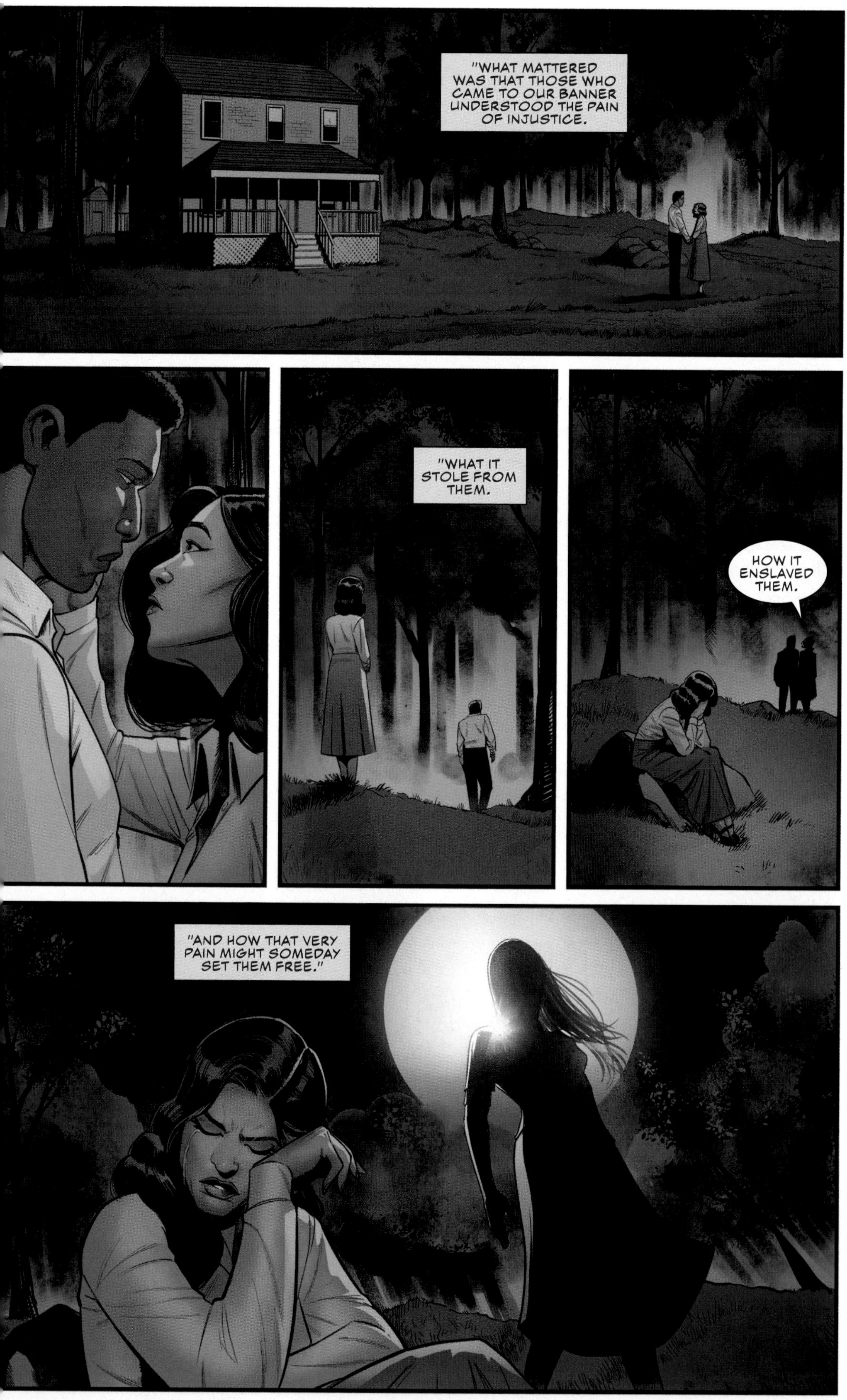
"WHAT MATTERED WAS THAT THOSE WHO CAME TO OUR BANNER UNDERSTOOD THE PAIN OF INJUSTICE.
"WHAT IT STOLE FROM THEM.
HOW IT ENSLAVED THEM.
"AND HOW THAT VERY PAIN MIGHT SOMEDAY SET THEM FREE."

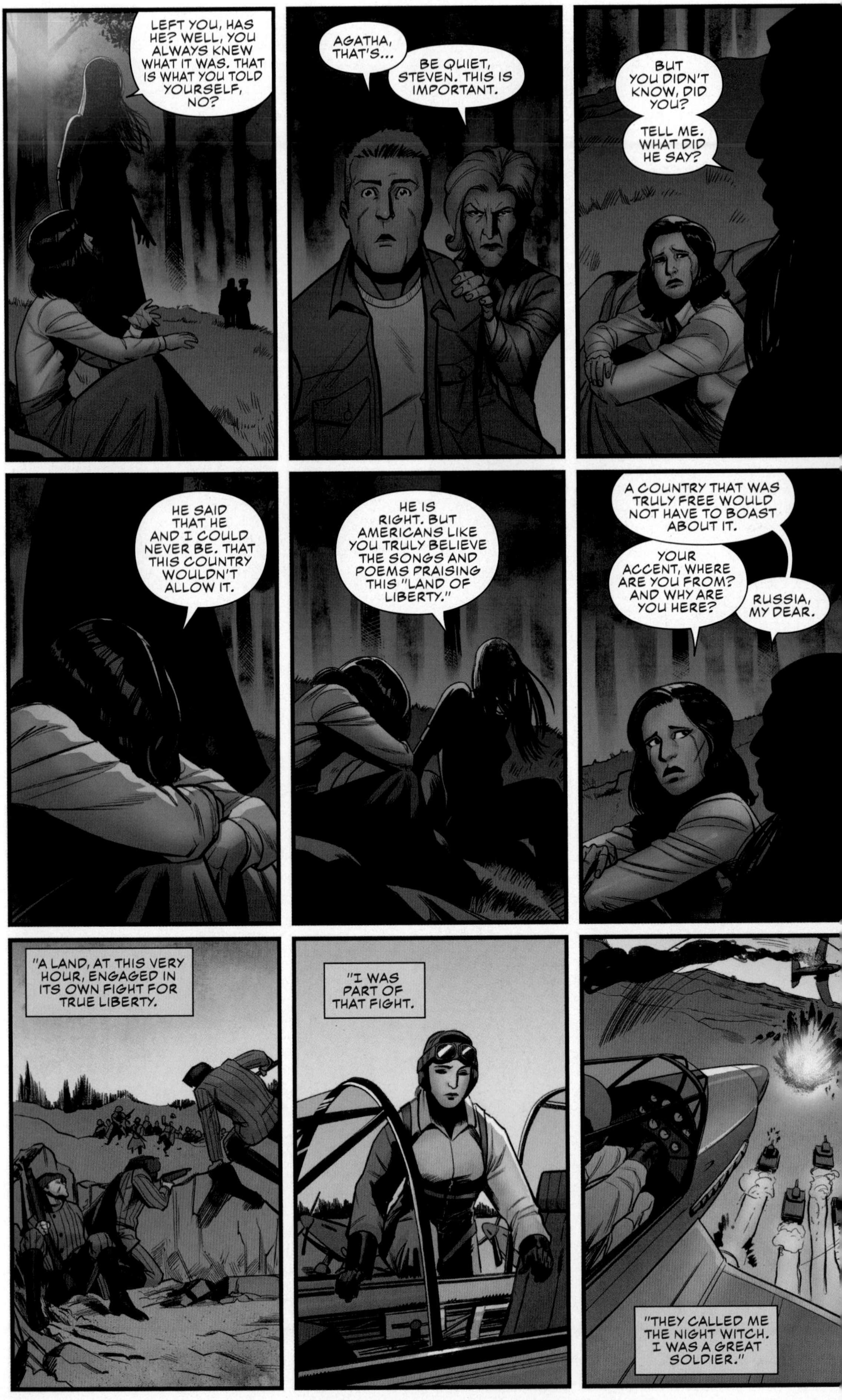

LEFT YOU, HAS HE? WELL, YOU ALWAYS KNEW WHAT IT WAS. THAT IS WHAT YOU TOLD YOURSELF, NO?
AGATHA, THAT'S...
BE QUIET, STEVEN. THIS IS IMPORTANT.
BUT YOU DIDN'T KNOW, DID YOU?
TELL ME. WHAT DID HE SAY?
HE SAID THAT HE AND I COULD NEVER BE. THAT THIS COUNTRY WOULDN'T ALLOW IT.
HE IS RIGHT. BUT AMERICANS LIKE YOU TRULY BELIEVE THE SONGS AND POEMS PRAISING THIS "LAND OF LIBERTY."
A COUNTRY THAT WAS TRULY FREE WOULD NOT HAVE TO BOAST ABOUT IT.
YOUR ACCENT, WHERE ARE YOU FROM? AND WHY ARE YOU HERE?
RUSSIA, MY DEAR.
"A LAND, AT THIS VERY HOUR, ENGAGED IN ITS OWN FIGHT FOR TRUE LIBERTY.
"I WAS PART OF THAT FIGHT.
"THEY CALLED ME THE NIGHT WITCH. I WAS A GREAT SOLDIER."

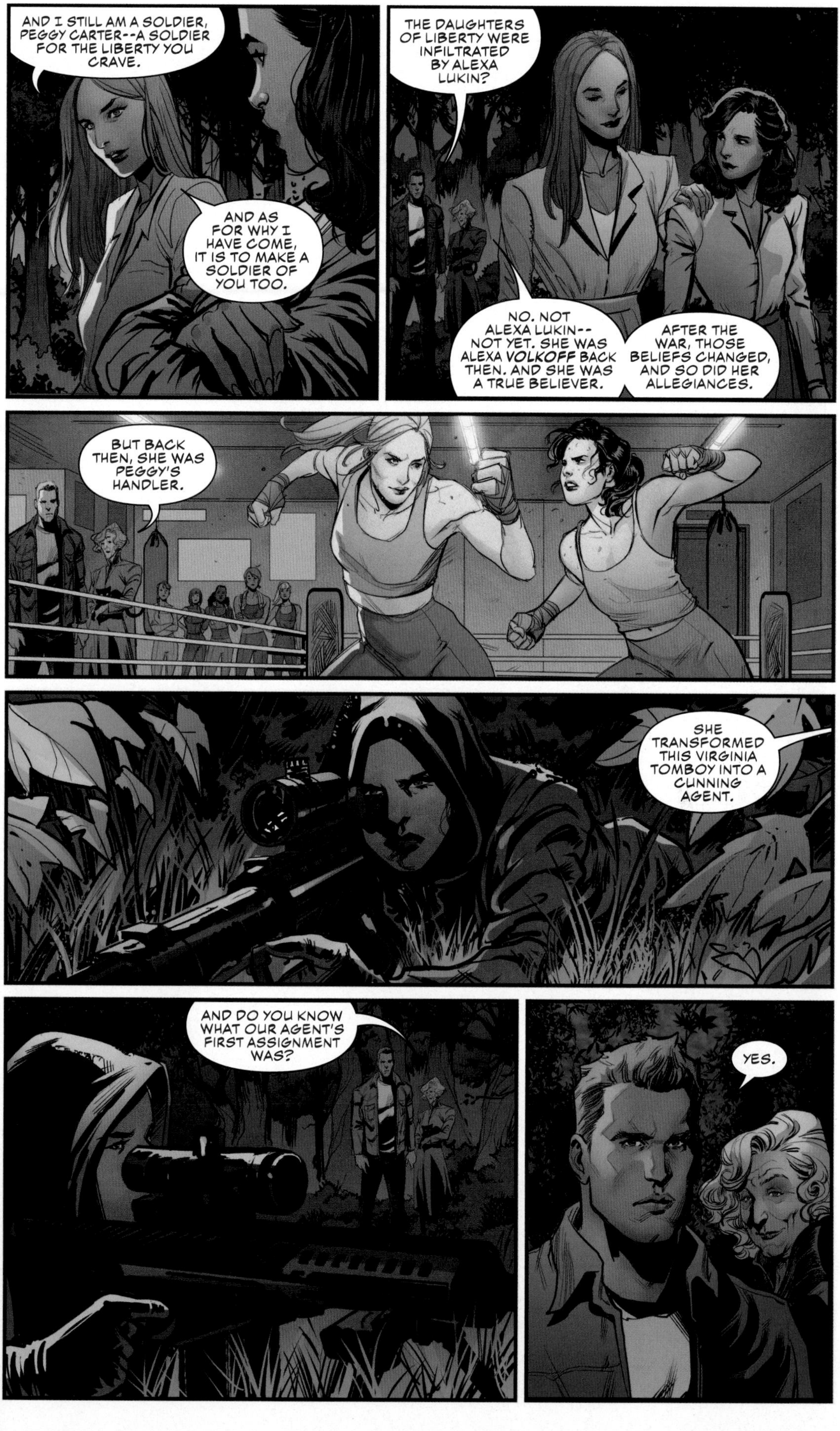
AND I STILL AM A SOLDIER, PEGGY CARTER--A SOLDIER FOR THE LIBERTY YOU CRAVE.
AND AS FOR WHY I HAVE COME, IT IS TO MAKE A SOLDIER OF YOU TOO.
THE DAUGHTERS OF LIBERTY WERE INFILTRATED BY ALEXA LUKIN?
NO. NOT ALEXA LUKIN--NOT YET. SHE WAS ALEXA VOLKOFF BACK THEN. AND SHE WAS A TRUE BELIEVER.
AFTER THE WAR, THOSE BELIEFS CHANGED, AND SO DID HER ALLEGIANCES.
BUT BACK THEN, SHE WAS PEGGY'S HANDLER.
SHE TRANSFORMED THIS VIRGINIA TOMBOY INTO A CUNNING AGENT.
AND DO YOU KNOW WHAT OUR AGENT'S FIRST ASSIGNMENT WAS?
YES.

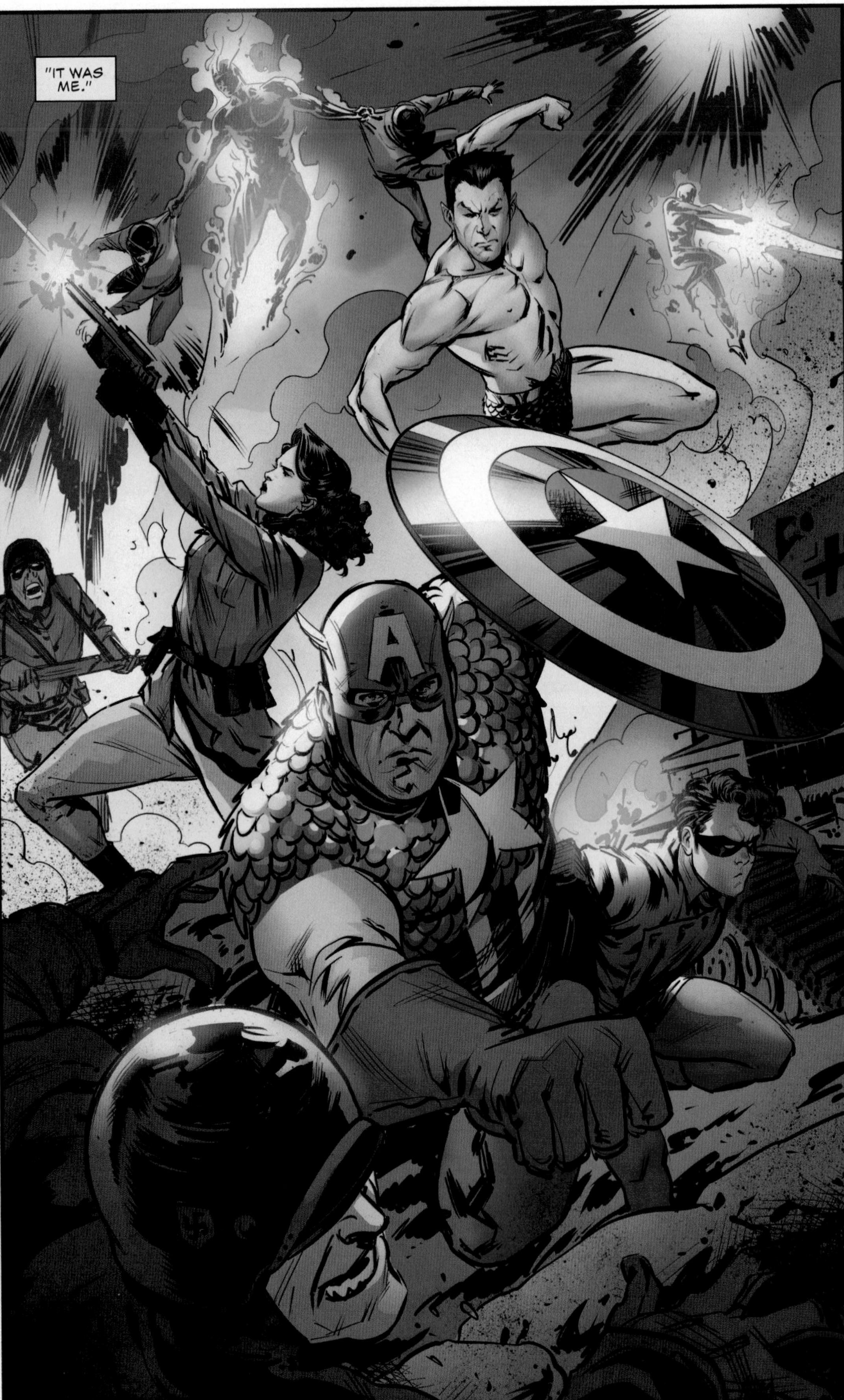
"IT WAS ME."

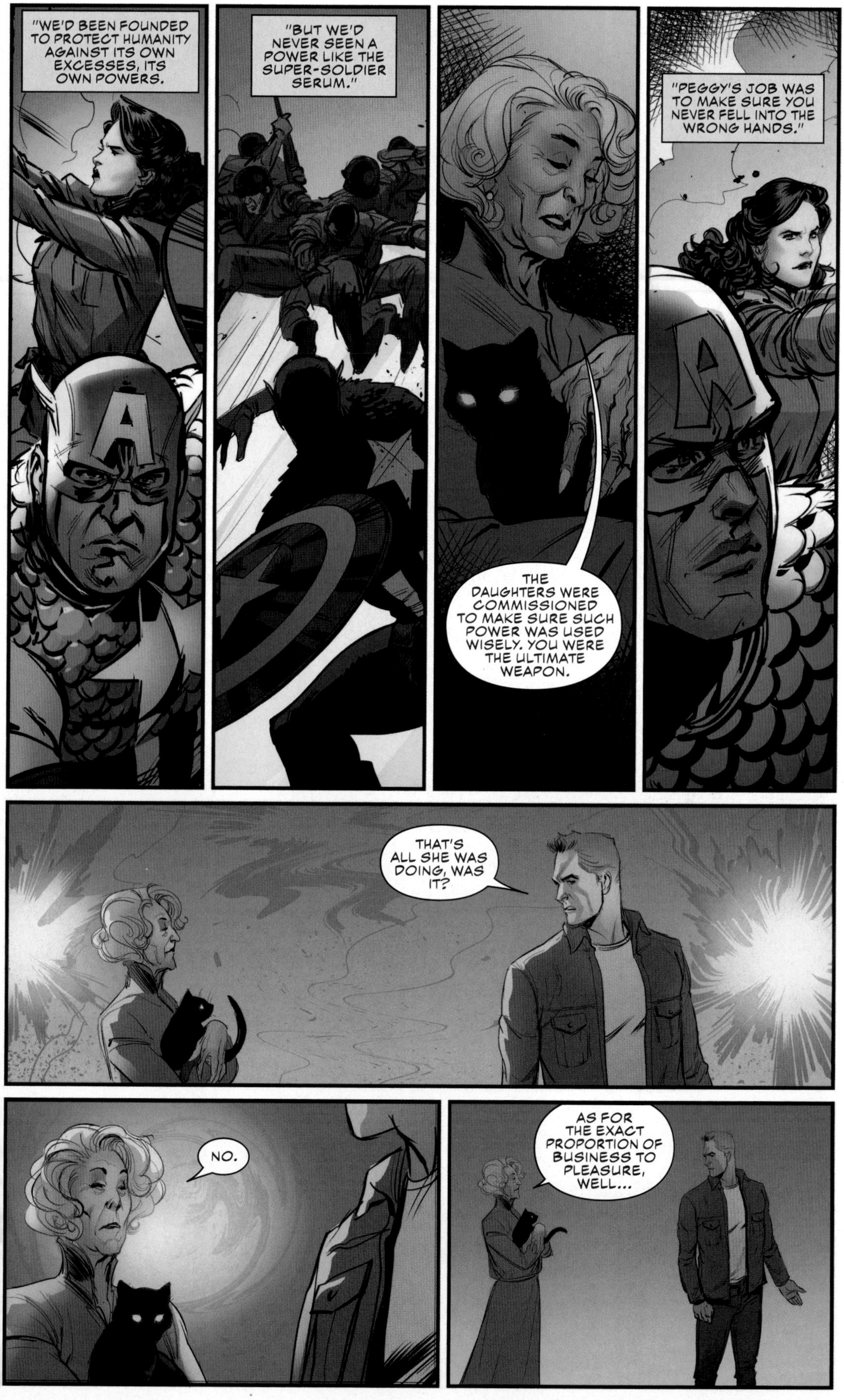
"WE'D BEEN FOUNDED TO PROTECT HUMANITY AGAINST ITS OWN EXCESSES, ITS OWN POWERS.
"BUT WE'D NEVER SEEN A POWER LIKE THE SUPER-SOLDIER SERUM."
THE DAUGHTERS WERE COMMISSIONED TO MAKE SURE SUCH POWER WAS USED WISELY. YOU WERE THE ULTIMATE WEAPON.
"PEGGY'S JOB WAS TO MAKE SURE YOU NEVER FELL INTO THE WRONG HANDS."
THAT'S ALL SHE WAS DOING, WAS IT?
NO.
AS FOR THE EXACT PROPORTION OF BUSINESS TO PLEASURE, WELL...

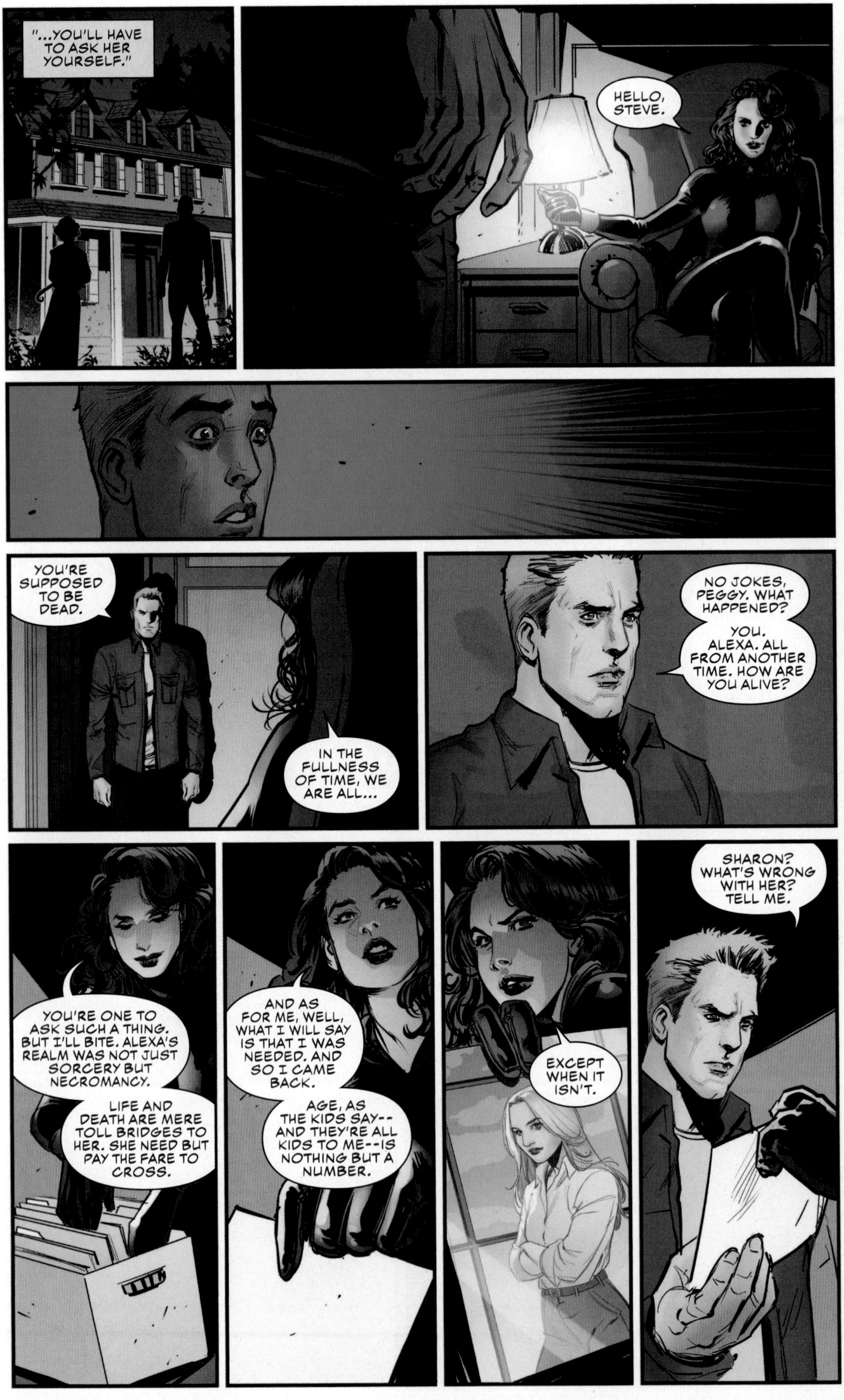
"...YOU'LL HAVE TO ASK HER YOURSELF."
HELLO, STEVE.
YOU'RE SUPPOSED TO BE DEAD.
IN THE FULLNESS OF TIME, WE ARE ALL...
NO JOKES, PEGGY. WHAT HAPPENED?
YOU. ALEXA. ALL FROM ANOTHER TIME. HOW ARE YOU ALIVE?
YOU'RE ONE TO ASK SUCH A THING. BUT I'LL BITE. ALEXA'S REALM WAS NOT JUST SORCERY BUT NECROMANCY.
LIFE AND DEATH ARE MERE TOLL BRIDGES TO HER. SHE NEED BUT PAY THE FARE TO CROSS.
AND AS FOR ME, WELL, WHAT I WILL SAY IS THAT I WAS NEEDED. AND SO I CAME BACK.
AGE, AS THE KIDS SAY-- AND THEY'RE ALL KIDS TO ME--IS NOTHING BUT A NUMBER.
EXCEPT WHEN IT ISN'T.
SHARON? WHAT'S WRONG WITH HER? TELL ME.

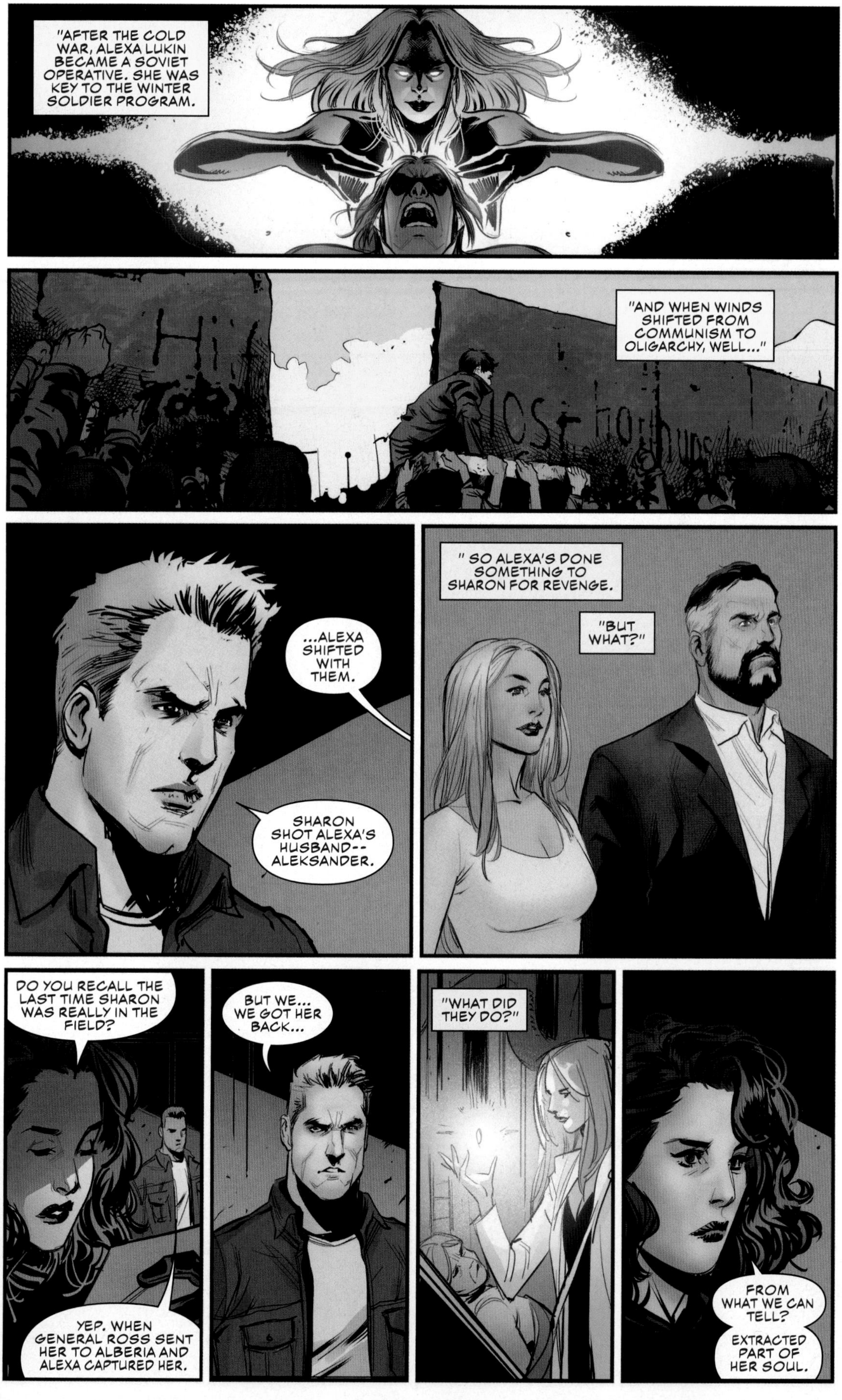
"AFTER THE COLD WAR, ALEXA LUKIN BECAME A SOVIET OPERATIVE. SHE WAS KEY TO THE WINTER SOLDIER PROGRAM.
"AND WHEN WINDS SHIFTED FROM COMMUNISM TO OLIGARCHY, WELL..."
...ALEXA SHIFTED WITH THEM.
SHARON SHOT ALEXA'S HUSBAND--ALEKSANDER.
" SO ALEXA'S DONE SOMETHING TO SHARON FOR REVENGE.
"BUT WHAT?"
DO YOU RECALL THE LAST TIME SHARON WAS REALLY IN THE FIELD?
YEP. WHEN GENERAL ROSS SENT HER TO ALBERIA AND ALEXA CAPTURED HER.
BUT WE... WE GOT HER BACK...
"WHAT DID THEY DO?"
FROM WHAT WE CAN TELL?
EXTRACTED PART OF HER SOUL.

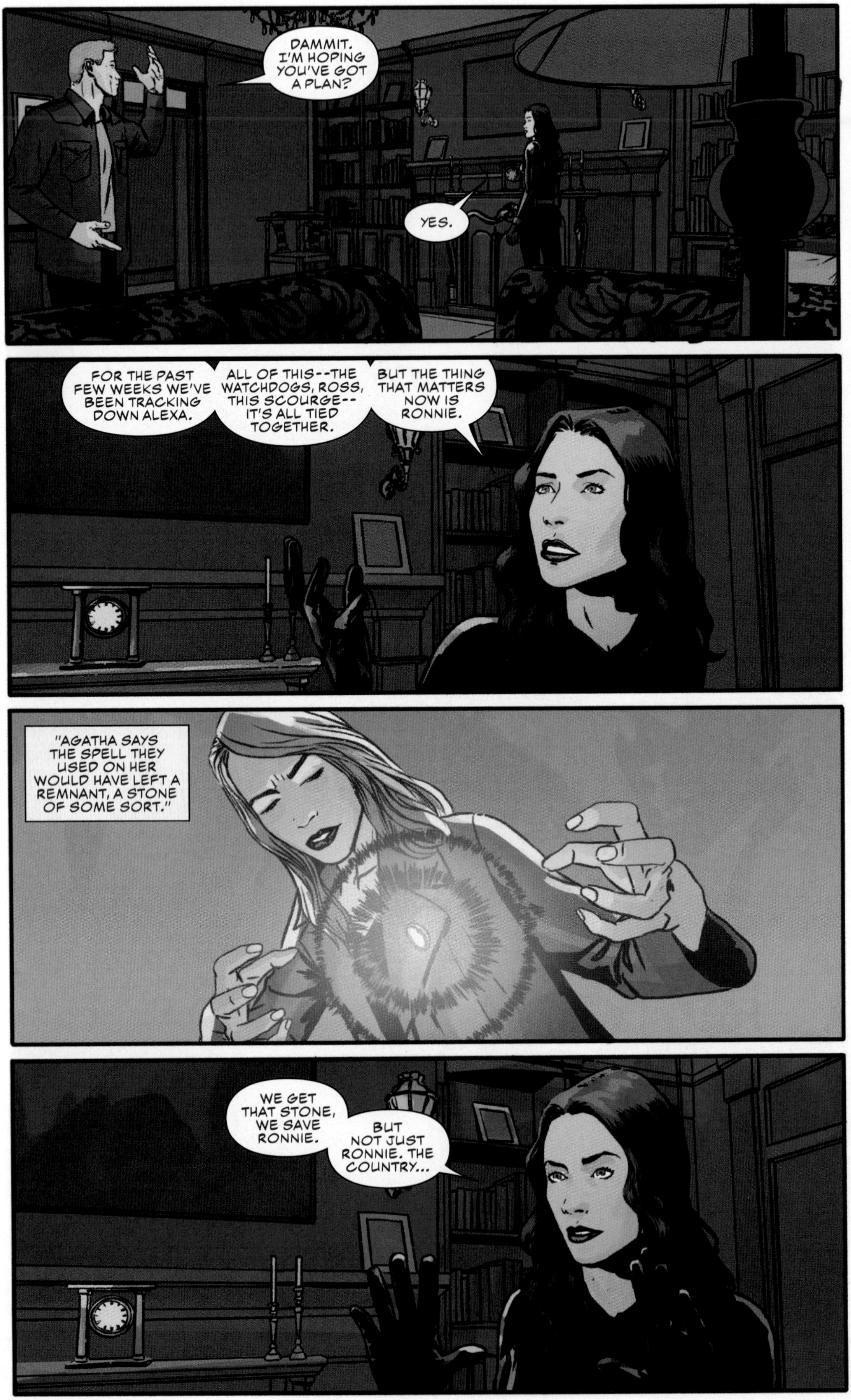
DAMMIT. I'M HOPING YOU'VE GOT A PLAN?
YES.
FOR THE PAST FEW WEEKS WE'VE BEEN TRACKING DOWN ALEXA.
ALL OF THIS--THE WATCHDOGS, ROSS, THIS SCOURGE--IT'S ALL TIED TOGETHER.
BUT THE THING THAT MATTERS NOW IS RONNIE.
"AGATHA SAYS THE SPELL THEY USED ON HER WOULD HAVE LEFT A REMNANT, A STONE OF SOME SORT."
WE GET THAT STONE, WE SAVE RONNIE.
BUT NOT JUST RONNIE. THE COUNTRY...

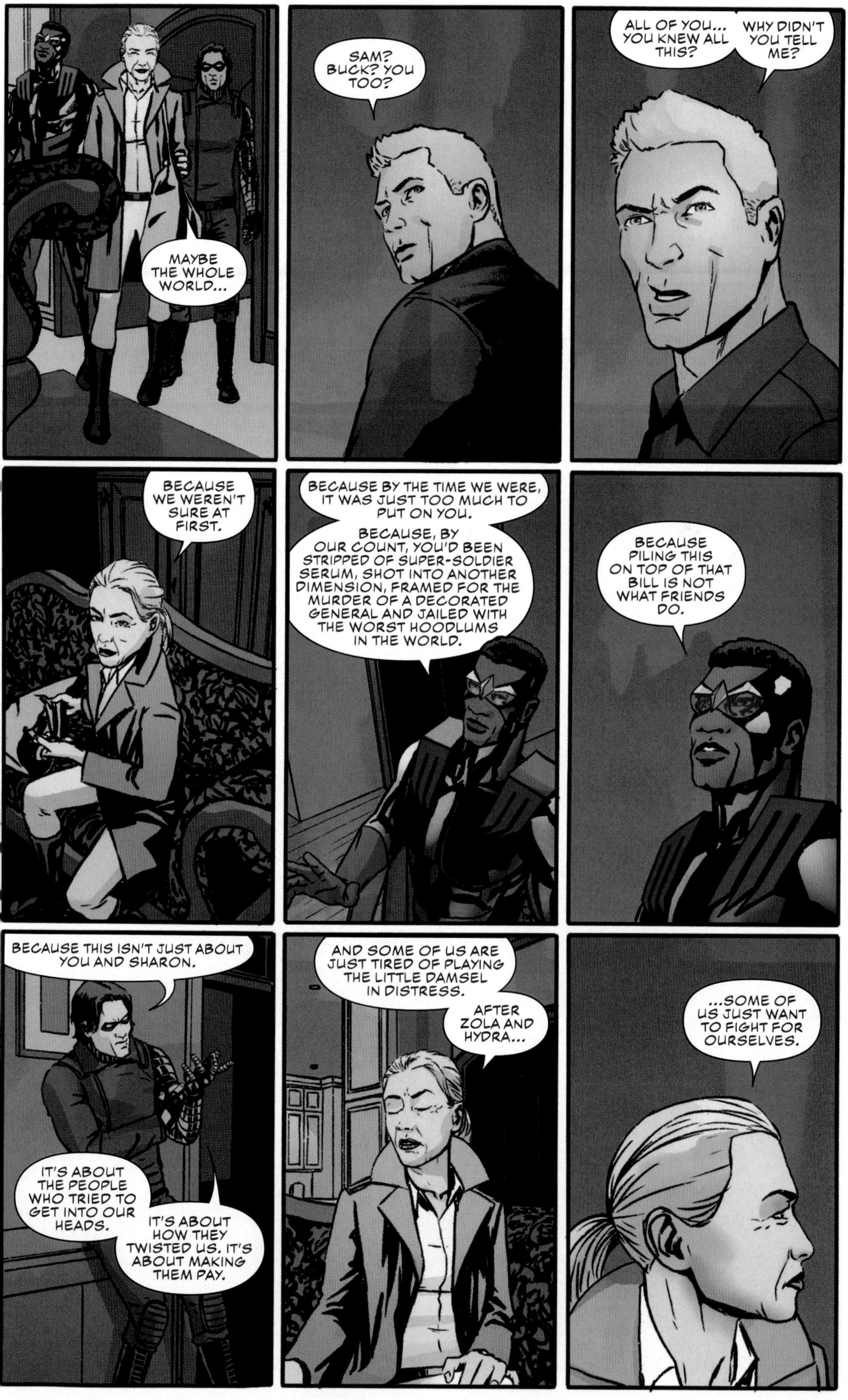
MAYBE THE WHOLE WORLD...
SAM? BUCK? YOU TOO?
ALL OF YOU... YOU KNEW ALL THIS?
WHY DIDN'T YOU TELL ME?
BECAUSE WE WEREN'T SURE AT FIRST.
BECAUSE BY THE TIME WE WERE, IT WAS JUST TOO MUCH TO PUT ON YOU.
BECAUSE, BY OUR COUNT, YOU'D BEEN STRIPPED OF SUPER-SOLDIER SERUM, SHOT INTO ANOTHER DIMENSION, FRAMED FOR THE MURDER OF A DECORATED GENERAL AND JAILED WITH THE WORST HOODLUMS IN THE WORLD.
BECAUSE PILING THIS ON TOP OF THAT BILL IS NOT WHAT FRIENDS DO.
BECAUSE THIS ISN'T JUST ABOUT YOU AND SHARON.
IT'S ABOUT THE PEOPLE WHO TRIED TO GET INTO OUR HEADS.
IT'S ABOUT HOW THEY TWISTED US. IT'S ABOUT MAKING THEM PAY.
AND SOME OF US ARE JUST TIRED OF PLAYING THE LITTLE DAMSEL IN DISTRESS.
AFTER ZOLA AND HYDRA...
...SOME OF US JUST WANT TO FIGHT FOR OURSELVES.

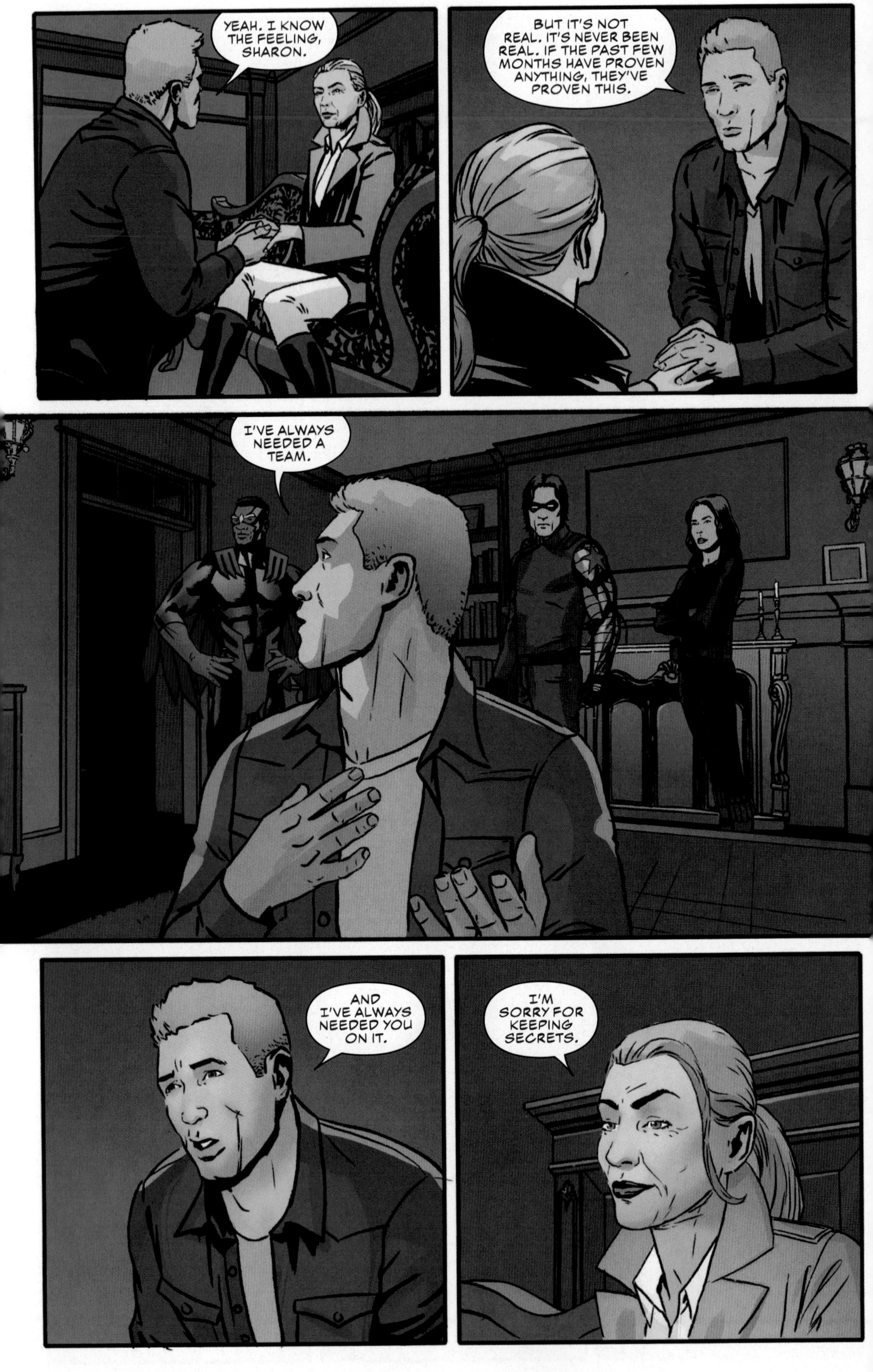
YEAH. I KNOW THE FEELING, SHARON.
BUT IT'S NOT REAL. IT'S NEVER BEEN REAL. IF THE PAST FEW MONTHS HAVE PROVEN ANYTHING, THEY'VE PROVEN THIS.
I'VE ALWAYS NEEDED A TEAM.
AND I'VE ALWAYS NEEDED YOU ON IT.
I'M SORRY FOR KEEPING SECRETS.

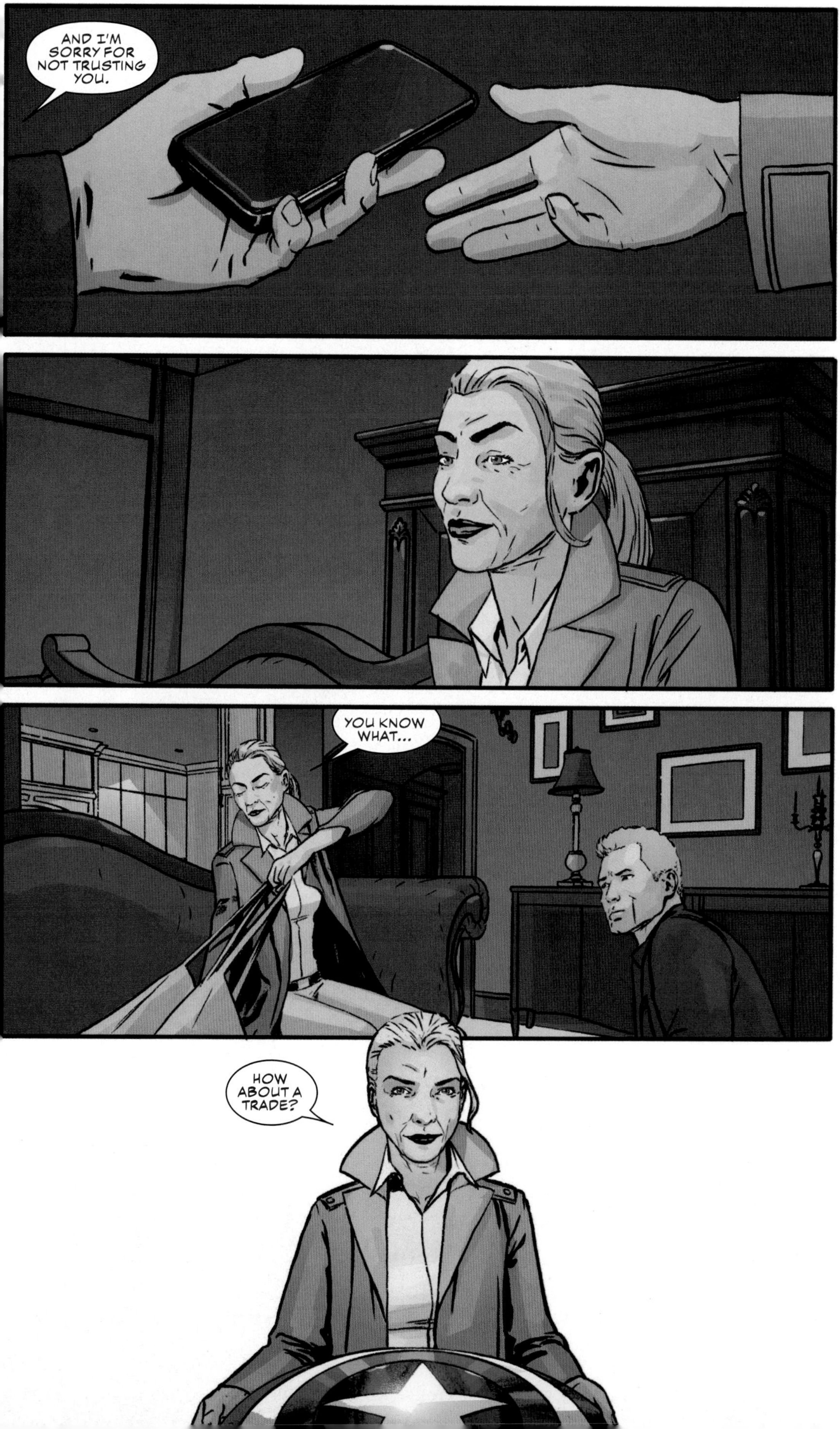
AND I'M SORRY FOR NOT TRUSTING YOU.
YOU KNOW WHAT...
HOW ABOUT A TRADE?

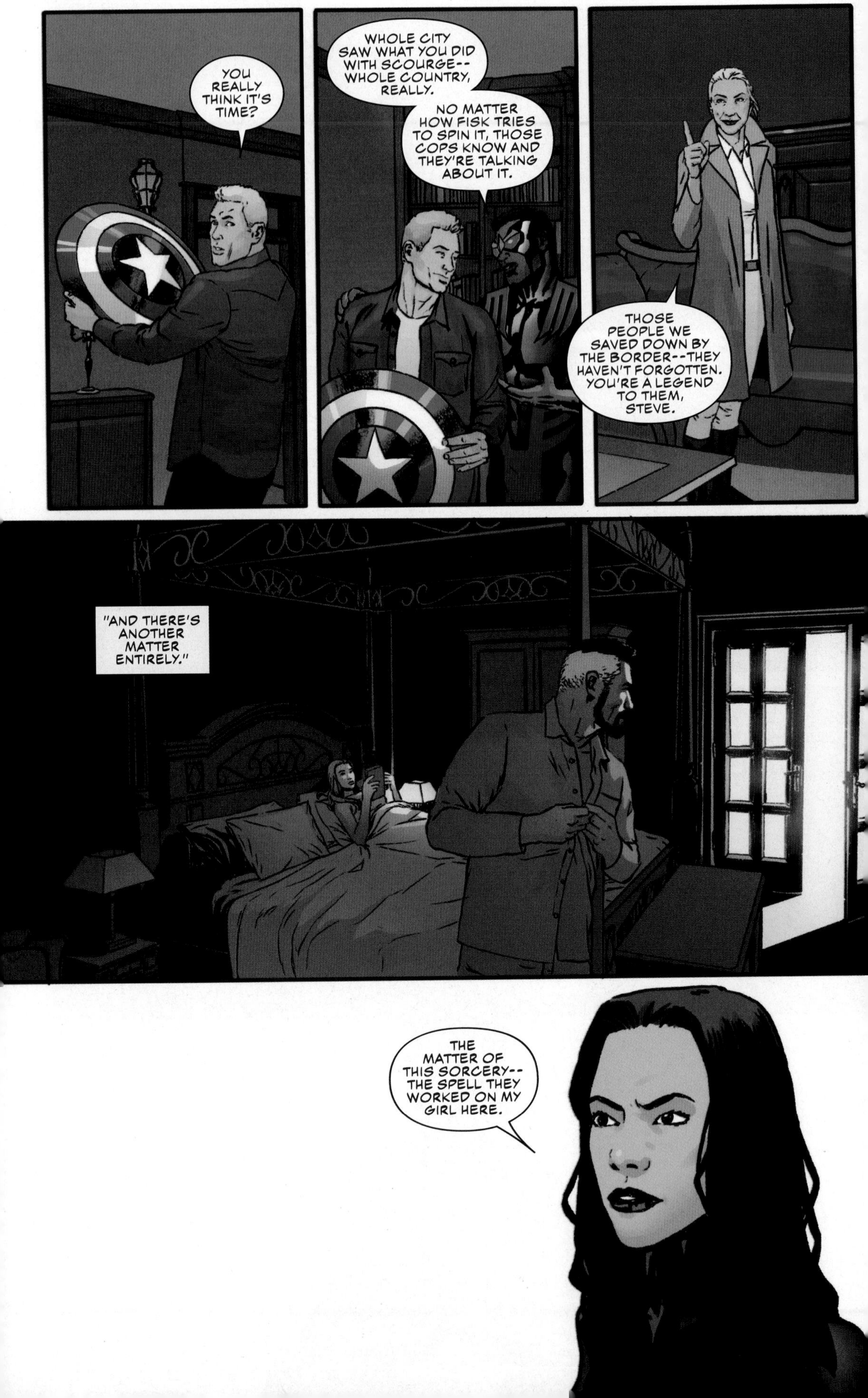
YOU REALLY THINK IT'S TIME?
WHOLE CITY SAW WHAT YOU DID WITH SCOURGE-- WHOLE COUNTRY, REALLY.
NO MATTER HOW FISK TRIES TO SPIN IT, THOSE COPS KNOW AND THEY'RE TALKING ABOUT IT.
THOSE PEOPLE WE SAVED DOWN BY THE BORDER--THEY HAVEN'T FORGOTTEN. YOU'RE A LEGEND TO THEM, STEVE.
"AND THERE'S ANOTHER MATTER ENTIRELY."
THE MATTER OF THIS SORCERY-- THE SPELL THEY WORKED ON MY GIRL HERE.

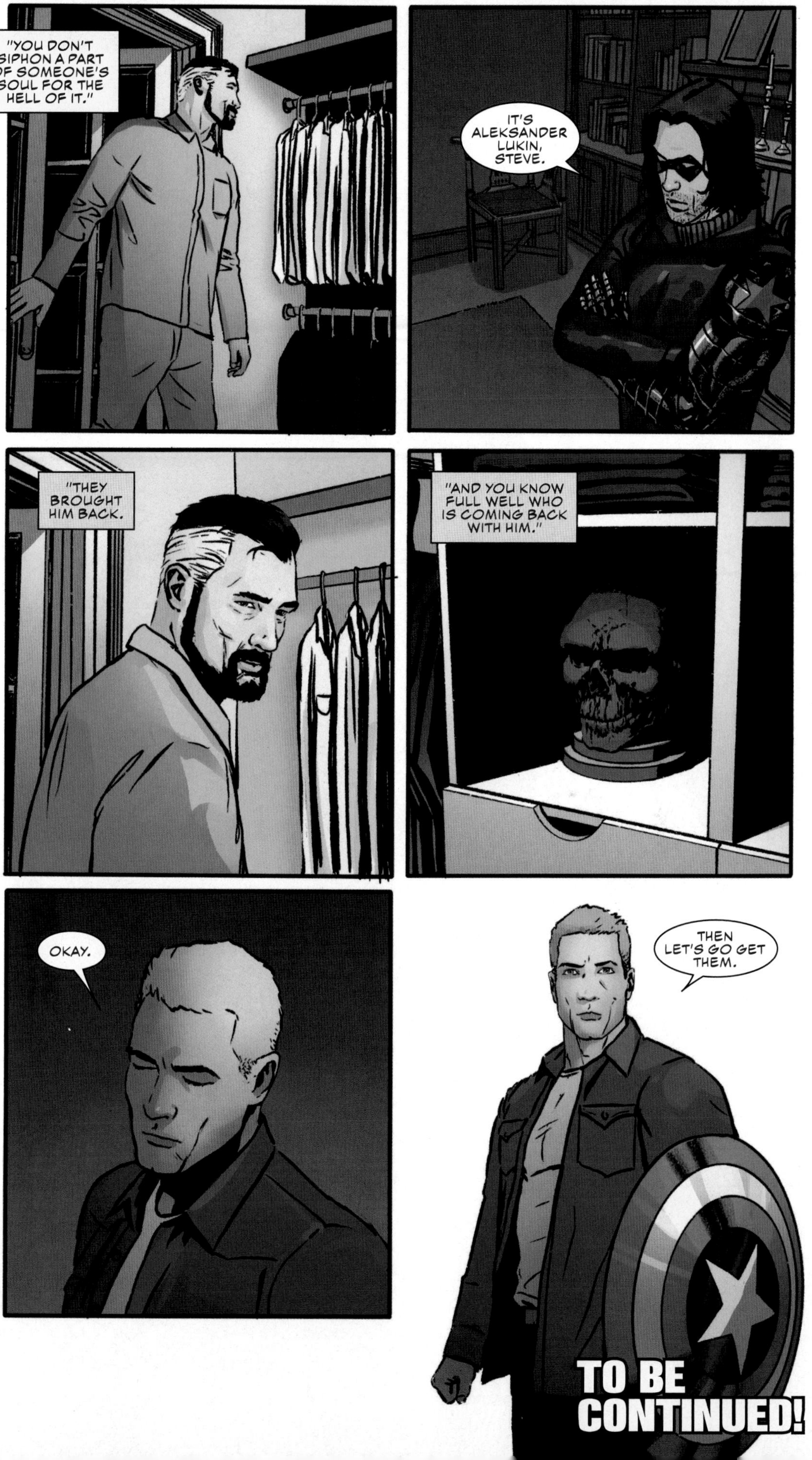
"YOU DON'T SIPHON A PART OF SOMEONE'S SOUL FOR THE HELL OF IT."
IT'S ALEKSANDER LUKIN, STEVE.
"THEY BROUGHT HIM BACK.
"AND YOU KNOW FULL WELL WHO IS COMING BACK WITH HIM."
OKAY.
THEN LET'S GO GET THEM.
TO BE CONTINUED!

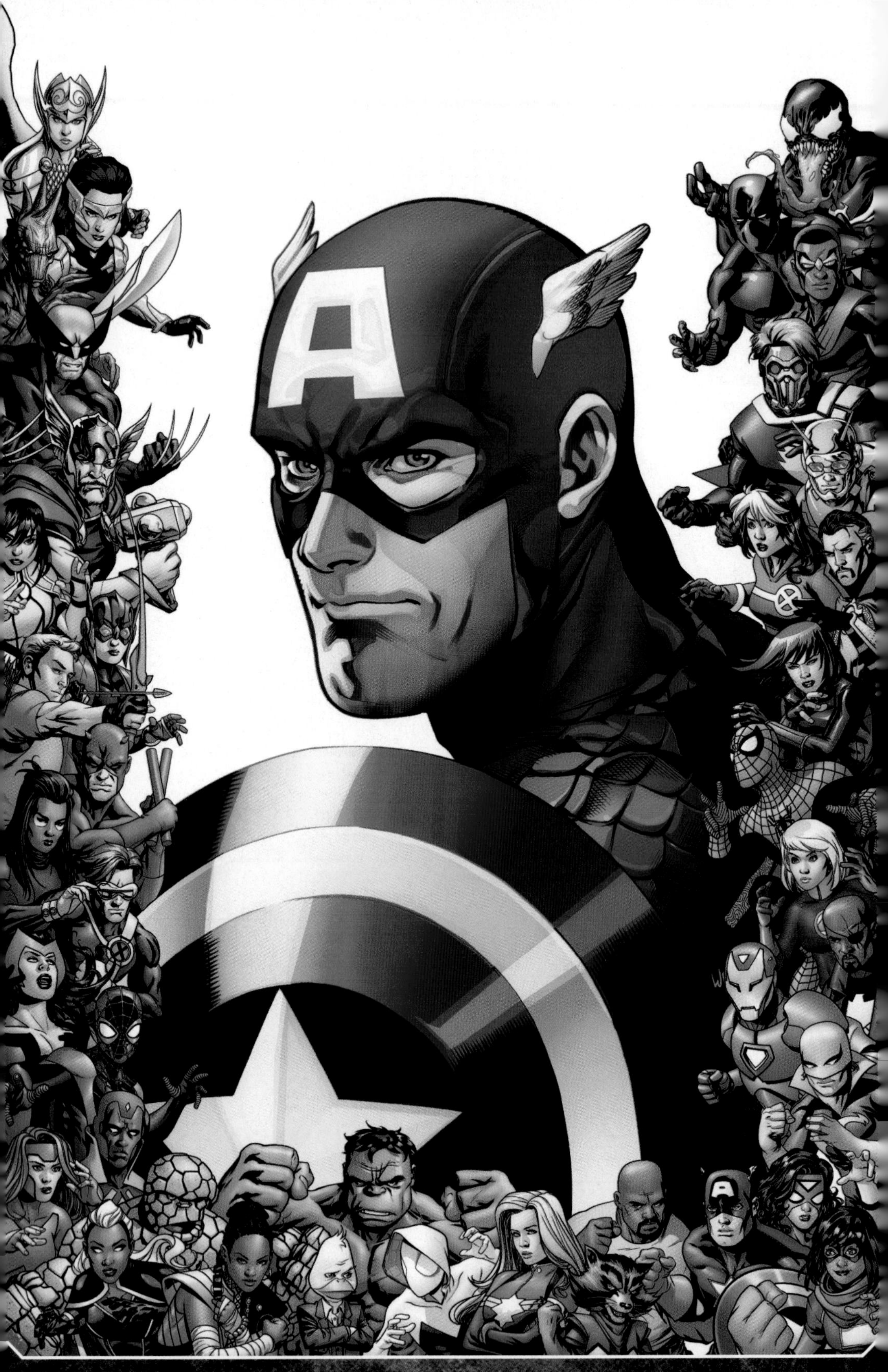

EMA LUPACCHINO & DAVID CURIEL WITH MIKE McKONE & EDGAR DELGADO

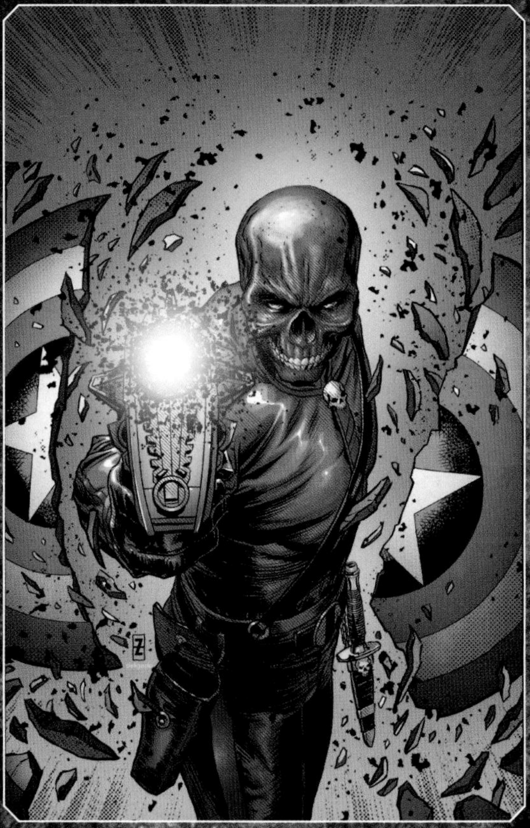

PATCH ZIRCHER & EDGAR DELGADO
13 BRING ON THE BAD GUYS VARIANT

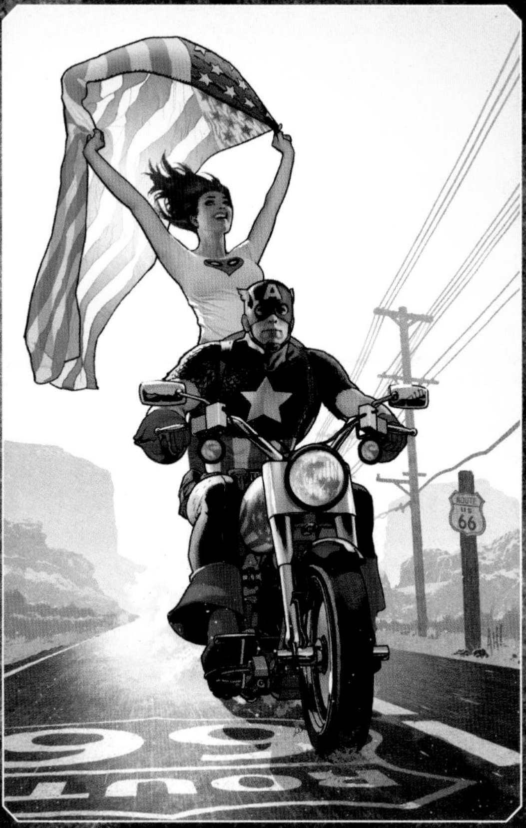

ADAM HUGHES
15 MARY JANE VARIANT

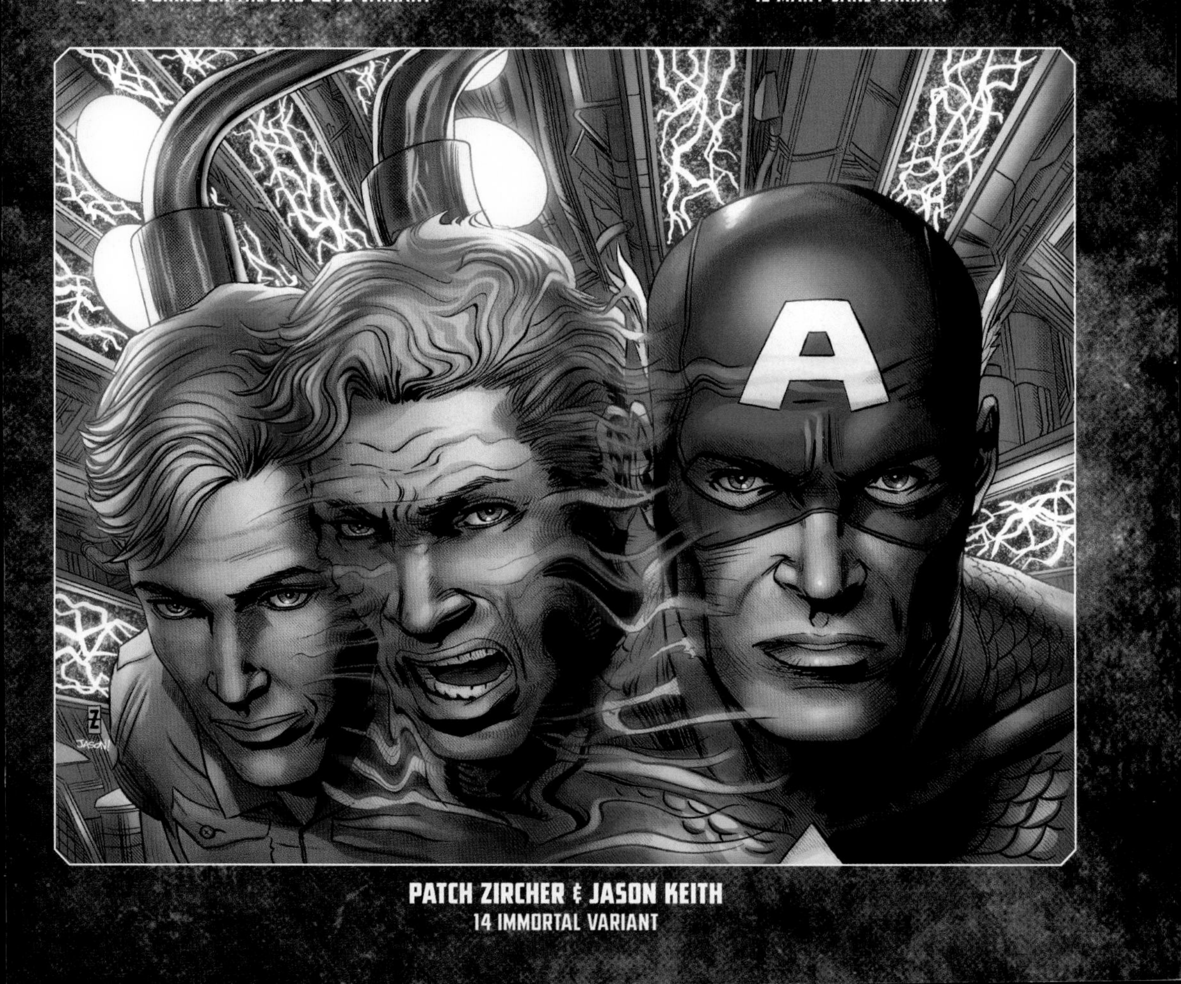

PATCH ZIRCHER & JASON KEITH
14 IMMORTAL VARIANT

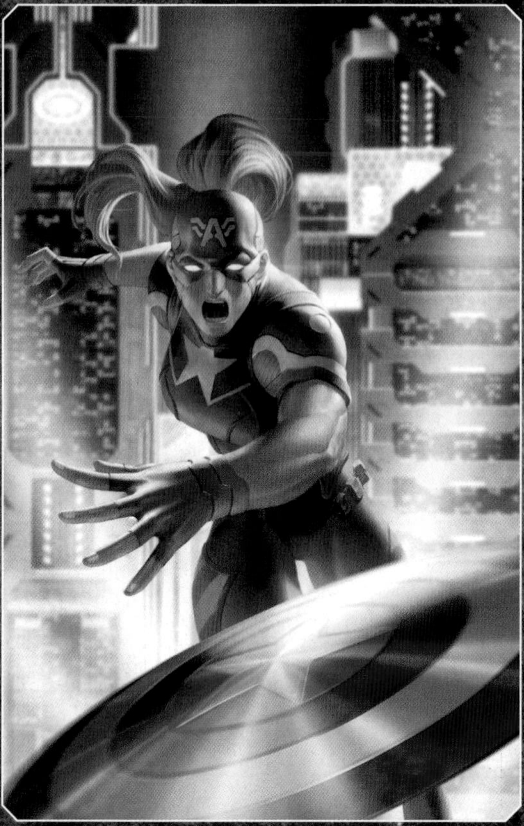

JUNGGEUN YOON
16 2099 VARIANT

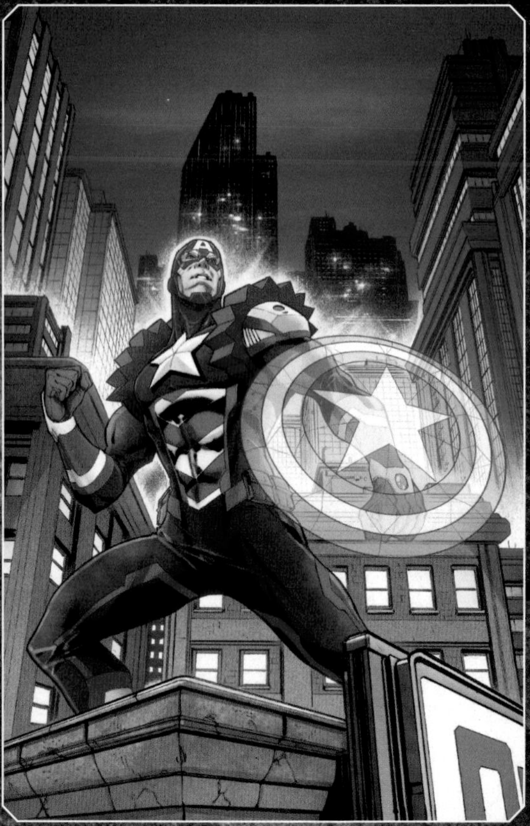

IBAN COELLO & MORRY HOLLOWELL
17 2020 VARIANT

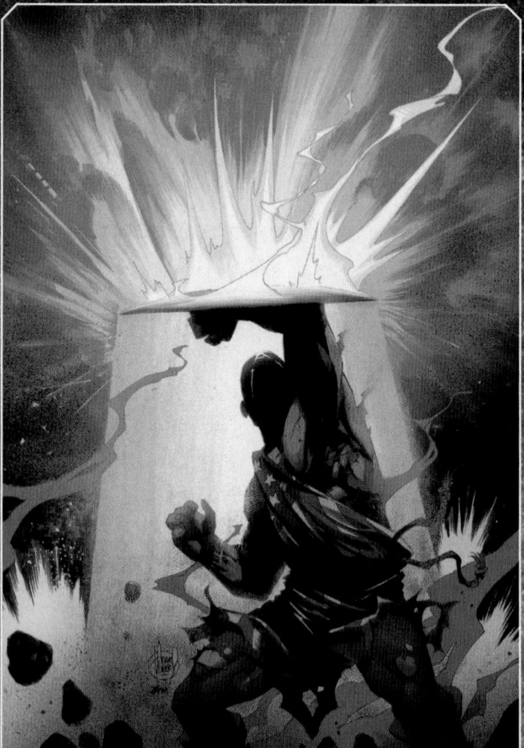

ADAM KUBERT & FRANK MARTIN
18 *MARVELS X* VARIANT

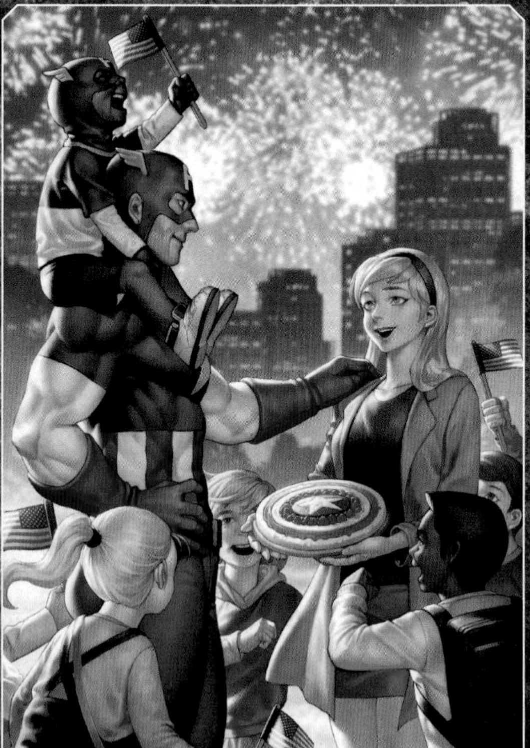

JUNGGEUN YOON
19 GWEN STACY VARIANT